Chaves

Rediscovering the Religious Factor in American Politics

Conclus:
rel. diffs influence: - level of activists (voting)
- partisanship
- attitudes
- content of pol. in church (150)
(civic skills - Verba et al)
- content of pol. preaching - 238

65 - statement of clergy assoc w/ partisanship,
issue positions, + voting patterns -
- our contribution is to show comments w/
political style -

236 - w clergy diffs in content that could
be interpreted as diffs in style -
- content diffs but not level diffs -

Rediscovering the Religious Factor in American Politics

David C. Leege
Lyman A. Kellstedt

With the Collaboration of
John C. Green
James L. Guth
Ted G. Jelen
Corwin E. Smidt
Kenneth D. Wald
Michael R. Welch
Clyde Wilcox

M.E. Sharpe
Armonk, New York
London, England

Library of Congress Cataloging-in-Publication Data

Leege, David C.
Rediscovering the religious factor in American politics /
David C. Leege and Lyman A. Kellstedt with the collaboration
of John C. Green . . . [et al.].
p.   cm.
Includes bibliographical references (p.   ) and index.
ISBN 1-56324-133-1 (cloth)
ISBN 1-56324-134-X (pbk)
1. Religion and politics—United States—History—20th century.
2. United States—Religion—1965–
3. United States—Politics and government—20th century.
I. Kellstedt, Lyman A.
II. Title.
BL2525.L44   1993
261.7′0973—dc20
92-34293
CIP

Printed in the United States of America

The paper used in this publication meets the minimum requirements of
American National Standard for Information Sciences—
Permanence of Paper for Printed Library Materials,
ANSI Z39.48–1984.

BM (c) 10 9 8 7 6 5 4 3 2 1
BM (p) 10 9 8 7 6 5 4 3 2 1

Contents

About the Authors

John C. Green is associate professor of political science and director of the Ray C. Bliss Institute at The University of Akron. His work on religion and politics has appeared in anthologies and journal articles, and he is the co-editor (with James Guth) of *The Bible and the Ballot Box: Religion and Politics in the 1988 Election* (1991). He is currently engaged in research on the Protestant clergy and the membership of evangelical interest groups.

James L. Guth is professor and chair of political science at Furman University. In addition to numerous articles in scholarly journals and anthologies, Guth has co-edited (with John Green) *The Bible and the Ballot Box: Religion and Politics in the 1988 Election*. He, along with several other collaborators on this book, is currently engaged in a massive survey of the membership of religion-based political interest groups and in the analysis of the political attitudes and roles of pastors.

Ted G. Jelen is professor of political science at Illinois Benedictine College. He is the author of numerous articles on religion and politics, voting, and public opinion in scholarly journals. Jelen edited a volume entitled *Religion and Political Behavior in the United States* (1989), and is the author of *The Political Mobilization of Religious Belief* (1991) and (with E. Cook and C. Wilcox) *Between Two Absolutes: Public Opinion and the Politics of Abortion* (1992). His current research addresses problems in democratic theory.

Lyman A. Kellstedt is professor of political science at Wheaton College. His published works, which focus especially on the political behavior of evangelicals, have appeared in several influential anthologies in the religion and politics field and in sociology of religion and political science journals. He chaired the Religion and Politics Section of the American Political Science Association in

1989–90. He is currently the co-director of two major surveys: one of religious activists and the other of the mass public, the latter with a particular focus on religion.

David C. Leege is professor of government and director of the Program for Research on Religion, Church, and Society at the University of Notre Dame. Co-author (with Wayne Francis) of *Political Research: Design, Measurement, and Analysis*, Leege directed the massive Notre Dame Study of Catholic Parish Life and wrote its 15-part *Report* series. His current articles on cultural theory, religion, and politics have appeared in anthologies and sociology of religion and political science journals. He serves on the Board of Overseers of the National Election Studies and chaired its 1992 Presidential Election Study planning committee.

Corwin E. Smidt is professor of political science at Calvin College. His work on religion and politics has appeared in a variety of scholarly journals and books, and he has edited a volume entitled *Contemporary Evangelical Political Involvement*. His current research involves two joint endeavors: a study of political activism among Protestant clergy and a study of political activism among members of evangelical groups.

Kenneth D. Wald is professor and chair of the Department of Political Science at the University of Florida. He has written *Religion and Politics in the United States* (2nd edition, 1992) and *Crosses on the Ballot* (1983), a study of religious influences in British elections. In addition to these books, he has published numerous book chapters and articles exploring the religious dimensions of mass political behavior. He has held research grants from the National Science Foundation and National Endowment for Humanities and was a Fulbright scholar at the Hebrew University of Jerusalem. From 1991–93, he chaired the Religion and Politics Section of the American Political Science Association.

Michael R. Welch is associate professor of sociology at the University of Notre Dame. He has published numerous articles on measurement and deviance, but has concentrated principally on the sociology of religion and religion and politics. Topics include the connection between religiosity and social control, and the link between religious values and political behavior among American Catholics. At present, he is examining the influence of attitudes toward abortion on the political mobilization of Catholics, and is at work on a book with David Leege on parishes as moral communities and a book with Chenggang Zhu and David Leege on the subcultural context of abortion attitudes.

Clyde Wilcox is associate professor of government at Georgetown University. He is the author of *God's Warriors: The Christian Right in 20th Century Amer-*

ica (1992), *Between Two Absolutes: Public Opinion and the Politics of Abortion* (with E. Cook and T. Jelen, 1992), and *Public Attitudes on Church-State Issues* (forthcoming). He has written a number of articles on religion and politics in political science, sociology, history, and psychology journals. His other research interests include gender politics, racial differences in public attitudes, and campaign finance.

Preface

From the outset we make what may appear to be an outlandish claim: social scientists who want to explain American elections, literate citizens who want to understand American politics, and ambitious politicians who want to win elections would be fools to ignore the subject matter of this volume. The volume addresses whether and how religion and religious institutions affect American politics.

For some time analysts have argued that the conflicts of the New Deal era rendered cultural differences trivial and placed economic interests at the top of the political agenda. We think not. Particularly as the New Deal coalitions have fragmented, the two-tiered alignments of the electorate have emerged, and presidential campaigns have symbolically manipulated wedge issues, we are aware that culture counts. And whenever we address culture, we look to the institutions that have specialized in the creation, propagation, and maintenance of values, namely, churches. Religious worldviews are still insinuated in American political institutions, and religious institutions still are points of reference long after the death-of-God has passed from the scene. Think what you wish about the obituary, but the American people continue to act as though the rumors of God's demise were greatly exaggerated.

Origins of the Volume

This volume began out of frustration: (1) social scientists who write about voting behavior were routinely ignoring religious explanations; (2) social scientists who sensed religion is important in American politics did not know what it was about religiosity that mattered; (3) those who were attuned to religious measurement were beginning to fragment into camps favoring this or that measure; and (4) the general-population survey organizations—the National Election Studies (NES), the General Social Survey (GSS), and the Gallup Poll—had some messy religiosity measures with untested and unknown properties.

The first breakthrough in confronting that frustration came with the National Election Studies. One of the senior authors of this book petitioned the NES

Board of Overseers to clean up its existing measures and to try a variety of new ones. Through the foresight of its funder, the National Science Foundation, NES conducts off-year pilot studies to experiment with alternate measures and get a first cut at new topics.

The NES Board had also noted frustration with religiosity measures among some of its users and observed the developing payoffs in religion and politics research, based on special purpose surveys. NES created the Working Group on Religious Measures consisting of Lyman A. Kellstedt, Wade Clark Roof, and Kenneth D. Wald, and chaired by David C. Leege. The group interacted with Santa Traugott, Steven Rosenstone, Donald Kinder, and Warren Miller of NES and emerged with recommendations for the 1989 Pilot Study. Most were placed on the instrument and have formed the core of this volume.

Leege, Kellstedt, and Wald prepared evaluations of the items in papers presented to the NES board and to annual meetings of the Midwest Political Science Association and the Society for the Scientific Study of Religion, all in 1990. Leege was placed on the planning committee for the 1990 Congressional Election Study, and several of the modified or new items appeared on the instrument for the 1990 study. This 1990 NES, together with earlier presidential and congressional studies and GSS data, provides most of the other resources used in this volume.

The other breakthrough came from an informal "Apalachin" meeting in early 1991, involving several of the scholars who were making the most extensive use of survey data to understand religion and politics. Having just roughed each other up a bit over measurement issues at a conference, they gathered for a conference postmortem, and this volume's other senior author proposed that these scholars work on a common project. It would involve state-of-the-art assessment of measures of religiosity in the context of new findings about the effects of religion on American politics. The 1989 Pilot Study beckoned, Leege, Kellstedt, and Wald having staked no informal claim to it. To the surprise of many, an agreement was made to write a thoroughly collaborative work. Its design differs from the usual anthology in that teams of authors address problems and have benefited from critiques not only from team members but from many others in the project.

The senior authors developed a prospectus, and the collaborators staked out their primary writing assignments. The prospectus was sent to several publishers. We were delighted not only that Michael Weber and M.E. Sharpe, Inc. showed interest but that the collaborators voted unanimously to accept their contract.

One of the senior authors then negotiated a grant from the Lilly Endowment, Inc., to defray research expenses involved in preparing the chapters. Dr. James Wind, a religion division program director at the endowment, realized the potential of the project for readers not only among social scientists and political journalists but also among theologians, seminarians, and religious leaders. He has been most encouraging.

Drafts of eight chapters were first delivered to two working sessions of the 1991 annual meeting of the Society for the Scientific Study of Religion in Pittsburgh, where we benefited from deadlines, collaborators' critiques, and audience reactions.

Plan of the Volume

The volume, and part I, begin with a chapter that attempts to place the study of religion and politics in a historical, theoretical, substantive, and normative context. It makes the case for *why* political scientists should incorporate religion into their analyses of American political behavior. Chapter 2 is also contextual, but the focus is on measurement strategies and their implications for the study of religion and politics. The chapter anticipates some of the innovations in the chapters that follow as well as the difficulties that will be encountered.

Part II of the volume begins the substantive analyses that constitute the major portions of the book. Chapter 3 argues the case for careful measurement of denominational affiliation and shows that, once this has been achieved, denominations can be combined into larger aggregates called *religious traditions*, which serve as important sources of political attitudes and behavior. Chapter 4 examines a psychological component of religious affiliation, called *religious group identification*, and argues for its importance in understanding political behavior. Chapter 5 concludes this section of the volume with a look at denominational changes over the life cycle. We believe this effort is the first time that denominational switching and its links to political behavior have been examined by political scientists.

Part III turns to an examination of religious practices. Chapter 6 explores the linkages between church involvement, or the public aspect of religious practices such as church attendance and other forms of church-related activity, and political behavior. In particular, church involvement makes a significant difference in levels of voting turnout. Chapter 7 looks at private devotional acts like prayer and Bible reading and their relationships to politics. Political scientists have given far less attention to this aspect of religious practice than to the more public acts. Yet the chapter demonstrates their importance. Part III concludes with chapter 8, addressing measures of the salience or importance of religion in the lives of Americans and its relevance for political behavior. It demonstrates the value of the NES measure of religious guidance and shows how it can combine fruitfully with parts of the measures discussed in the two preceding chapters.

Part IV looks at doctrinal, experiential, and religious worldview considerations. Chapter 9 focuses attention on measures of biblical literalism and inerrancy and shows that, despite the high level of social desirability attached to these survey items, they are strongly related to political behavior, particularly for evangelical Protestants. Chapter 10 attempts to sort out the conceptual meaning and empirical import of the born-again phenomenon. Surveys routinely ask Americans if they are born again or have had a born-again experience. This chapter points out the pitfalls of uncritical measurement of this phenomenon and its potential when properly understood. Chapter 11 takes this section in a direction not addressed as yet in the general-purpose surveys like NES and GSS. Are underlying religious worldviews, essentially of an individualist or communitarian nature, related to political behavior? The chapter answers the question affirmatively while placing the concept of religious worldviews into a biblical and social scientific framework.

Having established in parts II–IV of the volume that religion matters politically, in part V we initiate exploration of the sources of religious socialization and mobilization. Chapter 12 examines the role of clergy as one source of political cue giving. The results show that the way parishioners perceive cues varies by political content, political interest, and religious tradition. Chapter 13 looks at the impact of religious television as another source of political stimulus. Again, we find variation by religious tradition but discover the strength of religious television in resolving cross-cutting cues. Both chapters make it clear that research into understanding the causal sources of religious outlooks is only in its initial stages.

Finally, chapter 14 provides both a look backward at what has been accomplished in research in religion and political behavior, as exemplified by the preceding chapters, and a look ahead at the agenda still facing scholars in the field.

Acknowledgements and Dedication

We are especially grateful to Tracy Cabello and Mary Lister, who processed the manuscript skillfully and patiently; Tom Trozzolo who reliably ran data; Joan Blauwkamp, who assiduously spotted errors and awkward syntax; and to our many professional colleagues who through the years have probably thought we were some kind of evangelists without collars.

We also acknowledge our wives, Pat and Char. Their love, their spirit, their religious convictions, their courage in adversity, and their support have been special gifts of grace for both of us. We would like to dedicate this book to our children, David, Lissa, and Kurt; Anne and Paul. Many Americans are taught that you should not argue about religion or politics. For better or for worse, our children were brought up in a climate where religion and politics were the principal subjects of discussion and controversy. We are delighted that, in their individual ways, each is both deeply religious *and* strongly political.

We think the book we have dedicated to our children and their generation of "seekers after understanding" demonstrates that there is a reality worth understanding in the religion-politics nexus. We think the book shows that how that reality is measured and modeled has consequences for what we conclude about religion in American politics. At a minimum we have cleaned up misunderstandings for our colleagues in voting behavior, related social sciences, and political journalism. Better still, we hope we have created new opportunities for measuring the various aspects of religion that matter to voters.

For two decades, quantitative historians have been telling us that ethno-cultural and religious factors *were* most of the story in American political history. We think this book tells us that religious factors *are* important in the current story. We will be satisfied if the book helps social scientists and those who read us to rediscover the religious factor.

David C. Leege
Lyman A. Kellstedt

Part I

Why Study Religion
in the Context of Politics

Chapter 1

Religion and Politics in Theoretical Perspective

David C. Leege

Religion in Studies of the American Electorate

There are many reasons why social scientists should examine religion in studies of the American electorate (see Wald 1992, 7–38). Most American adults—between three-fifths and three-fourths—"belong" to churches, synagogues, or other religious assemblies. This is a much larger proportion of Americans than is attracted to any other kind of voluntary organization, whether it be unions, professional associations, neighborhood groups, alumni associations, clubs, or lodges. Depending on which survey one examines, somewhere between 82 and 93 percent of all adult Americans are willing to use some religious designation—Protestant, Catholic, Jewish, or other.

Religion is not only an affinity. It is something that people act out in public and private ways. In a normal week, 29–39 percent of Americans, depending on the survey, attend religious services, and 48–89 percent, again depending on the survey, offer prayer to God; smaller proportions watch religious television and listen to religious radio.

Churches inculcate beliefs and shape worldviews. They provide plausibility structures—i.e., ways of dealing with life's puzzles—and they offer social norms. They make different assumptions about the innate goodness or depravity of humankind, formulate rationales for the design and purpose of political systems, and generate expectations about the end of time and the outcomes of salvation. Some religious worldviews are world affirming, while others are world denying. Some churches and belief systems are universalistic and tolerant. Others are particularistic and shun all those who fail to follow their singular way. Some show respect and compassion to all human beings, but others see the hand of a judging God in the misfortunes of others.

Churches often are contexts for the development of consciousness-of-kind. Such group identities may come from credal precepts, ritual sharing, or social exchanges. Churches usually provide many opportunities for interaction beyond worship services; most have collective instruments for governance, ministries, programs, and activities. Consciousness-of-kind may also develop through stigmatization. When others in the larger society, particularly the elites, discriminate against people because of their religious affiliations, beliefs, or practices, those stigmatized share a common bond and often interpret their religious life through metaphors of deliverance.

Religious institutions often overlay ethnic or regional backgrounds. For most Americans, historically, religion did not precede politics; politics preceded religion. That is, if they came from Ireland or Italy or Poland, they were Catholic; from Saxony or Hanover or Scandinavia, they were Lutheran. If they grew up in Utah or the Great Basin, they were Mormon, or if they lived in the Deep South they were Southern Baptist. As Garrison Keillor, the modern-day cultural commentator, queried, "Why would you move to Lake Wobegon if you don't believe in God?" Everything around you falls in place and is nicely summarized by a religious affiliation.

Religion is also important in American politics because, if all politics is local, surely much of religion is local. In the early 1980s, religious leaders worried that the electronic church would replace the local assembly, but these fears turned out to be groundless when it was realized that the effect of religious television was not substitutional but cumulative. Even the Roman Catholic Church in the United States, often considered the epitome of organizational hierarchy, experienced a republican phase; until about the 1830s, it was a loosely connected collection of parishes and house-churches under lay trusteeship, which the Irish church leadership eventually consolidated into dioceses (Dolan 1985). Still, local parish loyalties are much more significant in the minds of Catholic parishioners than the church at large (Leege 1987).

American religious culture can be described as a marketplace (Stark and Bainbridge 1985; Hertzke 1988). In any given locale, a person who feels called by the Holy Spirit can hang out a shingle for preaching and other services. While charisms are routinized by denominational hierarchies and ordination is required in most churches through time, it is still the local congregation that determines how effectively those charisms can be used.

Local religious structures parallel the many points of access and the diffusion of power in the American political system. Even elected Beltway insiders must develop a home style if they want to remain in the seats of the powerful. And because of an antistatist political culture, Americans are prone to think of other institutions such as local churches when it comes to solving social problems—George Bush's "points of light" metaphor, for example, has its origin in the Psalms.

There is good reason to think, then, that the dimensions of American religion constitute fertile soil for explanations of the American electorate. There are, however, several reasons why social scientists ignore religion as an explanatory factor.

American social science, and American political science in particular, has imbibed deeply from the wells of (1) the German university as a model; (2) economic interpretations of society, whether Madisonian or Marxist; and (3) the progressive movement. The German university model is philosophically rooted in those manifestations of Hegelianism incorporated in *Kulturprotestantism.* At an earlier time, so goes this version of Hegelianism, the divine Mind was known through Scriptures and churches. In the progress of human history, however, the Spirit is manifested in all human institutions, but particularly those that rely on reason and science. The state, the university, the administrator, the theologian, the scientist—all read and implement the divine plan for an age. Many American universities—state and private—began as sectarian institutions with emphasis on chapel and rectitude; most of their presidents and many of their professors were clergy. In the spirit of deism and transcendentalism, however, they could be transformed—still serving the Spirit of God through sanctified yet secular learning (Marsden and Longfield 1992). The Hopkins History Seminar under Daniel Coit Gilman and Herbert Baxter Adams (Somit and Tanenhaus 1967, 1–35) and the Chicago School of Social Sciences under Charles E. Merriam (Merriam 1925) both justified their "missions" through Hegelian language.

The religious consensus that drove the major academic institutions until the late nineteenth century—what we now call *mainline* Protestantism—dissolved from its own secularizing reinterpretation, the rise of explicitly *state* institutions, new national needs, and the presence of many more Catholics, Jews, and eventually non–Judeo Christians in the professoriate and student body. Religion became a boring subject at best, a curious hangover from a past put aside. Rooted in superstition and tribalism, it was thought that religion would soon give way to the inevitable secularization of society. But it did not. Much of the resurgence of interest in religion and politics has come through (1) the realization that a golden age had not arrived through the collaboration of state and university, (2) disillusionment with the notion that a divine Spirit is unfolding in both imperialistic wars and well-meaning social programs, (3) the recognition that the general American public never did secularize, (4) the reinstitution of religious studies programs on state and private campuses, and (5) the acknowledgment that, in a culturally diverse society, religion can be a force that alternately unifies and tears asunder, and, therefore, we ought to know something about it.

Economic interpretations of American history have also had long acceptance in American social science. The Madisonian impact on American political institutions was based on assumptions about the acquisitive nature of humans. Left to their own deserts, factions would rule in their own economic interests. Thus, the scope of governmental activity needed to be limited, and interest needed to check interest. Yet, the assumption that humans are acquisitive also had a positive value: it drove people to seek power and thus created the capacity to govern. Societies could achieve collective goals. But unrestrained governance is always dangerous.

From Charles A. Beard to Frederick Jackson Turner, Madisonian assumptions about the economic underpinnings of American society and the American political system have held sway in the academy. Under the circumstances, it was at least plausible to take Karl Marx seriously, because social class was a form of faction and class rule was itself evidence that the system of checks and balances had become a facade behind which the "real" system, based in industrial capitalism, operated. Even if one is not a thoroughgoing Marxist, long-term trends in participation and electoral choice appear intelligible as the consequence of hegemonic economic institutions and the lack of true partisan, i.e., class-based, conflict (Burnham 1965).

Further, economic assumptions appealed to American social scientists because of their architectural elegance. For example, in Downs's (1957) theory of democracy, only three concepts need to be manipulated: *rationality, uncertainty,* and *ideology.* Economic terms could easily be integrated into both formal arguments and mathematical estimates. The behaviors of bureaucrats, policymakers, and voters alike could be understood by retrenching from the concept of rationality to the concept of *satisficing,* i.e., settling for the first acceptable alternative (Simon 1957; Fiorina 1981). On the other hand, religious worldviews and group identifications are more clumsy; often social scientists do not know what it is about religion that should be measured or how to measure it; and certainly no government agency—no Bureau of Religious Statistics in the U.S. Department of Religious Beliefs—would devote tax funds to collecting such statistics.

The progressive movement also discouraged the examination of religion and politics, except as a pathology. Many progressives, almost in a German idealist or New England transcendentalist tradition, became secular carriers of essentially mainline Protestant values. While their church was something of the past, their social and political reforms bristled with religious images (cf. Crunden 1982). Two types of religion remained problematic for them—Catholicism and evangelicalism. Both demanded particularistic credal commitments and drew their adherents' attention away from problems of the here-and-now to faithful preparation for the afterlife. The progressive ethos was more universalistic and found true religion in the commitment to *social* reform.

Implicated in the progressives' anti-Catholicism was a substantial amount of nativism. The Catholic ethnic groups that had flooded American cities late in the nineteenth century were easily kept by priests, so it was thought, and politicians. The corrupt machines, it seemed, were headed by Irish or other Catholic ethnic bosses, and the church was in cahoots with them. (Never mind that Boss Tweed of Tammany was of Presbyterian stock or that Baptist bosses emerged in the South.) In time, *public-regardingness,* i.e., all those good things associated with urban reform, indexed the extent to which WASPs or WASP values had reasserted control over civic life and public policy. So long as mainline Protestants did not take religion seriously, i.e., particularistically, they would rule for the public good.

The evangelicals, on the other hand, were from the backwoods and small towns of America. They still lived by prescientific notions that ill fit progress as defined by progressives. Since political scientists in the founding era of the discipline were heavily influenced by progressive ideals, to ignore the effects of religion on politics was actually a decision rooted in judgments about the religion of ethnic tribe and primitive superstition. It was distasteful for earlier generations of American political scientists to study religion. And yet mainline Protestant beliefs were imbedded in the "deep culture" of the social science of their day.

Further, it was thought dangerous to the fabric of society to give religion much credence in political interpretations. Religion seemed to divide people. Populist politicians played to the ignorance of people through the use of religious metaphors in campaigns. A people so diverse, so heterogeneous, could be divided irreconcilably by religion. The "wall of separation" of church and state took on a meaning different from its meaning for Thomas Jefferson (Dreisbach 1991). The later generations of constitutional scholars who had moved beyond the secularizing ethos of the first generation of progressives and social scientists began to see the "wall" argument as "no advantage for religion over irreligion" rather than "no advantage for one religious body over another." By the 1970s and 1980s, First Amendment issues remained but were overshadowed by one of the most divisive issues of the era—abortion. The abortion policy crisis became the fulcrum for concern about the mingling of religion and politics.

While many social scientists would rather ignore religion in explanations of the American electorate, neither voters nor politicians think it is irrelevant. A recent typology of the American electorate (Ornstein, Kohut, and McCarthy 1988) moves beyond the traditional measure of party identification ranging from Strong Democrat through Independent to Strong Republican; it uses a wide range of value, interest, and issue questions to construct groups and then relate them to the core and periphery of each party. In the Republican core are the Enterprisers and the Moralists, the latter being defined primarily by particularistic religious beliefs and being quite intolerant of other ascriptive groups. In the Democratic core are New Dealers, 60s Democrats (peace and justice Democrats), the Partisan Poor, and the God and Country Democrats. The first three Democratic groups are well defined by religious values, ranging from the economically welfarist but socially intolerant New Dealers to the economically welfarist but socially tolerant 60s Democrats. The God and Country Democrats are disproportionately black evangelicals from the South. Thus, in both parties' cores are voters who resonate to religious positions; swing voters among the Democrats in 1988 came disproportionately from the ranks of those for whom religion and life-style were salient (Times-Mirror 1988, 22–42, 1990).

Political elites develop campaign themes and use religious imagery to build coalitions based, in part, on religious appeals. In the 1960s a handful of conservative activists reacted to the defeat of Barry Goldwater by merging militant anticommunism, free market economics, and cultural traditionalism (Crawford 1980; Blumenthal 1986); the resulting New Right has dominated the national agenda beginning with the election of Ronald Reagan. Kellstedt and Noll (1990) have traced the realignment of the fastest-growing religious tradition, evangelical Protestantism, from Democratic identification to Republican identification. The shift is every bit as important to Republican presidential candidates as was the earlier realignment based on race (documented by Carmines and Stimson 1989). The mobilization of African-American voters under the Democratic banner since 1964 has been an important task for black churches (Lincoln and Mamiya 1990). Just as Democratic candidates work the black churches in the current era, so Republican candidates work white evangelical churches and religious media. Liberal language deeply embedded in the American political culture—like "freedom to choose"—is used by Republican politicians and evangelical activists alike to mobilize voters, not on abortion but on school-related issues: prayer, vouchers, secular humanism, etc. Supreme Court nominations become the bait for attracting moral traditionalists in all church bodies. In short, current American politics involves symbiotic relationships between elites and voters not only on economic issues but on issues that connect religious worldviews and church mobilization.

Social scientists should not be surprised that religion, like economic interest, is an important electoral force. Social theorists have long pointed to religion as the glue that holds society together, legitimates social change, and defines many of our basic expectations of the political order. The remainder of this chapter examines the treatment of religion by selected social theorists in literatures as diverse as anthropology, sociology, psychology, philosophy, and political science.

The Place of Religion in Cultural Theory

The function of culture is social control. Geertz (1973, 44) describes culture not simply as a repository of customs, usages, traditions, and habits, but as "a *set of control mechanisms*—plans, recipes, rules, instructions—for the governing of behavior." Culture brings predictability to both the physical universe and social relationships (Douglas and Wildavsky 1983). When the physical universe acts in violent and haphazard ways toward humans, or threatens to do so, culture rationalizes unpredictability through (1) *superstition*, such as fate or divine will; (2) *ritual*, such as exorcism, blessing the soil and showing gratitude for the harvest, safe travel, or whatever; and (3) *science*, observing repeated occurrences of phenomena until both the odds of counteroccurrences and the mechanisms that predict the occurrence are known.

Culture also nurtures predictability in social relations through (1) *making assumptions about human nature* that are then propagated, (2) *prescribing norms for appropriate social conduct*, (3) *establishing identity,* and (4) *maintaining boundaries* so that outsiders or nonconforming insiders cannot destroy predictability. Culture operates not only through norms that require conformity but through tolerable limits on nonconformity. A culture that has no room for the latter would become too static; it could not adapt to changing material and social conditions that result from modifications in the physical universe or from expanding contact with new biological organisms or adjacent social groups.

Religious beliefs and religious groups are at the foundation of a culture. Religious worldviews give transcendental meaning to the mundane. Religious worldviews consist of values that lay unique claim to truth while rationalizing social relationships and community objectives. Geertz (1973, 90) defines religion as "a system of symbols which acts to establish powerful, pervasive, and long lasting moods and motivations in men by formulating conceptions of the general order of existence and clothing these conceptions with such an aura of factuality that the moods and motivations seem uniquely realistic." Regarding the content of religious worldviews, Geertz argues (131), "both what a people prizes and what it fears and hates are depicted in its worldview, symbolized in its religion, and in turn expressed in the whole quality of life."

Religion derives staying power and its political import from the belief that the sacred is behind its social norms. Emile Durkheim argued ([1915] 1965, 261), "Religious force is only the sentiments inspired by the group in its members, but projected outside the consciousness that experienced them, and objectified." Religious force depends on the inseparable relationship between religious worldviews and religious groups. Group socialization, group ritual, and group pressure create both the capacity to believe and the impetus to conform. For Durkheim, moral authority is society's projection of its own need for order, for stability and predictability in social interactions. Through religious ritual people interact with the sacred, perceived to be at the center of an interacting community.

Philosophers and psychologists accept the Durkheimian notion that the moral force and political importance of religion derive from the common beliefs, interactions, and sacred projections of a group. Most philosophers of religion and some psychologists, however, argue beyond a sociological interpretation. They claim that individuals seek the divine. Otto (1950) argued that innate to every human is a sense of the *numinous*, an awareness of when a feeling or a presence is extraordinary, outside the human. The psychologist William James (1902) examined and cataloged such religious experiences, based on documents, diaries, and depth interviews. The sociologists Glock and Stark (1965, 42) classify them as (1) *confirming* the presence of the divine or of evil force; (2) *responding* to the presence of salvation or temptation, miracle or damnation, sanction or curse; (3)*entering an affective state* of ecstasy or terror; or (4) *perceiving oneself as in possession* of a revelation or possessed by the diabolical. Studies of individual religious experience always note the presence of both positive and negative—an important component of the capacity for boundary maintenance. While examining many avenues to intense, personal religious experience, empirical studies of the phenomenon (Glock and Stark 1965; Poloma and Gallup 1991; McCready and Greeley 1976) often note that individuals need to affirm such experiences as *religious* by processing them with fellow believers or by reference to sacred writings and prescribed devotional rituals. Thus, it is conceivable that the capacity to intuit the divine is innate to the individual and that is why religion has such centrality and psychological force in human life. But it certainly gains cultural and political force when affirmed and interpreted by religious groups, and that is what we can observe.

People become something more than ordinary mortals when they share a sacred community. People become empowered, they develop the self-confidence to *act* in concert. Religions specify what actions to take, and religious beliefs create the obligation to act (Hoge 1974, 92).

Religion, then, meets all the basic functions of a culture from the perspective of groups and individuals: (1) *identity*, it tells us who we are and who I am; (2) *norms*, it tells us how we ought to behave; and (3) *boundary-maintenance*, it tells us who or what behaviors are not "of us" (cultural criteria from Wildavsky 1987). But potentially, religion has greater salience *for the religious adherent* than any other social identity, norm, or boundary because it characterizes its answers as sacred, eternal, implicated with the ultimate meaning of life.

Not all cultural values, Durkheim notwithstanding, are religious values, and not all social groups can be defined by religious values. There are many alternate and accepted modes of social solidarity that may be quite irreligious. Therefore, not all political conflict should be thought of as religious conflict. In the American political culture, for example, (1) the notion of *original sin* or the depravity of human beings becomes embedded in limited government, separation of powers, and distrust of politicians; (2) *covenant theology* justifies both the constitutional order and the right to revolt; (3) the sense of a *chosen people* is evident in national purpose, manifest destiny, economic imperialism, and the export of democracy. All are religious ideas (Wald 1992, 45–68) that have political consequences. It might also be argued that beliefs in the divine creation of human beings, each with the imprint of God, led to arguments about *equality* before the law (and even equality of condition). They became embedded in the Declaration of Independence, were elaborated in many constitutional amendments, and have given energy to the later stages of the Civil War, the recent civil rights movement, and the current antiabortion movement.

Many other deep values evident in American political culture can be thought of as *religious*, however, only in the sense that they were originally counterreligious. Derived from the enlightenment—Scottish, French, or German—their purpose was to break the stranglehold on cultural values exercised by religious worldviews and institutions. These include notions of human progress through the perfectibility of humankind, the progressive revelation of the Spirit through human institutions to the point where the divine is indistinguishable from the mundane, the application of scientific knowledge to all human problems, the acquisition of private property through unfettered economic self-interest, and libertarian stances toward "moral" behavior that allow no claim to be subject to community standards. Several of these notions have stimulated both conservative and liberal movements in recent decades. Often they are syncretized by the moralistic ethos of American political discourse so that what was essentially antireligion in its origins becomes sanctified as the religious rationale for a secular objective.

The commingling of both religious and originally antireligious values in American political culture oftentimes leads to conflict evident in political discourse about *capitalism* and *freedom*. In its origins, capitalism challenged the established feudal order of (1) church, (2) knights and landed gentry, and (3) serfs, serving each of the first two orders. The ascendancy of cities and widespread commerce across political and maritime boundaries created new realities not well rationalized by medieval philosophy and theology. Insofar as the church became the cultural protector of the precapitalist *ancien regime*, the philosophers of capitalism, particularly those associated with the Scottish enlightenment, offered arguments challenging the hegemony of the dominant religious worldview (cf. Schneider 1967, especially selections from Hutcheson, Hume, Ferguson, and Smith). The philosophies associated with liberal individualism and utilitarianism emerged. But from the Protestant Reformation itself came new sects that also turned religious assumptions topsy-turvy.

In Catholic rationales for the feudal order, attention was focused on one's destiny in the next world, which was mediated sacramentally by the church; however, in the present world one's caste was fixed. The followers of John Calvin, on the other hand, argued that one's fate in the afterlife is fixed by predestination and that the individual is the master of his or her own fate in this life (Glock 1972). Liberal capitalists and religious nonconformists could alternately offer secular and religious rationales for capitalist behavior and capitalist consequences. Diligence, thrift, and prudence are the virtues replacing contemplation, spirituality, and passivity. If inequalities in this life emerge, they are because the poor have chosen not to develop capitalist virtues. Since God created all humans equal in this life, personal irresponsibility must account for unequal outcomes. The poor must suffer their plight, perhaps even as punishment. The well-off, on the other hand, can attest a special measure of virtue by acting charitably toward the poor—but that is still an individual's decision, not a collective obligation imposed by the state. On one paramount point the liberal capitalists and the religious nonconformists could *agree*: the state's obligation is to assure freedom for individual action.

And so, liberal capitalists and religious capitalists offered nearly compatible rationalizations for the functions of the state and the proper behavior of citizens. Yet they were built on rather different assumptions about the nature of humans, divine intentions, and the claims of religious communities. The former found the claims of all religious institutions to be an impediment to human freedom and put their faith in reason, science, and action. The latter interpreted the God–human relationship as an essentially unmediated religious experience that manifests itself in the righteous behavior of the believer. Righteousness was evident in religious rectitude, economic diligence, and civic involvement. As chapter 11 of this book elaborates, such religious individualists share sufficiently in the political discourse of secular enterprise capitalists but feel uncomfortable when their political alliance involves the extension of the concept of liberty to behaviors that violate their sense of rectitude, e.g., abortion or the failure to recognize the religious basis for a political consensus manifested in schoolteaching, legislation, and judicial decisions. Therefore, on one paramount point the liberal capitalists and religious capitalists *disagree:* the state's obligation is to assure freedom for individual action in a civic order that nurtures a sensitive conscience and sets boundaries on unrighteous behavior. Thus, their political discourse about capitalism and freedom resemble each other, but their roots in different worldviews foretell political conflict.

In still another way, the conflict inherent in the commingling of religious and antireligious values in the American political culture can be seen in *civil religion.* David Hume traced the origin of the state not to a social contract, but to some collective violence that subdued a people under a sovereign. Yet a people is not satisfied for long with a "might makes right" rationale for its origins. This rationale is inherently unstable. Culture must offer a more stable, more benign ideological basis for a political community. A founding myth seems necessary. That is where religion has special utility.

The young leaders of the breakaway colonies of North America used a unique form of contractarianism to declare independence from the British throne. It is the obligation of a people to owe loyalty to their ruler—an obligation imposed by God. But it is the obligation of the ruler to rule justly—an obligation imposed by God. When the ruler breaks that trust, then the subjects owe it not simply to themselves but to God to rebel. That is the logic of the Declaration of Independence. And it is the logic that has undergirded civil disobedience and the many moral crusades of American political history to this day. A higher law gives purpose to the state. A state gains its legitimacy by invoking that higher law. The American nation is born in the crucible of religious obligation. To its national purposes are quickly attributed religious motivations. Its monuments become shrines, its coins and pledges invoke the divine, its national songs become hymns, its national holidays fill the heavens with starbursts of light and peels of thunder. But its citizens may be pious fools, deceived by sovereigns who manipulate a civil religion.

In another form, founding American myths contribute to civil religion. There is some reason to doubt that the overwhelming body of early settlers were unduly religious, despite the presence of established state churches in many colonies. Otherwise, religious leaders would not have launched the massive conversion campaigns that became known as the Great Awakenings in the 1790s and the 1830s. A large proportion of these settlers came here to escape jails, to seek economic opportunity, and to avoid military obligations. Yet the founding myth that sticks is one that combines the quest for religious freedom with the purpose of the new world–new nation. It is caught up in the enduring symbols of the Mayflower Compact and the City on a Hill. The Pilgrims, a band of nonconformists seeking freedom from a religious establishment, bonded together as equals in a contract setting rights and obligations. The Puritans, escaping the corruption and depravity of an old world, envisioned a New Israel. As God called a wandering Aramean and promised a chosen people set aside for God's purposes, so the passage to the new world was a modern vision of divine purpose—a people who would found a Christian community in the wilderness that would become a shining beacon to the world. American notions of self-governance, democracy, freedom, limited government—all get subsumed in a spiritual purpose. Civil religion as a spiritual purpose shows itself in manifest destiny, in emancipation, in the white man's burden and other forms of religious and economic imperialism, in wars to make the world safe for democracy, in the United Nations, and in a cold war against an evil empire. Again it is difficult to separate what is a spiritual purpose from a cynical rationale for "might makes right."

What is clear, however, is that civil religion in the American political culture has both *priestly* and *prophetic* functions (Bellah 1975). The priestly function bathes American policy in divine blessing and mobilizes the loyalty of the people through transcendent purposes. The prophetic function calls to task those leaders and policies that fail to live up to a divine purpose for the American nation. National sin, for example, is seen in the genocidal treatment of indigenous populations, in the enslavement of African Americans, or, as some now argue, in the convenient termination of unborn human life.

Civil religion is like playing with the fire of the gods. Wald (1992, 64–65) summarizes the pros and cons: (1) it "can ennoble a people by prompting generous instincts and commitment to a nation's principles"; (2) it can lead to "idolatrous worship of the state"; (3) it "can inhibit the skepticism and sef-criticism" that democratic politics needs; and (4) it can set standards so "rigid and unbending" that compromise is impossible.

We would argue that some form of civil religion—whether in the reverent pilgrimage past V.I. Lenin's body in Moscow or in the thoughtful reflection on Abraham Lincoln's speeches in Washington—is inevitable in all nation-states. Religious worldviews and political philosophies draw on the same stuff of human experience—the desire to make life predictable. Yet civil religion is also one of the most dangerous motivating forces in human behavior. That is the case because religion is collective memory and politics is collective action. Both are sources for identity, norms, and boundaries. When they become virtually indistinguishable in a political culture, that is, when politics becomes salvational and religion is solely an instrument of the state, the most repressive totalitarian system is born. To understand this problem we need to examine religion as a source of political stability and change and to conclude wih a discussion of religion as a mediating institution.

Religion, Political Stability, and Change

Religion has been treated by social theorists as a source of political stability. Glock (1972) argues that all social organizations involve hierarchical forms. Religious beliefs are typically used to warrant hierarchical inequities. In the absence of force and without supernatural justifications, people would not consent to such inequities. According to Glock, warranting beliefs usually specify or imply mechanisms of social control such as *sanctions*, *compensations*, and *ideology*.

Sanctions range from internalized instruments, such as habit and custom, to external instruments, such as law and force. In periods of great political stability, habit and custom are sufficient to maintain hierarchy, law settles disputes among interested parties, and force both punishes the recalcitrant and strikes fear in potential rebels. In chapter 12 we note how local religious institutions such as churches transmit political cues to their flocks, most of which remind people to maintain or return to the status quo in their behaviors. Even when preaching or formal propagandizing is absent, political scientists have found evidence of behavioral contagion among fellow parishioners (Wald, Owen, and Hill 1990); parishioners learn to like and dislike the same thing through the social context of their churches. In chapters 3, 5, and 12, and from Wuthnow (1988) and Roof and McKinney (1987) we learn that American denominationalism is not only increasingly voluntary but that the more religiously active people choose parish contexts that reinforce their moral precepts. Such precepts usually involve judgments about appropriate citizen behavior, public policies, and governmental stances. Increasingly, evangelical Protestants have taken a proactive stance in calling for a return to a political climate that reinforces traditional religious and "family" values. In this case religious institutions not only seek to reinforce habit and custom but seek laws and judicial sanctions to limit public behavior perceived to be out of bounds.

Compensations include a wide range of institutions and practices that divert people's attention from their current conditions to some other state of existence. They can include otherworldly religious yearning—what Marx labeled "religion as the opiate of the masses"—as evidenced in the old Negro spirituals or in gifts of the Spirit that turn inward to the religious community alone, e.g., speaking in tongues, chiliastic seizures. Or they might involve sports—with its intense collective loyalties and hero worship—or the entertainment industry generally, including politicians as celebrities. Finally, compensations could include drugs, ranging from legally acceptable mood-altering drugs such as tobacco, alcohol, and over-the-counter painkillers, to controlled substances, to hard drugs such as crack cocaine, which though illegal, are unequally sanctioned in different neighborhoods. Commonly in hierarchical systems with great inequities, compensations are disproportionately available and utilized by those most disenfranchised by the status quo. Pentecostal religion, athletic prowess, and tobacco, alcohol, cocaine, and heroin addiction are all more evident among historically oppressed minorities in the United States. By their very nature, most religions provide the ultimate compensation—answers to questions unanswerable in scientific discourse, namely, about life, death, and eternity.

Contrary to the expectations of social theorists, however, what began as compensatory religion can become transformed into a politically activating religion when infused with a *community*, rather than an *individualistic*, spirit. Chapter 7 points out how highly devotional black evangelicals show strong political commitments, and Lincoln and Mamiya (1990) tell the history of the civil rights movement through the black church. In the black church, oppression and deliverance are seen as collective properties, and collective mobilization is required to alter the status quo and provide opportunity. Arguing for a different political agenda—one that would return to putative traditions—white evangelicals, who were often among the dispossessed of the southern and border states and the northern migrations, also call for collective mobilization to replace individualistic withdrawal. World withdrawal is itself a form of anomie and is highly individualistic. Durkheim ([1915] 1965), as discussed earlier, treated religion as the collective and highest aspirations of a *people* displaced on a divine object. We might infer, then, that the anomic individual, one lacking social norms, would not long be compensated by religion. In time he or she would pass on to a form of withdrawal less social. By definition, religion would engage the individual in a community with both norms and sanctions—and with that, political values. Religious transformationism eventually involves the embrace of community purpose and mission.

Ideology, according to Glock (1972), is most significant in times of social change. Ideology is a vision, a verbal picture of the good society and the principal means of achieving it. Ideology does not settle for the status quo; it is an instrument of change. The left Hegelians, Ludwig Feuerbach and Karl Marx, saw religion as the primary source of alienation. For Feuerbach, the species essence of humankind could never be realized so long as humankind's best traits, its ideal self, were projected on a radically other, God. Christian religion was the enemy that a new ideology must displace because its trinitarian God and Gospel message of sin and grace were the most convincing counterideology to human potential. For Marx, the source of alienation was in material conditions—the relationships surrounding purposive, productive labor that separated value from the person who produced it. Yet so long as religion was used as compensation for alienation, it was a handmaiden to false consciousness and the tool of the oppressing class. The solution for both Feuerbach and Marx was the same—jettison the Judeo-Christian religion and replace it with an anthropocentric, human-affirming ideology.

The irony is that wherever ideologies derived from left Hegelianism rationalized social change, new institutions quickly took on a religious character. For National Socialism, the party became the church, non-Aryans became evil incarnate, and the Third Reich became the millennium that was attained through faithfulness during great struggle. For communism, the party also became the church, capitalists became the arch-enemy, and the withering away of the state would follow a period of leadership by the new clergy—the vanguard of the proletariat—who could interpret the laws of history. Both created their own deities in the name of an ideology that advanced human beings beyond the religious stage of progressive human self-realization.

Still another approach to ideology is found in the United States of the 1800s. It made conscious application of extant religion to measure its progress. It can be seen in the uses of Alexis de Tocqueville's *Democracy in America* ([1835, 1840] 1958). Amos (1992) argues that Tocqueville was seen not only as a great social scientist by American educators but as a source document both for founding myths and for shaping national identity. Tocqueville argued that religion in the United States undergirded the mores of its people. Religion could never become joined to the state, never become dominant politically through a single denomination, and never rationalize political movements that could lay sole claim to truth. Truth was not incorporated in political institutions; it was never to be found in a Kingdom of God on earth. Instead truth was always just beyond grasp, in transcendent religious principles. Justice had to emulate truth.

This conception of true religion shaped an ideology of political striving. It created a nation of people dedicated to the principal that no one was above the law and that no earthbound form of justice was indeed fully just. According to Amos, the story of Tocqueville's American character was told most effectively to educated elites—the nation's economic and political heirs-apparent—in times of greatest instability, heavy immigration and civil war. It told those who came from different ethnic stocks and religious traditions, particularly Catholicism, that this is who we are. Its interpretation of religion and politics in the United States became a blueprint, an ideology, that forged consensus in a time of great change. It allowed the incorporation of the equalitarian West, the expanding frontier from Andrew Jackson's time onward, into the established elites on the eastern seaboard. And it became so deeply embedded in the way we judged ourselves politically that Lincoln's prophetic religious imagery seemed only natural at our time of greatest national crisis. The use of Tocqueville as programmatic ideology began to lose its force during the period of massive urbanization and industrialization, but has had periodic renewals in times when Americans search for their national soul (for an argument similar to Amos, see Bellah et al. 1985).

It is not clear from the work of the great social theorists just how religion becomes a force to rationalize the status quo or a model for change. Glock (1972) suggests that the images by which people perceive God hold the key. As the religious imagination changes, so do acceptable social forms, and vice versa. This theme is later developed theologically by Tracy (1975, 1981) and sociologically by Greeley (1981, 1982).

Tracy follows a Hegelian notion that individuals, whether religious or secular, seek to affirm the worth of their lives in history. They use a vocabulary very similar to the religious concepts of love, truth, beauty, and God, a vocabulary that transcends human experience but is rooted in projections from human experience. Thus, beliefs embedded in religious worldviews have very mundane roots, and the stuff of theology and political philosophy is similar—nature, destiny, relationships, order, freedom.

Greeley (1982) develops Tracy's argument that the language we use for such religious projections is poetry, metaphor, and story. What we attribute to God and what we attribute to humans differs primarily in the intuitive nature of the former, but it is modeled in ordinary observations of the latter. Thus, benevolent or judgmental traits attributed to God often have their referent in maternal or paternal relationships we have experienced in primary groups. Sin, grace, hope—all derive from threatening, affirming, or challenging life experiences. They form a predogmatic religious worldview, i.e., an outlook that precedes and overrides substantive theological concepts, and they establish outlooks by which we respond to new economic, social, and political events.

These metaphors and stories in religious language tell us whether we can expect humans to be basically good or depraved, altruistic or greedy. They tell us what to expect from God. Sacred Scriptures also fill in these expectations. In the Bible, for example, the Genesis account makes it clear that humans were fashioned in God's own image and hence can be assumed to be basically good. Yet the first couple disobeyed God and ate the forbidden fruit—and thereafter, humans were fallen, depraved at birth, greedy, self-interested. Some religious traditions deriving from the Judeo-Christian sourcebooks emphasize the former, others the latter. Reflecting on both the secular and religious origins of religious metaphors, Greeley argues that it should be possible to tap images of God and images of humankind, and to construct people's fundamental outlooks on the social order. Greeley (1981) argues that the most important image of God is that of the maternal, nurturant, gracious God, and the corresponding image of humankind is one of hope in the crucible of misfortune. Empirically, Greeley finds that those who imagine God as maternal and nurturant show strong social concerns, have an active sense of the spiritual or other-worldly dimension of life, yet are slightly more involved in social causes and political activity.

A study by Welch and Leege (1988) contrasts the utility of religious imagery, devotional style, sense of closeness to God, and foundational religious beliefs (described in chapter 11) as predictors of political attitudes and behavior. In contrast to Greeley, they find an image of God as judge to be more powerful than the maternal, nurturant image (but their samples were very different) and the judge image proves to be a strong predictor across the spectrum of political issues. While the judgelike image is not so strong a predictor of political conservatism as is religious individualism (see chapter 11), it nevertheless is a useful tip-off to political ideology. Pictures of God as a companion also show important predictive relationship to specific issue positions and political ideology.

In short, there is every reason to believe Glock's (1972) contention that religious imagery bears a strong relationship to both political-philosophical orientations and to feelings about specific political issues.

Still other careful, controlled studies examine the American creed or ethos without making cultural assumptions involving the religious imagination or religious worldviews. Typically such studies specify some fundamental values such as individualism, egalitarianism, libertarianism or personal freedom, tolerance of pluralism and dissent, confidence in science and rationalism, notions of progress, the depravity or perfectibility of humans, compassion for the truly needy, or preferences for nongovernmental solutions. Then they contrast different segments of the population, untangling potential explanations of causes and consequences. Sometimes a measure of religiosity is selected for an explanation but, quite commonly, the analyst makes the *secularization assumption*—i.e., that religious worldviews have declined in importance in the United States and that the key to understanding current rationalizations for the status quo or ideologies of change is in secular classifications or assumptions.

Illustrative of the strengths and limitations of this genre, for our purposes, is an excellent study of attitudes toward capitalism and democracy (McClosky and Zaller 1984). Using survey data drawn from mass and elite samples the authors provide a contemporary map of the values dominant in American political culture. They do so by focusing on *capitalism*—a system of private ownership of the means of production in which self-interested entrepreneurs can pursue profit and have the right to unlimited gain through their economic effort—and *democracy*—a system in which all people possess equal worth and have the right to share in governance. Many of McCloskey and Zaller's items are versions of questions that could appear in measures of religious worldviews or implementing beliefs. Consider the following as examples: (1) "When people fail at one thing after another, it usually means (a) they weren't given a good enough chance to begin with, or (b) they are lazy and lack self-discipline"; (2) "I sometimes feel like laziness is a sin"; (3) "There is no such thing as being 'too strict' where conscience and morals are concerned"; (4) "If some people are born poor, the community (a) should help them to become equal with others, or, (b) should simply accept the fact that not everyone can make it."

McClosky and Zaller's discussions, particularly in chapters on the libertarian tradition, the cultural foundations of capitalism, and ideology and the American ethos either center on or touch religious worldviews, but often they pull back from an empirical analysis by citing trend data that religious leaders or religious ideas no longer hold sway over the American public. In some instances the variables for modest tests of the relationship between religious worldviews and political values appear to be present in the data set, but only in the chapter on libertarianism are they seen as relevant. Yet the potential for understanding linkages between religious worldviews and political philosophies of the status quo and of change is evident in such empirical studies. We develop the point in passing in several chapters and explicitly in chapter 11.

Religion as a Mediating Institution

A final theme vital to the understanding of religion and politics in social theory involves the *mass society hypothesis*, and the argument that religion is a mediating institution that can protect the citizen from an increasingly powerful modern state. It bears special relevance to the American political and religious cultures, again through the illumination of Tocqueville.

The dissolution of the feudal order left few people with protection from the state. No rival institution had either the force or the legitimacy to challenge the state when the state overstepped its previous bounds. Democracy made people direct participants in matters of state. Industrialization, urbanization, and concentration made citizens more dependent on regulations and services provided by the state. Communications and mass literacy put ordinary citizens in touch with transactions by the state's leadership. The decline of small face-to-face communities was thought to make citizens more dependent on the nation-state as a referent for personal identity. Thus, many of the putative benefits of liberal democracy could push citizens toward consummatory loyalties to the state. Many social theorists saw the rise of individualism and the decline of community as the problematique of the modern era.

Tocqueville wrote *Democracy in America* ([1835, 1840] 1958) from this problematique. He questions whether equality will inevitably lead to despotism in the United States. The American political culture shows promise, he argues, because the sovereign power has not yet destroyed mediating institutions. The critical mediating institutions he sees as: (1) the structure of the political system itself, (2) voluntary associations, and (3) religion. Government in the United States is highly decentralized, and power is shared through the township system; indeed politics is local, and power cannot readily concentrate in central national institutions so long as local government remains vital. Voluntary associations are everywhere in this nation of joiners; when a problem arises that is beyond the scope of self-help, people band together to solve it rather than turning directly to government. Such efforts build both community and attentiveness to the needs of other citizens, nurture deep loyalties to non-governmental institutions, build self-confidence and self-esteem, and render reliance on a central government less necessary (Tocqueville [1835, 1840] 1958, 243–58). Finally, religion, for Tocqueville, is the centerpiece in the struggle to keep equality from degenerating into despotism.

Religion in its American version treats eternity as one motif, but principally religion concerns itself with how to live daily life according to God's precepts. For Tocqueville, true religion requires adherence to dogma from all classes of citizens; in that respect it is a leveler and unifier (Tocqueville [1835, 1840] 1958,

311). (Hatch 1989 traces the democratizing effects of religion in the colonial and early republican periods.) Because religion, thus understood, does not compromise on its spiritual values—on how to live in harmony with God and humankind—it is less attentive to specific material conditions. Religion must remain relevant to life but cannot lose its transcendence of life. The more it becomes identified with specific institutional arrangements, the more it loses it transcendence. People come to look upon it as one of a welter of common opinions rather than as a revealed truth. The more it becomes allied with the state, the more it takes on the service functions of the larger society, replacing the family and voluntary associations. Religion must place itself at some distance from the state, encouraging limited loyalty to the state but reserving the right to judge. Religion can never replace the civil law because in so doing it becomes mundane, temporal; law derives from the sovereignty of the people, but justice derives from the sovereignty of humankind and its Creator. The higher law of justice is a hedge against majority tyranny (269–70). Tocqueville's language is reminiscent of Pauline metaphors in which Christians are "ambassadors for Christ"; they operate *in* the world, shaping it for good, but do not become *of* the world.

But much has happened to the United States and to the world since Tocqueville wrote about religion and other mediating institutions. The breakup of the feudal order in Europe spawned fleeting tyrannies in France but eventually culminated in two of the most totalitarian regimes known in modern times. Selznick (1960) and Neumann (1942) describe the concentration of power and loyalty achieved by the Bolsheviks and the National Socialists respectively. The situation in Germany is instructive.

Historically, postfeudal Germany developed three autonomous cultures: Catholic, bourgeois Protestant, and socialist. Citizens were born into one of these cultures and looked to their respective institutions for education, social welfare, youth groups, political parties, economic interest groups, etc. But these plural-cultural milieux were destroyed by the twentieth-century catastrophes of World War I, inflation, and the National Socialist revolution (and we might add, have remained in ashes as the result of World War II, American reconstruction designs, massive immigration, the economic miracle, and now the absorption of the East and new immigrations). The strategy of the National Socialists was (1) to take over the functions of each of these mediating institutions in the respective cultures, (2) to rationalize access to them in the name of equal treatment, and (3) to build consummatory loyalty to and dependence on the state. The party supplied the state with a mobilizing ideology and mission. The loss of mediating institutions would dismiss rivals for the loyalties of the citizenry. A new citizen could be shaped by a culture socialized by central institutions. While the historical details differed considerably in postrevolutionary Russia, the organizational design was similar.

In the United States, Kornhauser (1959) cautioned that mass society created a similar potential for totalitarian control. But several social scientists have argued that mediating institutions, particularly churches, offer the most effective protection against this slippery slope (Berger and Neuhaus 1977; Novak 1980). Their argument is that the emphasis on liberal individualism at the expense of communitarianism and on the homogenization of citizens leads to the disintegration of civil society. Civil society remains vital when mediating institutions are central to people's daily lives. Mediating institutions (1) protect the individual from an all-powerful, even if benevolent, state, (2) provide services that render dependence on state bureaucracies less necessary, (3) become centers of identity that rival or outstrip nation-state loyalties, and (4) nurture moral criteria for judging the performance of the state. No institution, to these social theorists, is better situated for these purposes than religion, particularly in its local churches.

Wald (1992) claims that church members derive five essential skills from active citizenship: (1) social skills in listening, mediating, and leading; (2) awareness of public issues from a moral perspective; (3) encouragement to join other civic and community betterment activities; (4) a conviction that there is a sacred character to social obligations that transcends self-interest; and (5) the self-esteem that derives from practice with public assignments. In short, not only are churches important mediating institutions in their own right, but they potentially contribute to the success of the other institutions in which Tocqueville placed his hope.

Succeeding chapters of this book will demonstrate what it is about religiosity that links churches to politics and analyze whether in the American setting that is healthy or unhealthy. Denominations and religious traditions, organizational life and social interactions, religious experiences and private spirituality, creeds and religious worldviews, and more assertive political cues by religious leades—all bear on the political life of Americans. Churches count, and politicians know it.

Thomas Jefferson, a deist, and John Adams, a congregationalist of Puritan stock, maintained a vigorous, sometimes disputatious, correspondence about the young republic, but they agreed on the necessity of religion: "true religion consisted of benevolent conduct toward one's fellow human beings" (see Wald 1992, 134ff.). They also agreed that dogmatic religion, when translated into a political program, could quickly subvert a fragile democracy.

Political theorists generally agree that democracy is a big gamble. As a set of procedures, democracy insists that all people affected by a policy have the right to register their preference on the policy, that each vote counts equally, and that the option generating a plurality or majority becomes public policy. In representative systems, democracy substitutes *candidate* for *policy* in these canons and asks that elected candidates be sensitive to the policy preferences of their constituents.

Procedural democracy offers little protection from itself. It makes two major assumptions about the citizenry: (1) a moral consensus operates among the citizenry that will protect both the system from self-destruction and the citizen from oppressive policies, and (2) the citizenry will inform itself about options and their consequences. The Founders who operated from *pessimistic* perspectives about human nature, derived from Puritan doctrine, were skeptical about these assumptions. In *Federalist* 10, James Madison argued eloquently about the threat of majority tyranny and the need for checks and balances in the Constitution. The Founders who operated from *optimistic* perspectives about human nature, rooted in enlightenment philosophy, based their hopes for democracy on social institutions. Thomas Jefferson was confident that religion could develop moral balance, that public schools could shape responsible, i.e., informed, citizens, and that local communities could nurture the desire for civic participation and educate citizens through civic action.

As small farms were replaced by huge factories, small communities turned into teeming tenements and anonymous suburbs, and public schools became combat zones and service providers directed to family pathologies, many have despaired that social institutions could carry the load. In a nation of joiners where interest groups were seen as organized sources for aggregating and articulating the needs and wants of citizens too little to count by themselves, many interest group leaders have come to be seen as part of the controlling elite. Political parties, as legions of foot soldiers, have been replaced by masters of mass media and purveyors of sound bytes.

Almost by default, churches are left with the heavy load of procedural democracy's assumptions. Unlike Western Europe and well beyond the death of God, churches in the United States have remained vital. As pointed out at the beginning of this chapter, all but about 15 percent of the population still maintain some identification with a religious tradition. While about 25 percent limit church attendance to festivals, crises, and family rituals, nearly 30 percent are in church every Sunday, often more than that, and the remainder of the population attends fairly frequently. In short, the opportunity for sensitizing citizens to moral concerns in public life remains in churches; the possibility of stimulating an information search as a prelude to informed judgment is within the churches' grasp. However, because churches sometimes are more concerned with the afterlife than this life, because they often promulgate particularistic beliefs about social issues, because they sometimes invoke divine sanctions against the nonconformist, or because their followers sometimes perceive their leaders as acting with supernatural authority, some observers, at best, grudgingly allow churches a role in the shaping of democratic citizens.

The last two decades have witnessed considerable conflict about the appropriate role of churches and the place of moral discourse in the public square. Some observers have viewed the rise of the New Christian Right, in particular, with alarm; they perceive devout followers of religious leaders as blinded to their information needs as citizens; whether the issue is abortion, school prayer, civil protections for homosexuals, censorship of textbooks, or the teaching of creationism, the religiously devout are seen as political puppets on a string controlled by local preachers or distant televangelists and popes. Other observers have argued that religious leaders perform important mediating roles in a democracy by placing moral concerns on the public agenda and encouraging followers to study the issues and gain information on the positions of political leaders and thus to make informed judgments in their political participation. The quest for peace and social justice, for example, involves long, complicated studies and widely varying judgments about "moral" policies among the faithful; differences are tolerable.

This volume hopes to illuminate whether and how religion matters in contemporary American politics. Social theorists have never overlooked religion as a political force and the Founders placed churches at the heart of the civic order. This volume not only offers a guide to measuring religion's effects, but it allows the reader to assess whether American religion continues to warrant the attention of social theorists and political actors.

References

Amos, Sigrid Karin. 1992. "The Reception of *Democracy in America*." Unpublished Ph.D. diss., University of Eichstätt, Germany.

Bellah, Robert N. 1975. *The Broken Covenant: American Civil Religion in a Time of Trial*. New York: Seabury.

Bellah, Robert N.; Madsen, Richard; Sullivan, William M.; Swidler, Ann; and Tipton, Steven M. 1985. *Habits of the Heart: Individualism and Commitment in American Life*. Berkeley: University of California Press.

Berger, Peter, and Neuhaus, Richard John. 1977. *To Empower People*. Washington, DC: American Enterprise Institute.

Blumenthal, Sidney. 1986. *The Rise of the Counter-Establishment: From Conservative Ideology to Political Power*. New York: Times Books.

Burnham, Walter Dean. 1965. "The Changing Shape of the American Political Universe." *American Political Science Review* 59:7–28.

Carmines, Edward G., and Stimson, James A. 1989. *Issue Evolution: Race and the Transformation of American Politics*. Princeton, NJ: Princeton University Press.

Crawford, Alan. 1980. *Thunder on the Right: The New Right and the Politics of Resentment*. New York: Pantheon.

Crunden, Robert M. 1982. *Ministers of Reform: The Progressives' Achievement in American Civilization, 1889–1920*. New York: Basic Books.

Dolan, Jay P. 1985. *The American Catholic Experience: A History from Colonial Times to the Present*. Garden City, NY: Doubleday.

Douglas, Mary, and Wildavsky, Aaron. 1983. *Risk and Culture*. Berkeley: University of California Press.

Downs, Anthony. 1957. *An Economic Theory of Democracy*. New York: Harper and Row.

Dreisbach, Daniel L. 1991. "In Pursuit of Religious Freedom: Thomas Jefferson's Church–State Views Revisited." Paper presented at the annual meeting of the American Political Science Association, Washington, DC.

Durkheim, Emile. [1915] 1965. *The Elementary Forms of Religious Life*. New York: Free Press.

Fiorina, Morris P. 1981. *Retrospective Voting in American National Elections*. New Haven, CT: Yale University Press.

Geertz, Clifford. 1973. *The Interpretation of Cultures*. New York: Basic Books.

Glock, Charles Y. 1972. "Images of 'God,' Images of Man, and the Organization of Social Life." *Journal for the Scientific Study of Religion* 11:1–15.

Glock, Charles Y., and Stark, Rodney. 1965. *Religion and Society in Tension.* Chicago: Rand McNally.

Greeley, Andrew M. 1981. *The Religious Imagination.* New York: Sadlier.

———. 1982. *Religion: A Secular Theory.* New York: Free Press.

Hatch, Nathan O. 1989. *The Democratization of American Christianity.* New Haven, CT: Yale University Press.

Hertzke, Allen D. 1988. *Representing God in Washington: The Role of Religious Lobbies in the American Polity.* Knoxville: University of Tennessee Press.

Hoge, Dean. 1974. *Commitment on Campus.* Philadelphia: Westminster Press.

James, William. 1902. *The Varieties of Religious Experience: A Study in Human Nature.* New York: Random House.

Kellstedt, Lyman A., and Noll, Mark A. 1990. "Religion, Voting for te President, and Party Identification, 1948–1984." In *Religion and American Politics,* ed. Mark Noll, 355–79. New York: Oxford University Press.

Kornhauser, William. 1959. *The Politics of Mass Society.* New York: Free Press.

Leege, David C. 1987. "The Parish as Community." *Notre Dame Study of Catholic Parish Life,* Report 10. Notre Dame, IN: University of Notre Dame.

Lincoln, C. Eric, and Mamiya, Lawrence H. 1990. *The Black Church in the African American Experience.* Durham, NC: Duke University Press.

McClosky, Herbert, and Zaller, John. 1984. *The American Ethos: Public Attitudes toward Capitalism and Democracy.* Cambridge, MA: Harvard University Press.

McCready, William C., and Greeley, Andrew M. 1976. *The Ultimate Values of the American Population.* Beverly Hills, CA: Sage Publications.

Marsden, George, and Longfield, Bradley J., eds. 1992. *The Secularization of the Academy.* New York: Oxford University Press.

Merriam, Charles E. 1925. *New Aspects of Politics.* Chicago: University of Chicago Press.

Neumann, Franz L. 1942. *Behemoth: The Structure and Practice of National Socialism.* New York: Oxford University Press.

Novak, Michael. 1980. *Democracy and Mediating Structures: A Theological Inquiry.* Washington, DC: American Enterprise Institute.

Ornstein, Norman; Kohut, Andrew; and McCarthy, Larry. 1988. *The People, the Press, and Politics.* Reading, MA: Addison-Wesley.

Otto, Rudolf. 1950. *The Idea of the Holy.* Trans. John W. Harvey. 2d ed. London: Oxford University Press.

Poloma, Margaret M., and Gallup, George H., Jr. 1991. *Varieties of Prayer: A Survey Report.* Philadelphia: Trinity Press International.

Roof, Wade Clark, and McKinney, William. 1987. *American Mainline Religion.* New Brunswick, NJ: Rutgers University Press.

Schneider, Louis, ed. 1967. *The Scottish Moralists: On Human Nature and Society.* Chicago: University of Chicago Press.

Selznick, Philip. 1960. *The Organizational Weapon: A Study of Bolshevik Strategy and Tactics.* Glencoe, IL: Free Press.

Simon, Herbert. 1957. *Models of Man.* New York: Wiley.

Somit, Albert, and Tanenhaus, Joseph. 1967. *The Development of Political Science.* Boston: Allyn and Bacon.

Stark, Rodney, and Bainbridge, William Sims. 1985. *The Future of Religion.* Berkeley: University of California Press.

Times-Mirror. 1988. "The People, the Press, and Politics: Post-Election Typology Survey." Occasional Report, November.

———. 1990. "The People, The Press, and Politics 1990: A Times-Mirror Typology." Occasional Report, September 19.

Tocqueville, Alexis de. [1835, 1840] 1958. *Democracy in America.* Trans. Phillips Bradley. New York: Vintage Books.

Tracy, David. 1975. *Blessed Rage for Order.* New York: Seabury.

———. 1981. *The Analogical Imagination: Christian Theology and the Culture of Pluralism.* New York: Crossroad.

Wald, Kenneth D. 1992. *Religion and Politics in the United States.* 2d ed. Washington, DC: Congressional Quarterly Press.

Wald, Kenneth D.; Owen, Dennis E.; and Hill, Samuel S., Jr. 1990. "Political Cohesion in Churches." *Journal of Politics* 52:197–215.

Welch, Michael R., and Leege, David C. 1988. "Religious Predictors of Catholic Parishioners' Sociopolitical Attitudes: Devotional Style, Closeness to God, Imagery, and Agentic-Communal Religious Identity." *Journal for the Scientific Study of Religion* 27:536–52.

Wildavsky, Aaron. 1987. "Choosing Preferences by Constructing Institutions: A Cultural Theory of Preference Formation." *American Political Science Review* 81:3–21.

Wuthnow, Robert. 1988. *The Restructuring of American Religion.* Princeton, NJ: Princeton University Press.

Chapter 2

Measurement Strategies in the Study of Religion and Politics

Kenneth D. Wald and Corwin E. Smidt

Like their colleagues in other social science disciplines, political scientists who study religion have embraced the empirical research methods associated with the "behavioral" revolution. Though researchers have not abandoned the philosophical, legal, and historical approaches dominant in the prebehavioral era, the political relevance of religion is increasingly appraised "scientifically." In practice, this means analyzing quantitative data obtained through sample surveys. Since the 1980s, when the resurgence of fundamentalist political concern virtually forced the topic of "religion and politics" onto the mainstream research agenda, academic journals and presses have increasingly published survey-based studies of religious influences on mass political behavior.

Surveys have gained ground on alternative research methods in this field for the same reasons they have been so widely employed elsewhere in the discipline: surveys represent a "mating of sampling theory and systematic interview techniques" that promises both precision and impressive analytic power (Turner and Martin 1984, xiii [Vol. 1]). In the field of religion and politics, data obtained from sample surveys have enriched such well-tilled research areas as church and state relations and greatly enhanced studies on the electoral impact of religious commitment, a subject once largely dependent on anecdote and hunch. This volume of essays is both a testament to the contribution of survey-based data in the study of religion and politics and an indicator of the issues and dilemmas that still confront researchers in this fascinating field.

For all their potential and power, surveys do not absolve the researcher of responsibility for careful conceptualization and thoughtful assumptions about the nature of social reality. Indeed, they demand it. It is good to be reminded occasionally that what we dignify with the somewhat grandiloquent label of *survey data* are nothing more than answers certain people give to specific questions. To make something meaningful out of these responses requires a prior theoretical framework, a system of interpretation. When behavioral techniques first began to spread among political scientists, critics were quick to point out the dangers of mere data-grubbing inherent in the new approach. To avoid mindless number-crunching, survey analysts must be guided by sound theoretical guidelines. As empirically oriented students of religion and politics, our first responsibility is to think systematically about how religious variables may influence political thinking and behavior.

The second task is to confront theory with data suitable for testing various formulations. Until quite recently, that effort was severely hampered by the traditional neglect of religion as the subject of political science research. Guided by the prevailing view that religion was either an unimportant or pernicious political influence, survey questionnaires seldom inquired beyond simple face-sheet religious measures such as denomination or church attendance. Lacking opportunities to collect their own data, students of religious influence on electoral politics had to take data where and in whatever form they could find it. In making do with studies conducted for other purposes, scholars had to use the theoretical assumptions and empirical measures of investigators for whom concern with the political impact of religion was, at best, secondary. Such was the case for the biennial surveys of the American population in the ongoing National Election Studies (NES), the most important data source for scholarship on electoral behavior. NES researchers had never attempted to assess the magnitude of measurement error in the few "religious" questions on the survey schedule or explored the implications of alternative conceptualizations of religious commitment for political behavior.

For students of religion and politics, discharging their responsibility will be easier thanks to the many new religious questions included in the NES 1989 Pilot Study. The Pilot Study protocol carried questions and design features expressly intended to assess the utility of different conceptions of religiosity. As part of this effort to explore new forms of religious influence in politics, the Pilot Study departed from NES conventions by asking respondents about their religious upbringing, probing more deeply about contemporary denominational attachment, exploring multiple denominational affiliation and attendance, assessing religious identity among persons who were not involved in organized religion, eliciting reactions to a checklist of personal and church traits, measuring other forms of both institutional and noninstitutional religious participation, and soliciting information about political themes encountered in church. Several of these innovations carried through to the 1990 NES and are strong candidates to join the pool of core items in future waves. These innovations permit us to investigate how different understandings of religion influence the findings of empirical research. The subsequent chapters make use of these new features to reveal the diverse paths and modes by which religious commitment exerts a political impact.

In this chapter, we look beyond the focused inquiries of our colleagues to explore the broader frameworks and assumptions that underlie the social scientific analysis of religion. We have purposely shied away from asserting that any particular set of questions or conceptualization of religion is optimal. The results of survey analysis inevitably bear the impact of decisions made by the researcher; such effects may be measured and anticipated but never eliminated. Accordingly, our task is not to identify the correct approach, a Holy Grail whose existence we doubt, but to alert scholars to the assumptions and implications associated with different analytic strategies. Nor is it our task to validate the truth or falsity of religious claims, a task beyond the competence of empirical research methods. Rather, our mission as authors of the various chapters is to identify different approaches to the study of religion and politics, to relate the study of religion and politics to other social scientific research agendas, and to assess the relative advantages and disadvantages, strengths and weaknesses, of different measurement items employed in the study of religion and politics. We want to suggest possibilities and complications rather than to foreclose options.

Why Conceptualization and Measurement Matter

The need for theoretical guidance arises from the complex and multifaceted subjects examined by survey research and the pronounced ambiguity that surrounds even the most familiar concepts in social research. For purposes of illustration, consider a study designed to tap attitudes about housing: a researcher might elicit respondent evaluations of the physical structure, the various subsystems in the shelter, the public services available in the environment, or the traits of the neighborhood where the structure is located (Newman 1984). The respondent's level of housing satisfaction might depend upon which of these aspects is elicited by the survey question. If a phenomenon as relatively tangible and discrete as housing presents so many possibilities for conceptualization and measurement, vaguer concepts offer even more choices to the researcher. Thus a phenomenon such as *ethnicity* might conceivably be indexed by self-identification, nationality, language use, family ancestry, membership in voluntary associations, or cultural practices (Smith 1984). Reliance on any one of these facets to the exclusion of the others might entice the researcher to misread or misinterpret the answer given by a respondent. There is no "correct" indicator, only measures that are more or less appropriate to the concept under study.

At first glance, religion might not seem especially problematic. Consider the nearly universal survey practice of assessing religious commitment by asking respondents to report the frequency of their church attendance. Seemingly, nothing could be simpler or more straightforward than telling an interviewer how often one attends worship services at church. Is not that what we mean by characterizing individuals as more or less religious? The inquiry certainly seems like an objective measure rather than a subjective matter that might be distorted by the respondent or conceptualized inadequately by the researcher. Yet even this relatively "hard" datum about church attendance partakes of a "quasi-factual" or "semiattitudinal" status midway between the extremes of subjectivity and objectivity (Turner and Martin 1984, 8–9 [Vol. 1]).

To begin with, church attendance presents serious conceptual difficulties as the sole marker of *religiosity*. Equating religious commitment with collective institutional worship ignores the religious consciousness exhibited by respondents who engage in private devotions, behave in accordance with religious mandates, maintain a worldview heavily influenced by religious conceptions, pray together with others outside of church, socialize intensively with co-religionists, participate in voluntary and charitable organizations, or subscribe to religious systems lacking an institutional basis. All but the last dimension of religious commitment may be positively related to church attendance but, even if that could be taken for granted, they are not identical to it. Moreover, even as an indicator of *church-type* religiosity, participation in formal worship services may provide less information about the extent of commitment than alternative measures such as the strength of psychological identification with the religious tradition, participation in the organizational and social life of the congregation, and level of religious knowledge gained through formal education and socialization to tradition (cf. Lazerwitz 1973).

Even if we could agree that religious commitment is best associated with church involvement of some sort, it is not altogether clear that the "simple" church attendance question envisioned provides us with accurate information. Survey research proceeds on the assumption that respondents harbor some piece of information—variously an attitude, belief, or bit of personal history—that can in principle be revealed accurately during an interview. Any lack of fit between the "true" measure—i.e., what the interview subject actually thinks or has experienced—and the information disclosed by the respondent during the interview is *error*.[1] The closer the fit between the respondent's answer and the actual piece of information solicited during the interview, the more valuable the resulting datum as a basis for study and research. Conversely, substantial discrepancies between the underlying "true value" of a variable and the answer provided to the interviewer threaten the validity of conclusions based upon personal interviews.

Errors may arise from sampling, transcription of interviews, data processing, and data analysis. But our concern here is with one particular class of survey errors that arise ultimately from decisions made by the researchers who formulate survey questions. The term *response effects* is reserved for any variables other than the respondent's opinion that affect the answer given to a survey question (Dijkstra and van der Zouwen 1982). Following Sudman and Bradburn (1974), response effects are normally attributed to characteristics of the interview process (such as the wording of questions), the respondent (e.g., a desire to impress or satisfy the partner in conversation), and the interviewer (including deviations from the text of the question, variations in intonation, or facial expression, etc.).[2] Response effects inhibit the accuracy of survey data.

The church attendance question seems a likely candidate to generate response effects. Respondents may not hear the question the interviewer intended to ask and may cast their response in a framework different from the interviewers. For example, when asked how often he or she attends worship services, one individual might consider the time spent volunteering at a soup kitchen or homeless shelter to be a form of church attendance—especially if the pastor encouraged it and the parishioner volunteered in church—while another respondent would think of *church attendance* in a more restrictive manner. Does *church attendance* fit the actions of a participant in a parenting workshop that meets in a church building and opens and closes with prayer? And what of the respondent who "attends" church in the privacy of the home, courtesy of religious services broadcast by television or radio? Is *church attendance* elastic enough to incorporate a prayer group that meets in a restaurant or private home? The ambiguity of the question is likely to color the value of responses.

In addition to its essential ambiguity, the church attendance question is particularly susceptible to *social desirability effects*—the overreporting of socially valued behavior (DeMaio 1984). Because religion retains such a positive valence in the United States, respondents might well put themselves on the side of angels by erring on the high side when reporting attendance. Faulty memory, willful distortion, and wishful thinking could all generate inflated reports. On the other hand, if a respondent assumed that the person asking the question was hostile to religion and did not wish to raise tensions, he or she might downplay the importance of religious ties and affiliation. Whatever the direction of the effect, a question that elicits social influence diminishes the quality of the resulting data.

Equally threatening, church attendance may not mean the same thing across different religious traditions—making it difficult to use the measure for comparison. Recognizing that "the significance of churchgoing varies from one denomination to another," Wilson (1978, 441) warned scholars against assuming the equivalence of attendance across religious traditions. The norms of some faiths and traditions place great emphasis upon collective worship and provide numerous opportunities for adherents to gather in prayer.[3] In others, greater priority is attached to individual devotion or other noncollective sacraments such as private confession. As many scholars contend, people can be religious in different ways; the analyst who utilizes a measure insensitive to such differences runs the risk of labeling as *irreligious* what is simply a different manner of expressing religious commitment. In the language of survey research, church attendance may be a biased indicator of religiosity.

This discussion suggests three levels of analysis that the researcher must confront before undertaking data analysis. At the macrolevel, we need to explore different analytical approaches to the understanding of religion and to acknowledge differences in approaches to religious phenomena that may be inherent within our particular studies on the relationship between religion and politics. If we or our respondents connote fundamentally different things as *religious*, the confusion will divert our attention from the contribution of religious forces to political behavior. Though our concern as political scientists is explaining political phenomena, the study of the relationship between religion and politics must obviously monitor theoretical and methodological developments that have occurred or are occurring in the study of religious as well as political phenomena. That means incorporating the insights associated with the sociology of religion and the field of religious studies generally.

Once we settle upon an understanding of the essence of religion as it affects politics, the analysis moves to an intermediate level where we must decide which forms of religiosity have potential political relevance. In practice, this level requires us to sort out the dimensions of religious commitment. Of the various expressions of religiosity, which are most likely to exert an impact upon behavior in the realm of politics? As an example, consider the possibility that church involvement encourages political participation, a topic explored in detail in chapter 6. The relationship may develop because the churchgoer encounters certain values associated with a religious ethic—such as a sense of stewardship and community responsibility—that similarly promote civic activism. Or it may be that participation in church activities is an empowering experience by virtue of the social skills it facilitates. Perhaps religion is significant in turnout simply because affiliation with a church signifies an investment in and attachment to the community. To complicate matters further, imagine that these mechanisms work at cross-purposes: religious values encourage civic involvement but the time demands of congregational membership discourage political action. The analyst who studies the link between turnout and religiosity with a measure of religious commitment that does not tap these potential linkage mechanisms—such as, for example, some indicator of denominationalism—may erroneously underestimate the political potency of religion. The same danger arises from the selection of dependent measures that have no obvious theoretical link to religion. With surveys that capture the richness and multidimensionality of religious commitment, there is both opportunity and responsibility to think through causal mechanisms.

At the microlevel, the issues typically arise in the context of specific questions. Assuming we agree on a conception of religion and have identified a form of religious expression likely to influence political outlooks, the next task is to evaluate the measures of religiosity available to us. This step involves subjecting the various measures to standard validity and reliability analysis and discovering which are truer to the concept under investigation.

Analytical Approaches to Religion

More than a century ago, Francis Galton argued that scientific research methods could assess the validity of religious claims—in effect turning theological arguments into testable hypotheses. He thus made the longevity of clergyman a critical test of whether prayers were answered! Much more modest than Galton, modern social scientists recognize that they do not study religion per se but rather the social outcroppings of religious commitment. The core of religion—

the realm of the transcendent, supreme beings, and the communication of divine mandates—is beyond the reach of social science. What we can do, however, is determine how the beliefs and institutions associated with religion influence the political behavior of adherents.

The interpretation of answers provided by interview participants depends crucially on the theoretical and conceptual assumptions of the scientific researcher. While the conceptualization of religion has varied across epistemological traditions, social scientists have generally employed one of two research strategies in the study of religion: (1) religion as a mental phenomenon—*believing*, or (2) religion as a social phenomenon—*belonging*.[4] These approaches correspond to a distinction between a *personal-subjective* understanding of religion, emphasizing individual faith and piety, and a *social-collective* perspective that stresses the community basis of religious identity and expression (Roof 1979, 19–20). The first approach traces its roots to the work of Max Weber, who emphasized the capacity of religious belief systems to guide and direct secular behavior by rewarding righteous conduct and sanctioning deportment that violated prescribed norms. The other approach reflects Emile Durkheim's stress on the importance of the group in religion and the behavioral ramifications of the belonging component of religion.

Religion as a mental phenomenon encompasses the "fundamental beliefs, ideas, ethical codes, and symbols associated with a religious tradition, including what others call a theology or belief system" (Wald 1992, 27). This research strategy emphasizes both the specific content of religious teachings and the associated package of values and acceptable behavior that the religious tradition encourages. Several presuppositions are associated with this approach: (1) that human thinking and behavior are governed predominantly by cognitive processes; (2) that individuals are related to the world around them primarily in an atomistic, rather than an organic, fashion; and (3) that the impact of religion on political thought and behavior is "immediate" and direct.

Within the personal-subjective understanding of religion, the analyst must choose between substantive and functional approaches in defining religious beliefs. The substantive approach limits the analysis of religious beliefs "to those systems of thought embodied in social organizations that posit the existence of the supernatural" (Stark and Bainbridge 1985, 3). More specifically, the substantive tradition stresses the content of religious beliefs. In the analysis of religiously influenced political behavior, such substantive religious doctrines as orthodoxy, fundamentalism, biblical literalism, and otherworldliness have been deployed as explanatory variables (see, for example, chapter 9). For the most part, these measures of traditional religious outlooks have been hypothesized to promote conservative political values or withdrawal from political activity altogether. More recently, scholars have explored broader religious worldviews with either individualistic or communitarian visions (see chapter 11). Rather than lend support to the *more religious, more conservative* framework, these more complex formulations explore the cognitive foundations of different political orientations.

In the competing functionalist tradition, religious beliefs are less significant for their content than for the manner in which they are held. In this tradition, the primal nature of religious beliefs is assumed to foster certain cognitive habits that may take on political relevance. Variables such as authoritarianism, dogmatism, intolerance of ambiguity, and hostility to outgroups represent religiously induced modes of reasoning that may spill over into the political realm. Once again, the presupposition of most researchers has been that closed and rigid cognitive traits are somehow conducive to conservative political traits. But as in the substantive approach, more recent work in this tradition has broadened from specific cognitive traits to explore more encompassing orientations associated with what Allport (1954, chap. 3) described as *mature* religious commitment. Allport and Ross (1967) introduced a famous distinction between those who hold religious views *instrumentally* and the *intrinsic* religious who fully internalize religious imperatives and incorporate the values in their behavior and attitudes. Building on this concept, Batson and Ventis (1982, 149–50) proposed a *quest* dimension that measures the capacity for "honestly facing existential questions in all their complexity, while resisting clear-cut, pat answers." With this broadening of perspective, scholars have identified a form of intense religious commitment that appears to contribute to such positive orientations as racial tolerance and political sophistication.

While some analysts of religion choose conceptual and measurement strategies based on mental models of human behavior, others emphasize how religion finds expression within social entities. Still, just how religion is to be viewed as a social phenomenon can vary significantly. Individuals can be analyzed as members of a religious group that is categorical in nature, as members of a socioreligious group, as members of a particular religious movement, or as members of a religious organization or institution. The choice of which type of group approach to employ depends on the particular theory one seeks to test and the empirical characteristics of the group members (e.g., their relative pattern of social interaction and the bases of their association) as well as the particular operational measures available to the analyst.

As a social phenomenon, religion may be expressed within social collectivities whose members may exhibit a common identity, a regular pattern of social interaction, or similar expectations (group norms) concerning belief and behavior. Because members of religious groups frequently share a common history as well as common experiences, they may respond to social and political events more in a collective, than in an individual, fashion. Since this approach emphasizes that religious beliefs, experiences, and practices are generally expressed within some larger social context, principles that govern other social groups are seen to apply to religious groups as well. Consequently, this approach suggests that the political thought and behavior of religious group members are not necessarily derived from their specific religious beliefs, experiences, or practices. Several presuppositions are associated with this approach: (1) that human thinking and behavior are governed largely by social, rather than cognitive, processes, (2) that individual responses to political phenomena are mediated by and through participation within social groups, and (3) that religion's impact upon political thinking and behavior is often more indirect than direct in nature.

To a degree, the differences between these two understandings of religion—as belief and belonging—mirror the important differences between *ritualist* and *pietist* religious traditions described by Kellstedt and Green in chapter 3. The ritualist-pietist distinction itself corresponds to Max Weber's famous division of religious organizations into *church* and *sect* archetypes. The *church-type* ritualist families, with highly developed and formalized religious structures, liturgies, and creeds, tend to arrange doctrine hierarchically and permit a range of acceptable beliefs on less important matters. Two such exemplars of ritualism, Catholicism and Judaism, strongly emphasize a communal or ethnic consciousness. Beliefs are not unimportant in either tradition, but the sacraments and ritual acts associated with Catholicism and Judaism tend to serve as markers of community membership more so than assertions of particular beliefs (Leege 1988; Liebman and Cohen 1990, 97; Himmelfarb 1975). There is considerable reliance in Catholicism, for example, on grace mediated by the sacraments that forgive and transform the backslider. Pietism, more *sectlike* in Weberian terms, is characterized by a more congregational polity, less-structured routines for worship, and an emphasis on unmediated confrontation between God and believer. Affiliation in the Protestant tradition where pietism is strong is first of all the embrace of particular and especially personal practices; indeed, pietistic traditions insist on adherence to orthodoxy and tend to reject diversity of interpretation and behavior. Personal vices that impair the religious standing of the individual in the pietist tradition are often regarded as unavoidable shortcomings that require absolution in the ritualist tradition (Gerth and Mills 1946, 320).

This difference of emphasis means that the same religious measure will not perform equally well in all religious settings. The *religion as belief* framework closely conforms to the more pietistic formulations of Protestantism while the *religion as belonging* label more closely characterizes Catholicism, Judaism, and those Protestant denominations with a close affinity to Catholic rituals and sacramental understanding such as Anglicanism and Lutheranism. It should be emphasized, however, that we are describing central tendencies and that all traditions mix elements of faith with sacrament. Nonetheless, belief-oriented measures that discriminate effectively among Protestants, accurately dividing them into gradations of religious commitment, may be less useful with the more sacramental traditions. For the latter, religious behavior, especially the observance of mandated rites and communal involvement, probably has greater utility.

Posing the *belief* and *belonging* approaches as the endpoints on a continuum or as two discrete perspectives obscures the possibility of interaction between them. It is possible for the two modes of religiosity to operate independently of each other. Certain religious beliefs may be meaningful and salient for an individual who does not belong to or otherwise engage actively with any particular religious group. Conversely, individuals may find themselves involved with a group yet not accept or internalize the beliefs that define group membership. In other words, there are different degrees of *believing* and *belonging*, and these variations may be systematically related to political behavior. More commonly, as noted in chapter 9, the relationship between the *believing* and the *belonging* components of religion remains unclear. While some have argued that the two are relatively independent of one another, others have suggested various ways in which they are related. The polar opposite possibilities, that religious beliefs lead to religious belonging (Alston and McIntosh 1979) and the reverse (White 1968; Welch 1981), are countered by those who argue that beliefs and belonging interact to form a single process (Davidson and Knudsen 1977; Roof 1978).

As the contributors to this volume demonstrate, empirical researchers seldom make a clear-cut choice between the two forms of religious commitment. Recognizing the complex interplay between membership and belief, it is more common to incorporate elements of both. Thus, in chapter 3, Kellstedt and Green demonstrate that political differences within denominations generally sharpen with controls for the level of religious salience. Similarly, the analyses presented by Kellstedt and Smidt in chapter 9 show that orientations toward the Bible—a type of belief measure—discriminate well between the more and less politically conservative members of common religious traditions. The composite measure of religious commitment developed in chapter 8 combines the salience of religion as reported by the respondent, private devotionalism, and church attendance. In other chapters, the contributors include measures associated with both approaches.

The personal-subjective and social-collective approaches to religion also posit different means of political influence. From the tradition that emphasizes belief as the driving force linking religion and other types of behavior, the constraint between belief and behavior is largely a product of internal psychology. According to theories of cognitive consistency, individuals whose beliefs stand in logical contradiction to each other experience some psychological pressure to bring the cognitions into consistency. For example, those who believe that the Bible is literally true may interpret its language to prohibit women's equality, freedom of choice on abortion, and homosexual rights. The strain toward consistency is likely to be especially severe for persons who hold to their beliefs with considerable intensity. Those who assign high levels of salience to their religious beliefs should feel more pressure to bring their political cognitions into congruence with their religious cognitions than those whose religious beliefs are less important to them (Hoge and de Zulueta 1985). Under such conditions, it may not be too surprising that *religiosity* (or *salience*, the term favored by several contributors) has been found to be a significant predictor of attitudinal constraint among different religious groups (Jelen, Kellstedt, and Wilcox 1990). In this volume, Guth and Green (chapter 8) find that salience increases the impact of religious tradition on partisanship and a variety of dependent variables.

This mentalist approach calls attention to the cognitive processes that underlie political thinking. The information-processing perspective explores strategies that individuals employ to cope with the flood of complex data that would otherwise overwhelm them. These strategies include categorization and the employment of schemata, techniques that involve, respectively, comparing new attitude objects with other objects whose characteristics are stored in memory, and developing a set of overarching cognitive images about concepts such as a "person, role, group, event, or other object" (Kuklinski, Luskin, and Bolland 1991, 1341). Religious beliefs may play a prominent role in these information-processing strategies with, for example, religious self-classifications serving as devices by which individuals filter and process political information (see chapter 4). So, too, various schemata may have religious roots, particularly when one recognizes that these schemata themselves may develop in social interactions (Doise and Machie 1981). Furthermore, the questions of what information is recalled and which schemata are deployed may also be related to religious variables. Socialization studies emphasize that what is learned early is retained and what is learned first helps to structure what is learned later. Because religious beliefs and outlooks are strongly emphasized by parents during their children's early years, these beliefs and outlooks may well shape the particular cognitive habits later used by voters. And even when religious beliefs are acquired later in life, the result of a conversion experience of the "Saul/Paul" variety, they are likely to be salient to the convert and powerful enough to override existing cognitive orientations.

Conversely, the social-collective approach finds the linkage between religion and politics forged primarily by the actions of religious and political elites and the operation of social influence processes. Because religious doctrines do not have straightforward political messages that can be discerned easily, churchgoers may need assistance deriving political conclusions from religious beliefs. Some guidance is supplied at the denominational or interdenominational level, where Washington-based offices, such as the National Association of Evangelicals or Baptist Joint Committee, lobby both "up" to political elites and "down" to the masses (Hertzke 1988). Two of the studies in this volume indicate that the local congregation also serves as a venue for the politicization process. As chapters 12 and 13 discuss, exposure to cues provided by ministers who make explicit links between certain religious beliefs and political thinking may enhance relationships between the two. The analysis in chapter 13 suggests that congregational cues are most potent behaviorally when they are reinforced by political messages from televangelists. Chapter 8 suggests that latent partisan propensities are more likely to become manifest for individuals who are religiously active in terms of attendance and devotionalism.

If the more intimate environment of the congregation or religious community provides opportunities for individuals to learn about the political implications of their religious affiliation, this process may depend on subjective norm assessments (Fishbein and Ajzen 1975), i.e., an individual's assessments concerning what relevant others expect him or her to do. Those expectations have their basis in frequency of social interaction, the pattern of social relationships that may constrain social interaction, or the content of transactions among individuals who are interacting (Kiecolt 1988, 384). Thus, for example, it may be that the political thinking or behavior of evangelicals may be contextually determined, i.e., those evangelicals who attend evangelical denominations may differ in their political thinking and behavior from those evangelicals who attend mainline denominations or who are Catholic (Welch and Leege 1991). The effect may be mitigated by the ready availability of politically conservative mass media sources rooted in the evangelical tradition (see the discussion of *mismatched* respondents in chapter 13).

More generally, the existence of a supportive religious community may encourage the individual to link religious and political values in certain ways. According to cultural norm theories, attitudes reflect the values of subcultural groups and are transmitted through socialization processes. Differences in attitudes within and across subcultural groups are tied to differences in social learning, social acceptance, and differential association (Kiecolt 1988, 383). Thus, studies analyzing the relationship between religion and politics can easily be cast within a *symbolic politics* approach that portrays political attitudes and behavior as "unthinking, reflexive, affective responses to remote attitude objects" (Sears et al. 1980, 681). Such attitudes are formed in the matrix of cultural environments that delimit the individuals. Different religious groups (e.g., evangelicals and Jews) interact predominantly within different subcultures; these different subcultures may, in turn, be largely religious in nature and origin. Hence, members of different socioreligious groups living within different subcultures may acquire different political attitudes and behavior through differences in the content of what is taught, and these differences may be further reinforced by differences in people with whom they associate.

Measurement Strategy

The selection of a model that emphasizes religious belief raises new questions about what should be measured and how. Most analysts using mental measures have focused on various propositional statements tapping religious beliefs or doctrines. In one of the earliest and most influential attempts, Stark and Glock (1968) developed an index of Christian orthodoxy including items about beliefs in a personal God, the divinity of Jesus, the authenticity of biblical miracles, and the existence of the devil. More recent efforts (e.g., Fullerton and Hunsberger 1982; Pecnik and Epperson 1985) have attempted to refine these measures for use across different religious groups or to adapt them to the particular belief systems of specific religious communities. Such efforts are driven by psychometric imperatives to produce valid and reliable measures equivalent to the best secular attitude scales. That is, the scales must actually measure the quality they purport to assess and must do so consistently.

In response to several difficulties associated with the doctrinal approach, scholars have recently developed alternative mental measures of religion. Basically, these alternative approaches have sought to move beyond doctrinal questions, which assess whether or not respondents conform to some a priori image of religiosity, to *pre-doctrinal* questions that assess worldviews on their own terms. This viewpoint, a response to the admonition to study *how* people are religious, respects the integrity of the individual's perspective even if it does not conform to doctrinal definitions of orthodoxy. One such approach focuses on the holding of religious images; this method asks whether there may be common ways of thinking about God that not only transcend different religious doctrines but that also spill over into politics. Using an attribute checklist, for example, will reveal whether respondents perceive God as a warm, caring, and nurturing force or rather as a cold, judgmental, and punitive deity. Preliminary research suggests that the images one associates with God, rather than doctrinal tenets per se, serve as strong predictors of social outlooks and political values (Greeley 1984, 1988; Hoffman 1985; Jelen 1985; MacIver 1990; Welch and Leege 1988).

Another approach that has attempted to move away from doctrinal measures is the focus on foundational beliefs. Foundational beliefs interpret and give meaning to individual perceptions of reality; they provide guidance concerning what is problematic about the world, offer ways to cope with it or avoid it, and provide ultimate solutions to such problems. Concretely, researchers have attempted to determine how the respondent understands the relationship between God and the world, the nature of salvation, the meaning of transcendence, and so forth. These views have subsequently been linked to different styles of political thinking and values (Benson and Williams 1982; Leege and Welch 1989a). This approach is explored in depth in chapter 11 with data from a study of Catholic parishioners and a study of church activists.

In measuring doctrinal and alternative foundational religious beliefs of respondents, scholars face the same strategic choices that confront researchers in any attitude study. One approach is more analytically deductive in nature; it first attempts to identify potentially important religious beliefs and doctrines and then develops operational measures to tap those beliefs that have been conceptually derived (e.g., the orthodoxy measure developed by Glock and Stark 1966). A second approach is more inductive in nature; it derives important dimensions of religious beliefs by looking for mathematical relationships among sets of items from a large pool of indicators (e.g., the orthodoxy dimension derived by King and Hunt 1972).[5] This choice is likely to affect both the relative level of abstraction concerning the concepts and variables that are analyzed and the nature and strength of one's findings. For example, while the first approach might analyze the political ramifications of belief in premillennial dispensationalism (e.g., Turner and Guth 1989; Wilcox, Linzey, and Jelen 1991), the second approach might seek to discern whether answers to questions tapping belief in premillennial dispensationalism are a component part of a broader dimension of religious beliefs, e.g., fundamentalism, which may affect political attitudes and behavior.

The social-collective approach to religion, a perspective that emphasizes belongingness, imposes similar choices upon the investigator. What does it mean to belong to a religious group, and what groups are denoted as religious communities? Taking the second question first, religious attachment can occur at several different levels. Many surveys limit affiliation to a preference for one of four broad religious groupings: Protestant, Catholic, Jewish, other. As gross as it is, the simple distinction between Protestants and the other three groups still influences electoral choice in presidential campaigns (Erikson, Lancaster and Romero 1989). It is possible to identify successively more intimate forms of religious affiliation that might better discriminate among religiously grounded political worldviews: the transchurch movement based on mainline Protestant and evangelical Protestant traditions (e.g., National Council of Churches, National Association of Evangelicals), the denomination, the congregation, trends or tendencies within the congregation. *Membership* in these various religious communities can entail several different forms of affiliation. In addition to formal membership with a particular congregation affiliated with a specific denomination, there is the option of formal membership with a particular congregation only. Others may choose not be formal members but may be affiliated with a particular denomination or congregation through regular attendance. People who maintain membership in a congregation may associate primarily with very specific communities of interest within the church—from well-organized fellowships of like-minded individuals to nascent comradeships organized around particular religious trends (e.g., Leege 1987; Warner 1988, chap. 2). Participation in these subgroups may reinforce identification with the larger congregation or emerge as the primary source of religious identity that competes with or even threatens loyalty to the larger community. These options in affiliation should prompt researchers to consider different levels of religious classification. Transcending the familiar trichotomy of Protestant-Catholic-Jew, which seems to have less utility in the modern period, scholars have developed more nuanced schemes that apportion individuals into meaningful denominational groups or into religious tendencies that incorporate several denominations (see chapter 3) or even to congregations that exert independent influence on religious values (Jelen 1991; Wald, Owen, and Hill 1988). These new taxonomies show much more power in structuring political choice than some denomination-based classification systems.

In addition to group membership per se, the political power of religion may also stem from "the web of allegiances and antipathies that individuals develop toward groups" (Kinder 1983, 405). Accordingly, the political beliefs and attitudes that people express may reflect simply a "badge of social membership"—a declaration, both to themselves and to others, of their social identity. The categories relevant in perception are typically defined by an individual's distinction between his or her own groups and other groups (Conover 1985, 142). Not only may such social identities influence what is relevant perceptually, they can also provide a basis for social comparison—comparison that in a very real sense helps to define a person's place and interests in society (Tajfel 1981). Given the relatively high level of church attendance evident among the American people (Wald 1992), many Americans are likely to develop religious identities that are highly salient to them—identities that may help to shape their political thinking. There is much speculation and some evidence that resentment over their cultural devaluation by secular elites has animated traditionalist Protestants to undertake restorationist political efforts (Wald, Owen, and Hill 1989). It has also been suggested that efforts to link these individuals in common political groups, such as the Moral Majority, were doomed by group antipathies (Wilcox and Gomez 1990). The more fundamentalist Protestant members found it difficult to cooperate with Roman Catholics, whom they traditionally stigmatized as an outgroup, and Catholics, in turn, were wary of joining with groups whom they perceived as hostile to their faith. Chapter 4 suggests that very specific forms of religious identification—self-selected labels such as *evangelical* or *fundamentalist*—exert powerful political impact on Protestants even when other markers of religiosity have been taken into account.

Whether conceived as positive commitment to a group or a form of boundary maintenance, religion as a form of social identity may be indexed in different ways. As we know from the social psychological study of reference groups, attachment to the group does not require formal membership, nor does the power of the group over the behavior of members necessarily depend on the strength of affective ties binding individuals to one another. Hence, it has been suggested that self-identification, the "mere" selection of a label or set of labels, may provide valuable clues about affiliation and reveal identities that play an important role in political behavior (see chapter 4 for references). At the same time, it is important to recognize that selection of some labels—such as *born-again Christian* among southern Protestants—may be culturally determined, if not reflexive, and therefore less discriminating in predicting political behavior (chapter 10).

The social-collective approach might also identify certain forms of behavior as the best marker of belonging to a group. These forms of behavior may encompass certain language forms (e.g., whether one is willing to describe oneself with a label such as *born-again Christian*), certain devotional practices (e.g., participation in prayer groups or Bible studies), ritual behavior (such as participation in various sacraments or observance of dietary laws), or certain forms of social behavior (e.g., refusal to participate in certain "worldly" forms of behavior such as drinking alcohol, smoking tobacco, attending movies, or playing cards). The badge of membership might literally be revealed in choice of clothing or in less overt denotations. As chapter 7 indicates, the extent of private religious practice may exert an independent influence on certain types of political behavior and attitudes. By performing various religious acts in the privacy of the home, individuals may link themselves to others in an "invisible church" that carries implications for behavior in the world outside.

The final point to be made about measurement strategy applies whether the researcher is guided by the Weberian or Durkheimian framework. Neither approach is well served by a single indicator. Religion as belonging clearly encompasses multiple forms of association—psychological identification with a religious tendency (chapter 4), affiliation with a denomination (chapter 3), perceived centrality of religion (chapter 8), participation in private devotions (chapter 7), and involvement in a specific religious organization (chapter 6). Though correlated, these are different forms of behavior exhibited in varying degrees by survey respondents. Treating these individual items as components of a more general construct, the research strategy illustrated in chapters 4 and 8 may generate a more authentic measure of religious commitment than simply designating any one item to represent the concept of religious belonging. Yet even such composite measures may simply aggregate a tendency peculiar to one tradition and should not be treated as the "best" single measure of religiosity across all religious traditions and faiths.

The same stricture applies to adherents of the religion as believing approach. Attitude psychology has long recognized that the general domain of belief includes the substance of the belief itself, the emotions engendered by the belief, and the value attached to the belief. Cognitive psychology has added concern about the manner in which belief is held in memory and deployed. In this volume, contributors honor that complexity by exploring the political role of beliefs about the Bible (chapter 9), the born-again experience (chapter 10), and the general salience that individuals attribute to their religion (chapter 8). The multivariate analyses indicate that all three forms of belief make independent contributions to political attitudes, underscoring the importance of treating belief as a multi-indicator variable.

Operationalization

After choices are made about the conceptualization and measurement of religion, after this realm is reduced to concrete attitudes and behavior, the researcher must evaluate the caliber of the specific questions on the interview protocol. That step is essential whether the researcher collects his or her data through a special-purpose survey or relies instead on data collected as part of other research projects. The first option is appealing because it offers the researcher considerable freedom in conceptualizing and measuring religion according to personal taste in theoretical assumptions (Leege and Welch 1989b). Notwithstanding the costs and demands of a special-purpose survey, several important data sets have been generated by scholars interested in the religious factor in American politics. These include the Evangelical Voter Study, the Notre Dame Study of Catholic Parish Life, periodic surveys of clergy in several traditions, and congregational surveys in various communities. These surveys have yielded important insights in peer-reviewed publications but are typically limited to specific religious groups or cover only limited geographic areas. Given these limitations and the cost of undertaking such efforts, most scholars will resort instead to secondary analysis of such large and institutionalized sources as the National Election Studies, General Social Survey, the Gallup Poll, or other polls conducted by private organizations but eventually released to the scholarly community.

Regardless of the data set, the research payoffs promised by survey methods may be compromised by limitations of measurement. Personal interviews, the most common method of data collection in political behavior research, are powerful but imperfect sources of social information. Instruction manuals on survey techniques commonly stress the imperfections associated with the process of sampling—covering everything from deficiencies in the sampling frame to non-response bias—and provide guidance about minimizing errors in transcription and coding. But as many survey researchers have come to recognize and their critics have long asserted, some of the most powerful threats to the validity of survey data are embedded in the very core of the interview process. As noted above, the term "response effects" is reserved for survey errors associated with interviewers, interviewees, and their interaction through standardized survey questions.

The impact of response effects is best assessed by comparing answers to questions posed at different times or to different samples, design features incorporated in the 1989 Pilot Study. First, the 1989 study was actually a series of *reinterviews* with respondents in the 1988 National Election Study. This arrangement permitted comparisons of answers given to questions in 1988 with the responses to variations on those questions in 1989. On the assumption that religious outlooks and behavior are stable over the short run, this *test-retest* method is one way to reveal the impact of variations in question form on the responses to survey questions. Second, questions were posed in different formats to subgroups of respondents in 1989. Assuming that subsamples should yield approximately the same attitude distributions to identical questions, this *split-ballot* technique also reveals the magnitude of influence associated with variations in the form of a question. Both types of experiments were undertaken to explore the impact of several aspects of question form: the use of *filter* items, the addition of qualifying clauses, different numbers and types of response options, and new follow-up questions to yield greater precision in response patterns.

Many of these innovations, first profiled in a working paper prepared for the National Elections Studies (Leege, Kellstedt and Wald 1990) are assessed in the accompanying research reports. What do they tell us about the behavior and properties of some of the perennial religious items included on the National Election Studies?

From the *religion as belonging* perspective, the critical measure of denominational affiliation clearly benefited from the methodological innovations first undertaken in 1989. The additional probes for specific church affiliation and the question about childhood affiliation revealed serious levels of misclassification in the pre-1989 formulation. When denominations were aggregated into religious families, the effect was in some instances to substantially misstate the true proportion. A careful examination of pentecostals revealed a 25 percent undercount due to misallocation of denominations. These errors were compounded when religious denominations were subsumed into broader traditions. Among Lutherans, for example, somewhere between one-fifth and one-third were improperly allocated on the evangelical vs. mainline divide due to ambiguities in denominational identification. The general error rate for all Protestants on this specific classification was around 14 percent. As illustrated in chapter 3, the net effect of improving denominational measurement and developing a nuanced scheme for classifying denominations by underlying tendencies is to reveal much more clearly how denomination exerts substantial electoral influence.

Our understanding of the other components of religion as a form of group membership also benefits from more careful assessment. The experiments in measuring religious identity in chapter 4 revealed that this concept is subject to the same problems of response set and measurement error that afflict such standard measures as party identification, ideological self-placement, and feeling thermometer scores. The use of screening questions in the 1989 church attendance series significantly altered the measurement of religious attachment by controlling for social desirability (Leege, Kellstedt, and Wald 1990, 21–32). Enabling respondents more easily to *dis*claim involvement with organized religion increased the percentage of the "unchurched" from the abnormally low rate of 8 percent found in other surveys to a figure of almost 18 percent, much closer to the estimates of those who contrast survey data with church membership data. Removing such false positives and correcting for the greater emphasis upon church attendance in the evangelical Protestant tradition helped to uncover a strong link between church involvement and voter turnout in chapter 6. At the same time, we learned that the phenomenon of attendance at multiple churches does not appear as significant as first imagined, nor is it likely to exert a political impact. On the evidence presented about religious television viewing in chapter 13, the use of more precise closed response options in questions about religious behavior may generate more accurate reports. Chapter 8 suggests that notwithstanding a truncated set of response options, there is predictive value in a measure of ascribed religious importance based on the amount of guidance respondents report receiving from religion.

Previous research has suggested that marginal distributions on belief items are extremely sensitive to variations in wording. The reports in chapters 9 and 10 confirm that finding and suggest improvements, such as increasing the number of response options for the Bible question to reduce the skewed distribution. While these changes seldom alter the direction of a relationship between a religious and a political variable, they often enhance the magnitude of the religious effect. In some cases, the change may be substantial enough to raise the religious factor to preeminence in the hierarchy of predictors. Even if our goal is to relate religion to politics rather than to profile religion, there is convincing reason to pay attention to the nuances of religious measurement.

The Case for Religious Influence in American Political Behavior

This chapter, and the entire volume in which it appears, is premised on the implicit assumption that religion—variously conceptualized and measured through opinion surveys—contributes fundamentally to the nature and character of the belief systems of Americans. That assumption alone justifies the elaborate efforts to obtain meaningful and accurate religious measures from the National Election Studies. While the case will be made—or not—by the research reports that follow this chapter and in subsequent efforts over the years, we need to make the assumption explicit and provide the underlying rationale.

The conventional wisdom concerning American political thinking has been that most Americans are largely indifferent to ideological concepts, lack a consistent perspective on most matters of public policy, and express authentic opinions on relatively few policy questions. This conventional wisdom has been challenged with the claim that a large proportion of the American electorate is capable, under proper circumstances, of thinking ideologically, that the American electorate has revealed greater cohesion in its stands on public policy since the early 1960s, and that opinion instability is more a reflection of unclear questions than unclear thinking. In the final analysis, however, it would appear that the fragmented, narrow, and diverse political thinking of the American electorate cannot be reduced solely to problems of measurement and environmental constraints. Rather, "instability reflects both fuzzy measures and fuzzy citizens" (Kinder 1983, 397).

If ideology does not constitute the taproot for political beliefs for most Americans, then what does serve as the root or roots of political beliefs evident among the American electorate? In a wide-ranging review of this issue, Kinder (1983) has noted five alternative sources of constraint: personality, self-interest, group identification, values, and inferences from history. We have already made reference to the potency of religion as a basis of group identification. For each of the other potential sources of constraint, religious variables could also be viewed as important components.

Personality theories frequently invoke religion as an important source of political socialization and attitude constraint. For example, political scientists who adopt a psychoanalytic approach to political thinking and behavior tend to see such thinking and behavior as shaped by unconscious motives that reflect "a displacement of intrapsychic needs that have little or nothing to do with politics" (Lau 1990, 299). We are reminded here of the classic yet much-maligned *authoritarian personality* syndrome that included a proto-fascist disposition in politics. Because this personality type supposedly developed as a result of growing up in a household characterized by heavy emphasis on repression and restraint, the authors linked, if only indirectly, a certain form of religious socialization with a very destructive form of politics. Other forms of religion might conceivably generate a different set of intrapsychic needs that shape the political thoughts and behavior exhibited by the individual and, thereby, help to interpret the specific political attitudes and behavior manifested by the individual.[6]

Just as was the case for personality variables, religious variables could easily serve as a mechanism for the operation of self-interest, another potential source of constraint. Stated concisely, self-interest analyses of policy preferences posit that "people support policies that promote their own material interests and oppose policies that threaten them" (Kinder 1983, 403). This *rational-choice* model credits individuals with "a coherent set of known and fixed preferences, and a consistent set of beliefs about the world" (Lau 1990, 303). However, such rational behavior need not be restricted to material concerns; rational behavior can be considered simply as the application of one's beliefs in some value-maximizing way to achieve goals tied to individual preferences—which may themselves be culturally determined (Wildavsky 1987). Again, religious concerns (whether they be the enactment of "symbolic" policies related to personal religious beliefs or the advancement of material resources related to membership within a socioreligious group) can serve as the mechanism by which such self-interest may be expressed. If self-interest is the cause, religious variables may be the vehicle by which it is expressed.

Values, too, are potential sources for political opinions. Some constructions of social behavior give a central role to values, defined as general and enduring standards. Indeed, Allport (1961) contended that attitudes were derived from preexisting social values. How is it that the American public may reason from values? As noted by Feldman (1988, 418), "policy preferences, performance judgments, and candidate assessments are all political evaluations." Policies and actions may be judged right or wrong, therefore, simply because of their implications with regard to deeply held values (Rokeach 1973). Once again, if values do serve an important role in shaping political evaluations, then it would not be surprising that religious values, particularly given their likely normative prescriptions, would serve as important factors helping to shape political evaluations.

Finally, historical events may help to shape political thinking. Events must always be interpreted, however. As a result, it may be that the meaning of salient historical events will be inferred, at least in part, "as they are filtered through the citizen's own needs, groups identifications, core values, and the like" (Kinder

1983, 411). Even interpretations of important historical events may therefore be affected by religious variables. If interpretations of historical events are indeed filtered through group identifications, core values, or personal needs, then such interpretations may still be shaped by religious factors associated with those filters.

Regardless of the route by which Americans arrive at their political preferences and dispositions, religious factors play an important role in shaping political thinking. While personality, self-interest, values, and historical experiences may be the proximate influences on political thinking, religious variables may serve as the vehicle through which they are expressed. That perception lends urgency to the task of conceptualizing religion intelligently, devising sound measurement techniques, and producing valid and reliable indicators for inclusion in empirical studies.

Notes

1. *Error* in this context does not connote mistake but simple divergence. Some error is inherent in surveys, i.e., sampling fluctuation, while others are in principle controllable or at least recognizable.

2. In practice, response effects cannot be restricted to this neat tripartite scheme. The well-known problem of *social desirability*—the tendency of respondents to give answers that make themselves look good—is a function of the question asked, the personality of the respondent, and the presence of the interviewer.

3. For example, evangelical Protestant congregations routinely offer group worship on Wednesday and Sunday evenings in addition to the Sunday morning service, and the Catholic tradition maintains days of obligation (Sundays and feast days) on which non-attendance is deemed sinful. The greater availability of worship and the strong imperative to attend may account for the pattern of greater evangelical Protestant and Catholic church attendance noted in chapter 6. The inclusion of a measure of church involvement other than worship corrected for this bias by recognizing a form of activity highly valued in mainline Protestantism.

4. The following paragraphs draw heavily upon material found in Guth et al. (1988).

5. Because it requires a large item pool and thus demands substantial space on questionnaires, this approach is not likely to become the standard technique when political scientists study religious influence.

6. This particular approach to attitude formation and political behavior, however, is ill suited for mass sample surveys. By necessity, it is a relatively individual, highly personalized approach, requiring detailed in-depth interviews—characteristics generally avoided in mass surveys.

References

Allport, Gordon. 1954. *The Individual and His Religion.* New York: Macmillan.
———. 1961. *Pattern and Growth in Personality.* New York: Holt, Rinehart and Winston.
Allport, Gordon, and Ross, J. Michael. 1967. "Personal Religious Orientation and Prejudice." *Journal of Personality and Social Psychology* 5:432–43.
Alston, Jon P., and McIntosh, William A. 1979. "An Assessment of the Determinants of

Religious Participation." *Sociological Quarterly* 20:49–62.

Batson, Daniel C., and Ventis, Larry W. 1982. *The Religious Experience: A Social-Psychological Experience.* New York: Oxford University Press.

Benson, Peter L., and Williams, Dorothy L. 1982. *Religion on Capitol Hill: Myths and Realities.* New York: Harper and Row.

Conover, Pamela Johnston. 1985. "The Impact of Group Economic Interest in Political Evaluations." *American Politics Quarterly* 13:139–66.

Davidson, James, and Knudsen, Dean. 1977. "A New Approach to Religious Commitment." *Sociological Analysis* 10:151–73.

DeMaio, Theresa J. 1984. "Social Desirability and Survey Measurement: A Review." In Turner and Martin 1984, 2:257–82.

Dijkstra, W., and van der Zouwen, J. eds. 1982. *Response Behavior in the Survey-Interview.* London: Academic Press.

Doise, Willem, and Machie, Diane. 1981. "On the Social Nature of Cognition." In *Social Cognition: Perspective on Everyday Understanding*, ed. Joseph Forgas, 53–83. London: Academic Press.

Erikson, Robert S.; Lancaster, Thomas D.; and Romero, David W. 1989. "Group Components of the Presidential Vote." *Journal of Politics* 51:337–46.

Feldman, Stanley. 1988. "Structure and Consistency in Public Opinion: The Role of Core Beliefs and Values." *American Journal of Political Science* 32:416–40.

Fishbein, Martin, and Ajzen, Icek. 1975. *Belief, Attitude, Intention and Behavior: An Introduction to Theory and Research.* Reading, MA: Addison-Wesley.

Fullerton, J. Timothy, and Hunsberger, Bruce. 1982. "A Unidimensional Measure of Christian Orthodoxy." *Journal for the Scientific Study of Religion* 21:317–26.

Gerth, Hans H., and Mills, C. Wright, eds. 1946. *From Max Weber: Essays in Sociology.* New York: Oxford University Press.

Glock, Charles Y., and Stark, Rodney. 1966. *Christian Beliefs and Anti-Semitism.* New York: Harper and Row.

Greeley, Andrew. 1984. "Religious Imagery as a Predictor Variable in the General Social Survey." Paper presented at the annual meeting of the Society for the Scientific Study of Religion, Chicago.

———. 1988. "Evidence That a Maternal Image of God Correlates with Liberal Politics." *Sociology and Social Research* 72:150–54.

Guth, James; Jelen, Ted; Kellstedt, Lyman; Smidt, Corwin; and Wald, Kenneth. 1988. "The Politics of Religion in America: Issues for Investigation." *American Politics Quarterly* 16:357–97.

Hertzke, Allen D. 1988. *Representing God in Washington: The Role of Religious Lobbies in the American Polity.* Knoxville: University of Tennessee Press.

Himmelfarb, Harold. 1975. "Measuring Religious Involvement." *Social Forces* 53:606–18.

Hoffman, Thomas J. 1985. "Religion and Political Change: The Impacts of Institutional Connectedness and Religious Imagery." Paper presented at the annual meeting of the American Political Science Association, New Orleans.

Hoge, Dean, and de Zulueta, Ernesto. 1985. "Salience as a Condition for Various Social Consequences of Religious Commitment." *Journal for the Scientific Study of Religion* 24:21–37.

Jelen, Ted. 1985. "Images of God as Predictors of Attitudes on Social Issues among Fundamentalists and Non-Fundamentalists." Paper presented at the annual meeting of the Society for the Scientific Study of Religion, Savannah.

———. 1991. *The Political Mobilization of Religious Beliefs.* New York: Praeger.

Jelen, Ted; Kellstedt, Lyman A.; and Wilcox, Clyde. 1990. "Racism and Religion: Some

New Evidence for an Old Question." Paper presented at the annual meeting of the Association for the Sociology of Religion, Washington.

Kiecolt, Jill K. 1988. "Recent Developments in Attitudes and Social Structure." *Annual Review of Sociology* 14:381–403.

Kinder, Donald R. 1983. "Diversity and Complexity in American Public Opinion." In *Political Science: The State of the Discipline*, ed. Ada Finifter, 389–425. Washington, DC: American Political Science Association.

King, Morton B., and Hunt, Richard A. 1972. *Measuring Religious Dimensions: Studies in Congregational Involvement*. Dallas: Southern Methodist University Press.

Kuklinski, James H.; Luskin, Robert C.; and Bolland, John. 1991. "Where Is the Schema? Going beyond the "S" Word in Political Psychology." *American Political Science Review* 85:1341–56.

Lau, Richard. 1990. "Political Motivation and Political Cognition." In *Handbook of Motivation and Cognition*, ed. E. Tory Higgins and Richard M. Sorrentino, 2:297–329. New York: Guilford Press.

Lazerwitz, Bernard. 1973. "Religious Identification and Its Ethnic Correlates: A Multivariate Model." *Social Forces* 52:204–20.

Leege, David C. 1987. "The Parish as Community." *Notre Dame Study of Catholic Parish Life*. Report 10. Notre Dame, IN: University of Notre Dame.

———. 1988. "Who Is a True Catholic? Social Boundaries on the Church." *Notre Dame Study of Catholic Parish Life*, Report 13. Notre Dame, IN: University of Notre Dame.

Leege, David C.; Kellstedt, Lyman A.; and Wald, Kenneth D. 1990. "Religion and Politics: A Report on Measures of Religiosity in the 1989 NES Pilot Study." Paper presented at the annual meeting of the Midwest Political Science Association, Chicago.

Leege, David C., and Welch, Michael R. 1989a. "Religious Roots of Political Orientations: Variations among American Catholic Parishioners." *Journal of Politics* 50:137–62.

———. 1989b. "Catholics in Context: Theoretical and Methodological Issues in Studying American Catholic Parishioners." *Review of Religious Research* 31:132–48.

Liebman, Charles S., and Cohen, Steven M. 1990. *Two Worlds of Judaism: The Israeli and American Experiences*. New Haven, CT: Yale University Press.

MacIver, Martha Abele. 1990. "Mirror Images: Conceptions of God and Political Duty on the Left and Right of the Evangelical Spectrum." *Sociological Analysis* 51:287–95.

Newman, Sandra J. 1984. "Housing Research: Conceptualization and Measurement Issues." In Turner and Martin 1984, 2:143–56.

Pecnik, Julia A., and Epperson, Douglas L. 1985. "A Factor Analysis and Further Validation of the Shepherd Scale." *Journal of Psychology and Theology* 13:42–49.

Rokeach, Milton. 1973. *The Nature of Human Values*. New York: Free Press.

Roof, Wade Clark. 1978. *Community and Commitment: Religious Plausibility in a Liberal Protestant Church*. New York: Elsevier.

———. 1979. "Concepts and Indicators of Religious Commitment: A Critical Review." In *The Religious Dimension: New Directions in Quantitative Research*, ed. Robert Wuthnow, 17–45. New York: Academic Press.

Sears, David; Lau, Richard; Taylor, Tom R.; and Allen, Harris M. 1980. "Self-Interest vs. Symbolic Politics." *American Political Science Review* 74:670–84.

Smith, Tom W. 1984. "The Subjectivity of Ethnicity." In Turner and Martin 1984, 2:117–28.

Stark, Rodney, and Bainbridge, William Sims. 1985. *The Future of Religion: Secularization, Revival, and Cult Formation*. Berkeley: University of California Press.

Stark, Rodney, and Glock, Charles Y. 1968. *American Piety: The Nature of Religious Commitment*. Berkeley: University of California Press.

Sudman, Seymour, and Bradburn, Norman. 1974. *Response Effects in Surveys: A Review and Synthesis*. Chicago: Aldine.

Tajfel, Henri. 1981. *Human Groups and Social Categories: Studies in Social Psychology*. Cambridge: Cambridge University Press.

Turner, Charles F., and Elizabeth Martin, eds. 1984. *Surveying Subjective Phenomena*. Vols. 1, 2. New York: Russell Sage Foundation.

Turner, Helen Lee, and Guth, James. 1989. "The Politics of Armageddon: Dispensationalism among Southern Baptist Ministers." In *Religion and Political Behavior in the United States*, ed. Ted Jelen, 187–208. New York: Praeger.

Wald, Kenneth. 1992. *Religion and Politics in the United States*. 2d ed. Washington, DC: Congressional Quarterly Press.

Wald, Kenneth D.; Owen, Dennis E.; and Hill, Samuel S., Jr. 1988. "Churches as Political Communities." *American Political Science Review* 82:531–48.

———. 1989. "Evangelical Politics and Status Issues." *Journal for the Scientific Study of Religion* 28:1–16.

Warner, R. Stephen. 1988. *New Wine in Old Wineskins: Evangelicals and Liberals in a Small-Town Church*. Berkeley: University of California Press.

Welch, Kevin W. 1981. "An Interpersonal Influence Model of Traditional Religious Commitment." *Sociological Quarterly* 22:81–92.

Welch, Michael R., and Leege, David C. 1988. "Religious Predictors of Catholic Parishioners' Sociopolitical Attitudes: Devotional Style, Closeness to God, Imagery, and Agentic-Communal Religious Identity." *Journal for the Scientific Study of Religion* 27:536–52.

———. 1991. "Dual Reference Groups and Political Orientations: An Examination of Evangelically Oriented Catholics." *American Journal of Political Science* 35:28–56.

White, Richard. 1968. "Toward a Theory of Religious Influence." *Pacific Sociological Review* 11:23–28.

Wilcox, Clyde, and Gomez, Leopoldo. 1990. "The Christian Right and the Pro-Life Movement: An Analysis of the Sources of Political Support." *Review of Religious Research* 31:380–89.

Wilcox, Clyde; Linzey, Sharon; and Jelen, Ted. 1991. "Reluctant Warriors: Premillenialism and Politics in the Moral Majority." *Journal for the Scientific Study of Religion* 30:245–58.

Wildavsky, Aaron. 1987. "Choosing Preferences by Constructing Institutions: A Cultural Theory of Preference Formation." *American Political Science Review* 81:3–21.

Wilson, John. 1978. *Religion in American Society*. Englewood Cliffs, NJ: Prentice Hall.

Part II

Religion as an Orientation toward Group

Chapter 3

Knowing God's Many People: Denominational Preference and Political Behavior

Lyman A. Kellstedt and John C. Green

Individual affiliation with a religious group or organization is central to a full understanding of the effects of religion on politics. Indeed, the usual first step in describing a person's religion is ascertaining his or her denominational preference, be it membership in a specific denomination, affiliation with a local congregation, association with a broad religious grouping, or no preference at all. Although scholars have routinely recognized gross denominational divisions in survey research, it has never been clear whether such measures refer to ethnic histories, doctrinal beliefs, social status, or social group attachments, and such measures have often been characterized by imprecision and social desirability effects as well. Indeed, political scientists have tolerated undesirable measurement properties in *religious denomination* because it was a standard face-sheet item inherited from the early days of opinion research, and many scholars were unconvinced that it mattered in any event. Recent theoretical and empirical work, however, has improved our understanding of denominational preference and suggests that "knowing God's many people" is valuable in analyzing political attitudes and behavior.

This chapter examines the use of denominational preference by political scientists. After briefly outlining its theoretical relevance, we discuss the measurement, aggregation, and use of denominational preference in data analysis and then illustrate its relationship to political attitudes and behavior. We find that aggregating denominational preference into appropriate religious traditions is particularly useful on theoretical, practical, and empirical grounds.

Denominational Preference and Political Behavior

A denomination is a set of religious institutions, principally local churches and related missionary, educational, and administrative agencies, that are formally linked to one another, and which share common beliefs, practices, and commitments. *Denominationalism* is one of the unique features of American society (Roof and McKinney 1987, 76–78), and denominations play a central role in American life (Greeley 1972). Indeed, more than four-fifths of American adults routinely express a denominational preference of one kind or another—more, in fact, than identify with a political party.

Any set of preferences that involves so many people collected into groups is bound to have a major impact on politics, much as identification with other kinds of social groups, ranging from labor unions to social clubs, has been found to be politically relevant (Lazarsfeld, Berelson, and Gaudet 1944). Yet identification with a denomination is by far the most common and intense form of group identification in the United States (Wald 1992, 9). In this regard, denominational preference is comparable in scope to other social reference groups, including gender, race, ethnicity, and social class. Denominational preference is, in fact, closely intertwined with such social characteristics (Roof and McKinney 1987, 106–47), but there are good theoretical reasons to expect it to influence political attitudes and behavior apart from other social characteristics (cf. Harrison and Lazerwitz 1982).

In recent years, scholars have increasingly found that cultural traditions have a strong impact on politics, and religion is among the most potent and persistent elements of culture (Leege, Lieske, and Wald 1991). Culture structures individual worldviews, helping to generate foundational beliefs, delineate appropriate behavior, and define personal identity (Wildavsky 1987), factors that are often central to political disputes, particularly in diverse societies such as the United States (Inglehart 1990). However, religion is more likely to be a source of social distinctiveness than most other group attachments.

After all, religious organizations are intimately involved in early and ongoing socialization, processes that produce and maintain common cognitions (Conover 1984). And as with other groups, continued membership and interaction within religious organizations creates and reinforces like-mindedness among participants (Tajfel 1981). These factors combine with more general social experiences to generate positive affect toward one's own religious group and negative affect toward rivals (Miller et al. 1981). All told, religious denominations are at root distinctive and concrete expressions of cultural traditions, and thus, at the individual level, denominational preference represents a personal attachment to a particular version of such a tradition.

Of course, denominational preference is not the only component of religion. Individuals may differ in their understanding, participation, and commitment to their own denomination, and, likewise, they may also share beliefs, practices, and commitments across denominational boundaries. However, the impact of these factors is likely to be enhanced once denominational preference is taken into account. For instance, while religious beliefs may be very important, their meaning and relevance are conditioned by the context in which they occur. Similarly, religious practices may matter a great deal, but the social environment in which such behavior takes place matters as well. And although religious commitment may be a crucial factor, it alone begs the question of commitment to what. Denominational preference may encapsulate differences in belief, practice, and commitment, even for individuals with nominal religiosity. Thus, we would expect denominational preference to influence political attitudes and behavior apart from other measures of religion, although the influence should be strongest for those who are more religious (Wald, Owen, and Hill 1988).

In this sense, denominational preference resembles party identification, the central predictor variable in the field of voting behavior. Like denominational preference, partisanship reflects a set of political beliefs, practices, and commitments. The power of partisanship in accounting for political behavior, however, stems from the fact that it can encompass any one or all of these things and more besides, representing in the last analysis attachment to a broader political tradition. And like denominational preference, the strength of an individual's partisanship varies: some partisans are highly ideological, active, and strongly committed, while others have only the most nominal attachments. While the attitudes and behavior of the former are most predictable, even for the latter party identification has an impact independent of other factors.

Parties and denominations, the institutional sources of partisan and denominational preferences, both owe their character to the U.S. Constitution and have been closely related to one another historically (Swierenga 1990). On the one hand, federalism, single-member plurality contests, and the electoral college have encouraged electoral forces to coalesce into two major parties. In contrast, the First Amendment, which denies the possibility of a state-sponsored church and at the same time guarantees the free exercise of religion, has encouraged the development of diverse and numerous denominations. In addition, parties and denominations share certain organizational dynamics. Parties are primarily organized around the limited access to power via the ballot and have often sought the support of religious groups in their quest for office. Denominations are primarily organized around their varied conceptions of the good life and have often sought assistance from the parties to defend or achieve their particular goals.

Thus, the combination of cultural diversity and constitutional order has produced an enormous diversity of denominations in the United States. While specific denominations often have distinct political outlooks, few are large enough to influence politics on their own, and thus practicality dictates that they form alliances with similar denominations for political purposes. This tendency is further encouraged by the limited number of political parties in the United States. The basic "building blocs" of these alliances have been religious traditions: alliances of specific denominations representing major cultural divisions and rivalries. Scholars have generally recognized six major religious traditions[1] (and perhaps a dozen minor ones)[2] in the United States, based on distinctive beliefs and ethos: these include two traditions among the politically dominant white

Protestants, often labeled *mainline* and *evangelical*, and four significant "minority" traditions: black Protestants, Roman Catholics, Jews, and the nonreligious or seculars.[3]

These religious traditions have been relatively stable elements in American electoral politics for more than 150 years as two grand ethnocultural alignments undergirded the major party coalitions: mainline Protestants in the Whig and Republican parties, and a collection of religious minorities—evangelical Protestants, Roman Catholics, and secularists, and more recently Jews and black Protestants—in the Democratic party (McCormick 1986). While these coalitions varied somewhat over time, from place to place, and even from issue to issue (Swierenga 1990, 157–61), these major religious traditions are still distinctive in contemporary politics. As Kellstedt and Noll (1990) have demonstrated, evangelical Protestants have largely moved into the Republican party coalition over the last forty years, while mainline Protestants have become less solidly Republican. During the same period, black Protestants have joined the Democratic coalition, Jews have remained loyal, and Catholics have become less Democratic. These changes reflect in part demographic and political shifts but contain an element of religious change as well. Indeed, the composition of the major religious traditions themselves varies over time, with older denominations evolving and new ones developing (Roof and McKinney 1987, 13–26).

Survey data can provide both a sense of the present size of these religious traditions and a notion of how they have changed in the recent past. The 1990 National Election Study reveals the following proportions of the American population: mainline Protestants, 24.1 percent; evangelicals, 23.5 percent; black Protestants, 9.8 percent; Catholics, 24.9 percent; Jews, 1.9 percent; seculars, 13.3 percent; and all other groups, 2.5 percent. This pattern presents a sharp contrast to the situation thirty years ago. Although the data are not entirely comparable (see below), the 1960 National Election Study shows mainline Protestants at 41.7 percent; evangelicals, 25.3 percent; black Protestants, 6.5 percent; Catholics, 19.5 percent; Jews, 3.4 percent; seculars, 1.2 percent, and all others 2.4 percent. Clearly, mainline Protestants and Jews have lost ground to black Protestants and Catholics and, most dramatically, to seculars. Despite the much discussed growth of many evangelical denominations (Kelley 1972), we find a small decline for the tradition as a whole.[4] When combined with recent political shifts, these data highlight the continued importance of religious traditions in party coalitions.

Assigning Denominations to Religious Traditions

Despite their bewildering diversity, most of the specific denominations in the United States (some 1,200 by recent count; cf. Melton 1989) can be allocated to one of the major religious traditions. Membership in some traditions, however, is easier to define than in others. For instance, due to its great size, doctrinal core, and institutional hierarchy, the Roman Catholic Church largely defines membership in the Catholic tradition, although there are actually many Catholic denominations (Stark and Bainbridge 1985). On the other hand, Protestant theology and institutional diversity make membership in the mainline and evangelical traditions much more difficult to determine. Understanding the origins and character of denominations can help categorize them into the appropriate religious tradition.

Most *specific denominations* developed out of religious innovations resulting from the interaction of denominational families and religious movements, the former representing cultural continuity and the latter cultural change. *Denominational families* refers to groups of denominations with a common historical origin, sharing basic beliefs regarding ecclesiology, ritual, and theology, and often embodying ethnic, quasi-ethnic, or racial distinctions as well (Greeley 1972, 115–19). Denominational families are numerous in the United States, particularly among Protestants (see Melton 1989), and derive from major cultural shifts, such as the Reformation in Europe and the Great Awakenings in the United States.

A common distinction is between *ritualist* and *pietist* families (Swierenga 1990, 151–52; cf. Sommerfield 1968). Ritualist families place greater emphasis on institutional mediation between humanity and God and to this end are characterized by centralized religious authority, formalized rituals, and official creeds. These families tend to maintain *pluralistic* denominations with room for variations in beliefs and local practices beyond their common creeds, central doctrines, sacraments, and standard liturgical forms. Among Protestants, the Episcopal and Lutheran families are good examples. In contrast, pietist families place greater emphasis on the unmediated contact between believers and God and are thus characterized by decentralized religious authority, informal worship, individual religious experience, and emphasis on righteous behavior. These families tend to maintain *particularistic* denominations with orthodox beliefs: great uniformity of interpretation and behavior within locally narrow, informal communities. Among Protestants, the Baptist and pentecostal families are good examples. Parallel distinctions can be found in other traditions as well.[5]

Defining and using categories based on denominational families is often problematic, however. The ritualist-pietist distinction is difficult to measure with precision, and such categories mask the changes that produce diversity within denominational family members. New denominations arise most often as the result of *religious movements*, which are conscious efforts to alter existing denominations. Such movements reflect a common ethos concerning the purity of doctrine, the behavior of members, and stance toward the outside world and often embody class, educational, or regional divisions (Wuthnow 1986). There have been enormous numbers of religious movements in the United States (McLoughlin 1978), and they have restructured the religious landscape by creating new connections between, and new cleavages within, existing families. Indeed, most denominational families arose from past religious movements.

A common distinction is between *church* and *sect* movements (Stark and

Bainbridge 1985). Church movements reduce the differences among denominational families by seeking accommodation with the broader culture. These movements tend to produce *liberal* denominations or ecumenical churches with an
adhesional ethos: an acceptance of individuals based on adherence to broad
values common to many cultures. Modernism, ecumenism, and the social gospel
are examples of important church movements among Protestants. On the other
hand, sect movements generate diversity within denominational families by
seeking separation from the broader culture. These movements tend to produce
conservative denominations or nondenominational churches with a conversionist
ethos: an acceptance of individuals based on commitment to narrow values specific to a particular cultural tradition. Fundamentalism, neoevangelicalism, and
charismatic renewal are examples of recent sectarian movements among Protestants. Parallel church and sect movements have occurred in other traditions as
well.[6]

Defining and using categories based on religious movements is not without its
problems either: the influence of religious movements on denominations is often
difficult to measure, and such categories often fail to recognize residual familial
influences. However, denominational families and religious movements can be
used together to define membership in *religious traditions*. Generally speaking,
the mainline Protestant tradition contains specific denominations from ritualist
families (the Episcopal Church), particularly those influenced by church movements (the Evangelical Lutheran Church in America), and denominations from
pietist families influenced by strong church movements (the United Methodist
Church). On the other hand, the evangelical Protestant tradition contains specific
denominations from pietist families (the Southern Baptist Convention), particularly those influenced by sect movements (the Assemblies of God) and those
from ritualist families influenced by strong sect movements (the Lutheran
Church—Missouri Synod). These differences among denominations produce the
subtle but important differences between the two wings of white Protestantism:
the modernism and tolerance of the mainline and the orthodoxy and separatism
of the evangelicals (Kellstedt, Smidt, and Kellstedt 1991).

Assigning specific denominations to religious traditions thus relies on a sensitive understanding of denominational families and religious movements, so that
specific denominations are combined according to comparable beliefs and ethos.
Membership in these categories varies as circumstances change, as families
evolve, and new movements arise. The appendix to this chapter lists the most
important specific denominations in each of the major religious traditions.

Measurement of Denominational Preference

Until very recently, the measurement of denominational preference was done in
a haphazard and inconsistent manner by all the major survey research organizations. Gallup surveys, for example, usually collect data only for major religious

traditions, such as Catholics, Jews, and Protestants, and, when a breakdown for Protestants occurs, it is usually by denominational families rather than specific denominations. Scholarly surveys have fared only slightly better. The National Election Studies (NES) did not attempt to distinguish among Protestants until 1960 but then routinely confused denominations and denominational families. Recent improvements have occurred in the NES studies, however (see below). The General Social Surveys (GSS) recognized smaller denominations from its inception in 1972 but did not distinguish specific denominations among major denominational families until 1984. Since then, the GSS has grouped denominations in a threefold classification (liberal, moderate, and fundamentalist), reflecting a limited understanding of major religious movements, although the data on specific denominations have been preserved. Unfortunately, neither the GSS nor other major surveys contain questions that allow for a precise classification according to religious movements. Thus, a few special-purpose surveys aside, the scholarly community has not had access to reliable data on denominational preference, and as a result, attempts to use denominational data have not produced consistently robust findings.

As with many concepts, the key to valid measurement of denominational preference is specificity (Smith 1990). Once data are collected on specific denominations, they can be aggregated by denominational families, religious movements, or religious traditions in a useful fashion. Indeed, such data allow researchers to investigate *any* aggregation of denominational preference and to respond to religious and political change, such as the unexpected mobilization of evangelical Protestants in recent times. The costs of nonspecific denominational data are serious, undermining otherwise comprehensive studies, such as the recent National Survey of Religious Identification (Kosmin and Lachman 1991).

Specific denominational data are not easy to obtain, however. First, questions should be preceded by a screening question to reduce social desirability effects. Since it is still normative in American society to be religious, many respondents who have no behavioral or cognitive links to a religious group will nonetheless express a *preference*, particularly if they are not given the option to express the *lack* of such a preference. A screening question that allows for a variety of *no preference* responses is very effective in this regard. The alternative is to seriously underestimate the secular population. Second, questions must go beyond undifferentiated categories such as *Protestant* or *Presbyterian* because such categories mask important within-group differences. Third, because of the diversity of denominations and the confusion on the part of some respondents as to the name of their specific denomination, ambiguous responses (e.g., Baptist) must be followed up with probes to ascertain more detailed information. Fourth, denominational probes must be carefully constructed, and interviewers must be specially trained to use them effectively. And fifth, some respondents will not be able to give a specific denominational preference, but nonetheless identify with a denominational family (Methodist), religious movement (Fundamentalist), or tradition (Jewish). Such respondents can be classified as *no further specifics* within the category mentioned by the respondent. Any classification of denominations must be flexible, however, and take into account the inevitable change in denominations and membership in religious traditions (cf. Leege, Kellstedt, and Wald 1990).

Even if reliable data on denominational preference are collected in surveys, there are some practical problems associated with their use. The first problem is related to sample size: most national surveys contain only a few cases for many small denominations, particularly among white Protestants but also for blacks and Jews. It may be necessary to pool surveys over time to study smaller traditions, families, or specific denominations. In addition, respondents from larger denominations do not constitute random samples of the population in question, and thus the data for subsamples may be seriously biased (Leege and Welch 1989). And finally, given the difficulties in obtaining specific denominational data, measurement error may be a serious problem. One way to cope with all of these problems is to aggregate denominations into relatively large categories. This solution provides an additional pragmatic argument for aggregation by religious tradition. Once aggregated by whatever criteria, denominational preference can be used in data analysis either by means of categorical controls (Kellstedt, Smidt, and Kellstedt 1991) or by constructing scales that reflect relevant attitudinal patterns (Green and Guth 1991b).

The 1989 NES Pilot Study tested a new set of questions on denominational preference, including screens to correct for social desirability effects and probes to obtain specific data (cf. Leege, Kellstedt, and Wald 1990). Building on the result of this effort, the 1990 NES Congressional Election Study incorporated a new battery of screens, questions, and probes on denominational preference and developed a new master code for denominations. Because of the more reliable data and the large sample ($N = 2,000$), the 1990 survey can be used to explore the impact of denominational preference on political attitudes and behavior.

Analysis of Denominational Preferences

As a first cut at the relationship between denominational preference and political variables, Table 3.1 presents data on eight Protestant denominations that are large enough to investigate individually; the first four are mainline (United Methodist Church, Presbyterian Church USA, Evangelical Lutheran Church in America [ELCA], and Episcopal Church); while the second four are evangelical (Lutheran Church—Missouri Synod, Southern Baptist Convention, Assemblies of God, and nondenominational evangelicals).[7] The table reports on a range of political attitudes and behavior: percentage vote for George Bush in 1988, mean self-identified partisanship and ideology, and mean abortion attitudes. These data are presented directly and then subjected to controls for demography (region, gender, education, and age), and religious salience.[8]

Table 3.1 reveals both the value of denominational preference and the frustrations associated with analyzing unaggregated data. First, there are clear political distinctions between the mainline and evangelical denominations in the uncontrolled data (first row for each denomination). Overall, mainliners tend to be less Republican and conservative than evangelicals, although the differences are somewhat muted if compared to non-Protestants (see Table 3.2 below). For example, United Methodists and Presbyterians were much less supportive of Bush in 1988 than the Assemblies of God and nondenominational evangelicals. There are some modest anomalies, however, such as Missouri Synod Lutherans and Southern Baptists, who voted less for Bush than ELCA Lutherans and Episcopalians. Party identification shows very much the same pattern, but once again, there are some important exceptions, such as Southern Baptists, who are more Democratic than other evangelicals, and ELCA Lutherans, who are more Republican than the other mainline churches. There is a similar but stronger pattern for self-identified ideology, and an even more striking pattern for abortion attitudes: mainliners are more liberal than the evangelicals.

What accounts for the exceptions to the underlying pattern among the religious traditions? One potential source of these exceptions, demographic differences, is quickly disposed of. Controls for demography have only modest impact on these patterns (second row for each category). For instance, in terms of party identification, Episcopalians become more Democratic and Southern Baptists more Republican (reflecting controls for region), while ELCA Lutherans become more liberal and Assemblies of God become more conservative (reflecting controls for education), but these changes do not alter the relative positions of the denominations. Clearly, denominational preferences are more than reflections of demography.

Significant differences appear when religious salience is controlled along with demography (third row for each category), but the underlying patterns remain largely intact. The mainline denominations show a more mixed pattern compared to evangelicals. Although the most religious members of each denomination voted in greater numbers for Bush, and highly religious United Methodists become more Republican, conservative, and prolife across the board, the other denominations show occasional exceptions (ELCA Lutherans and Episcopalians on partisanship, Presbyterians and Episcopalians on ideology, and ELCA Lutherans on abortion). In contrast, the most religious members of the evangelical denominations are uniformly more supportive of Bush, more Republican, conservative, and prolife. As might be expected, mainline Protestants contain fewer members to whom religion is salient: the more religious account for 25 percent of the mainline as compared to 60 percent among the evangelicals. This finding helps account for the solid and enhanced conservative pattern among evangelicals, since highly committed members are more likely to receive and assimilate political cues (Wald, Owen, and Hill 1988).

Measurement error may account for some of these findings as well. The

Table 3.1

Denominational Preference and Political Behavior
Major Protestant Churches

Denomination	Bush Vote* 1988	Mean Partisan	Mean Ideology	Mean Abortion Attitudes	N
United Methodist	62%	3.02	4.35	1.79	151
+Demography	62	3.07	4.34	1.77	151
+Salience	72	3.34	4.60	2.04	38
Presbyterian USA	66%	3.00	4.25	1.58	50
+Demography	66	2.93	4.24	1.61	50
+Salience	68	3.05	3.87	1.74	13
ELCA Lutheran	70%	3.71	4.15	1.94	55
+Demography	70	3.64	4.14	1.98	55
+Salience	76	3.48	4.22	1.88	15
Episcopal	70%	3.49	3.83	1.78	37
+Demography	71	3.34	3.38	1.85	37
+Salience	95	2.82	3.56	2.10	8
MO Synod Lutheran	59%	3.08	4.64	2.31	39
+Demography	59	2.97	4.64	2.36	39
+Salience	86	4.17	4.99	3.06	18
Southern Baptists	69%	2.84	4.65	2.37	137
+Demography	69	3.17	4.62	2.21	137
+Salience	71	3.20	4.84	2.63	60
Assemblies Of God	76%	4.26	5.11	2.97	32
+Demography	76	4.37	5.18	2.92	32
+Salience	87	4.88	5.65	3.28	23
Non-Denominational	83%	4.32	4.56	2.88	34
+Demography	81	4.36	4.93	2.85	34
+Salience	85	4.65	5.19	3.19	26

Source: 1990 National Election Study.

+Demography = controls for gender, region, age, and education.

+Salience = religion is *important* and gives *great deal of guidance*, plus demographic controls.

* Partisanship ranges from 0 to 6, where 0 = strong Democrat, 3 = independent, and 6 = strong Republican. Ideology ranges from 1 to 7, where 1 = extremely liberal, 4 = moderate, and 7 = extremely conservative. Abortion measure ranges from 1 to 4, where 1 = abortion should "*always*" be permitted, and 4 = abortion should "*never*" be permitted.

number of cases for each denomination is very small, with only two denominations having more than one hundred. Even these larger subsamples raise questions: clearly Southern Baptists are more numerous in the country than United Methodists (Roof and McKinney 1987, 150), but in this sample there are more United Methodists. These sorts of factors may also account for the data on Lutherans, where, contrary to some expectations, the Missouri Synod as a whole is less Republican than the ELCA. A similar situation may occur for the small group of more religious Episcopalians who combine near-unanimous vote for Bush with Democratic party leanings and prochoice sentiments on abortion. On the other hand, George Bush is a highly visible Episcopalian, and communal sentiment may draw co-religionists to him, as it did with Catholics to John Kennedy and Southern Baptists to Jimmy Carter.

Of course, it is also possible that these exceptions reflect denominational distinctiveness. After all, liberal Republicanism is quite consistent with the worldviews of ELCA Lutherans and Episcopalians, and the liberal nature of Presbyterian theology has been well documented. Likewise, the "establishment" character of United Methodists in the Midwest and Southern Baptists in the South may help account for their greater diversity compared with other denominations, while the uniform conservatism of nondenominational evangelicals and Assemblies of God is consistent with their theological orthodoxy. Thus, specific denominations may well have specific political profiles. But the differences between the mainline and evangelical Protestant traditions are clearly more important than the differences among specific denominations.[9]

Analysis of Religious Traditions

Table 3.2 presents the relationships among the same political variables as in Table 3.1, but with denominational preference aggregated into the six major religious traditions. The results for vote choice and party identification for the uncontrolled data are striking: evangelical Protestants voted most heavily for Bush in 1988, modestly ahead of mainline Protestants, followed by Catholics, seculars, Jews, and black Protestants. A similar pattern holds for partisanship, although mainline Protestants surpass evangelicals, and seculars surpass Catholics in the Republican direction.

In terms of self-identified ideology, evangelicals are the most conservative and seculars the most liberal. Abortion attitudes show a different pattern, however: evangelicals, blacks, and Catholics lean in a prolife direction, while mainline Protestants, seculars, and Jews favor a prochoice position. The gap between prolife and prochoice groups is important: these data suggest that different issues underlie self-identified ideology, for example, social issues for evangelicals and economics for the mainline (Kellstedt, Smidt and Kellstedt 1991).

As before, controls for demography make only a few important changes. Demographic controls push evangelicals, Jews, and blacks in a Republican direc-

Table 3.2

Denominational Preference and Political Behavior
Major Religious Traditions

Religious Tradition	Bush Vote* 1988	Mean Partisan	Mean Ideology	Mean Abortion Attitudes	N
Evangelical					
Protestant	70%	3.09	4.74	2.57	413
+ Demography	70	3.37	4.77	2.55	413
+ Salience	79	3.60	4.97	2.94	216
Mainline					
Protestant	67%	3.24	4.22	1.76	431
+ Demography	67	3.13	4.21	1.78	431
+ Salience	74	3.05	4.24	2.04	103
Roman Catholic	54%	2.41	4.13	2.26	356
+ Demography	54	2.22	4.11	2.27	356
+ Salience	62	2.20	4.31	2.64	94
Secular	43%	2.64	3.68	1.67	210
+ Demography	42	2.58	3.69	1.68	210
+ Salience	59	3.08	4.53	2.03	25
Jewish	38%	1.42	3.73	1.44	36
+ Demography	45	1.77	3.99	1.70	36
Black					
Protestant	21%	.93	3.87	2.43	271
+ Demography	19	1.02	3.80	2.30	271
+ Salience	19	.92	3.87	2.59	126

Source: 1990 National Election Study.

+Demography = controls for gender, region, age and education.

+Salience = religion is *important* and gives *great deal of guidance*, plus demographic controls. Jews are excluded due to less than 10 cases.

* Partisanship ranges from 0 to 6, where 0 = strong Democrat, 3 = independent, and 6 = strong Republican. Ideology ranges from 1 to 7, where 1 = extremely liberal, 4 = moderate, and 7 = extremely conservative. Abortion measure ranges from 1 to 4, where 1 = abortion should *"always"* be permitted, and 4 = abortion should *"never"* be permitted.

tion, and mainline Protestants, Catholics, and seculars in a Democratic direction. In fact, evangelicals are the most Republican group when demographic controls are instituted, supplanting mainline Protestants at the core of the Republican coalition.

The additional control for religious salience makes much more difference, generally strengthening the underlying pattern. For example, highly religious evangelicals become much more Republican and conservative, while their mainline counterparts become more Democratic, revealing the recent political change of each tradition. Strongly religious Catholics become both more Democratic and more conservative, highlighting an important political tension among them. And religious salience moves all the groups in a prolife direction compared to their co-religionists. For instance, the small number of seculars who claim no denominational preference but who say that religion provides them *a great deal of guidance* are more likely to support George Bush, to identify as Republicans and conservatives, and to have prolife views on abortion than seculars as a whole.[10]

The results in Table 3.2 are striking, with controls for demography and religious salience demonstrating the strong conservative flavor of evangelicals and the moderation of the Protestant mainline. And both traditions stand in contrast to the historic minority traditions, although the controls lessen the gap between them. Clearly, the failure in much contemporary scholarship to distinguish among denominational traditions is a serious error, and one that is commonly made. To cite one example, Abramson, Aldrich, and Rohde (1990, 125) report that two-thirds of all Protestants voted for Bush in 1988, a figure that masks the greater Republican vote among evangelicals. Accurate measurement of specific denominational preferences should be a high priority in survey research.

Conclusion: Knowing God's Many People

The foregoing analysis has established a strong warrant for the value of "knowing God's many people" in the study of political attitudes and behaviors, and a brief restatement of our argument is in order. Simply put, denominational preference matters in politics because denominations are important: they are central to religious life, objects of deeply held commitments, and, together with their component institutions, the most common form of voluntary association in the United States. Denominations are characterized by all of the processes that create and maintain group identification, and the core of such identification is attachment to broader cultural traditions. As a result, members of denominations develop particular political outlooks, and denominational preferences are systematically associated with partisanship, issue positions, and voting patterns. The poor measurement of denominational preference in survey research has thus obscured a potentially important factor in understanding political alignments.

However, practicality dictates that specific denominations join broader alliances for political purposes, a tendency that is further encouraged by the two-party system. While these alliances might well take many forms, in the United States the most enduring involve religious traditions. Religious traditions aggregate the values of large numbers of individuals, local congregations, denominations, denominational families, and religious movements in a way that can be more easily processed by the political system. For many citizens, religious traditions serve as a point of conscious identification and a potent source of political attitudes and behavior.

Of course, neither religion nor politics is static in the United States. Specific denominations grow and decline, new ones are born and old ones merge, churches shift between traditions and new traditions are formed. And the political environment changes as well: new candidates, issues, and party coalitions replace older ones, presenting new alternatives to religious groups and undermining previous alliances. These points are relevant to the "decline of denomination" discussed in the literature: older denominational distinctions may be waning due to religious and political change (Wuthnow 1988). Much of our evidence supports this kind of change.

On the other hand, our data also suggest that denominational distinctiveness is still strong and important and that whatever changes are occurring strengthen the major religious traditions. Indeed, the past generation has witnessed an increase in the importance of religious traditions in politics. Evangelicals have held their own in relative numbers and shaken off their southern and lower-class character to identify with the Republican party, while the greater education and cosmopolitan nature of the mainline has led them away from church and the GOP. Meanwhile the mobilization of black Protestants and the growth of the seculars have added new elements to the Democratic coalition, even as Catholics have increased and wavered in their traditional partisanship. These patterns bespeak a profound restructuring of the connections between religion and politics in which the major religious traditions will remain crucial "building blocs" in party coalitions for many years to come (Green and Guth 1991a). For better or worse, God's many people are in politics to stay.

Notes

1. Roof and McKinney (1987, 85–99) offer an excellent discussion of the six major religious traditions. Note, however, that they use the term *family* instead of *tradition* and divide the mainline tradition into *liberal* and *moderate* categories. For our purposes, their distinctions confuse denominational families, religious movements, and religious traditions.

2. Minor religious traditions are usually less relevant to survey research because few cases appear in national samples, but for the sake of completeness a brief description is in order. First, there are at least five significant minor traditions found among American Christians: Eastern Orthodox churches (with their many ethnic variations), the Church of Jesus Christ of the Latter Day Saints (Mormons), Jehovah's Witnesses, Church of Christ Scientist, and Unitarian-Universalists. Only a little is known about the politics of these groups: the Orthodox tend to behave like traditional Roman Catholics; Mormons and

Witnesses resemble highly sectarian evangelicals; while Christian Scientists and Unitarians are close to the liberal mainline. In addition, there are growing numbers of non–Judeo-Christian groups in the United States: Muslims, Buddhists and other Asian religions, and a host of new religious groups and cults, such as the Unification Church and the New Age groups. Even less is known about the politics of these groups. Overall, great care must be taken in combining these minor traditions with major traditions because of their religious differences.

3. Describing even major religious traditions is difficult to do with precision. For a general understanding of these traditions, see Dayton and Johnston (1991) on evangelicals; Hutchison (1976) on the mainline; Lincoln and Mamiya (1990) on black Protestants; Greeley (1990) on Catholics; Heilman and Cohen (1989) on Jews; and Turner (1985) on seculars.

4. A different pattern emerges if we consider the regularly attending church population, the people most likely to be affected by religious cues. In 1960, mainline Protestants made up 36.8 percent of regular attenders; evangelicals, 23.8 percent; and Catholics, 36.6 percent. By 1990, mainliners had declined to 21.3 percent of regular attenders, while evangelicals had expanded to 40.8 percent, and Catholics remained nearly constant at 34.1 percent.

5. Roman Catholics are perhaps the archetype of a ritualist family and Jews also have these tendencies, while most black Protestants resemble white pietists.

6. Church and sect movements have occurred among Catholics, black Protestants, and Jews as well, generating a continuum of *liberal* and *conservative* denominations within these traditions.

7. Nondenominational evangelicals represent a rapidly growing group of largely pietist Protestants who consciously operate outside of denominational boundaries (Kellstedt and Noll 1990). In some cases, these groups are hostile to religious institutions in principle, but in other cases, they may represent the birth of new denominations. Here this group is identified by nondenominational preference, literal or inerrant view of the scriptures, and born-again status.

8. The religious salience measure is a composite index (see chapter 8) based on two variables: whether religion is important to respondents' lives and a follow-up question on how much guidance religion provides them. In Tables 3.1 and 3.2, *high salience* people are defined as those to whom religion was *important* and provided *a great deal of guidance.*

9. Analyses similar to Table 3.1 were conducted for categories based on denominational families (i.e., all Methodists, Presbyterians, and so forth), and the effects of religious movements (liberal, moderate, and conservative denominations). Although quite interesting, these results were not as strong as categories based on religious tradition.

10. The pure category of seculars, those with no religious commitment (65 percent of the total), voted for George Bush and held liberal ideology at the same rate as seculars as a whole. At the same time, however, they were slightly more Democratic and prochoice on abortion. Jews show similar results, but are excluded from Table 3.2 because of the small number of cases.

References

Abramson, Paul R.; Aldrich, John H.; and Rohde, David W. 1990. *Change and Continuity in the 1988 Elections.* Washington, DC: Congressional Quarterly Press.

Conover, Pamela Johnston. 1984. "The Influence of Group Identification on Political Perceptions and Evaluations." *Journal of Politics* 46:760–85.

Dayton, Donald W., and Johnston, Robert K. 1991. *The Variety of American*

Evangelicalism. Knoxville: University of Tennessee Press.

Greeley, Andrew M. 1972. *The Denominational Society*. Glenview, IL: Scott, Foresman.

———. 1990. *The Catholic Myth: The Behavior and Belief of American Catholics*. New York: Scribner's.

Green, John C., and Guth, James L. 1991a. "The Bible and the Ballot Box: The Shape of Things to Come." In Guth and Green 1991, 207–26.

———. 1991b. "Religion, Representation, and Roll Calls: A Research Note." *Legislative Studies Quarterly* 16:571–84.

Guth, James L., and Green, John C., eds. 1991. *The Bible and the Ballot Box: Religion and Politics in the 1988 Election*. Boulder, CO: Westview Press.

Harrison, Michael I., and Lazerwitz, Bernard. 1982. "Do Denominations Matter?" *American Journal of Sociology* 88:356–77.

Heilman, Samuel C., and Cohen, Steven M. 1989. *Cosmopolitans and Parochials: Modern Orthodox Jews in America*. Chicago: University of Chicago Press.

Hutchison, William R. 1976. *The Modernist Impulse in American Protestantism*. Cambridge, MA: Harvard University Press.

Inglehart, Ronald. 1990. *Culture Shift in Advanced Industrial Society*. Princeton, NJ: Princeton University Press.

Kelley, Dean M. 1972. *Why Conservative Churches Are Growing*. New York: Harper and Row.

Kellstedt, Lyman A., and Noll, Mark A. 1990. "Religion, Voting for the President, and Party Identification, 1948–1984." In Noll 1990, 355–79.

Kellstedt, Lyman A.; Smidt, Corwin E.; and Kellstedt, Paul M. 1991. "Religious Tradition, Denomination, and Commitment: White Protestants and the 1988 Election." In Guth and Green 1991, 139–58.

Kosmin, Barry A., and Lachman, Seymour P. 1991. "The National Survey of Religious Identification 1989–90." Research Report, Graduate School and University Center of the City University of New York.

Lazarsfeld, Paul F.; Berelson, Bernard F.; and Gaudet, Helen. 1944. *The People's Choice*. New York: Columbia University Press.

Leege, David C.; Kellstedt, Lyman A.; and Wald, Kenneth D. 1990. "Religion and Politics: A Report on Measures of Religiosity in the 1989 NES Pilot Study." Paper presented at the annual meeting of the Midwest Political Science Association, Chicago.

Leege, David C.; Lieske, Joel A.; and Wald, Kenneth D. 1991. "Toward Cultural Theories of American Political Behavior: Religion, Ethnicity, Race, and Class Outlook." In *Political Science: Toward the Future*, ed. William Crotty, 3:193–238. Evanston, IL: Northwestern University Press.

Leege, David C., and Welch, Michael R. 1989. "Catholics in Context: Theoretical and Methodological Issues in Studying American Catholic Parishioners." *Review of Religious Research* 31:132–48.

Lincoln, C. Eric, and Mamiya, Lawrence H. 1990. *The Black Church in the African American Experience*. Durham, NC: Duke University Press.

McCormick, Richard L. 1986. *Party, Period and Public Policy*. New York: Oxford University Press.

McLoughlin, William G. 1978. *Revivals, Awakenings and Reform*. Chicago: University of Chicago Press.

Melton, J. Gordon, ed. 1989. *The Encyclopedia of American Religions*. Detroit: Gale Research.

Miller, Arthur H.; Gurin, Patricia; Gurin, Gerald; and Malanchuk, Oksana. 1981. "Group Consciousness and Political Participation." *American Journal of Political Science* 25:494–511.

Noll, Mark, ed. 1990. *Religion and American Politics*. New York: Oxford University Press.

Roof, Wade Clark, and McKinney, William. 1987. *American Mainline Religion*. New Brunswick, NJ: Rutgers University Press.

Smith, Tom W. 1990. "Classifying Protestant Denominations." *Review of Religious Research* 31:225–45.

Sommerfield, Richard A. 1968. "Conceptions of the Ultimate and the Social Organization of Religious Bodies." *Journal for the Scientific Study of Religion* 7:178–96.

Stark, Rodney, and Bainbridge, William Sims. 1985. *The Future of Religion: Secularization, Revival, and Cult Formation*. Berkeley: University of California Press.

Swierenga, Robert P. 1990. "Ethnoreligious Political Behavior in the Mid-Nineteeth Century: Voting, Values, and Cultures." In Noll 1990, 146–71.

Tajfel, Henri. 1981. *Human Groups and Social Categories: Studies in Social Psychology*. Cambridge: Cambridge University Press.

Turner, James. 1985. *Without God, Without Creed: The Origins of Unbelief in America*. Baltimore: Johns Hopkins University Press.

Wald, Kenneth D. 1992. *Religion and Politics in the United States*. 2d ed. Washington, DC: Congressional Quarterly Press.

Wald, Kenneth D.; Owen, Dennis E.; and Hill, Samuel S., Jr. 1988. "Churches as Political Communities," *American Political Science Review* 82:531–48.

Wildavsky, Aaron. 1987. "Choosing Preferences by Constructing Institutions: A Cultural Theory of Preference Formation." *American Political Science Review* 81:3–21.

Wuthnow, Robert. 1986. "Religious Movements and Counter-Movements in North America." In *New Religious Movements and Rapid Social Change*, ed. James A. Beckford, 1–28. Beverly Hills, CA: Sage Publications.

———. 1988. *The Restructuring of American Religion*. Princeton, NJ: Princeton University Press.

Appendix

Major Denominations Organized by Religious Traditions and Denominational Families

White Evangelical Protestants	White Mainline Protestants	Black Protestants*	Roman Catholics	Jewish
Baptist: Southern Baptist Convention American Baptist Churches USA Baptist General Conference	Anglican: Episcopal Church	Baptist: National Baptist Convention USA National Baptist Convention of America Progressive National Baptist Convention	Roman Catholic Church	Conservative Reform
	Congregational: United Church of Christ			
Holiness: Christian and Missionary Alliance Church of the Nazarene Free Methodist Church Salvation Army Wesleyan Church	Lutheran: Evangelical Lutheran Church in America	Methodist: African Methodist Episcopal Church African Methodist Episcopal Zion Church		
	Methodist: United Methodist Church			
	Nondenominational Mainline	Pentecostal: Church of God in Christ Church of God in Christ, International		
Lutheran: Missouri Synod Wisconsin Synod	Presbyterian: Presbyterian Church (USA)			
Nondemoninational Evangelical				

Pentecostal:
Assemblies of God
Church of God (Cleveland, TN)

Presbyterian:
Presbyterian Church in America
Orthodox Presbyterian Church

Reformed:
Christian Reformed Church

Restorationist:
Churches of Christ

Others:
Seventh Day Adventists
Mennonite Church
Evangelical Free Chruch
Evangelical Covenant Church
Plymouth Brethren

Reformed:
Reformed Church in America

Restorationist:
Christian Church
(Disciplies of Christ)

*Black denominations only are mentioned.
A more complete listing of denominations is available from the authors.

Chapter 4

Religious Group Identifications: Toward a Cognitive Theory of Religious Mobilization

Clyde Wilcox, Ted G. Jelen, and David C. Leege

During the 1980s, political scientists rediscovered the importance of group identities. After nearly two decades of concentration on party identification, scholars
in the 1980s began to focus on identification with other social groups. The
concept of group identification was posited to include two components: an
awareness of membership in a group, and a psychological attachment to the
group (Tajfel 1981). Those who felt a psychological attachment to a group but
were not objectively members of the group were defined as exhibiting group
sympathy (Conover 1986).[1] Conover (1984) reported that group identifications
were significant predictors of political attitudes. She argued that politically significant group identifications usually emerged slowly through normal socialization processes, but that dramatic political events might lead to more rapid
change.

Group identification was posited as one component of group consciousness—
a necessary but not sufficient condition. A number of scholars posited that group
consciousness included group identification, power discontent (the belief that
your group has less power than it deserves), system blaming (the belief that your
group is disadvantaged by the system and does not deserve its subordinate position), and an orientation toward collective action (Miller, Gurin, and Gurin 1980;
Gurin, Miller, and Gurin 1980; Miller, et al. 1981; Gurin 1985; Klein 1984;
Cook 1989). A few other studies have included polarized group affect—that is,
affinity toward members of one's own group and hostility toward members of
other groups—as a component of group consciousness. All these studies generally found that group consciousness facilitates political participation, and a few
studies have reported that group consciousness is also related to candidate preference (Cook 1993).

Group identification is the cognitive component of group consciousness. Individuals are thought to identify with a group and to perceive a common fate with
other members of the group. Those who perceive a common fate will subse-

quently perceive a common political interest and support at least some of the policies that group leaders advocate as a means of advancing the common group interest. Although these self-schema (Conover 1984) are usually characterized as purely cognitive, it seems likely that identification implies at least some affect as well (Conover and Sapiro 1992).

Group-related attitudes have come to occupy a central place in the study of public opinion because they have been shown to be efficient ways of organizing diverse bits of political information. Most citizens are *cognitive misers* (Brady and Sniderman 1985; Sniderman, Brody, and Tetlock 1991) who do not devote substantial psychological resources to public affairs. Attitudes toward highly visible groups in society (either positive or negative) are an effective means of simplifying the world. An identification with a social, political, or religious group helps citizens sort out political issues and candidates and more easily determine the course of their political behavior.

A variety of religious identifications appear important to doctrinally conservative Protestants. The most inclusive religious identification is that of *evangelical*. Some scholars have used the term *evangelical* to denote all doctrinally conservative Protestants, including fundamentalists, charismatics, and pentecostals (see Kellstedt and Smidt 1991; Wilcox 1992). Marsden (1984, xi) suggests that the term *evangelical* refers to "a religious fellowship or *coalition* of which people feel a part."

In other usages, the term *evangelical* is used to delimit a set of relatively "accommodating" (see Hunter 1983, 1987) conservative Christians different from fundamentalists, who are less willing to compromise (see Falwell 1981). In a similar vein, Wilcox (1992) refers to *other evangelicals* as the residual category of theologically conservative Christians after fundamentalist and pentecostal evangelicals are isolated.

By contrast, the concept of *fundamentalism* is typically employed to describe a subset of conservative Protestants who are often considered to have a separatist orientation and who regard the Bible as literally true (see Kellstedt and Smidt 1991; Jelen 1987). Fundamentalists are generally considered as a subset of evangelicals associated with membership in a few denominations such as the Baptist Bible Fellowship. Other denominations, including the Southern Baptists, include both fundamentalist and more moderate evangelical members.

Both charismatics and pentecostals are also considered a subset of evangelicals, with both groups emphasizing spiritual gifts such as glossolalia (speaking in tongues), faith healing, and prophecy. While the terms *charismatic* and *pentecostal* are often used interchangeably (see Smidt 1989a), the charismatic movement is generally thought to have a more ecumenical basis, while pentecostalism carries a more particularistic connotation (see Wilcox 1988; Jelen 1991a). There are charismatic groups in many mainline Protestant churches and in the Roman Catholic Church, but pentecostals are generally associated with a particular set of denominations such as the Assemblies of God.

The schismatic propensities of Protestantism and the heterogeneity of doc-trinal traditions within American denominations have exerted strong pressures on analysts to devise identification measures more precise than denominational family or religious tradition for *Protestants*. But American Catholics operate in the same American culture and religious marketplace. Various studies (Greeley 1977; Gremillion and Leege 1989) have also noted great differences among *Catholics* and within Catholic parishes, depending on ethnic backgrounds and devotional movements. While the Roman Catholic Church is a *church-type* rather than *sect-type* religious institution, it nevertheless has either encouraged or tolerated many charisms, spiritual gifts, and devotional emphases. Its historic success as a world-church is found in its capacity to maintain a core doctrinal system and authority structure while permitting adaptations to local cultures. Should we, then, not expect meaningful religious identities *within* the Catholic tradition?

Lacking an extensive measurement literature on the religious identities of Roman Catholics, it is more difficult to determine which sets of terms might best discriminate among different subgroups of Catholics. Through the centuries some Catholics have identified themselves with the charisms and devotional emphases of various religious orders (e.g., Franciscans, Benedictines, Jesuits, Sacred Heart). More recently the doctrinal emphases and liturgical updatings of the First (1871) and Second (1963–65) Vatican Councils have symbolized differ-ences that are captured in the terms *traditionalist* (pre-Vatican II) and *post-Vatican II*. In part as a result of the Second Vatican Council's "open window" to spiritual renewal, many Catholics have become identified with the charismatic movement (which is not limited to any of the three Christian traditions) and are quite willing to call themselves Catholic *charismatics*. Finally, many Roman Catholics identify with particular ethnic or racial groups within the faith (e.g., Irish Catholic, German Catholic, Polish Catholic, Latino Catholic).

Scholars who study the relationship between religion and politics have re-cently become interested in the question of religious identity. This interest stems in part from the energetic inquiry into operational definitions of evangelicalism (Kellstedt 1989; Smidt 1989b; 1991; Smidt and Kellstedt 1987; Wilcox 1986a; Wilcox 1992); in addition to doctrine and denomination, a third possibility is to define as evangelicals all citizens who identify themselves as such. Most of the scholarly interest to date has focused on fundamentalism (Smidt 1988; Wilcox 1989; Jelen 1991b; Beatty and Walter 1988; Kellstedt and Smidt 1991), where research has demonstrated that self-identified fundamentalists are more conser-vative than other evangelicals, even after controls for religiosity and doctrine. Other scholars have investigated the consequences of other religious identities, including evangelical, pentecostal-charismatic, and conservative (Wilcox 1986b; Smidt and Penning 1991; Jelen 1990; Green and Guth 1988; Jelen and Wilcox 1992; Wilcox 1990a). Little attention has gone into the sources of religious identity (but see Wilcox 1989) or to the meaning that these labels have for respondents. To date, little systematic research has explored the sources or consequences of alternate religious identities among Catholics.

None of this research has attempted to examine the more inclusive concept of a politicized religious consciousness, although some studies have included some components of group consciousness. Jelen (1990) shows that religious identification, religious affect, and polar group affect interact in politically important ways. Wald, Owen, and Hill (1989) have examined status discontent, a concept related to power discontent. Although no surveys to date combine all of the items that could measure religious consciousness, this kind of combination may not be necessary. Cook (1989) has shown that a parsimonious two-indicator scale does quite well in measuring feminist consciousness and is strongly correlated with all the other components of group consciousness.

Measurement Issues

Nearly all the research on religious identification to date has used samples of elites. Wilcox (1986b) surveyed members of the Ohio Moral Majority, Smidt (1988), Kellstedt and Smidt (1991), and Wilcox (1989) used data from a national survey of evangelicals, Green and Guth (1988) surveyed political contributors, Smidt and Penning (1990) examined the responses of activists in Michigan Republican politics, and Beatty and Walter (1988) examined data from their survey of pastors. As Ammerman (1988) has noted, these studies have demonstrated that religious identity is a meaningful concept for well-educated, religiously and politically informed citizens. Although Jelen (1991a) has shown that religious identification is a meaningful concept for regular churchgoers in Putnam County, Indiana, whether it is a useful concept for studies of the general population remains to be demonstrated.

Religious identity has been measured in these studies in a number of ways. Wilcox (1986b) asked Moral Majority members whether they thought of themselves as fundamentalist, evangelical, both, or neither. The *Evangelical Voter* study (Rothenberg and Newport 1984) asked evangelicals whether they thought of themselves as fundamentalists. Guth and Green (1988) asked political contributors to check any label that they applied to themselves, then listed many possible religious identities. The Green and Guth measures were adopted by Jelen and Wilcox (1992)[2] and by others.

In the National Election Studies (NES) 1989 Pilot Study, Protestant respondents who attended church at least occasionally were asked whether each of the following terms described (1) their churches and (2) their own religious views: *fundamentalist, evangelical, pentecostal or Spirit-filled, conservative*, and *liberal*. Responses ranged from 1 (the term describes the church or person very well) to 4 (not well at all). Catholics were offered a different list of identities: *traditionalist, supportive of the reforms of post-Vatican II, ethnic* (Polish, Italian, Hispanic, etc.), and *charismatic or Spirit-filled*.

Routinely we find that respondents experience more difficulty rating their parishes through these terms than themselves. Catholics experience the greatest difficulty applying the terms to their parishes (26 percent unable to rate parish on these identifications); mainline Protestants show the next greatest difficulty (19 percent on the five identifications discussed previously); and evangelical Protestants show the greatest facility in using the terms to describe their churches (only 13 percent cannot do it). The same pattern is evident in apparent response sets—that is, using identical values across all four or five terms—with Catholics at 11 percent, mainline Protestants at 5 percent, and evangelical Protestants at 4 percent. Such findings are not measurement artifacts, however; they reflect the difficulty of the task. The average Catholic parish has 2,330 members, a figure seven to eight times the average membership of a Protestant church. Each Catholic parish incorporates many styles of religiosity and of liturgical and devotional celebrations (Gremillion and Leege 1989). Mainline Protestant churches, while much smaller than Catholic parishes, often convey less ideological clarity than is found in the evangelical churches; particularism appears to be valued more in the evangelical churches than in the mainline.

To use the data on self-identification in the 1989 Pilot Study, it is important to deal with the problem of missing data. The filtering out of those who do not attend church regularly creates problems, for the total missing data on these questions is more than 60 percent. Approximately one-third of the respondents are filtered out, and an additional third or more are unable to answer one or more of the questions. Analysis of the response patterns of these two groups suggests that it is possible to bring those who are filtered out back into the analysis, coding them where the label fits *not well at all*. These filtered respondents are not especially religious, and identities such as *fundamentalist* and *charismatic* are not likely to apply to them.[3]

Many of those who are genuinely unable to answer the questions are, however, devoutly religious, and some are doctrinally orthodox.[4] Some analysts may choose to code these orthodox respondents who cannot decide how well these theological labels fit them as nonidentifiers. We have chosen to treat these responses as missing data, since a sizable subset is otherwise indistinguishable from those who claim one of these identities. This means that between one-third and 40 percent of the population is missing on any religious identity item. (In contrast, a quarter of respondents are unable to place themselves on the general political ideology question. There are therefore more missing data on religious identity than on ideological self-placement, but the differences are not large.) With a large national sample, these missing data would not pose an insurmountable problem, although they do pose analytic difficulties for the smaller number of cases in the 1989 Pilot Study.

In the 1990 NES, Protestant respondents were asked to choose the word that best described their kind of Christianity: *fundamentalist, evangelical, charismatic-pentecostal,* or *moderate to liberal.* Approximately 12 percent were unable to respond to the question, but among those who did, 21 percent chose *fundamentalist*, 24 percent chose *evangelical*, 12 percent chose *charismatic or pentecostal*, and 42 percent chose *moderate to liberal*.

A well-established body of research suggests that religious identities, doctrines, and practices have different political implications in the white and African-American communities. Although white evangelicals, pentecostals, and fundamentalists are generally conservative on all issues, among blacks evangelicalism is sometimes associated with support for civil rights activism, for gender equality, and economic liberalism along with social issue conservatism (Wilcox 1992). For this reason, we examine only white respondents in this chapter. The NES 1989 Pilot Study and the 1990 NES study contain too few black respondents for separate analysis. The data reported in Tables 4.1–4.4 are confined to white Protestants. We have duplicated the analysis for white Catholics and report that analysis in the text of the chapter rather than in the tables.

Validating the Questions: Can the Public Apply These Labels?

The various items on religious identity were contiguous in the 1989 Pilot Study, and substantial percentages of respondents showed multiple religious identities. By itself, this pattern is not evidence of a response set, for several of the religious identities are compatible. Several studies have shown that those who combine identities as fundamentalists, charismatics, and evangelicals are not necessarily responding inappropriately to religious identity questions. Green and Guth (1988) reported that a simple additive index of a series of orthodox religious identities (including charismatic, fundamentalist, and evangelical) was an effective measure in predicting support for Marion ("Pat") Robertson. In a series of studies (Wilcox 1990a, 1990b; Cook and Wilcox 1990; Wilcox and Thomas 1992) examined the impact of three religious identities (fundamentalist, evangelical, and charismatic) on the political beliefs and behaviors of blacks in Washington, D.C. Wilcox and his colleagues reported that religious identity was a significant predictor of political attitudes and behaviors but that for some dependent variables the three identities had different implications, while for others they were additive as Green and Guth (1988) had reported.

Two of the five religious identities for Protestants are incompatible, however. Those who identify as both *liberal* and *conservative* Christians are likely responding to the religious identity items in an inappropriate manner. Approximately 11 percent of respondents identified as both a liberal and conservative Christian. In contrast, 8 percent of respondents rated political conservatives and liberals above 70° on feeling thermometer items, and 2 percent indicated that they felt especially close to both liberals and conservatives. In short, the religious identity items show a slightly higher rate of response set than similar political items. For the remainder of this chapter, we have assigned those respondents who identify as both liberal and conservative Christians in the 1989 Pilot Study to a missing data code. Some analysts may also wish to code as *missing* those respondents who claim to be liberal Christians and also claim one of the more orthodox identities, although we have not done so in this paper. A religious identity as a liberal Christian and a fundamentalist are clearly incompatible, but we believe that the *liberal* label is contaminated with political meaning. Some fundamentalists who accept a liberal identity may be signaling their political beliefs.

In Table 4.1, the last column shows the percentages of Protestant respondents who adopt each religious identity; data are presented for both 1989 and 1990. In addition, the table validates the religious identity items with other relevant religious variables. The data show that a large percentage of Americans respond to labels such as *fundamentalist, pentecostal or Spirit-filled*, and *evangelical*, regardless of a multiple-option for forced-choice format. Few scholars who study American religious life would think of more than one-fifth of all church-connected Americans as strong fundamentalists; doubtlessly some response error is present. Yet the data do show the predicted patterns, at least for the three theological identifications. The relationship between *pentecostal, fundamentalist*, and *evangelical* identity on the one hand, and the belief in a literal Bible and a born-again experience on the other, is monotonic. The relationships are more complex for the religious salience and church attendance measures, for highly religious Americans can strongly reject these identities. Indeed, those who report that these three identities fit them *not well at all* show higher levels of religious salience and attendance than those who merely say they fit *quite well* or *not too well*. Highly religious liberals strongly reject these labels.

These relationships suggest that the public is generally responding appropriately to these measures but that up to one-third of the respondents who claim a *fundamentalist, evangelical,* or *charismatic* identity lack some of the theological beliefs and practices that are usually associated with those labels.

Also included in Table 4.1 are a similar set of relationships for the respondents to the 1990 NES.[5] The 1990 item, unlike the 1989 item, forced Protestant respondents to make a choice among four identifications (fundamentalist, evangelical, charismatic-pentecostal, and moderate to liberal). Once again most respondents seem to be responding to these labels in a manner that is generally consistent with expectations. Somewhat surprisingly, those for whom the fundamentalist identity is most important are less likely than charismatics to take a literal view of the Scriptures. This relationship is, however, replicated in the contributor data with a more comprehensive Bible item, in which respondents were given the choice of a literal or an inerrant Bible.[6] Charismatics are also more likely to find religion highly salient to their lives, but on most other variables the three theological groups are quite similar. It is also interesting to note that a sizable minority of those who adopted a *moderate to liberal* religious identity believed the Bible to be literally true, and reported a born-again experience. This finding suggests that religious identities such as *moderate, liberal,*

Table 4.1

Validating the Religious Identity Questions
(white Protestants only)

1989 NES Pilot Study	Religion High Salient	Bible Literal	Born Again	Attend >Weekly	% Total
Fundamentalist					
very well	71%	67%	67%	35%	22%
quite well	41%	56%	45%	23%	26%
not too well	35%	40%	38%	9%	24%
not well at all	48%	32%	30%	23%	29%
Evangelical					
very well	73%	65%	69%	40%	22%
quite well	46%	53%	44%	24%	25%
not too well	34%	41%	49%	12%	24%
not well at all	47%	31%	27%	19%	28%
Charismatic					
very well	64%	81%	69%	31%	23%
quite well	41%	60%	50%	16%	23%
not too well	34%	30%	35%	8%	19%
not well at all	50%	30%	34%	30%	34%
Conservative					
very well	60%	57%	50%	29%	33%
quite well	42%	48%	46%	21%	36%
not too well	40%	44%	36%	13%	17%
not well at all	49%	38%	42%	19%	15%
Liberal					
very well	57%	53%	45%	23%	20%
quite well	35%	45%	37%	10%	21%
not too well	39%	45%	41%	17%	29%
not well at all	59%	49%	52%	35%	29%

1990 NES	Religion High Salient	Bible Literal	Born Again	Attend >Weekly	% Total
Fundamentalist	47%	61%	63%	29%	21%
Evangelical	57%	58%	58%	28%	24%
Charismatic/Pentecostal	67%	76%	75%	25%	12%
Moderate to Liberal	22%	32%	26%	11%	42%

	Read Bible Daily +	Pray >Daily	Civil Religion
Fundamentalist	28%	40%	39%
Evangelical	27%	43%	44%
Charismatic/Pentecostal	29%	47%	28%
Moderate to Liberal	7%	18%	26%

Source: 1989 NES Pilot Study, 1990 NES.

and *conservative* are contaminated by the political meaning of these terms. Some orthodox Christians may call themselves religious liberals or moderates to reflect their political views.

We have also examined the relationship between these religious variables and the four Catholic identities, although we do not show the results in Table 4.1. Many of the religious variables in Table 4.1 are not especially relevant to Catholic religiosity: only a small minority of Catholics believe the Bible is literally true or report a born-again experience. However, post-Vatican II Catholics are much more likely than other Catholics to indicate that religion is highly salient to their lives and to attend religious services regularly. Traditionalist Catholics are more likely than others to believe in the authority of the Bible and to attend religious services regularly, but they do not exhibit higher levels of religious salience. Charismatic Catholics are more likely to report high levels of religious salience, to believe in the authority of the Bible, and to report a born-again experience, but not to attend religious services.

In Table 4.2, we show the mean values for four political variables that are useful in validating the scales. The first two scales measure moral traditionalism and social issue conservatism. These scales have been normalized, and high scores reflect more conservative positions. The final two items reflect affect toward Marion ("Pat") Robertson and the Moral Majority. These scores are adjusted to reflect individual differences in responses, with positive scores indicating warm responses and negative scores indicating negative affect.[7] At the bottom of the table, we present similar information for the 1990 forced-choice religious identity item. We have constructed similar scales measuring moral traditionalism and social issue positions and constructed measures of affect toward the women's movement and antiabortionists.

Again, the general patterns suggest that the Protestant public is responding to most of these items in a meaningful pattern. Those who take a *fundamentalist*, *evangelical*, or *pentecostal* identity are more morally traditionalistic and conservative on social issues. They are less cool toward Pat Robertson and the Moral Majority, although even those who indicate that the terms *fundamentalist* or *pentecostal* fit them *very well* are generally cool to the Moral Majority and Robertson. It should be noted that among whites, these three identities are associated with more conservative positions on all social issues, including an equal role for women in society. Other studies among African Americans report a different result, suggesting that the political meaning of religious identities may be at least partially mediated by religious and political elites (Wilcox 1989; Wilcox 1990a). The two sets of findings also parallel the racial differences reported in chapter 7.

In the 1990 data we find a similar pattern. Fundamentalists, evangelicals, and charismatics are all more conservative on these scales than those whose religious identity is moderate to liberal. Charismatics are the most conservative, followed by fundamentalists and then evangelicals. Those who opt for a moderate to

Table 4.2

Validating Religious Identity: Political Measures
(white Protestants only)

1989 NES Pilot Study	Moral Tradition	Social Issues	Affect Robertson	Affect Moral Majority
Fundamentalist				
very well	.90	.37	-14	-8
quite well	.32	.10	-14	-12
not too well	-.03	-.11	-20	-17
not well at all	-.22	-.19	-32	-26
Evangelical				
very well	.57	.29	-12	-5
quite well	.65	.21	-12	-9
not too well	.01	-.22	-24	-23
not well at all	-.26	-.22	-33	-27
Pentecostal				
very well	.41	.36	-8	-1
quite well	.42	.21	-10	-10
not too well	-.09	-.27	-25	-20
not well at all	-.13	-.17	-31	-27
Conservative				
very well	.63	.24	-19	-14
quite well	.51	.11	-15	-12
not too well	-.13	.12	-25	-20
not well at all	-.34	-.22	-32	-27
Liberal				
very well	-.42	.00	-31	-19
quite well	-.21	-.11	-23	-23
not too well	.22	.07	-18	-15
not well at all	-.00	-.07	-28	-23

1990 NES	Moral Tradit.	Social Issues	Affect Women Mvt	Affect Anti-Abort
Fundamentalist	.36	.23	-4	9
Evangelical	.27	.18	-4	4
Charismatic	.44	.34	-5	11
Moderate/Liberal	-.14	-.24	5	-16

Source: 1989 NES Pilot Study, 1990 NES.
Mean score on normalized scales for each group. Moral traditionalism and social issue scales are normalized for all whites, and high scores indicate more conservative positions. Affect toward Robertson and the Moral Majority represent degrees below each group of respondents' mean feeling thermometer score that these Christian Right figures were rated.

liberal religious identity are markedly more liberal politically than the respondents who adopt the other three religious identities. Those white Protestants who call themselves fundamentalist, evangelical, or charismatic are somewhat cool toward the women's movement and warm toward antiabortion activists, while those who adopt a moderate to liberal religious identity reverse this pattern.

Once again, we have examined the relationships for the four Catholic identities in the 1989 Pilot Study, although we do not present them in this table. There are fairly large relationships between the Catholic identities and political attitudes. Charismatic and traditionalist Catholics take significantly more conservative positions on the moral traditionalism scale than do other Catholics, while post-Vatican II Catholics take more liberal positions. Charismatics, traditionalists, and post-Vatican II Catholics all take more conservative positions on social issues than do Catholics who do not adopt these labels. Charismatic Catholics are more supportive of Pat Robertson and the Moral Majority, while post-Vatican II Catholics are somewhat more cool toward these New Christian Right figures. The term *ethnic* Catholic does not discriminate well politically.

Taken together, the data in Tables 4.1 and 4.2 suggest that the Protestants are responding to the three theological identities in a manner consistent with our expectations. The appropriate religious public is capable of responding to these items, albeit with some response error. The exception is the identity as a *liberal* Christian in the 1989 Pilot Study, which seems to have no theological meaning. Further analysis (Leege, Kellstedt, and Wald 1990) suggests that this label induces responses that combine theological and political meanings and is therefore not useful as a religious identity.[8] In the 1990 NES, however, those who chose *moderate to liberal* Christian are markedly different theologically from those who chose one of the other labels. For most of this chapter, we will focus our attention on Protestant identities with clear theological meaning: *fundamentalist, evangelical,* and *Spirit-filled or pentecostal.*

Recoding the Identification Items in the Pilot Study

Analysts often seek to isolate fundamentalists from evangelicals, or pentecostals from both groups. Because the 1989 Pilot Study used four-category items, any attempt to isolate fundamentalists, evangelicals, or charismatics from each other, or to distinguish post-Vatican II Catholics from traditionalist Catholics, will inevitably involve recoding. The data in Tables 4.1 and 4.2 make it clear that those who believe that an identity fits them *very well* are the closest to our conventional understanding of fundamentalists, evangelicals, and pentecostals. Yet there are few respondents who report this strong level of identification. Only 55 respondents feel that the label *fundamentalist* fits them *very well*: the comparable figure for pentecostal is 65 and for evangelical 55. The figures are even smaller for the Catholic identities, because there are fewer Catholic respondents to the survey. Any attempt to identify, for example, "true" fundamentalists by responses to the Bible or born-again items would further reduce these numbers. This problem arises in part because of the smaller number of respondents to the Pilot Study; in a larger national survey we might expect four times as many respondents who would indicate that these terms describe them *very well*.

Analysts using the 1989 Pilot Study data may wish to recode the religious identities into dichotomies with those who report that an identity fits them *very well* or *quite well* coded as identifiers. Should these items be used in a larger survey with substantially more cases, isolating those who select *very well* would seem preferable. For multivariate analysis, however, recoding the identification items results in substantially lower correlations, since the marginals are badly skewed. For Pearson's correlations, multiple regression, probit, logistic regression, or other techniques, the unrecoded items offer stronger relationships.[9]

Dealing with Multiple Identifications

The group identification literature in political science has not dealt well with the question of multiple group identifications. All published studies focus on single social or political identities for each respondent without taking into account other identifications that the respondent might report. Conover (1984), for example, chooses the identity that the respondent holds most strongly and ignores other social identities for that respondent. Clearly, most Americans have complex social identities and feel close to several social and political groups. Indeed, multiple cross-cutting identities are an important part of pluralist theories of how society remains civil in the face of important political conflicts.

Yet many accounts of the politics of the evangelical community stress the sectarian nature of religious strife. Wilcox (1992) has argued that religious particularism among fundamentalists prevented them from building a wider coalition with pentecostal, charismatic, or evangelical Protestants and conservative Catholics. He suggested that Baptist Bible Fellowship ministers in the Moral Majority made their religious prejudices known, and nonfundamentalists were made to feel less than welcome. Several scholars (Green and Guth 1988; Smidt and Penning 1990; Wilcox 1992; Jelen 1991a) have reported that Pat Robertson's campaign attracted strong support from pentecostals and charismatics but little backing from fundamentalists or other evangelicals, and the most likely explanation for this pattern is particularism.[10] The generally cool reception of Robertson among fundamentalists is thought to result from fundamentalist skepticism about the spiritual gifts that charismatics and pentecostals regularly claim (Wilcox 1988). Jelen (1991a) has reported a symmetrical negative affect among charismatics, pentecostals, evangelicals, and fundamentalists, with each group relatively cool toward the others. Thus a major line of recent scholarship has stressed the negative affect toward various evangelical subgroups and non-evangelical groups engendered by religious particularism. Religious elites have provided considerable evidence for this line of scholarship: Jerry Falwell (1981) has criticized pentecostals, charismatics, and evangelicals, and did not endorse fellow Baptist televangelist Pat Robertson in his bid for the presidency.

Yet a substantial portion of the respondents in the 1989 Pilot Study chose more than one of these religious identities. Fewer than 25 percent of those who identified themselves as fundamentalist did not identify as either an evangelical or a pentecostal. Only 14 percent of pentecostals held that identity only, while fewer than one in four evangelicals did not identify as either fundamentalist or pentecostal. Nearly one-quarter of those who chose one of these three theological identities identified as all three.[11]

How are we to interpret these multiple identities? The 1989 Pilot Study data do not contain sufficient cases to reliably examine the seven possible combinations of Protestant theological identities. In an analysis of religious identity among political contributors, Jelen and Wilcox (1992) found that those who identified as only fundamentalists clearly did not fit the pattern of doctrinally pure separatists, for they were not especially likely to take a "high" (i.e., inerrant or literal) view of the Scriptures.[12] The authors did find that fundamentalists supported the Baptist-based Moral Majority, while charismatics supported the charismatic Pat Robertson. In a study of religious identity among those who contributed to evangelical political groups, Smidt (1991) reported that those who held a charismatic identity only were the least doctrinally orthodox and that although those with multiple identities were more doctrinally conservative, there were complex interactions among the various religious identifications.

Clearly, more research is needed to understand these multiple religious identities. While fundamentalist elites are preaching that the gifts of the Spirit that are common in charismatic services are illegitimate and dangerous, a majority of those who identify as fundamentalists in the 1989 Pilot Study data also identify themselves as charismatics. Jelen (1990) reported that nearly two-thirds of churchgoers in Putnam County who called themselves *fundamentalists* also called themselves *charismatics* and *pentecostals*. Smidt (1991) similarly reported that fully 40 percent of evangelical activists who called themselves *fundamentalists* also adopted the identity of *pentecostal* or *charismatic*.

As Smidt and Penning (1991, 121) argued, "Certain religious self-classifications appear, based on historical emphasis and theological emphasis, to be 'logically' incompatible. For example, dispensational premillenialism is a theological perspective which is widely evident within fundamentalism . . . , but a theological perspective which is inconsistent with charismatic understandings." Most dispensationalist accounts suggest that the gifts of the Spirit were confined to an earlier religious era. Yet in the 1989 Pilot Study data, approximately half of all who took the *pentecostal* label also identified as *fundamentalist*.

Such results starkly confront all published work on particularism among evangelicals. There is a fairly substantial body of theory and research to suggest that religious particularism among evangelical subgroups is widespread. There is much observational evidence of fundamentalist pastors criticizing sharply the spiritual practices of pentecostals and charismatics (e.g., Ammerman 1988; Jelen 1991a; Wilcox 1992). Much of the scholarship on fundamentalism, including writings by fundamentalist elites, stresses the separatist nature of fundamentalism.[13] And yet multiple identities persist.

The single-choice item in the 1990 NES avoids but does not solve this problem; indeed, it avoids the problem by making it impossible to measure. With the available data we are unable to solve this theoretical puzzle, but we can suggest some directions for future research. First, it might be helpful if some future survey would allow respondents to choose multiple religious identities, then include a follow-up question asking respondents what they mean by the terms *fundamentalist, charismatic*, and *evangelical*. Such a probe has proved useful in helping decipher the meaning of *liberalism* and *conservatism* in NES data (Conover and Feldman 1984). Second, it might be useful in some future national survey to include both the questions from the 1989 Pilot Study and the item in the 1990 NES. By combining these items we could learn which of the religious identities is most salient for multiple identifiers.[14]

Third, it is possible to measure feelings toward groups with which the respondent does not identify via items asking whether the respondent feels *close* to members of a particular group or through more standard feeling thermometers (Wilcox, Sigelman, and Cook 1989). Nonidentification with a particular group may conceal a variety of feelings toward that group, including sympathy, ignorance, indifference, or hostility, and future research might profitably take up these differences. Jelen (1990, 1991a) has shown that, among a rural, white sample, negative affect toward certain cultural and religious groups was a much more powerful predictor of feelings toward figures of the New Christian Right than was simple group identification.

Wilcox (1986b) argued that those Moral Majority members who identified as both *evangelicals* and *fundamentalists* were primarily evangelicals who used the fundamentalist label to identify their belief in the Bible. Although his data did not permit a direct test, he suggested that the *evangelical* label would be most salient for those Moral Majority members. It may be that among multiple identifiers we would find several distinct subgroups who hold different identities as the most salient. Perhaps many of those who hold all three identities are charismatics who use the label *fundamentalist* to describe their beliefs about the Bible and the term *evangelical* to describe their commitment to personal evangelism. Without a measure of charismatic experience, we cannot test this hypothesis with the 1989 Pilot Study data. In the contributor data, however, fully 93 percent of those who accepted all three labels reported a charismatic experience (e.g., speaking in tongues).

A different conceptual approach to the multiple identity problem would be to follow Conover (1986) and others and to suggest that only those who objectively belong to a group exhibit *group identity*, while others exhibit *group sympathy*. Thus a Baptist who believes the Bible is literally true and who has never had an ecstatic religious experience could show a *fundamentalist* identity, but her closeness to charismatics would be classified as *religious group sympathy*.

Although we have argued that these items exhibit only slightly more evidence of response set than other similar types of questions, it is also clear that some of the multiple-identification problem is due to response error. At least some of the respondents who indicate that the terms *fundamentalist, pentecostal,* and *evangelical* fit them *very well* are probably reflecting their high levels of religiosity rather than agreement with a particular doctrine.

The small number of Catholics in the 1989 Pilot Study make an understanding of the meaning of multiple religious identities difficult to interpret. There is substantial overlap among the religious identities, with more than one-third of traditionalist Catholics also accepting an identity supportive of post-Vatican II reforms, although these identities would seem to be contradictory. A number of Catholics even identify multiply as traditionalist, post-Vatican II, and charismatic. Further research with larger samples of Catholics is needed to sort out the meanings of multiple Catholic identifications.

The Sources of Religious Identification

The political science literature on group identification is generally weak on the sources of these identities. Conover (1984) merely asserts that political socialization produces most political identities, although a few are created by dramatic political events. Yet surely the "consciousness raising" of feminists and African-American leaders in the 1960s and 1970s led to a sharp increase in the two most frequently studied political identities: feminist and racial. Political entrepreneurs and interest groups attempt to build a sense of common fate in their prospective members and to link that common fate to policies that they advocate. During the 1980s, prominent televangelists and political-religious interest groups attempted to build a larger sense of religious identity and to politicize that identity into consciousness. Thus Falwell argued that fundamentalists (and to a lesser extent evangelicals) share a common religiously based political agenda and that collectively they could strongly influence politics. For evangelicals, however, Falwell (1981, 222) first recommended taking on a fundamentalist identity: "reacknowledge your fundamentalist roots."

We argue that religious identities come primarily from two sources: religious affiliation and religious doctrine. We have estimated a series of regression equations to predict Protestant religious identities from the 1989 Pilot Study data (not shown). In the first set we included religious doctrine (born-again status, belief in the Bible), religious denomination (fundamentalist,[15] pentecostal, other evangelical), religiosity (salience, attendance), and viewing of televangelists. In the second set we included an additional set of measures that asked respondents whether the church they attended was fundamentalist, pentecostal, and/or evangelical.[16]

The strongest predictors of all three religious identities in the first set of equations was religious doctrine. Those who attended pentecostal or holiness churches were more likely to take the charismatic identification, but fundamentalist churches were not more likely to instill a fundamentalist identity, nor were other evangelical churches likely to facilitate an evangelical identity. Our measure of fundamentalist denomination is badly skewed, for few respondents belonged to such churches, and such distributions can suppress the magnitude of coefficients. When we *equiweighted* the correlation (Bruner 1984), membership in a fundamentalist church is a significant predictor of a fundamentalist religious identity.

In the second set of equations, the strongest set of predictors were the respondents' classification of their local churches. Although we think it likely that the causal connection between local church theology and religious self-identification is somewhat overstated by these equations,[17] they do point to the importance of taking into account local congregations in assessing the connection between religion and politics. Other studies (Wald, Owen, and Hill 1988, 1990; Jelen 1992) have reported that local churches are important sources of political cues. This study shows that they are also important sources of religious self-identities. One way that Christians come to know to label themselves as *fundamentalists* is when their local pastor uses the label in his or her sermon.[18]

Unfortunately, neither the 1989 Pilot Study nor the 1990 NES contained measures of charismatic religious experiences. Numerous special-purpose surveys have included such items, along with measures of religious identification. In data from Jelen's (1991a) survey of Greencastle churchgoers, from Brown, Powell, and Wilcox's (1990a, 1990b) survey of political contributors, and from Wilcox's (cf. Jelen and Wilcox 1992) survey of African Americans in Washington, D.C., a charismatic religious experience is a powerful predictor of a charismatic or pentecostal religious identity. Among the contributors in the Brown, Powell, and Wilcox survey, 93 percent of those who took a *charismatic* label reported some type of charismatic experience.

If local churches are one important source of religious identities, what of those respondents who hold orthodox doctrinal views but do not attend churches that call themselves fundamentalist, pentecostal, or evangelical? How do these Christians learn the correct religious identities? Wilcox (1989) reported that for those respondents who held fundamentalist doctrinal beliefs but who did not attend fundamentalist churches, exposure to televangelists or to religious publications was a strong predictor of religious identity. In other words, those who were not informed by their local pastors that their religious beliefs qualified them as fundamentalists or charismatics or evangelicals could learn this from televangelists.

The data from the 1989 Pilot Study confirm this result, although the smaller number of cases makes inferences tentative. Separate regression equations were estimated, with an interaction term between exposure to televangelists and doctrine included in the analysis. Those who regularly view televangelists, do not attend pentecostal churches, but hold orthodox religious views are significantly more likely to identify as pentecostals, and there is also a strong interaction between doctrine and exposure to religious television among those who do not attend fundamentalist churches, but who hold fundamentalist doctrine. Thus doctrine is the basis of religious identity, but most Christians do not know that their beliefs qualify them as charismatics or evangelicals or fundamentalists unless their local church or religious television provides this information. Such a finding is well grounded in earlier research in the sociology of religion. Glock and Stark (1965) show that people who claim to have had an intense religious experience did not interpret it as a *religious* experience until fellow church members interpreted it as such. Co-religionists create a *plausibility structure* for interpreting experiences. The finding is also well grounded in Laing's psychology of self and other (1970) and in studies of contextual reinforcement of communications effects (Katz and Lazarsfeld 1955).

If some Americans adopt an orthodox religious identity in response to the language used in their local church, then it is likely that at least some of them will lack the prerequisite theological beliefs that generally fit that label. Some churchgoers, without actually holding fundamentalist views of the Bible, will call themselves *fundamentalists* merely because their pastor says that their church is *fundamentalist*. In contrast, those who attend mainline churches and adopt these labels should be more likely to actually hold the orthodox doctrinal beliefs and report the religious experiences that fit the religious identity. Many self-identified fundamentalists who attend mainline Protestant churches will hold fundamentalist beliefs, for it is these beliefs, interpreted by some other religious figure such as a televangelist, that will lead to the religious identity.

The data in the 1989 Pilot Study support this expectation. Among those who attend evangelical churches, the correlation between the three orthodox religious identities (fundamentalist, evangelical, pentecostal) and beliefs in the Bible and a born-again experience are generally modest: the average is .14. In contrast, among mainline Protestants, the average correlation was .39. In part, the higher correlations among mainline Protestants are due to the greater variation in religious identities and religious doctrine and experience. Yet after adjustments for the unequal marginals, the correlations are still significantly higher among mainline Protestants. A similar pattern holds for some political variables. The average correlation between the three orthodox identities and the social issue index is .11 for those who attend evangelical churches, .23 for those who attend mainline churches. For the moral traditionalism scale the difference is .16 to .24.

The Consequences of Religious Identification

Do religious identities help us predict political attitudes and behaviors? To answer this question, we have computed a series of partial correlations for each religious identity, controlling for demographic variables (sex, age, region, rural birth, education) and other religious variables (denomination, salience, attendance, frequency of prayer, doctrine). The data are in Table 4.3.

Religious identity remains a strong source of political attitudes and orientations, even after controls for demographic and other religious variables. Much of this effect is mediated through party and ideology, for additional controls for these two variables substantially reduce the magnitude of many of these correlations. Yet this finding does not diminish the importance of religious identity, for these correlations show that religious identification is an important source of political cues.

Among the three theological labels, our results show that a fundamentalist identification is a somewhat better predictor of conservative values, attitudes, and group affect than an evangelical identity, which is, in turn, a stronger predictor than a pentecostal identity. Surprisingly, a fundamentalist identity is a slightly stronger predictor of warmth toward Robertson than a pentecostal identity, while a pentecostal identity is a much better predictor than a fundamentalist identity of warmth toward the Moral Majority in this set of results.

It is also obvious from these correlations that the labels *liberal* and *conservative* Christian are contaminated with political meaning—that is, some respondents choose these labels according to their political ideology. Constructing cumulative indices of religious identity that include *conservative* (and a recoded *liberal*) identity will inflate correlations, but do so primarily through measurement error.

Group consciousness is more frequently used to predict political behavior than political attitudes. Our results show that religious group identity by itself is a poor predictor of turnout and only a weak predictor of vote choice. Controls for ideology and partisanship wipe out the correlations between fundamentalist and evangelical identity and vote in 1988. It is possible that a fuller model of religious group consciousness (including the other components discussed above) would provide more predictive power.

Additional analysis (not shown) reveals that for the 1989 Pilot Study data, the relatively high correlations among these three religious identities effectively wipe out any significant correlations once all three are simultaneously in an equation. In other words, a fundamentalist identity is a significant predictor of political attitudes only if we do not control for an evangelical identity or a pentecostal identity.[19] Of course, the problem does not exist where the identities have been derived from a forced-choice item, as in 1990 NES.

We have calculated a similar set of partial correlations for the four Catholic identities. The small number of Catholics in the study is further reduced by multivariate controls, so these results must be interpreted as preliminary. Despite the small sample size, however, we do find a number of statistically significant differences. Moreover, the absolute magnitude of these partial correlations is substantial. Catholics who take the traditionalist identity are significantly more

Table 4.3

The Consequences of Religious Identity
(white Protestants only)

	Funda-mentalist	Evan-gelical	Charis-matic	Conser-vative	Liberal
General Orientations					
Nationalism	-.03	.08	.03	.06	-.02
Anti-Communism	.24**	.09	.09	.31**	-.13*
Moral Traditionalism	.19*	.08	-.04	.31**	-.27**
Equality Values	.08	.05	.02	.20**	-.08
Partisanship	.19**	.10#	.03	.29**	.01
Ideology	.26**	.11#	-.01	.39**	-.24**
Issue Attitudes					
Social Issues	-.00	.04	.03	.17*	-.26**
Death Penalty	.10#	.04	.11#	.22**	-.18*
Economic Issues	.14*	.23**	.12#	.32**	-.12#
Spending for Poor	.15*	.24**	.07	.29**	-.06
Racial Issues	.11#	.08	.07	.05	-.03
Defense Spending	.10	-.00	.02	.16*	-.15*
Detente, USSR	-.01	.19**	-.02	.15*	-.14*
Affect					
Moral Majority	.18**	.26**	.31**	.28**	-.05
Robertson	.23**	.17*	.21**	.23**	-.05
Feminists	-.15*	-.07	-.06	-.09	.04
Homosexuals and Lesbians	-.21**	-.11*	-.13*	-.27**	.11*
Catholics	-.09#	.05-	.02	.09#	-.02
Jews	.01	.04	-.05	-.07	-.05
Fundamentalists	.23**	.13*	.14*	.23**	-.07
Civil Rights Leaders	-.12*	-.03	.05	-.10#	.00
Blacks	-.07	-.00	-.02	-.05	.03
Political Behavior					
Turnout	-.03	-.02	-.07	-.02	-.10#
Vote Choice	.13*	.13*	.03	.32**	-.02

Source: 1989 NES Pilot Study.

Entries are partial correlation coefficients, holding constant sex, age, region, rural birth, education, denomination (a dummy measure of evangelical denomination), religious salience, frequency of church attendance and prayer, and doctrine. # = $p < .10$; * = $p < .05$; ** = $p < .01$.

conservative on nationalism and more conservative on economic issues, racial attitudes, spending for the poor, and ideology. They are warmer toward civil rights leaders. Reflecting their greater policy liberalism, they are more Democratic and more likely to have voted for Michael Dukakis. Charismatic Catholics are more conservative on moral traditionalism, nationalism, and general equality values and are more conservative in general and on social issues, racial attitudes, and attitudes toward relations with the former Soviet Union. They are much warmer toward Robertson and cooler to civil rights leaders. Post-Vatican II Catholics are significantly more liberal on moral traditionalism and more liberal on economic issues, spending for the poor, defense spending, and racial attitudes, cooler toward Robertson and toward Catholics in general, and warmer toward blacks. Those who identify as ethnic Catholics are significantly cooler toward Robertson and warmer toward homosexuals, a result perhaps best attributed to random error. Such findings obviously point to considerably more political variance explained through knowing the specific identity of a Catholic (beyond just *Catholic*); perhaps political scientists would be well advised to devote attention to Catholic identities to the degree that they have addressed the more conservative of the Protestant identities. Catholics, after all, constitute 24.9 percent of adult Americans but more than one-fourth of the *active* electorate.

Religious Identification in a Measurement Model: An Alternative Conceptualization

Most studies have viewed religious identity as a cognitive component of a constellation of religious variables and have attempted to assess the independent impact of identifications. The analysis above has followed this model. Yet it is also possible to model religious identification as merely one more imperfect measure of evangelicalism, fundamentalism, or pentecostalism.

Many studies use denomination as a single indicator of evangelicalism, and it appears to be a reasonably good single indicator of the concept. Yet it is clear that there is measurement error through this approach. In the border states, some mainline Protestant churches (especially Methodists) preach fundamentalist doctrine. In the African-American community, Baptists are often pentecostals. At Ohio State University, the Southern Baptist congregation was theologically very liberal.

A second measurement approach has been to use measures of doctrine to identify evangelicals, fundamentalists, and charismatics. This approach often encounters a different type of measurement error, in which a sizable portion of those who meet a doctrinal test never attend church or read the Bible. In the 1990 NES, fully 61 percent of those who took a "high" view of the Scriptures read their Bible weekly or less. Most of these types of respondents are responding with the socially desirable answer that they are Christians, without any discrimination in doctrine.

In the 1989 Pilot Study, a third approach is newly available, in which respondents describe their local congregation as *fundamentalist, evangelical, pentecostal, conservative,* or *liberal.* Finally, we have religious identification, which is also measured with error as discussed above. Instead of conceiving of these as separate religious variables (whose collinearity often wipes out very real religious effects), it may be better to model these as separate imperfect indicators of the same concepts.

Such a measurement model would incorporate religious doctrine and experience, denomination, the respondent's label for his or her local church, affect for fundamentalists, and religious self-identity as indicators of evangelicalism, fundamentalism, and pentecostalism. By allowing for correlated measurement error, we could better measure these concepts. The appropriate statistical technique for this approach would be latent structure modeling. In this paper, we will use LISREL.[20]

We have estimated two different LISREL confirmatory factor models using the 1989 Pilot Study data and two models using the contributor data, to determine how best to model religious identity. In the first model, we view denomination, doctrine, local congregational identity, and religious self-identity as different measures of evangelicalism, fundamentalism, and pentecostalism. In the second model, we posited that denomination, doctrine, religious self-identity, and local congregational identity were separate sets of variables. In both models, we allowed for correlated errors of measurement among sets of similarly worded items.

The data show a much stronger fit for the first model. For the data from the 1989 Pilot Study, a model that posits that religious identity is one additional measure of membership in one or another evangelical theological community, and that all of the available measures contain significant error, is confirmed by the data. A similar model gives the best fit for the contributor data of Brown, Powell, and Wilcox.[21] The results are shown in Table 4.4.

If religious identity is but another imperfect measure of religious communities, then it might seem that measures of identity are superfluous in building models of political attitudes and behavior. Inspection of the parameter estimates, however, suggests that religious identity is a stronger predictor of these latent religious concepts than either denomination or the theological label applied by the respondent to her or his local church, although religious doctrine is more important than religious identity. These results are confirmed in the LISREL analysis of the contributor data, although the measure of a charismatic experience loads more strongly on the latent measure of pentecostalism. In short, religious identity is an important additional measure of these concepts and may contain less measurement error than other measures of the same underlying construct.

To further test the utility of religious identity, we estimated a series of somewhat more complex LISREL models, one set including the religious identity

Table 4.4

LISREL Results
(white Protestants only)

	Fundamentalist	Pentecostal	Evangelical
Fundamentalist Denom.	.33		
Pentecostal Denom.		.42	
Other Evangelical Denom.			.34
Affect, Fundamentalists	.50		
Fundamentalist ID	.49		
Pentecostal ID		.75	
Evangelical ID			.50
Fundamentalist Church	.42		
Pentecostal Church		.33	
Evangelical Church			.33
Bible Belief	5.10	3.81	-.50
Born Again	1.36	.23	-8.12

Adjusted Goodness of Fit = .99
Root Mean Square Residual = .05

	Contributor Data		
Fundamentalist Denom.	.20		
Pentecostal Denom.		.57	
Other Evangelical Denom.			.60
Fundamentalist ID	.86		
Pentecostal ID		.72	
Evangelical ID			.61
Charismatic Experience		.93	
Bible Belief	.22	.19	-1.07
Born Again	.84	.13	-.13

Adjusted goodness of fit = .99
Root mean square residual = .03

Standardized lambda X values for best fitting LISREL models.
Source: 1989 NES Pilot Study.

items and the other set excluding them. We used a least-squares model to regress the latent religious variables on latent variables that tapped several types of political attitudes, including social issues, foreign policy issues, economic issues, racial issues, moral traditionalism, equality values, anticommunism, nationalism, and affect toward outgroups. Our results show a significant improvement in explanatory power from including measures of religious identity in measuring membership in these theological communities for anticommunism, moral traditionalism, economic issues, and outgroup affect.[22] This finding suggests that measures of religious identity add to our understanding of the connection of religion and politics, even in models in which they are used merely to improve the measurement of theological communities. Measures of religious identity significantly improve our ability to measure membership in theological communities.

Future Research

Religious identification thus appears to suggest a promising research strategy for investigating the relationship between the religious and the political. For many citizens, identification as *fundamentalist, pentecostal*, or *post-Vatican II Catholic*, for example, may provide a cognitive shortcut with which political information may be organized and may provide a psychological link between membership in a particular congregation and affiliation with larger political movements. The LISREL results described above how that the measurement properties of religious group identification lend themselves to relatively simple survey items, with less measurement error than alternative approaches.

There seem to be at least *four* important sets of questions that remain to be answered concerning religious identity. First, what do individuals mean when they use labels such as *fundamentalist, evangelical*, and *charismatic*, or *traditionalist* and *supportive of post-Vatican II reforms*? Although this type of question is difficult to answer with mass-based surveys, some well-placed probes on phone surveys coupled with in-depth interviews are needed to help us understand what these labels mean to people. Such research may help us refine our wording of religious identity questions and understand more fully the nature of the concept. It would be useful to pose the identities of evangelical and fundamentalist to Catholics as well, since research has shown that an important minority of Catholics practice their religion in an evangelical style (Welch and Leege 1991) and that some Catholics hold evangelical doctrinal views and call themselves evangelicals (Wilcox 1992). Although a debate exists in the literature on whether Catholics can properly be considered evangelicals (see Welch and Leege 1991 for a review), this seems to be at least in part an empirical question that can best be answered with a complete set of data.

Second, what are we to make of multiple religious identities among evangelical subgroups? How can we integrate the results from these items into our theoretical and empirical work on religious particularism? What do these data tell us about the way rank-and-file Christians think of themselves and their theology?

Third, what is the meaning of nonidentification? More elaborate measurement strategies, in which hostility, indifference, or sympathy are distinguished would enhance our understanding of group-related religious attitudes considerably. What sorts of stereotypes do people hold about religious traditions with wich they do not identify? Since the political importance of religious particularism is a prominent theoretical development in the religion and politics literature, more research on attitudes toward religious outgroups is clearly warranted.

Finally, it may be profitable to attempt to measure religious group consciousness. This measurement would entail using questions about support for collective action, polarized group affect, perception of political disadvantage, system blaming, and other related concepts. It is possible that such an endeavor would provide a truly cognitive theory of religious mobilization.

Notes

1. Some research has shown that group sympathy has an almost identical set of predictors, and of political consequences, as group consciousness. See Cook and Wilcox 1991.

2. The data on which the Jelen and Wilcox (1992) paper was based were provided from a survey conducted by Clifford Brown of Union College, Lynda Powell of the University of Rochester, and Clyde Wilcox.

3. In future surveys, it would be best to allow respondents to answer these questions and to then allow analysts to filter them out as they choose. Adding these filtered respondents back into the sample results in only one important change in the patterns of correlations. With these respondents out of the analysis, there is no correlation between an identity as a liberal Christian and doctrinal orthodoxy. With them in the sample, a significant correlation emerges.

One other change is necessary to use these data. Those who attended more than one church were asked the question at a slightly different point in the survey from those who attended only one church, and the 1989 Pilot Study data record the answers to these questions separately. Analysts should combine these two sets of religious identity questions.

4. For example, those who were unsure whether to apply the fundamentalist label were almost as likely as those who said the label fit very well to believe that the Bible is literally true.

5. The *civil religion* measure is the percentage of respondents who indicated that believing in God is extremely important to being a true American.

6. Unfortunately, the 1990 NES survey did not allow respondents to choose between a literal and an inerrant interpretation of the Scriptures but instead used a split-half approach with one item asking for a literal and the other an inerrant Bible. It is possible to ask respondents to choose directly between these two levels of biblical authority, instead of indirectly approaching this point through a split sample. See Jelen, Smidt, and Wilcox 1990 for an account of such a measure. The relationships reported in that paper are

replicated in the contributor data discussed in this paper and are also found in contributor data collected by John Green and James Guth.

7. Specifically, the two issue scales have been normalized by subtracting the mean score for whites and dividing by the standard deviation. The resulting score reflects the number of standard deviations above or below the mean that reflects each group's average response. The feeling thermometers are adjusted by subtracting the average score for each respondent to a series of similar items for other political groups. For a discussion of the necessity of adjusting feeling thermometer scores, see Wilcox, Sigelman and Cook 1989.

8. The item is useful, however, in weeding out response sets.

9. An intermediate possibility is to recode the items so that those who report that the labels fit them *very well* or *quite well* are classified as *fundamentalists*, *charismatics*, or *evangelicals*, and others are called *nonidentifiers*. This practice does not produce as pure a category, but the correlations are higher than a more stringent recode.

10. Others have reported that Pat Robertson had strong support among fundamentalists. See, for example, McGlennon 1989.

11. This analysis is based on a recoding where those who reported that the label fit them *very well* or *quite well* are coded as having a particular identity.

12. In a personal communication, John Green and James Guth confirm these results in their studies of political contributors.

13. The counterintuitive results from religious identity measures are not limited to the question of particularism. Jelen (1991a) reports an entire congregation that reported they were pentecostals but not charismatics.

14. Wilcox (1990a, 1990b) included both types of items in his survey of African Americans in Washington, but the relatively small number of cases made precise analysis impossible.

15. The variable that measured fundamentalist denominations was coded at 1 for most of the small Baptist denominations and for other fundamentalist churches and coded at 0.5 for Southern Baptists. Southern Baptists were also coded at 0.5 for the variable that measured other evangelical denominations.

16. The equations did a fair job of predicting religious identity. The adjusted R^2 was highest for a charismatic identity (.28) and lowest for a fundamentalist identity (.22). The difference here was that the measure of fundamentalist churches was not a significant predictor of fundamentalist identity, while pentecostal churches exhibited a much higher rate of charismatic identity.

17. There is doubtlessly correlated measurement error between the items that ask respondents to place their church and themselves on theological scales. The items were identically worded and contiguous in the survey.

18. One of us grew up attending a fundamentalist Methodist church. Most denominational coding schemes would place Methodists as mainline Protestants, but the local context in that church was quite different.

19. We experimented with a variety of methods of modeling religious identity, including additive indices of conservative religious identities.

20. LISREL is a statistical technique that resembles factor analysis. The technique is especially useful for circumstances in which there are strong theoretical expectations concerning the underlying measurement error. LISREL separately estimates the measurement error and the underlying structure among the variables after that error has been parceled out. It allows researchers to specify that certain sets of variables will have correlated measurement error because they have been measured in a similar manner.

21. In that second model, there were no measures of the theology of the local church. We were able to include a measure of charismatic experience, however.

22. Interestingly, the structural coefficients suggest that fundamentalism consistently

leads to greater conservatism, but that once fundamentalism is controlled, evangelicalism and pentecostalism do not consistently lead to conservative policy positions or values.

Bibliography

Ammerman, Nancy. 1988. *Bible Believers*. New Brunswick, NJ: Rutgers University Press.

Beatty, Kathleen, and Walter, Oliver. 1988. "Fundamentalists, Evangelicals and Politics." *American Politics Quarterly* 16:43–59.

Brady, Henry E., and Sniderman, Paul. 1985. "Attitude Attribution: A Group Basis for Political Reasoning." *American Political Science Review* 79:1061–78.

Bruner, Jere. 1984. "What's the Question to That Answer: Measures and Marginals in Cross-Tabulation." In *Theory-Building and Data Analysis in the Social Sciences*, ed. Herbert B. Asher, Herbert F. Weisberg, John H. Kessel, and W. Phillips Shively, 211–36. Knoxville: University of Tennessee Press.

Conover, Pamela Johnston. 1984. "The Influence of Group Identifications on Political Perceptions and Evaluations." *Journal of Politics* 46:760–85.

———. 1986. "Group Identification and Group Sympathy: Their Political Implications." Paper presented at the annual meeting of the Midwest Political Science Association, Chicago.

Conover, Pamela Johnston, and Feldman, Stanley. 1984. "Group Identification, Values, and the Nature of Political Beliefs." *American Politics Quarterly* 12:151–75.

Conover, Pamela Johnston, and Sapiro, Virginia. 1992. "Gender, Feminist Consciousness, and War." Paper presented at the annual meeting of the Midwest Political Science Association, Chicago.

Cook, Elizabeth Adell. 1989. "Measuring Feminist Consciousness." *Women and Politics* 9:71–88.

———. 1993. "Feminist Consciousness and Candidate Preference, 1972–1988." *Political Behavior* (forthcoming).

Cook, Elizabeth Adell, and Wilcox, Clyde. 1990. "Religion and Political Attitudes among Black Americans in Washington, D.C." *Polity* 22:527–39.

———. 1991. "Feminism and the Gender Gap: A Second Look." *Journal of Politics*. 53:1111–22.

Falwell, Jerry. 1981. *The Fundamentalist Phenomenon*. Garden City, NY: Doubleday.

Glock, Charles V., and Stark, Rodney. 1965. *Religion and Society in Tension*. Chicago: Rand McNally.

Greeley, Andrew M. 1977. *The American Catholic: A Social Portrait*. New York: Free Press.

Green, John, and Guth, James. 1988. "The Christian Right in the Republican Party: The Case of Pat Robertson's Supporters." *Journal of Politics* 50:156–65.

Gremillion, Joseph, and Leege, David C. 1989. "Post-Vatican II Parish Life in the United States: Review and Preview." *Notre Dame Study of Catholic Parish Life*, Report 15. Notre Dame, IN: University of Notre Dame.

Gurin, Patricia. 1985. "Women's Gender Consciousness." *Public Opinion Quarterly* 49:143–63.

Gurin, Patricia; Miller, Arthur; and Gurin, Gerald. 1980. "Stratum Identification and Consciousness." *Social Psychology Quarterly* 43:30–47.

Hunter, James Davison. 1983. *American Evangelicalism: Conservative Religion and the Quandary of Modernity*. New Brunswick, NJ: Rutgers University Press.

———. 1987. *Evangelicalism: The Coming Generation*. Chicago: University of Chicago Press.

Jelen, Ted G. 1987. "The Effects of Religious Separatism on White Protestants in the 1984 Presidential Election." *Sociological Analysis* 48:30–45.

———, ed. 1989. *Religion and Political Behavior in the United States.* New York: Praeger.

———. 1990. "The Political Consequences of Religious Group Identification." Paper presented at the annual meeting of the Midwest Political Science Association, Chicago.

———. 1991a. *The Political Mobilization of Religious Beliefs.* New York: Praeger.

———. 1991b. "Politicized Group Identification: The Case of Fundamentalism." *Western Political Quarterly* 44:209–19.

———. 1992. "Political Christianity: A Contextual Analysis." *American Journal of Political Science* 36:692–714.

Jelen, Ted G.; Smidt, Corwin E.; and Wilcox, Clyde. 1990. "Biblical Literalism and Inerrancy: A Reconsideration." *Sociological Analysis* 51:307–15.

Jelen, Ted G., and Wilcox, Clyde. 1992. "The Effects of Religious Self-Identifications on Support for the New Christian Right: An Analysis of Political Activists." *Social Science Journal* 29:199–210.

Katz, Elihu, and Lazarsfeld, Paul F. 1955. *Personal Influence: The Part Played by People in the Flow of Mass Communications.* Glencoe, IL: Free Press.

Kellstedt, Lyman A. 1989. "The Meaning and Measurement of Evangelicalism: Problems and Prospects." In Jelen 1989, 3–22. New York: Praeger.

Kellstedt, Lyman A., and Smidt, Corwin E. 1991. "Measuring Fundamentalism: An Analysis of Different Operational Strategies." *Journal for the Scientific Study of Religion* 30:259–78.

Klein, Ethel. 1984. *Gender Politics.* Cambridge, MA: Harvard University Press.

Laing, R. D. 1970. *Self and Others.* New York: Pantheon.

Leege, David C.; Kellstedt, Lyman A.; and Wald, Kenneth D. 1990. "Religion and Politics: A Report on Measures of Religiosity in the 1989 NES Pilot Study." Paper presented at the annual meeting of the Midwest Political Science Association, Chicago.

McGlennon, John. 1989. "Religious Activists in the Republican Party: Robertson and Bush Supporters in Virginia." Paper presented at the annual meeting of the American Political Science Association, Chicago.

Marsden, George. 1984. *Evangelicalism and Modern America.* Grand Rapids, MI: William B. Eerdmans.

Miller, Arthur; Gurin, Patricia; and Gurin, Gerald. 1980. "Age Consciousness and Political Mobilization among Older Americans." *Gerontologist* 20:691–700.

Miller, Arthur H.; Gurin, Patricia; Gurin, Gerald; and Malanchuk, Oksana. 1981. "Group Consciousness and Political Participation." *American Journal of Political Science* 25:494–511.

Rothenberg, Stuart, and Newport, Frank. 1984. *The Evangelical Voter.* Washington, DC: Free Congress Research and Education Foundation.

Smidt, Corwin E. 1988. "Evangelicals within Contemporary American Politics: Differentiating between Fundamentalist and Non-Fundamentalist Evangelicals." *Western Political Quarterly* 41:601–20.

———. 1989a. "'Praise the Lord' Politics: A Comparative Analysis of the Social Characteristics and Political Views of American Evangelical and Charismatic Christians." *Sociological Analysis* 50:53–72.

———. 1989b. "Identifying Evangelical Respondents: An Analysis of the 'Born-Again' and Bible Questions Used across Different Surveys." In Jelen 1989, 23–43.

———. 1991. "Religious Self-Identifications among Evangelical Political Activists: An Analysis of Two Measurement Approaches." Paper presented at the annual meeting of

the American Political Science Association, Washington.
Smidt, Corwin E., and Kellstedt, Lyman A. 1987. "Evangelicalism and Survey Research: Interpretative Problems and Substantive Findings." In *The Bible, Politics, and Democracy*, ed. Richard J. Neuhaus, 81–102, 131–67. Grand Rapids, MI: William B. Eerdmans.
Smidt, Corwin E., and Penning, James. 1990. "A Party Divided? A Comparison between Robertson and Bush Delegates to the Michigan Republican State Convention." *Polity* 23:127–38.
————. 1991. "Religious Self-Identification and Support for Robertson: An Analysis of Delegates to the 1988 Michigan Republican State Convention." *Review of Religious Research* 32:321–36.
Sniderman, Paul M.; Brody, Richard A.; and Tetlock, Philip E. 1991. *Reasoning and Choice: Explorations in Political Psychology.* New York: Cambridge University Press.
Tajfel, Henri. 1981. *Human Groups and Social Categories: Studies in Social Psychology.* Cambridge: Cambridge University Press.
Wald, Kenneth; Owen, Dennis; and Hill, Samuel, Jr. 1988. "Churches as Political Communities." *American Political Science Review* 82:531–48.
————. 1989. "Evangelical Politics and Status Issues." *Journal for the Scientific Study of Religion* 28:1–16.
————. 1990. "Political Cohesion in Churches." *Journal of Politics* 52:197–215.
Welch, Michael, and Leege, David C. 1991. "Dual Reference Groups and Political Orientations: An Examination of Evangelically Oriented Catholics." *American Journal of Political Science* 35:28–56.
Wilcox, Clyde. 1986a. "Fundamentalists and Politics: An Analysis of the Impact of Differing Operational Definitions." *Journal of Politics* 48:1041–51.
————. 1986b. "Fundamentalists vs. Evangelicals in the New Christian Right." *Journal for the Scientific Study of Religion* 25:355–63.
————. 1988. "The Christian Right in Twentieth Century America: Continuity and Change." *Review of Politics* 50:659–81.
————. 1989. "The Fundamentalist Voter: Politicized Religious Identity among American Evangelicals." *Review of Religious Research* 31:380–89.
————. 1990a. "Religious Sources of Politicization among Washington, D.C. Blacks." *Journal for the Scientific Study of Religion* 29:387–95.
————. 1990b. "Blacks and the New Christian Right: Support for the Moral Majority and Pat Robertson in Washington, D.C." *Review of Religious Research* 32:42–56.
————. 1992. *God's Warriors: The Christian Right in Twentieth Century America.* Baltimore: Johns Hopkins University Press.
Wilcox, Clyde; Sigelman, Lee; and Cook, Elizabeth Adell. 1989. "Some Like It Hot: Individual Differences in Response to Group Feeling Thermometers." *Public Opinion Quarterly* 53:246–57.
Wilcox, Clyde, and Thomas, Sue. 1992. "Religion and Feminist Attitudes among African-American Women: A View from the Nation's Capitol." *Women and Politics* 12:19–40.

Chapter 5

From Lambs to Sheep: Denominational Change and Political Behavior

John C. Green and James L. Guth

During the 1970s and 1980s, scholars rediscovered the impact of religion on American politics. Much attention was focused on the renewed political vigor of evangelical Protestants and their dramatic shift toward the Republican party. But at the same time, leaders in the mainline Protestant churches, once the anchor of the GOP, redoubled their involvement with reform politics and edged toward the Democratic party, joining there many of their historic opponents, such as Catholic liberals and militant secularists. Scholars were quick to note that these events paralleled changes in the size and composition of denominations: the growth of evangelicals, the decline of the mainline, the upward mobility of Catholics, and the expansion of secularism (Hadaway 1978).

This chapter is a preliminary look at the relationship between denominational change and political behavior. Using a unique data set, we investigate the change from "lambs to sheep" for the four largest religious traditions in the United States (evangelical and mainline Protestants, Catholics, and seculars). Overall, we find that movements between and within denominations sharpen the political distinctiveness of the religious traditions. Although stability by tradition is evident, shifts within and between denominations within the same tradition are quite important. In contrast, movement between traditions is much less common, with the largest numbers of switchers moving to secularism. These shifts are restructuring American religion and its connection to political alignments. If left unchecked, these trends will produce increased political polarization based on religious affiliation.

Denominational Change and Its Political Implications

Changes in the size and composition of denominations are politically relevant because denominational preferences matter in politics. At root, such affiliations represent attachments to broader cultural traditions undergirding individual political beliefs, affiliations, and behaviors (Leege, Lieske, and Wald 1991). While denominational preferences can influence politics in many ways, their most prominent and durable impact is through religious traditions, groupings of denominations with comparable beliefs and ethos, as noted in chapter 3. The major religious traditions have been significant "building blocs" of American party coalitions for the last 150 years, and their political attachments have varied over time, reflecting in part fluctuations in the number and character of their adherents (Kellstedt and Noll 1990).

In theoretical terms, the distribution of denominational preferences results from three processes: residual childhood socialization, adult resocialization via life experiences, and anticipatory socialization accompanying change. These concepts closely parallel Hirschman's (1970) formulation of *exit, voice, and loyalty* and Tajfel's (1981) notions of social *stability, mobility, and change.* Taken together, these processes provide a framework for understanding denominational change and its political implications.

Despite the enormous flux in American religion, denominational preferences have been relatively stable: large portions of the population spend their lives in their childhood denomination or closely related ones (Roof and McKinney 1987, 168–69). Such stability reflects the powerful influence of early socialization, which inculcates religious worldviews, group identifications, and standards of behavior. The residues of this socialization constrain the direction and magnitude of denominational change. Indeed, residual socialization gives religious traditions their enduring influence in politics.

Residual socialization does not, however, preclude changes in the size and composition of denominations. Instead, it channels change in particular directions. For example, natural increase via birth rates and the absorption of immigrants can change the number and character of denominations, and both are conditioned by religious values. Both phenomena are part of the broader process of cultural adaptation to societal change. Indeed, residual socialization sets the context for such adaptation, so that the members of denominations move together through social transformations.

Some sources of change are more challenging to residual socialization than others. Chief among these are life cycle factors: the typical sequence of life experiences provides many opportunities for denominational change (Roof and McKinney 1987, 151–57). While many individuals remain in their childhood denomination, many undertake modifications of their original beliefs, and still others adopt new religious affiliations (Hadaway and Marler 1991). Age summarizes many of these opportunities for change, such as the tendency of young adults to test both secularism and religious experimentation. Marriage and children provide similar opportunities, particularly if the partners come from different backgrounds. Gender is also an important factor. Not only are women generally more religious than men, but age, marriage, and children often have a greater impact on their lives. Thus life cycle factors interject diversity into even the most stable denominations.

Students of religion note that the effects of residual socialization and associated life cycle factors account for most denominational change (Hoge and Roozen 1979), and in the long run, produce new social and political attachments. Denominational *loyalty* is, in fact, commitment to an evolving institution, and *social stability* is itself a process. But even relatively slow and constrained changes can generate great stress, and the rapid pace of change common in modern societies can create enormous tension. These problems are often associated with the appearance of religious movements, which are deliberate attempts to alter existing denominations. Such movements include both *church* movements, which seek greater accommodation with the broader society, and *sect* movements, which seek greater distinctiveness or separation (Stark and Bainbridge 1985). Residual socialization can thus become a source of denominational change, as rival interpreters of a common heritage battle over future directions.

Such *voice* in favor of *social change* can resocialize individuals away from their childhood religion. The winners in such disputes have incentives to remain loyal, while the losers have incentives to change. The easiest kind of change is to a more compatible local church within the same denomination. But if dissatisfied enough, individuals can switch denominations, moving most easily within the same tradition and with more difficulty to a different tradition. Such *exit* and *social mobility* are facilitated by the internal pluralism of many denominations, the great diversity among denominational families, and the frequent founding of new denominations. In addition, the cost of denominational switching is relatively low for most Americans.

Thus denominational change moves individuals away from the dominant traits of, and trends within, their childhood denomination and toward more congenial settings. Life cycle factors and religious movements do not occur in a vacuum, however, and there are many experiences that can spark, reinforce, or independently produce these kinds of change. Scholars have identified two important sets of factors with opposite effects: high social status and religious intensity.

Among the most tangible effects of the modern world are individual gains in social status, including greater occupational prestige, income, and education, and these experiences can resocialize individuals, though their impact on religious values is usually indirect (Stark and Glock 1968). High social status often renders traditional religious worldviews implausible (Roof 1978), motivating individuals to switch to denominations with churchlike orientations, such as those within mainline Protestantism and to some extent Catholicism. Historically, this process produced the "social sources of denominationalism," a hierarchy of denominations based on social status (Niebuhr 1929). Some view the end point of this process as the abandonment of organized religion altogether (Roof and McKinney 1987, 163–64).

Despite the secularizing tendencies of modern society, intense religious consciousness is still common, and such experiences can alter an individual's religious values directly (Roof and Hoge 1979). Historically, conversions and revivals have made traditional religious worldviews more plausible, motivating individuals to switch to denominations with sectlike orientations, such as those within evangelical Protestantism (Nelson and Bromley 1988). Some scholars argue that such phenomena reflect the deep spiritual and social alienation common in modern societies (Greeley 1972), perhaps related to the church movements in many denominations (Kelley 1972). Others suggest it results in large part from a "circulation of the saints," as particular kinds of religious people move among compatible denominations in search of new religious experiences (Bibby and Brinkerhoff 1973).

While all these factors can provide an impetus to switch denominations, most individuals must make a deliberate decision to do so, choosing a particular alternative to their present situation. Once such a choice is made, switchers often internalize the values and norms of their new denomination, engaging in anticipatory socialization and producing the "zeal of the convert" (Homans 1950). But given the strength of residual socialization and the importance of resocializing experiences, it is most probable that switchers will stand between their new and old denominations in attitudes and social characteristics.

What are the political implications of these processes? First, residual socialization maintains the political distinctiveness of religious traditions even as their allegiances evolve in response to life cycle factors as well as other sources of change. And second, resocializing experiences and anticipatory socialization further sharpen such distinctiveness by moving individuals into more compatible groups. The specific political impact of these trends depends, of course, on the prior political alignments of religious groups.

Data and Methods

The National Election Studies (NES) Pilot Study offers a unique opportunity to study the political effects of denominational change. For the first time, an NES survey included data on childhood and adult denominational preference. Of even greater importance were several innovations in the questions asked about religion. First, an effort was made to ascertain denominational preference with great specificity, using a series of probes for ambiguous answers and a more accurate and detailed denominational code. Second, to reduce social desirability effects, the items on adult denomination preference were preceded by a set of screening questions to identify nonreligious respondents. And third, respondents were asked about the religious identity of the church they attended most often in childhood and as an adult.[1]

The great drawback of the 1989 Pilot Study is the small sample size ($N =$ 494). And although the full battery of NES political questions is available from the 1988 study (from which the 1989 sample was drawn), some data relevant to denominational change are not available, such as the denominational preference of spouses. Thus, we will supplement the analysis with data from the 1988 General Social Survey (1988 GSS). While not entirely comparable, this survey was administered during the same general time frame, had a larger sample ($N = 1,481$), more extensive demographic data, and special questions on denomination switching.

The analysis proceeds as follows. First, childhood and adult data in the 1989 Pilot Study and 1988 GSS are classified into the four major religious traditions (evangelical Protestant, mainline Protestants, Catholics, and seculars). This effort reflects the theoretically driven definition of religious tradition and the painstaking analysis of the data developed in chapter 3. Second, a measure of change between specific denominations is calculated by comparing childhood and adult preferences (e.g., from Baptist Bible Fellowship to Southern Baptist). Third, childhood and adult preferences are aggregated by religious tradition and again compared, producing a measure of change between traditions (e.g., from evangelical to mainline Protestant). Fourth, an additional category of change is calculated for the 1989 Pilot Study only: change in the type of church attended within specific denominations (e.g., from a *fundamentalist* Southern Baptist church to a *liberal* one). This calculation involved combining the church identities into major types and then comparing the childhood and adult data.[2]

All together, these measures generate six potential categories for each of the traditions: a *standpat group* with no change at all; two groups involving internal change within a tradition (shifts *between church type within a specific denomination*, and shifts *between specific denominations within a particular tradition*); and then, three groups of switchers *between traditions*, one from each of the three other traditions. However, the characteristics of Catholics and seculars reduced their categories to five. Table 5.1 lists the categories used and gives their relative size for the 1989 Pilot Study.

Table 5.2 summarizes some relevant sociological characteristics of each category. The entries are mean factor scores for life cycle variables (age, marital status, number of children, and their age); social status variables (income, education, occupational status, and social mobility, measured by the difference between the respondents' occupational status and their fathers'); and religious variables (church attendance, membership, religious salience, and frequency of prayer). Each factor score was produced in a separate analysis, all had eigenvalues greater than 1, and all factor loadings were greater than .5. Table 5.3 provides political data for each category, including mean party and ideological self-identification, mean abortion attitudes, percent vote for George Bush in 1988, and percent turnout in 1988. Data on political participation beyond voting were also analyzed and the results closely resemble turnout (data not shown).

Patterns of Denominational Change

What do these data tell us about the amount and nature of denominational change? Although the small sample size mandates caution, three important findings emerge. First, stability by tradition is evident, but it masks large shifts within most traditions. Second, switchers between traditions are less common, with the largest number moving to the secular categories. Third, other kinds of movement between traditions are smaller and tend to offset each other. Thus overall, seculars show large net gains, evangelicals have a very small decline, followed by Catholics and mainliners with larger net losses.

Table 5.1 reveals the continued importance of stability by religious tradition (Roof and McKinney 1987, 167), with the exception of the seculars. For example, 69 percent of evangelicals, 76 percent of mainliners, and 81 percent of Catholics remain in their childhood tradition. These figures are derived by adding the first three categories for the Protestant traditions and the first two for Catholics. However, this overall stability masks enormous changes within traditions. While standpat groups are generally the largest, ranging from one-fourth to two-fifths of each tradition, changes between church type within denominations and between denominations within traditions are larger when combined.

Approximately one-sixth of evangelicals and mainliners showed change between church type, and one-quarter experienced change between denominations within their traditions. While this sample makes it difficult to ascertain the exact nature of these changes, they appear to be very different: change between church type is toward theologically liberal local churches, while denominational change within traditions is toward theologically conservative denominations. The data suggest that such shifts may be associated with church and sect movements, respectively. In any event, there certainly seems to be a "circulation of the saints" among conservative Protestants (Bibby and Brinkerhoff 1973).

Change between church type is also quite common for Catholics, but since Catholicism allows for very few shifts between denominations, this category probably contains both churchlike and sectlike changes. Indeed, this figure for Catholics is only slightly larger than the combined internal change for Protestants. Such a higher rate of internal change may reflect the greater ethnic identity of many Catholics and the related costs of moving outside of Catholicism.

Switching between traditions is less common than internal change: the largest category is movement to the secular category, which gained equal shares from the mainline, evangelical, and Catholic traditions. Looked at another way, Protestants lost roughly one-sixth and Catholics more than one-fifth of their original numbers to the ranks of nonadherents. On the other hand, standpat seculars are rare, accounting for only about one-sixth of the total. And those outside organized religion are the least stable group, with more than one-half of the original numbers switching to other traditions. But overall, seculars have made large net gains at the expense of other traditions (cf. Hadaway and Roof 1988).[3]

The two Protestant traditions resemble each other closely in switching patterns: each draws about one-fifth of its adherents from the other, and a similarly small proportion from Catholics and seculars. Evangelicals show a slight net gain via switching and the mainline a small net loss. Catholics have also lost to

Table 5.1

Profile of Denominational Change

	(N)	% Distribution
EVANGELICAL PROTESTANTS	(145)	100%
Standpat	(42)	29
Change Church Type	(20)	14
Within Evangelical	(38)	26
From Mainline	(27)	19
From Catholic	(10)	7
From Secular	(8)	5
MAINLINE PROTESTANTS	(113)	100%
Standpat	(40)	35
Change Church Type	(16)	14
Within Mainline	(30)	27
From Evangelical	(19)	17
From Catholic	(5)	4
From Secular	(3)	3
CATHOLICS	(98)	100%
Standpat	(33)	34
Change Church Type	(46)	47
From Mainline	(11)	11
From Evangelical	(5)	5
From Secular	(3)	3
SECULARS	(79)	100%
Standpat	(12)	15
From Mainline	(23)	29
From Evangelical	(22)	28
From Catholic	(22)	28

Source: NES 1989 Pilot Study.

evangelicals and gained from the mainline, but these shifts are even smaller, while converts from the secular group resemble the Protestant categories. The 1989 Pilot Study and 1988 GSS surveys also provide some tantalizing evidence on multiple church attenders, multiple switchers, and participants in para-church organizations. These behaviors tend to reinforce the dominant patterns of change.[4]

While these findings generally resemble those of other surveys (Roof and McKinney 1987; Stark and Bainbridge 1985), there are some interesting differences with the 1988 GSS data, most of which can be attributed to the measurement innovations in the 1989 Pilot Study. First, the 1988 GSS data show more stability, with the standpat categories 8 percent larger for mainliners, 10 percent for Catholics, and 18 percent for evangelicals. The GSS data also reveal fewer switchers from evangelical to mainline and from mainline to Catholic. These differences result in large measure from the 1989 Pilot Study's innovations: the greater number of denominational categories, more precise measurement of denomination, and church identity data. Indeed, both surveys offer similar estimates for change within the mainline (27 percent and 24 percent), where the denominational categories are most alike.[5]

Second, the 1989 Pilot Study finds twice as many seculars overall as the GSS (16 percent to 8 percent), and one-half as many standpat seculars (15 percent to 30 percent). These differences result largely from the 1989 Pilot Study's screening questions that reduce the social desirability effects of denominational preference. But despite such differences, the two surveys agree on the equal proportion of switchers to secularism from evangelicals, mainliners, and Catholics.

The 1988 GSS asked respondents if they had ever switched denominations, and these data, when suitably adjusted, suggest that the two surveys tapped the same phenomenon. When asked directly, 35.4 percent of the GSS sample reported having switched denominations. This figure is higher than the 30.8 percent derived from comparing childhood and adult denomination in the GSS, but much lower than the comparable estimate of 49.5 percent for the 1989 Pilot Study. When both GSS measures are cross-tabulated, however, 2.8 percent of the sample claimed to have switched but reported no change in denomination, while 7.2 percent claimed not to have switched but reported a change in denomination. If one subtracts the former number and adds the latter to the percentage of self-identified switchers, one arrives at an estimate of 39.8 percent switching denominations. And if one were to add the greater number of seculars identified in the 1989 Pilot Study (8 percent), this estimate rises to 47.8 percent. This figure is very close to the 1989 Pilot Study results, even taking into account the possible forms of error.

In sum, then, Table 5.1 reveals three major patterns of denominational change. First, while there is a great deal of stability by tradition, there are also large internal shifts, including change between church type and between denominations. Second, switching between traditions is generally smaller than internal change, and switching to secularism is the most common category. Third, switchings between the other traditions are even smaller and tend to offset each other.

Factors Associated with Denominational Change

What social factors lie behind these changes? Evidence from life cycle variables suggests the importance of common challenges to residual socialization, while religious and social status variables reveal the impact of resocializing experiences. Among the latter, social status variables are most associated with changes between church type, switching to secularism, and switching to churchlike traditions. On the other hand, religious variables are most associated with denominational change within traditions and switching to sectlike traditions. Despite differences in measurement, the 1988 GSS and 1989 Pilot Study produce similar findings.

The mean factor scores for life cycle variables in Table 5.2 summarize evidence of challenges to residual socialization occasioned by age, marital status, children, and gender. Larger, positive coefficients indicate more younger, married women with children in a category, while large, negative coefficients indicate more older, married men, and coefficients that lie in between represent various combinations of these factors. The pattern in these data is striking: denominational change is systematically associated with deviations from the social characteristics of the standpat groups in each tradition. This finding is particularly true for the large categories of internal change. For example, among evangelicals, the shifts between church type and denominations within the tradition include many more younger married women with children (.32 and .29), particularly when compared to the standpat group (.12). Similar findings obtain for mainliners, although those changing church type are somewhat less often female, and the greater age of the mainline mutes the pattern somewhat.

Catholics follow an opposite pattern: younger married men are more likely to be engaged in internal change (–.10) compared to the standpat group (.11). And much the same holds for those moving to secularism. Although secular switchers show the traits of their origins, they include more younger, unmarried men (–.16, –.15 and –.14, respectively), particularly compared to the standpat group (.15). Standpat secularists include more younger, unmarried women, a pattern that appears also for switchers from seculars to mainline and Catholic (.10 for both). Similarly, switching between other religious traditions closely resembles the internal change within their destinations: evangelicals and mainliners recruit younger, married women with children from each other (.24 and .15) and from Catholics (.20 and .25), while Catholics recruit younger, married family men from the Protestant ranks (–.15 and –.14). The one exception to these patterns is switchers from seculars to evangelicals, which also include more younger, married men (–.08).

Data from the GSS support these findings in two important ways. First, when asked why they switched denominations respondents most often mentioned life

Table 5.2

Factors Associated with Denominational Change*

	N	Lifecycle Variables	Social Status Variables	Religious Variables
EVANGELICAL PROTESTANTS	(145)	.12	-.08	.49
Standpat	(42)	-.19	-.16	.60
Change Church Type	(20)	.32	.10	.12
Within Evangelical	(38)	.29	-.08	.58
From Mainline	(27)	.24	-.07	.54
From Catholic	(10)	.20	-.09	.54
From Secular	(8)	-.08	-.10	.22
MAINLINE PROTESTANTS	(113)	-.01	.26	.04
Standpat	(40)	-.24	.39	.07
Change Church Type	(16)	.05	.35	-.07
Within Mainline	(30)	.12	.18	.10
From Evangelical	(19)	.15	.15	.13
From Catholic	(5)	.25	.06	-.29
From Secular	(3)	.10	-.06	-.33
CATHOLICS	(98)	.03	.14	-.04
Standpat	(33)	.11	-.11	.26
Change Church Type	(46)	-.10	.30	-.13
From Mainline	(11)	-.15	.23	-.25
From Evangelical	(5)	-.14	.25	-.42
From Secular	(3)	.10	-.03	-.69
SECULARS	(79)	-.10	.18	-.77
Standpat	(12)	.15	-.11	-.60
From Mainline	(23)	-.16	.21	-.90
From Evangelical	(22)	-.15	.23	-.70
From Catholic	(22)	-.11	.24	-.80

Source: NES 1989 Pilot Study.

*Table entries are mean factor scores for each of the categories of denominational change. Higher scores indicate, respectively, more younger, married women with children, higher social status, and greater religious intensity. See text for description of variables.

cycle factors, such as marriage, family, friends, and local church location, far outpacing concerns about clergy or theology. For example, for all the evangelical categories, the mean life cycle mentions were 55 percent compared to 20 percent for clergy and theology. Second, mixed marriages are strongly associated with switching between traditions. For example, among the relevant evangelical categories a mean of 60 percent were raised in a denomination different from their spouse, compared to 11 percent for those not changing traditions. The only exception are the seculars, who are less likely to be married.

The mean factor scores for higher social status in Table 5.2 complement our findings on life cycle factors and reveal the historic status differences among traditions (larger coefficients indicate higher social status and greater upward mobility). As a group, evangelicals have lower social status, particularly regarding upward mobility and education. However, those changing church type score the highest on these variables. For the mainline, internal change shows the same general pattern: change between church type is associated with high social status, nearly matching the standpat group, and change within the tradition is associated with lower status. Differences in education also parallel these patterns, but given the high status of the Protestant mainline, upward mobility is not very important.

Like the mainline, internal shifts among Catholics are also related to higher social status, particularly upward mobility and education. And this pattern appears for those moving to secularism as well, although these categories have higher income and education and show less upward mobility. Standpat seculars and those switching from secular to other traditions have much lower levels of social status. Switchers between traditions resemble their destinations: those who switched to evangelical Protestantism show lower status, and to Catholicism and mainline Protestantism, higher status.

The mean factor scores for religious variables in Table 5.2 are also associated with important patterns of change (large coefficients indicate greater religious intensity). The two streams of internal changes have divergent patterns: evangelicals changing between church type are much less religious (although still more religious than other traditions), while those changing denominations within the tradition approach the strong religious commitment of the standpat group. Mainliners show a very similar pattern for internal shifts, as do Catholics. As suggested above, change between church type is reminiscent of church movements, while denominational change within traditions resembles sect movements.

As might be expected, switchers to secularism exhibit the near-absence of religiosity, although the standpat group shows some slight residual spirituality. Secularists changing to other traditions show a mixed pattern: those moving to mainline Protestantism and Catholicism are not very religious at all, while those shifting to evangelicalism are much more so. Switchers between the other traditions resemble their destinations once again: those going to evangelicalism are very religious, while those moving to Catholicism and mainline Protestantism are much less so. The one modest exception are evangelicals moving to the mainline, who retain considerable religious commitment. The GSS data on reasons for switching support these patterns: mentions of clergy and theology are most frequent among categories with greater religiosity, while those that are less religious most often failed to answer the question at all.

In sum, then, Table 5.2 shows evidence of the processes that underlie denominational change. Residual socialization is clearly very strong, inhibiting change and channeling it in particular directions. Life cycle factors and resocializing experiences lie behind the largest shifts within and across traditions. Social status variables are strongly associated with change between church type, switching to secularism, and shifts to more churchlike traditions. And religious intensity is strongly associated with denominational change within traditions and switching to more sectlike traditions. The tendency of many switchers to resemble their destination suggests the presence of anticipatory socialization.

Denominational Change and Political Behavior

What effect does denominational change have on political attitudes and behaviors? These data reveal the political distinctiveness of the core of each tradition and suggest that denominational change further sharpens these tendencies. Shifts between church type and switching to churchlike traditions generate greater Democratic and liberal attitudes, while change within traditions and switching to sectlike traditions generate greater Republican and conservative leanings (cf. Swierenga 1990 for historical evidence on this point). The 1989 Pilot Study and 1988 GSS data show very similar results.

The standpat groups within each tradition display the expected political characteristics described in chapter 3. Standpat evangelicals are strongly Republican and very conservative, matching the standpat mainline, but voting much more heavily for George Bush. Indeed, only the lower evangelical turnout leaves the mainline with greater influence in the GOP. In contrast, standpat Catholics are more Democratic and liberal and have high turnout. Standpat seculars tend to be independent and moderate, but their great liberalism on social issues, such as abortion, produces Democratic votes. Their impact is muted, however, by their low turnout. These data point to the importance of residual socialization: the core of each tradition has clearly changed politically quite apart from denomination switching (Kellstedt and Noll 1990), but changed in a consistent fashion so that its political distinctiveness vis-à-vis other traditions has been largely maintained.

Among evangelicals, internal changes have opposite political effects: those changing church type are less Republican and conservative, vote less for Bush, and vote less frequently, running counter to the standpat group. On the other hand, those changing denominations within the tradition are more Republican and conservative than the standpat group, nearly as supportive of Bush, and have even higher turnout. These patterns surely reflect the differential concerns of the higher status, less religious women in the former category, and the middle status,

Table 5.3

Denominational Change and Political Behavior

	N	Mean Party ID	Mean Ideology	Mean Abortion Attitude	% Bush Vote	% Turnout
Evangelical Protestants	(145)	3.17	4.65	2.53	66	78
Standpat	(42)	3.26	4.65	2.61	72	79
Change church type	(20)	3.05	4.46	2.55	67	60
Within evangelical Protestant	(38)	3.31	5.00	2.71	70	90
From mainline Protestant	(27)	3.48	4.52	2.33	60	78
From Roman Catholic	(10)	2.30	4.50	2.10	38	60
From Secular	(8)	2.50	4.16	2.50	60	63
Mainline Protestants	(113)	3.48	4.67	1.98	57	82
Standpat	(40)	3.27	4.68	1.75	47	90
Change church type	(16)	3.44	4.72	1.87	54	75
Within mainline Protestant	(30)	3.68	4.80	2.40	60	80
From evangelical Protestant	(19)	3.63	4.59	2.21	63	84
From Roman Catholic	(5)	4.00	4.00	1.00	50	80
From Secular	(3)	3.67	4.00	1.67	33	33
Roman Catholics	(98)	2.25	4.26	2.32	35	80
Standpat	(33)	2.03	4.10	2.72	31	91
Change church type	(46)	2.26	4.20	2.21	39	74
From mainline Protestant	(11)	2.90	4.25	1.72	50	64
From evangelical Protestant	(5)	1.80	4.25	2.40	0	80
From Secular	(3)	3.00	5.00	1.67	33	100
Seculars	(79)	2.98	4.00	1.85	56	62
Standpat	(12)	3.00	4.00	1.36	33	25
From mainline Protestant	(23)	2.56	3.50	1.74	40	74
From evangelical Protestant	(22)	3.33	4.52	1.86	64	68
From Roman Catholic	(22)	3.09	4.07	2.22	64	64

Source: NES 1989 Pilot Study.
*For Party ID: 0 = Strong Democrat, 3 = Independent, 6 = Strong Republican; for Ideology: 1 = extremely liberal, 4 = moderate, 7 = extremely conservative; for abortion attitudes: 1 = prochoice, 4 = prolife.

highly religious women in the latter.

The mainline shows a similar pattern, but change runs entirely counter to the standpat group. Those changing church type are actually modestly more conservative, Republican, and pro-Bush. This pattern bolsters the moderate wing of the Republican party and reflects the concerns of the middle-aged, high status, and less religious people in this group. Those changing denominations within the tradition are markedly more Republican, conservative, and pro-Bush, as befits the older, higher status, religious women who make up this group. However, both categories have lower turnout than the standpat group.

These patterns reveal the deep tensions among Protestants (Wuthnow 1988). Each tradition has (1) a large group seeking a closer accommodation with society, and (2) another group seeking greater distinctiveness or separation. The key difference is that the former are dominant in the mainline, while the latter are dominant among evangelicals. At the moment, the GOP is the clear beneficiary of these changes, since it retains the support of most mainliners and has gained substantial backing among evangelicals.

Internal changers among Catholics also look quite different from their standpat co-religionists. These trends generate greater Republicanism and support for Bush, without a loss in turnout. Such findings are consistent with the historic patterns of ethnic assimilation, as younger married men gain in social status and move away from their ethnoreligious heritage. These movements could bode ill for the Democratic party if the aggregate political effects were to increase, particularly given the relative size and youth of this group.[6]

Much the same pattern holds for those switching to secularism. But the overall Democratic leanings of this tradition mask the different sources of change. Mainline to secular switchers are the most Democratic, resembling the standpat seculars, while evangelical and Catholic switchers to secularism show the opposite tendency, exceeding their standpat co-religionists in Republicanism. But all of the seculars display greater liberalism than their former traditions and have lower turnout (Nelson 1988). Thus, Democratic gains from the growth of secularism are muted by low turnout. Seculars who join other traditions show the same effect in reverse. These patterns are certainly consistent with the values of the highly educated, young men who dominate the secular category and the values of the lower status men and women who have moved to organized religion.

Anticipatory socialization is evident in these data, with switchers approaching the political values of their new group. These effects are clearest among switchers between traditions. For instance, those moving to Protestantism and Catholicism tend to resemble their destinations in partisanship, ideology, and voting behavior. Overall, these switches make each religious tradition more distinctive, as Republican elements leave Democratic traditions for more Republican venues and vice versa. And such switching is consistent with their demography: lower status, religious women join the evangelicals, while upper status women shift to the mainline, and their male counterparts become Catholics. Chapter 12 argues that both political cue giving and social interaction effects are likely to bolster anticipatory socialization.

Conclusions

In the transition from lambs to sheep, most Americans stay in or near their original folds, although there is considerable milling about the pens. Very few stray to distant pastures, and the largest number of these are lost, becoming indifferent or hostile to the Good Shepherd. And the overall effect is to increase the purity of the flocks. The political implications of these trends are straightforward: denominational change as well as changes in political values by the stand-pat core of each tradition maintains the political distinctiveness of traditions vis-à-vis one another, and these tendencies forecast increased political polarization based on religious affiliation.

The tendency of denominational change to enhance the political distinctiveness of religious traditions reflects the power of residual socialization, even in the face of major social transformations. In all probability, natural increase and the absorption of immigration have a greater political impact than denominational change, and cultural adaptation alone may be more significant than switching between traditions. Thus, the internal dynamics of groups with stable religious affiliation are particularly important. Indeed, the largest shifts are internal to the traditions themselves, reflecting intramural disputes as much as outside intrusions. Of course, the church and sect movements that apparently underlie this foment are far older and more powerful than most present-day influences, dating from the very beginning of the modern era. Now, as in the past, they operate in opposite directions, constantly restructuring religious life (Wuthnow 1988).

The switching among traditions that does occur can be thought of as extensions of these internal disputes. The most important form of switching is the most recent in historical terms: the growth of secularism. Increases in social status have eroded the ranks of the other traditions, removing the least religious people and thus moving all traditions in a more religious direction. This process adds a new element to political alignments, and one that potentially favors the Democratic party. However, seculars appear to be unpredictable allies (Guth and Green 1990). Lacking the institutional structure of the church, they tend to participate less in politics, and their loosely structured groups offer fewer and less consistent political cues. But beyond short-term politics, seculars may not socialize their offspring to any particular set of values, and hence they more frequently switch to other traditions as adults. On the other hand, the effects of high social status do not uniformly favor Democrats: increases in social status erode ethnic loyalties among Catholics, potentially benefiting Republicans.

The growth of secularism and the decline of ethnic identities may create an opportunity for religious conversion and revival, activities in which sectlike denominations excel. Evangelicals and perhaps the more traditionalist elements of other traditions may eventually balance the shifts between organized religion and apostasy. Already evangelical and mainline Protestants have reached such a rough balance, and a similar situation with Catholics may not be far behind. Indeed, the interaction between residual socialization and the most common resocializing experiences creates a vast religious marketplace from which a great variety of people can pick and choose (Stark and Bainbridge 1985).

Religious intensity as a source of denominational change is strongly evident in these data, although it does not yet rival the influence of high social status.

The social issue conservatism of religious people offers the GOP a great opportunity, particularly given their high rates of participation, deep involvement in cue-giving institutions, and intergenerational stability. However, such gains may turn the GOP into a crucible for conflict over issues such as abortion and the role of women (Kellstedt, Smidt, and Kellstedt 1991).

These data also reveal the "collapse of the center" of American religion (Roof and McKinney 1987, 25–26). Large, pluralistic denominations such as the United Methodist and Roman Catholic churches are under assault from all sides. These traditions have lost many adherents to secularism and are also net losers to evangelicals. In addition, the people they recruit tend to have low levels of religious commitment. Internal dissension and organizational decline among these broad-based institutions robs political alignments of important moderating influences. The twin engines of denominational change, high social status and religious intensity, compounded by anticipatory socialization, may forecast the end of the "social conscience" wing of the GOP and "God and Country" Democrats, both key elements in past party coalitions. Indeed, were it not for the ballast of residual socialization, these forces would produce more rapid and severe polarization. But if left unchecked, political polarization based on religious affiliation will be the shape of things to come (Green and Guth 1991b).

Notes

1. The denominational preference items first ascertained religious traditions and then branched into a series of questions on specific denominations, including probes for ambiguous answers. Prior to ascertaining their present denomination, respondents were asked three questions to screen out nonreligious people: if they attended church for more than occasional ceremonies, if they thought of themselves as belonging to a particular religious tradition, or if they considered themselves a "religious person." Christian respondents were also asked the religious identity of the church they attended as a child and as an adult. The Catholic identities, as noted in chapter 4, were *post-Vatican II, traditionalist, ethnic,* and *charismatic*; Protestant identities were *fundamentalist, evangelical, pentecostal, conservative,* and *liberal.* Each item had four response categories, ranging from *very well* to *not well at all* (cf. Leege, Kellstedt, and Wald 1990).

2. The identity measures were first recoded so that the *very well* and *quite well* equaled 1 and the rest 0, and then all of the identities were summed to produce a single measure of church identity. This complex measure was then recoded into four categories for Protestants (fundamentalist, evangelical, liberal, and no identity) and Catholics (traditionalist, ethnic, post-Vatican II, and no identity), giving priority to the most conservative identities (i.e., if fundamentalist and liberal, the case was coded fundamentalist). While quite interesting, this measure surely underestimates change within denominations.

3. There is some dispute among scholars as to whether seculars return to organized religion as adults. For example, Greeley (1972) believes they do, while Hadaway and Marler (1991) argue they do not.

4. The 1989 Pilot Study data reveal that 8 percent of the sample were multiple church attenders and that 11 percent participated in some kind of para-church group; the GSS reveals that 8 percent engaged in multiple switching. Multiple attenders and switchers follow the patterns described in the text: both were most common where change was

occurring already and mostly occurred between denominations in the same tradition. Para-church participation is less clear, but with the exception of standpat evangelicals, involvement in such organizations was most common where change was occurring already. Politically, multiple attenders tend to stand halfway between the churches they attend, while multiple switchers and para-church participants show the same tendencies as other members of the categories of change to which they belong, but to a greater extent.

5. For these purposes, the GSS denomination codes leave a lot to be desired. For example, nondenominational Protestants, one of the fastest growing segments of evangelicalism, are combined with *Protestant, no denomination*, also a growing group of nearly secular mainliners. But more problematic is the collapsed categories for smaller denominations in major denominational families, such as *Other Baptists* and *Other Methodist*.

6. Similar analyses for black Protestants and Jews show them to resemble Catholics: high levels of internal change, largely associated with upward mobility, but very little shifts between traditions. Although these groups are far more Democratic and liberal politically, the individuals engaged in internal change are more Republican. The data are not shown because of small N.

References

Bibby, Reginald W., and Brinkerhoff, Merlin B. 1973. "The Circulation of the Saints: A Study of People Who Join Conservative Churches." *Journal for the Scientific Study of Religion* 12:273–83.

Bromley, David G., ed. 1988. *Falling from Grace: The Causes and Consequences of Religious Apostasy.* Beverly Hills, CA: Sage Publications.

Greeley, Andrew. 1972. *The Denominational Society.* Glenview, IL: Scott, Foresman.

Guth, James L., and Green, John C. 1990. "Politics in a New Key: Religiosity and Participation among Political Activists." *Western Political Quarterly* 43:153–79.

———. 1991a. *The Bible and the Ballot Box: Religion and Politics in the 1988 Election.* Boulder, CO: Westview Press.

———. 1991b. "The Bible and the Ballot Box: The Shape of Things to Come." In Guth and Green 1991a, 207–26.

Hadaway, C. Kirk. 1978. "Denominational Switching and Membership Growth: In Search of a Relationship." *Sociological Analysis* 39:321–37.

Hadaway, C. Kirk, and Marler, Penny L. 1991. "All in the Family: Religious Mobility in America." Paper presented at the annual meeting of the Society for the Scientific Study of Religion, Pittsburgh.

Hadaway, C. Kirk, and Roof, Wade Clark. 1988. "Apostasy in American Churches: Evidence from National Survey Data." In Bromley 1988, 29–46.

Hirschman, A.O. 1970. *Exit, Voice, and Loyalty.* Cambridge, MA: Harvard University Press.

Hoge, Dean R., and Roozen, David, eds. 1979. *On Understanding Modern Church Growth.* New York: Pilgrim Press.

Homans, George C. 1950. *The Human Group.* New York: Harcourt, Brace and World.

Kellstedt, Lyman A., and Noll, Mark A. 1990. "Religion, Voting for the President, and Party Identification, 1948–1984." In Noll 1990, 355–79.

Kellstedt, Lyman A.; Smidt, Corwin E.; and Kellstedt, Paul M. 1991. "Religious Tradition, Denomination, and Commitment: White Protestants and the 1988 Election." In Guth and Green 1991a, 139–58.

Kelley, Dean M. 1972. *Why Conservative Churches Are Growing.* New York: Harper and Row.

Leege, David C.; Kellstedt, Lyman A.; and Wald, Kenneth D. 1990. "Religion and Politics: A Report on Measures of Religiosity in the 1989 NES Pilot Study." Paper presented at the annual meeting of the Midwest Political Science Association, Chicago.

Leege, David C.; Lieske, Joel A.; and Wald, Kenneth D. 1991. "Toward Cultural Theories of American Political Behavior: Religion, Ethnicity, Race, and Class Outlook." In *Political Science: Toward the Future*, ed. William Crotty, 3:193–238. Evanston, IL: Northwestern University Press.

Nelson, Lynn D. 1988. "Disaffiliation, Desacralization, and Political Values." In Bromley 1988, 122–39.

Nelson, Lynn D., and Bromley, David G. 1988. "Another Look at Conversion and Defection in Conservative Churches." In Bromley 1988, 47–61.

Niebuhr, H. Richard. 1929. *The Social Sources of Denominationalism*. New York: Henry Holt and Co.

Noll, Mark A., ed. 1990. *Religion and American Politics*. New York: Oxford University Press.

Roof, Wade Clark. 1978. *Community and Commitment: Religious Plausibility in a Liberal Protestant Church*. New York: Elsevier.

Roof, Wade Clark, and Hoge, Dean R. 1979. "Church Involvement in America: Social Factors Affecting Membership and Participation." *Review of Religious Research* 21:405–26.

Roof, Wade Clark, and McKinney, William. 1987. *American Mainline Religion*. New Brunswick, NJ: Rutgers University Press.

Stark, Rodney, and Bainbridge, William Sims. 1985. *The Future of Religion: Secularization, Revival, and Cult Formation*. Berkeley: University of California Press.

Stark, Rodney, and Glock, Charles Y. 1968. *American Piety: The Nature of Religious Commitment*. Berkeley: University of California Press.

Swierenga, Robert P. 1990. "Ethnoreligious Political Behavior in the Mid-Nineteenth Century: Voting, Values, and Cultures." In Noll 1990, 146–71.

Tajfel, Henri. 1981. *Human Groups and Social Categories: Studies in Social Psychology*. Cambridge: Cambridge University Press.

Wuthnow, Robert. 1988. *The Restructuring of American Religion*. Princeton, NJ: Princeton University Press.

Part III

Religion as a Set
of Public and Private Practices

Chapter 6

Church Involvement and Political Behavior

Kenneth D. Wald, Lyman A. Kellstedt, and David C. Leege

When asked why he robbed banks, the legendary Willy Sutton replied, "Because that's where the money is." In much the same way, political scientists who study religion pay attention to churches because that is where the parishioners are. By joining churches in large numbers, attending them frequently, and funding church activities generously, Americans have made religious association the single most frequent form of voluntary organizational affiliation in the United States. As a result, the religious sector enjoys a dynamism and pervasiveness unmatched in other advanced industrial societies. Describing the United States memorably as "a nation with the soul of a church," G.K. Chesterton recognized the deep imprint of religious attachment on the national culture.

What difference does religious attachment make to civic life? At one extreme, theorists like Alexis de Tocqueville have treated churches as the incubators of the distinctive American political character. In their churches, Tocqueville opined, Americans learned beliefs and practices that undergirded the democratic tenor of political life. Historians have adduced strong evidence of a connection between religion and political choice over the course of American national development (Noll 1990). Notwithstanding the historical record and contemporary empirical evidence, many political scientists continue to regard church membership or religion generally as factors of little or no political significance. Guided by this secular presumption, contemporary studies frequently omit religious variables from models of political behavior or, at best, work with such gross distinctions as Protestant-Catholic-Jew or frequent vs. infrequent attendance.

This chapter focuses on the political consequences of church involvement. For reasons to be set out in the next section, we distinguish this form of religious commitment from religious beliefs, denominationalism, private actions of devotion, or the salience of religious identity. Rather than confuse what is potentially an independent dimension of religiosity with other forms of religious attachment, we examine only the *public* form of attachment to formally constituted religious organizations. Chapter 7 deals with *private* devotionalism.

Church Involvement: Theoretical Considerations

The ties between religion and political behavior are to some degree the product of what goes on in the churches that Americans join and support so abundantly. By *churches*, we refer to the characteristic form of religious organization in the United States, voluntary congregations that may be components of a larger religious network or stand alone as independent assemblies.[1] These churches, some 300,000 or more, have a number of qualities that enhance their potential as political learning environments. The mere fact that so many Americans spend time in church offers a potential audience for communicating political messages. That potential includes direct efforts at political suasion, when religious authorities capitalize on the opportunity presented by attentive congregants, as well as informal political communication among parishioners. According to surveys of the clergy and churchgoers, as attested in chapter 12, the former frequently transmit messages with overt political content and the latter recognize the political dimension of what they hear. The churchgoer also encounters symbolic political messages as part of the religious socialization process and may well obtain politically relevant cues from discussion and interaction with other congregants.

Do these explicit and latent messages "take"? If asked to describe the formative influences on their political views, most Americans do not identify the church or clergy as influential sources, and many decisively, indeed indignantly, reject the very idea of clerical political guidance on the principle of church–state separation. Yet the persistence of political distinctiveness among religious groups suggests that the messages do penetrate to some degree. That is hardly surprising given that several aspects of the church—its voluntary character, high public esteem, and apparent distinterestedness—are qualities likely to confer considerable *source credibility* upon church authorities and trusted friends in the congregation (Cohen 1964, 23–29). Churches also appear to be excellent environments for the operation of social influence processes.

The emphasis on churches as potential sources of political influence cuts against the rationalist and individualist assumptions that dominate so much of contemporary social science. Without fully exploring an argument that has been developed elsewhere (cf. Ennis 1962), modern social scientists usually posit the autonomous individual as the core unit of analysis and treat the individual as the sum total of personal traits. One "explains" a vote choice from this perspective by identifying all the forces that drive an individual to select a candidate—the voter's age, education, race, partisan commitment, ideological views, and so on. This individualist perspective, revealed most starkly in economic models of behavior (Downs 1957), conflicts with another tradition emphasizing the social and communal character of humankind (Przeworski 1974). Viewing individuals as embedded in environments that mold behavior, this alternative approach suggests that the individual's attitudes may respond to social forces in the particular context that the individual inhabits. The environment may render certain traits politically relevant or diminish their influence in the voter's calculus. The voter is not only the sum of individual traits but a participant who is shaped by and reacts to other people in the vicinity.

In the case of religion and politics, this alternative contextualist perspective raises doubts about the capacity or inclination of isolated individuals to reason through connections between abstract religious doctrines and "appropriate" political manifestations. Indeed, world religions are so comprehensive and multifaceted that they can be—and have been—connected to a wide range of political programs. Rather, we suppose that individuals who link their politics and religion make the connection in church. In Berger's (1967) phrase, churches are *plausibility structures*, environments that help the individual make sense of the world and learn how to cope with it. In such an environment, where the individual expects to receive moral counsel, it is not farfetched to suppose that he or she will also obtain guidance about the relevance of religious doctrine to contemporary public issues. That is why the search for religious influence on political behavior increasingly takes account of church involvement (Gilbert 1991).

Recognizing the potential significance of religious environments is only the first step in studying the political influence of religious involvement. The second step is establishing church involvement as a distinct and separate dimension of religion. As noted in chapter 2, the phenomenon of *religion* encompasses a variety of different activities or referents. The three modes of religion commonly recognized in the literature—religion as a body of ideas and ritual obligations, a social collectivity with routine patterns of interaction, or an organization with prescribed rules, norms, and infrastructure—are indexed by different measures that may exert unique influence on political behavior. The distinctions among modes of religious influence are more commonly recognized than practiced. Empirical researchers typically utilize a global measure of religiosity, mixing components associated with different conceptualizations, or take one single manifestation of religious behavior—most commonly, church attendance—to represent the multifaceted phenomenon of religious commitment. The unique contributions of different forms of religiosity are lost with composite indicators, and the effects of religion in toto are probably underestimated.

The methodological innovations in the National Election Studies (NES) Pilot Study provide a means to assess the political impact of different forms of religious commitment. We tke advantage of these innovations to explore the political impact of religious association, measured by the level of involvement in formal religious organizations. The organizational-associational dimension of religious commitment was recognized in the pioneering empirical investigations of modern religious sociology.

Gerhard Lenski's *The Religious Factor* (1963), perhaps still the best and most theoretically sophisticated treatment of involvement with organized religion, argued for a multidimensional approach to religious measurement. To guide his survey-based investigation of religion in a modern urban environment, Lenski proposed three different forms of religious commitment—orientation, communalism, and associationalism—which correspond to the theological, social, and organizational dimensions discussed above. The *orientation* dimension encompassed both agreement with church doctrines and frequency of private communication with the divine. By *communalism*, Lenski referred to the commonality of religious identification among family and friends. *Associationalism*, equated with public involvement in corporate religious organizations, was measured by attendance at collective worship and other activities conducted under the aegis of churches.

Lenski (1963, 174) analyzed the political impact of associationalism on the assumption that "those who are more active in a group usually conform to the norms of that group more faithfully than do marginal and peripheral members." When he linked associational involvement to political behavior, he found important and interesting patterns. Greater church involvement exerted measurable effects on the partisanship, political values, racial attitudes, and moral preferences of the major religious groups, although not always in the direction predicted by social theory. Similarly though not without exception, higher levels of religious involvement enhanced the level of electoral participation. Consistent with his multidimensional view of religious commitment, Lenski found that the other forms of religious behavior were sometimes unimportant for selected dependent variables, frequently reinforced the associational impact, or occasionally worked against it. Thus, for Catholics, communal involvement correlated with commitment to the Democratic party, but associationalism bred Republicanism, an anomaly that Lenski traced to the different political priorities of the Catholic community and its hierarchy. The former, viewing politics as an arena to pursue class and status interests, regarded the Democrats as most representative of their views, while the church as church regarded the Republicans as the most faithful standard-bearers of conservative personal morality. The two different forms of Catholicism, the community and the church, provided conflicting cues that translated into different partisan commitments.

Church involvement was also accorded significance in Stark and Glock's (1968) celebrated survey of parishioners from Northern California churches. In that study (82), church involvement was deemed salient primarily for the public opportunity to celebrate ritual: "It is largely through rituals that religion constitutes a truly social phenomenon, a gathering of persons for religious reasons to take part in religious activities. Such social circumstances provide the occasions and the means for a collective reaffirmation of the meaning and sacredness of religion, for it is most commonly in such circumstances that people *feel* religious." Using *ritualism* to describe public affirmations of religious commitment, Stark and Glock included public worship, membership in a church and church-related organizations, financial contributions to church-supported causes, and the saying of table grace in the home as exemplars of involvement. A ritualism index composed only of church attendance and table grace was significantly related to other forms of religious commitment but not strongly enough to challenge its status as an independent dimension. Though Stark and Glock never examined the effect of religious commitment on social behavior, they clearly anticipated that ritualism would exert significant impact independent of other forms of religious attachment.[2] We shall explore that possibility by analyzing data from the NES 1989 Pilot Study.

The Measurement of Religious Involvement

Commitment to organized religion reflects identification with a religious tradition, affiliation with its tangible expression, and participation in church-related activities. The NES 1989 Pilot Study provided new opportunities to assess these factors. In common with previous investigations, the core of our measure of commitment to organized religion is frequency of attendance at corporate worship services. But the measure also reflects the willingness of respondents to identify with a religious tradition, maintenance of formal membership in a religious organization, and participation in church activities other than organized worship. These three additional elements provide both greater precision and a more well-rounded view of organizational involvement than can be attained by church attendance alone.

The particularities of questionnaire design precluded the creation of a simple additive scale or a psychometrically driven cumulative scale.[3] Instead, we produced an index of church involvement with five levels ranging from *irreligious* at one extreme to *very religious* at the other. Of the 494 respondents polled during the second wave of the 1989 Pilot Study, 472 provided sufficient information to classify them on the church involvement measure. As the first column of Table 6.1 indicates, respondents were distributed normally among the five categories.

The *irreligious* respondents disclaimed any cognitive loyalty to churches, religious traditions, or denominations; reported they never attended services outside of weddings and funerals; and did not think of themselves as religious persons. At the other pole, the *very religious* identified with a church or tradition, maintained formal membership in it, attended services at least once a week, and also reported membership in religious organizations outside the church. The cutoff points for the three middle categories reflected investigator judgments about the significance of different forms of attachment. Membership in all three intermediate categories required some form of identification with religion. To be coded as *minimally religious*, respondents had at least to embrace a self-designation as a religious person and at most to attend services less than once a month. The *moderately religious* category comprised nonmembers who attended services at least monthly (but not weekly) and church members who attended anywhere

Table 6.1

Distribution of Respondents in NES 1989 Pilot Study on Index of Church Involvement

	All Respondents %	Evangelical Protestant %	Mainline Protestant %	Roman Catholic %
Irreligious	9	0	0	0
Minimally religious	23	14	21	23
Moderately religious	35	37	51	35
Religious	25	37	22	33
Very religious	8	12	6	10
N	(472)	(148)	(121)	(89)

from less than monthly to monthly. Membership in the *very religious* category required formal church membership and attendance at least weekly.

This index offers several advantages over competing indicators of church involvement, enabling it to offer a truer picture of the contribution of church involvement to political behavior. This index is normally distributed and unskewed, hence making it suitable for inclusion in multiple regression analysis. On grounds of face validity, it encompasses the domains of identification, affiliation, and participation in both corporate worship and other types of organizational activity. The core element of the index, church attendance, benefited from several innovations of the 1989 Pilot Study that enhanced validity by screening out false positives (see Leege, Kellstedt, and Wald 1990, 21–23, for details). The measure also appears to be reliable: of the thirty-nine respondents who denied any religious identification when first interviewed in 1988, all but three fell in the lowest two categories of the measure constructed on the basis of information collected during 1989 interviews.

In addition, the measure of church involvement is compatible with the multidimensional understanding of religiosity. Given the centrality of churches in American religion, we were not surprised to find significant correlations between the church involvement index and other forms of religious commitment. Predictably, the salience attributed to religion, the guidance received from religion, and a composite measure of private devotionalism discussed in the following chapter all rose monotonically with the level of church involvement. Notwithstanding these correlations, the index is sufficiently independent to represent a distinct dimension of religiosity. A multiple regression of church involvement upon a full set of religious predictors—a composite salience index, private devotionalism, attitude toward the Bible, and identification with a major religious tradition—accounted for only a bit more than one-third of the variance. This finding leaves sufficient variation for the index to attain predictive significance—if we are indeed correct in suspecting church involvement as a political influence.

Finally and most important, the measure is not strongly biased in favor of any particular religious tradition. That quality is essential if multivariate analysis is to distinguish between the political consequences of church involvement and identification with a religious tradition. Note from Table 6.1 how the three major religious traditions broken out of the survey—Catholics, evangelical Protestants, and other mainline Protestants—had very similar profiles across the church involvement index.[4] The relative independence of the church involvement index from religious tradition, signified by a *tau-b* of only 0.15, constitutes a substantial advance over measures that conflate church involvement with evangelical affiliation—primarily a consequence of the greater emphasis on and opportunity for group worship in the evangelical tradition. This finding can best be illustrated by contrasting the findings in Table 6.1 (above) with parallel analysis of denominational differences on an alternative involvement measure (not shown but see Leege, Kellstedt, and Wald 1990, 21–32). On a seven-point scale based on identification and church attendance variables included in the 1988 wave of the NES, a plurality of evangelical respondents were located in the extreme cell representing identification with a religious tradition and more than weekly church attendance. By contrast, a plurality of respondents from the mainline Protestant and Roman Catholic traditions were placed in a cell below the scale midpoint, a location representing church identification but less than monthly church attendance.[5] Such a distinctive pattern would obscure the independent effects, if any, of religious tradition (specifically, evangelical Protestantism) and church involvement.

The independence of the church involvement index from measures of religious affiliation stems from two aspects of its construction. The coding of church attendance, the core item in the index, included a common category for both weekly and more than weekly church attenders. This strategy blunts evangelical distinctiveness by giving less emphasis to the pattern of multiple attendance that sets evangelicals apart from mainline Protestants and Roman Catholics.[6] The other significant factor is the item querying whether respondents participated in religious organizations or activities outside the church. Even though the item was marked by considerable measurement error, it seems to tap types of mainline Protestant and Catholic religious involvement that are functionally equivalent to the midweek worship services in the evangelical tradition.

Religious Involvement as an Independent Variable: Hypotheses

What aspects of political behavior might we expect church involvement to explain, and in what manner? The strongest evidence links church involvement to another form of social activity, electoral participation (see Wald 1992, 35–37). Based on previous research, *we expect to find a positive relationship between the index of church involvement and turnout.* The studies that have linked church involvement and electoral participation have found that the rule applies only to the least demanding form of participation—casting a vote—and does not hold for forms of participation that require greater investments of time and energy. A few investigators have even contended that high levels of church commitment inhibit political activism. This pattern may stem from the inability to serve two masters or simple conflicts of time and resources. Whatever the source, *we hypothesize that church involvement will be negatively related to political activism other than voting.*

Religiosity has also been linked to political values and preferences across a wide array of policy questions. We want to see whether a particular mode of religious commitment—level of involvement with organized religion—similarly contributes to a diverse set of dependent variables. These variables have been grouped into three categories—indicators of fundamental political identity (vote choice, partisanship, and ideological self-description), matters of social regulatory policy (traditionalism, moralism, and abortion), and a diverse set of political attitudes covering the former Soviet Union, civil rights, poverty, and capital punishment. Our expectations are not so clear-cut on these substantive variables as they are for electoral participation. The strongest evidence links church-based involvement with conservative values on questions of personal morality, the so-called social issues of sexuality, civil liberties, and public order (Hoge and de Zulueta 1985; Wuthnow 1973). Though the evidence is not nearly so strong or the rationale so compelling, others have asserted a more global linkage between conservatism in religion and politics. Following those who regard churches as incubators of conservative values, *we predict a positive relationship between church involvement and conservative preferences on the set of attitudinal measures.*

The hypotheses address the *direction* but not the expected *form* of the relationship between church involvement and the political measures. Treating church involvement as an independent variable assumes it exerts a direct and independent effect on certain variables, an effect that does not depend on whether the involvement takes place in a Roman Catholic cathedral or a pentecostal assembly. In other words, there is something inherent in church involvement or the type of people who get involved in churches that promotes uniform political behavior. That assumption may be valid for some attitudes, but it certainly does not exhaust the theoretical possibilities. To consider only one plausible alternative, church involvement may also be a moderator variable, a factor that affects the relationship between another independent variable and the dependent variable (Jaccard, Turrisi, and Wan 1990, 9). Lenski's (1963) hypothesis, that highly integrated members of a religious community adhere more closely to group norms than persons on the margin, provides a warrant for exploring the interaction between church involvement and religious tradition. Accordingly, we shall include a series of interaction measures in the multivariate equations. These will allow us to determine whether church involvement has different consequences in the three major Christian traditions.

Data and Results

Table 6.2 reports the relationship between church involvement and two measures of political action in the 1988 general election—voter turnout and campaign activity. Turnout was based on self-report, while campaign activism was measured by a scale based on reported participation in several forms of electioneering in 1988: proselytizing on behalf of a candidate, displaying public support, attending meetings, volunteering, and contributing money to a candidate, party, or election-related group. The seven-item scale had a standardized reliability coefficient of 0.70. Because of the heavy skew toward inactivity, the item was dichotomized. This step, in turn, mandated the use of logistic regression analysis.

The first hypothesis, linking church involvement and turnout, was largely confirmed in Table 6.2. In the univariate analysis reported in the first row, church involvement made a substantial positive contribution to the probability of casting a vote in the 1988 presidential election. The pattern persisted with only slight diminution in a multivariate analysis that included other measures of religiosity and a set of demographic and political variables long associated with electoral participation.[7] The inclusion of correlated religious measures undoubtedly accounts for the coefficient of church involvement just missing the .05 level of significance. Of the control variables, only identification with an evangelical Protestant denomination and family income joined church involvement as significant and positive influences on turnout, while southern residence and race diminished it.

The second column of Table 6.2 reports the coefficients for campaign activity. The expectation that religious involvement would depress this form of political involvement was weakly supported at best. In the univariate equation, the coefficient for church involvement was almost indistinguishable from zero. The relationship assumed the expected negative form in the multivariate equation but still fell short of statistical significance. Based on this analysis, all we can say with confidence is that church involvement neither encourages nor inhibits participation in more demanding forms of electoral activity. What is more surprising about this analysis is the finding from Table 6.2 that devotionalism—a measure of private religious observance—joined education as the only other significant stimulus to electioneering. By exerting a strong and positive impact on campaign activism, a relationship different in both magnitude and direction from other measures of religious commitment, the power of devotionalism underscores the importance of distinguishing among modes of religious activity. We leave to chapter 7 a discussion of devotionalism as a stimulus to political activity.

The third hypothesis posited that church involvement would exert a conserva-

Table 6.2

Impact of Church Involvement on Political Participation

	Turnout	Campaign Activity
Church involvement	.45**	.06
Church involvement	.53	-.19
Devotionalism	.04	.08**
Religious salience	-.07	.03
Biblical literalism	.33	.18
Evangelical Protestant	.60*	-.08
Mainline Protestant	.17	-.14
Roman Catholic	.20	.07
Female	.24	-.15
Nonwhite	-.88**	-.42
South	-.60**	-.04
Age	.02	-.01
Education	.16	.43**
Family income	.10**	.04
Conservatism	-.12	.06
Republicanism	.02	-.02

Source: NES 1989 Pilot Study.
*$p < .05$.
**$p < .01$.

Note: Coefficients are derived from logistic regression equations.

tive influence upon a range of political attitude items. For ease of analysis, we classified these variables in three sets: (1) the political identity items of presidential vote in 1988, party preference, and ideological self-description; (2) questions of social regulation including composite scales representing support for moral norms (social policy), endorsement of traditional values on "family" issues (moral traditionalism), and a single item measuring policy preferences on abortion; and (3) the secular policy areas of capital punishment, attitudes toward the former Soviet Union, evaluations of civil rights leaders, and feelings about federal aid to poor people. These dependent variables were regressed first on church involvement alone and then on the full set of predictors listed in Table 6.2. To

Table 6.3

Impact of Church Involvement on Selected Political Attitudes

	Univariate Equation	Multivariate Equation
Bush vote	.01	-.30
Republicanism	.01	.02
Conservatism	.22**	.01
Moral traditionalism	.43**	.24*
Social policy	.47**	.35**
Abortion (pro-life)	.36**	.15
Anti-Soviet Union	.22**	.09
Civil Rights (too fast)	.01	.04
Poverty (decrease aid)	-.05	-.04
Pro-Capital punishment	.25**	-.13

Source: NES 1989 Pilot Study.
*p < .05.
**p < .01.
Note: Except for Bush vote and capital punishment, which were analyzed using logistic regression, the coefficients are derived from OLS analysis. See Table 6.2 for a list of controls used in the multivariate analysis.

conserve space, only the coefficients for the church involvement index are repro-duced in Table 6.3.

The measure of particular interest in this chapter—church involvement—had no significant impact on any of the three political identity items. The only signif-icant coefficient from the univariate analysis of the three measures—the positive contribution of church involvement to conservatism—disappeared with the intro-duction of controls. The same pattern of nonrelationship was observed for the four items representing secular conservative concerns. Again, the univariate analysis left the impression that church involvement contributed substantially to opposition to the Soviet Union and support for capital punishment. In both cases, the inclusion of the full set of predictor variables drove these relationships to insignificance.

The findings are quite different when we shift to the issue area where reli-gious commitment has frequently been linked to political attitudes—the social issues. The univariate analysis in the first column of Table 6.3 reveals the strong, conservative influence of church involvement on each of the three policy questions. As expected, church involvement enhanced commitment to social traditionalism, moralism, and the prolife side of the abortion debate. Though reduced in magnitude, two of the three measures retained significance in the multivariate equation, and the third—the coefficient for abortion—just missed significance by the narrowest possible margin. The direction was stable, indicating that involvement in a church, regardless of type, promoted support for conservative social morality. Taken together, these findings reaffirm those scholars who have identified aspects of the *plausibility structure* of Christian churches conducive to social conservatism. At the same time, the lack of findings in other policy areas suggests caution before generalizing too widely about the inherent conservative impact of involvement with organized religion. The impact of church involvement is concentrated heavily on questions of sexual and social morality, much less evident on other important issues on the national agenda.

The magnitude of the church involvement coefficients in the multivariate analysis is impressive on two counts. First, by including some very powerful attitudinal predictors such as partisanship and ideological identification and strong demographic influences like race and region, we have stacked the deck against religious predictors. Under the circumstances, the church involvement measure has passed a stringent test. Specifying a model with indirect effects might reveal an even stronger influence for church involvement. Second, the relationship between church involvement and social attitudes held despite the conjoint influence of the other religious variables included in the equation (but not shown in Table 6.3). On the moral traditionalism scale, for example, church involvement worked together with biblical literalism to raise scale scores. The two measures had the same effect on social policy, where they competed with the contrary influences of identification as a Roman Catholic or mainline Protestant. The disposition to favor restrictions on abortion was also encouraged by high levels of religious salience, biblical literalism, and devotionalism. On that measure, however, identification with a Protestant denomination, whether mainline or evangelical, contributed to a prochoice orientation.

By virtue of the model specification embodied in Tables 6.2 and 6.3, church involvement was assumed to have the same effect regardless of the religious tradition to which it was attached. As mentioned above, that assumption may not hold, as all churches do not send out the same message on the same issues. To consider that possibility, the equations were reestimated with three additional variables representing the interaction of church involvement with identification as a mainline Protestant, evangelical Protestant, and Roman Catholic. Where interaction among two variables is suspected, statisticians differ over whether it is appropriate to include both interaction terms and the variables representing the components of the interaction (see Jaccard, Turrisi, and Wan 1990, 14–15). We are persuaded that both main effects and interaction measures are meaningful and have thus included in the new equations both the interaction terms and the

Table 6.4

Impact of Church Involvement × Religious Tradition on Attitudes to Civil Rights and Abortion

	Civil Rights	Anti-Abortion
Church involvement	.25*	-.04
Devotionalism	-.01	.03*
Religious guidance	-.03	.16**
Biblical literalism	.12	.33**
Evangelical Protestant	.62	-.71
EP x Church involvement	-.22	.13
Mainline Protestant	.87*	-.02
ML x Church involvement	-.33*	-.09
Roman Catholic	.29	-1.84**
RC x Church involvement	-.18	.63**

Source: NES 1989 Pilot Study.

*p < .05.

**p < .01.

Note: High positive scores represent conservative positions—i.e., dislike of civil rights leaders, support for the prolife position.

original measures of church involvement and denominational identification. In such an equation, the main effect will signify the impact of the average value of the variable.

For the most part, the inclusion of additional measures did not alter the findings reported in Tables 6.2 and 6.3. That is not surprising, because interaction terms frequently fail to attain significance due to high correlations with their component terms. But the two exceptions, the equations where coefficients did shift significantly in the presence of interaction between church involvement and religious tradition, are worthy of comment because of the issues they encompass. In Table 6.4, we have presented the reestimated equations for civil rights and abortion, omitting the coefficients for the control variables but reporting the performance of the full set of religious predictors. Recall that both variables were coded so that high scores represented conservative positions—dislike of civil rights leaders and support for the prolife position.

On these two measures, it did matter where a respondent was religiously involved and how intensely he or she was engaged with the church. Note the difference controlling for involvement makes for mainline Protestants on attitudes toward civil rights leaders. Simply identifying with a mainline denomination makes the respondent, on average, significantly less supportive of civil rights leaders than the comparison group of the nonreligious. But according to the interaction coefficient, higher levels of involvement in mainline churches turn the relationship around, making respondents more positive toward civil rights leadership.[8] A similar pattern differentiates nominal and involved Roman Catholics on the abortion question. Identification as a Catholic actually moves respondents significantly to the prochoice end of the spectrum. But when religious involvement is factored in (and all other traits are controlled), the pattern reverses and Catholic involvement drives respondents to the prolife position.

These patterns make a great deal of sense given the content of church cues.[9] To a substantial degree, the mainline Protestant churches made civil rights their defining social issue during the 1960s and 1970s. Outside the South, the Protestant clergy took a strong position in favor of the movement. In the same way, the Roman Catholic church became identified in the public mind with the prolife movement in the aftermath of *Roe* v. *Wade*. What we find on these issues is a pattern consistent with Lenski's (1963) hypothesis about differential fidelity to group patterns depending on level of church integration. The pro–civil rights message of the mainline clergy did not "take" with nominal congregants, who were actually quite hostile to the leaders of the movement, but did reach church members who were most deeply involved in their religious community. Similarly, Catholics per se were significantly more prochoice than the nonreligious but turned against liberal abortion laws as a consequence of high levels of church involvement. In both cases, the message transmitted by the church was apparently perceived and internalized by the strongly involved congregant. Alternatively, perhaps some of the noninvolved Protestants and Catholics, respectively, were turned away by the strong pro–civil rights and prolife position preached by chrch leaders. Whatever the precise linkage, this finding lends weight to the hypothesis that political messages are likely to be absorbed only by the most attentive congregants. They are both more likely to hear the cues and to take them to heart—as data in chapter 12 elaborate.

Summary

We began by speculating that church involvement matters for politics and matters regardless of how the respondent scores on other dimensions of religious commitment. By and large, this speculation was warranted. So, on at least two issues, was our speculation that involvement might matter more in some traditions than others or for some congregants more than others. Hence the findings permit us to offer measurement advice to scholars who wish to continue the exploration of religious influences on political behavior.

First, to the extent a data-set allows, researchers should distinguish church involvement from other forms of religious commitment. It is important to treat church involvement as only one of several forms of religious influence on political behavior, an independent variable separable from such manifestations of religiosity as private devotionalism, salience, denominational affiliation, or beliefs about the Bible. Like early researchers, we treated *religion* as a multifaceted concept and further postulated that its influence upon politics would vary with different modes of commitment. That approach, long suspected but seldom investigated, was empirically confirmed utilizing new measures first developed in the NES 1989 Pilot Study. To the extent religious commitment is indexed by church involvement, it is clear that voter turnout and several "family" issues bear a strong religious imprint. Had a researcher equated religion with some other form of religious commitment, the findings would have generally supported a different conclusion. By the same token, models of voter turnout that omit church involvement are clearly misspecified.

Second, church involvement is not the same thing as church attendance. The inclusion of two new items on the interview schedule—church membership and involvement in religious activities other than worship—as well as a measure of identification with a denomination allowed us to create an index that more faithfully represented church involvement. Even if these additional measures are not available in a data set, and they seldom are, researchers must still be sensitive to the biases associated with sole reliance upon church attendance. Evangelical Protestants attend services more frequently than other Christians, so a church attendance measure used in isolation may credit attendance with an influence that is actually due to identification with the evangelical tradition. This skewing can be combated in two ways. By using an attendance scale with fewer categories at the high end, the researcher will diminish the uniqueness of the evangelical respondents. At the same time, the equation should include separate variables for attendance and attachment to a religious tradition. In that way, the analysis may reveal the effects of both attendance and attachment.

Third, to be fully sensitive to the nature of religious influence, it is advisable to include interaction terms. By including both church involvement and its interaction with the three major religious traditions, we could explore differences between the religious and nonreligious and also between the least and most committed congregants in a common religious tradition. On a number of issues, particularly in the social regulatory sphere, the religiously involved were strikingly different from the uninvolved (see Wald 1989 for similar patterns). On two issues, abortion and civil rights (respectively), the most intensely affiliated Catholics and mainline Protestants differed significantly from their co-religionists. This pattern is explicable in terms of social influence theory and also accords with Allport and Ross's (1967) famous distinction between *extrinsic* and *intrinsic* religious motivation. Assuming that distinction is captured by church involvement, we found two issues where the extrinsically oriented were deaf or even hostile to the message emanating from the church while the intrinsically religious absorbed the guidance provided by the clergy.

We must also acknowledge findings that challenge our general theory, particularly the large number of issues in which church involvement did not matter whether used alone or in concert with attachment to any particular religious tradition. We are working toward satisfactory explanations for two anomalies—the significant positive contribution of devotionalism to campaign activism (discussed in chapter 7) and the equally puzzling attraction of evangelical Protestants to the prochoice position in a controlled multivariate equation. We do not understand why the differential impact of church involvement, so marked for mainline Protestants and Catholics on civil rights and abortion, respectively, did not similarly show up for evangelical Protestants on social issues. If future surveys take heed of the methodological innovations introduced in the NES 1989 Pilot Study, researchers will have the data to explore these questions in great detail.

Notes

1. We use the term *church* to refer conceptually to any organized group that meets regularly for worship and prayer. It includes Jewish synagogues and temples, Muslim mosques, and the buildings used for similar purposes by other non-Christian faith communities. Because there were so few adherents of non-Christian faiths in the NES 1989 Pilot Study sample, they have been excluded from the empirical analyses reported in this chapter. Nothing in our argument would preclude application of our arguments to these religious traditions.

2. In an earlier study, Glock and Stark (1966, 137–38) found a complex relationship between religious bigotry and a ritualism measure including both church attendance and private prayer. This measure of ritualism confounded what we regard as independent dimensions of religiosity—private devotionalism and public involvement. As they noted (16 n. 5), the high correlation between these two domains was probably the result of using a sample of active church members. Among a more heterogeneous group of respondents, the two forms of religious activity are not so closely linked.

3. In the 1989 Pilot Study, the section on current religious affiliation began with a question asking respondents if they ever attended church apart from such events as weddings and funerals. The respondents who answered in the affirmative were then asked to identify their primary church. Those who answered the screening question negatively were asked if they nonetheless identified with a religious tradition. If so, they were asked the same identity sequence as other respondents. If not, they were then asked if they thought of themselves as religious people.

4. Respondents who claimed any religious tradition were by definition placed in one of the four highest categories. The three traditions in Table 6.1 comprise almost 95 percent of all respondents.

5. The Roman Catholics were actually bimodally distributed with pluralities on values 3 and 6 of the seven-point scale.

6. Specifically, evangelicals are about twice as likely to attend services at least weekly as mainline Protestants but are only slightly more devout on this measure than Roman Catholics. In terms of attendance on more than a weekly basis, however, evangelicals outpace mainline Protestants and Catholics by a ratio of roughly 4:1.

7. Even with the eight demographic and social control variables, the turnout model in Table 6.2 does not include all factors conceivably linked to participation. It omits, in particular, psychological factors such as political efficacy and cognitive measures like political information. A fully specified model of participation would also allow for both direct and indirect influences, something not currently possible with a logistic regression technique. In the calculation of religious tradition, separate dummy variables were created for adherents of Roman Catholicism, mainline Protestantism, and evangelical Protestantism. Those adhering to non-Christian faiths were excluded from the analysis. The comparison category consisted of the nonreligious respondents.

8. The same pattern was observed on attitudes toward capital punishment, which has also been the subject of severe criticism among clergy from the mainline Protestant churches. The coefficients just failed to attain statistical significance.

9. We had anticipated that the same pattern might emerge for evangelical Protestants on the social issues which have received such emphasis in that community. On the assumption that the pattern might be obscured by the inclusion of a measure of biblical literalism and the presence of nonwhite respondents, the equations were reestimated for white respondents only and without biblical literalism. But these changes did not make any difference.

References

Allport, Gordon, and Ross, J. Michael. 1967. "Personal Religious Orientation and Prejudice." *Journal of Personality and Social Psychology* 5:432–43.

Berger, Peter. 1967. *Sacred Canopy*. Garden City, NY: Doubleday-Anchor.

Cohen, Arthur R. 1964. *Attitude Change and Social Influence*. New York: Basic Books.

Downs, Anthony. 1957. *An Economic Theory of Democracy*. New York: Harper and Row.

Ennis, Phillip. 1962. "The Contextual Dimension in Voting." In *Public Opinion and Congressional Elections*, ed. William McPhee and William A. Glaser, 180–211. New York: Free Press.

Gilbert, Christopher P. 1991. "Religious Environments and Political Actors." Ph.D. diss., Washington University, St. Louis.

Glock, Charles Y., and Stark, Rodney. 1966. *Christian Beliefs and Anti-Semitism*. New York: Harper and Row.

Hoge, Dean R., and de Zulueta, Ernesto. 1985. "Salience as a Condition for Various Social Consequences of Religious Commitment." *Journal for the Scientific Study of Religion* 24: 21–37.

Jaccard, James; Turrisi, Robert; and Wan, Choi K. 1990. *Interaction Effects in Multiple Regression*. Newbury Park, CA: Sage Publications.

Leege, David C.; Kellstedt, Lyman A.; and Wald, Kenneth D. 1990. "Religion and Politics: A Report on Measures of Religiosity in the 1989 NES Pilot Study." Paper presented at the annual meeting of the Midwest Political Science Association, Chicago.

Lenski, Gerhard. 1963. *The Religious Factor: A Sociological Study of Religion's Impact on Politics, Economics, and Family Life*. Garden City, NY: Doubleday-Anchor.

Noll, Mark A., ed. 1990. *Religion and American Politics*. New York: Oxford University Press.

Przeworski, Adam. 1974. "Contextual Models of Political Behavior." *Political Methodology* 1: 27–61.

Stark, Rodney, and Glock, Charles Y. 1968. *American Piety: The Nature of Religious Commitment*. Berkeley: University of California Press.

Wald, Kenneth D. 1989. "Assessing the Religious Factor in Electoral Behavior." In *Religion in American Politics*, ed. Charles W. Dunn, 105–22. Washington, DC: Congressional Quarterly Press.

―――. 1992. *Religion and Politics in the United States*. 2d ed. Washington, DC: Congressional Quarterly Press.

Wuthnow, Robert. 1973. "Religious Commitment and Conservatism: In Search of an Elusive Relationship." In *Religion in Sociological Perspective*, ed. Charles Y. Glock, 17–132. Belmont, CA: Wadsworth.

Chapter 7

The Public Dimension of
Private Devotionalism

David C. Leege, Kenneth D. Wald,
and Lyman A. Kellstedt

For many believers in the United States, the essence of religion is noninstitutional private devotionalism. It involves the reception of religious stimuli and the expression of religious feeling through such private or intimate-group acts as prayer, Bible reading and discussion, sharing the faith with others through evangelization, and seeking God's guidance for life's personal problems. The American religious culture provides fertile ground for devotionalism. Based on sect-style religion rather than church-style religion, it allows the suppliant to approach God directly without sacramental rituals or priestly intermediaries. And as Max Weber argued (Gerth and Mills 1946), since the evidence of true religion was to be found not simply in articles of faith and frequent church attendance but also in righteous *behavior*—acts that put one in daily touch with God—American religious norms stimulate private devotionalism. But it has never been clear to scholars whether such private acts have independent social and political import or are simply measures of intensification for other religious dimensions such as church affiliation, church involvement, or religious beliefs.

A Capsule History of Devotionalism in the Christian West

Records of the early Christian community make it difficult to isolate public ritual from private devotion. The Acts of the Apostles (2:24, KJV) says that the followers of Jesus "continued steadfastly in fellowship, the breaking of bread, and in prayer." At another point in the Scriptures it says "where two or three are gathered together in my name, there am I in the midst of them" (Matthew 18:20, KJV). Apparently, the early Christian communities were small gatherings characterized by daily, intense, face-to-face interactions. They held property in common as well as faith and ritual. Awaiting an early return of their Lord, they were not for the most part deeply involved in leadership of the civic order. Subject to growing persecution, they found security in small groups. Emissaries linked one group to another. But nothing spreads like an idea martyred.

Surely the concentrations of Christianity in the large cities and the declaration of Christianity as the religion of the realm, first in Eastern regions such as Armenia and shortly thereafter in the Western empire, changed the character of religious life. Charisms became routinized, only priestly specialists performed public ritual, councils promulgated doctrine, and the scope of private religiosity—religion practiced in noninstitutional settings—grew. Because of early Christianity's noninstitutional nature, it is never clear to what extent these practices reflected the personal religious experience of the individual striver or whether they reiterated prescribed rituals of the larger religious community.

In time, monastic orders specialized in nurturing private devotional life and personal growth in righteousness. The writings of great saints from this period attest to the mingling of institutionally prescribed ritual and unique religious experience. But the growth of individualism in the Renaissance and the contention that each person must be justified before God in the Reformation placed new emphasis on noninstitutional settings for religious devotion. The Council of Trent also recognized that the sacraments and liturgies of the Church, while the pinnacle of religious life, did not constitute the single way of the ordinary believer. Instead, each should develop regimens of private prayer, devotions to saints, and contemplation of the Christian mysteries. While such devotionalism had a strong institutional thrust, it took quite different nuances in the religious life of the individual. It became a problem for the Church to discern when some popular devotions derived simply from the superstitions of the people or when they attested a new gift of the Spirit. The Marian apparitions are a case in point.

In the New World, the ever-expanding frontier offered rich soil for religious individualism and noninstitutional devotionalism. Hertzke (1988) characterized the American religious culture as pluralistic and entrepreneurial. Organized religion grew from bottom up, not top down. While older denominations set strictures for ordination, basically any individual who felt called by the Spirit through his or her intense devotional life and who had a capacity to attract followers could become a religious leader. In time, of course, these charisms were also routinized. Thus, there is always an interplay between those devotional practices and private disciplines encouraged by churches and those that stem from the individual's own experience or experiences shared among noncanonical groups.

Under such circumstances, it is no surprise that sociologists of religion have recognized private devotionalism as an important dimension of religiosity but have reached little consensus on how to define and measure it. Further, while they have often viewed private devotionalism as a measure of religious intensity and have related it to the beliefs and practices of sponsoring churches (cf. D'Antonio et al. 1989), they have been slow to note connections between private devotionalism and *civic* life. We know much about the connections among denominations, beliefs, and social and political attitudes. We know little about the connections between private devotionalism and politics. Yet, devotional measures of one kind or another typically appear on both special-purpose religious surveys and general-purpose surveys.

This chapter seeks to redress that imbalance. It reviews the conceptual confusion and empirical montage of previous studies, and then addresses variables that appear in the National Election Studies (NES) 1989 Pilot Study and 1990 Congressional Election Study. It asks whether private devotionalism is a unique religious dimension that contributes to the understanding of politics or whether it is simply a supplement to denominational affiliation and attendant belief systems.

Devotionalism: The Research Tradition

The earliest work of Glock and Stark (1965) includes the *ritualistic* as one of the five dimensions of religiosity. *Religious practice*, which is used interchangeably with the ritualistic dimension, focuses on what people do and, by inference, the meaning of such acts for them. Glock and Stark (1965, 29–30) make no distinctions at this stage between public and private acts, elaborating a list including "worship, prayer, scripture reading, penance, obeying dietary laws, confession, tithing, and many more." It is clear from their conceptual discussion that they think of prayer as a religiously deeper practice than attendance at corporate worship, but even the depth of prayer fluctuates greatly by content and style. Curiously, their discussion of the *experiential* dimension, i.e., religious feeling, includes reference to other acts such as conversion, speaking in tongues, or being visited by the Spirit. Such occurrences or acts involve elements of "(1) concern, (2) cognition, (3) trust or faith and (4) fear" (31). What distinguishes these acts from religious practices is not altogether clear since both are likely to involve trust in the efficacy of a divine power.

By the time Stark and Glock published *American Piety: The Nature of Religious Commitment* (1968), however, they began to make both conceptual and empirical distinctions among practices. *Ritual* was defined as practices of a formal and public character. *Devotionalism* was reserved for "relatively informal and typically private acts" (81). Operationally, *ritual* was measured by the frequency of (1) attendance at Sunday worship services, (2) listening to religious services on radio or television, (3) attendance at Holy Communion, (4) involvement in church organizations, (5) financial support of the church, (6) saying grace at mealtime, and (7) importance of church membership to the respondent. A two-item ritual index was formed from church attendance and saying grace. Although it would appear that both saying grace and listening to religious radio and television fit the definition of private acts, Stark and Glock introduced a new defining criterion by claiming that saying grace is encouraged by all churches. Thus, conceptually, it appears that *ritual* refers to public religious acts or those private acts encouraged by all denominations.

Stark and Glock measured *devotionalism* by frequency of (1) Bible reading,

(2) private prayer, (3) asking forgiveness of sins, and evaluations of (4) the importance of prayer, and (5) the efficacy of prayer. A two-item index was derived from frequency and importance of prayer. Again conceptual boundaries are crossed, in that both *behaviors* and *evaluations* of behaviors are treated as acts and that religious behaviors widely encouraged by churches (grace, prayer, Bible reading) appear on both of the *distinct* dimensions. There is some overlap between the two indices, as witnessed by a product-moment correlation of .360 for Protestants and .365 for Catholics; yet there is much evidently distinct between them, because the correlation is far from unity.

These dimensions become independent variables in the explanation of religious orthodoxy, religious particularism, and ethicalism. They are stronger predictors of religious orthodoxy and particularism than ethicalism, the latter showing modest correlations on ritual and only slightly higher on devotionalism (Stark and Glock 1968, 177–80). Although Stark and Glock never published he final book of the series devoted to the *consequential* dimension, one may extrapolate these findings to suggest that perhaps those who score higher on devotionalism may be slightly less tolerant of others; at the same time one may draw modest connections between religious values and public morality.

Both Fukuyama (1961) and Lenski (1963) developed devotionalism indices that hinted at political consequences. Fukuyama used a three-item devotionalism measure (daily Bible or devotional reading, faith in the power of prayer, and belief in the necessity of conversion) that was clearly distinguished from his measure of associational activities. People scoring high on devotionalism were more likely than those scoring high on other dimensions of religiosity to want religion to be taught in public schools and less likely to want their ministers to preach on controversial subjects. Lenski's two-item devotionalism measure (prayer, seeking God's will) showed relationships with upward class mobility, positive attitudes toward work and other "capitalist virtues," and "humanitarian" policies on foreign aid, school integration, and government involvement in social problem-solving. None of these political consequences was associated with doctrinal orthodoxy. While Lenski noted the paradoxes in findings, the crudeness of his measures, and the lack of controls for explanatory factors other than race, class, and Protestant–Catholic, his findings suggest that devotionalism may merit attention as a distinct religious variable with different political consequences from other dimensions of religiosity, particularly beliefs.

In a study of Lutherans in the Detroit area, Kersten (1970) made a clean distinction between *associational involvement*—including frequency of attendance and participation in church activities—and *religious practices*—including grace at mealtime, efforts to evangelize, and seeking God's guidance for personal decisions (42–46). The *religious practices* (devotionalism) items not only predicted significantly to six other variables that have often been used in devotionalism scales but also showed some, but nowhere near complete, overlap with other dimensions of religiosity.

The special attraction of the Kersten study (1970) is the wide range of political dependent variables to which devotionalism predicts. Those Lutherans scoring high on devotionalism were more likely to be Republicans, to have voted for Republican presidential candidates, to be intolerant of the civil rights of homosexuals, to object to sex or violence on television, and to be politically suspicious of nonbelievers. Devotionalism, however, did not distinguish attitudes toward social welfare, war, divorce, or the role of women. Kersten's observed relationships were all bivariate, so it is impossible to tell whether any of the connections between devotionalism and politics are unique or whether they mask other religious variables such as beliefs, attendance,communal involvement, or other demographic indicators such as education, age, or gender. And his findings for one religious family sometimes conflict with Lenski's findings across several denominations in the Detroit area.

King and Hunt (1972) moved beyond the summated index models of the early scholars to factor-analytic derivations of the dimensions of religiosity. One of ten factor scales was labeled *devotionalism*; it included items about frequency of (1) private prayer, (2) asking for forgiveness, and (3) seeking God's will on personal decisions, and evaluations of (4) the personal importance of prayer, and (5) closeness to God through prayer, public worship, and important moments in life. While the individual items showed correlations with the factor ranging from .74 to .59 for the fifth item, they obviously mingled reported behaviors and assessments. Devotionalism correlated highly (.71) with another factor scale called *growth and striving*, which included such staples of devotionalism scales as frequency of Bible reading, reading religious literature, understanding the faith and the moral life, etc. Devotionalism also correlated highly (.71) with a *salience* factor that included common items among the three factors. In short, although separate factors were labeled, there is substantial overlap among three of them that describe devotional behaviors, their intentions, and their impacts. The study does not draw political consequences from devotionalism.

Political consequences are most thoroughly studied through factor analytic models of devotionalism by Welch and Leege (1988, 1991). Using a specialized data set of American Catholic parishioners, the authors addressed twenty-one items measuring the frequency of public and private religious practices known to Catholics. All were reports of *behavior*. Five distinct factors emerged including two that are done in *public* settings—*minimal traditional practices* (attending Mass, receiving communion) and *exclusively Catholic public devotions* (e.g., confession, communal penance, public rosary, stations of the cross, benediction, novenas). Three factors describe behaviors done in *noninstitutional* settings: religious media monitoring, faith sharing and evangelization, and evangelical-style devotionalism (saying grace, reading the Bible alone or studying it with friends, praying with family, sharing religious beliefs with others). Each had a coefficient *alpha* exceeding .70 and eigenvalue exceeding 1.0; extracted from principal factor analysis, each appears to summarize an analytically and conceptually distinct set of behaviors for Catholics.

Welch and Leege (1988) then set these measures of devotionalism into equations with four factor-based images of God, two factor-based measures describing situations when one feels close to God, and a measure of foundational worldviews ranging from religious *individualism* to religious *communitarianism* (see chapter 11 for elaboration). Multiple regression analyses linked these independent variables to dependent variables including political ideology, religion-based voting, sociopolitical attitudes, and policy positions, with controls for age, gender, education, income, race, region, and urban-rural locale. Significant relationships emerged on two of the devotionalism factors: (1) *evangelical-style devotionalism* with religious voting, capital punishment, school prayer, abortion, premarital cohabitation, and male breadwinner roles; and (2) *religious media monitoring* with school prayer, nuclear freeze, and busing. In particular, Welch and Leege found that the devotionalism measures were often stronger than such proven variables as religious imagery (Greeley 1984; Benson and Williams 1982) and foundational worldviews (Benson and Williams 1982; Leege 1989).

The evangelical-style devotionalism measure had many attractive qualities according to Welch and Leege. It seemed to answer the call of Guth et al. (1988) for a *behavioral* measure of evangelicalism, not rooted in a specific denominational affiliation or a set of religious beliefs. It could transcend rather different faith traditions and thus move beyond institutional prescriptions for an appropriate private devotional life.

The measure proved so attractive it appeared in a later study that traced anomalies in liberal and conservative issue positions among evangelical-style Catholics to dual reference groups (Welch and Leege 1991). The data confirmed test expectations so nicely that Welch and Leege argued strongly for attention to devotional style as a politically important variable alongside denominational affiliation, beliefs, associational involvement, etc. Their findings are all the more promising when one notes that significant relationships to issue positions and religious voting remain beyond controls for all of the standard demographic predictors, as well as church attendance, parish loyalty, and parish organizational involvement. Devotionalism, depending on its measurement, can be a uniquely important religious variable in explanations of politics.

It is worth noting that the most suggestive of these studies involve special-purpose samples of Lutherans or Catholics for a limited area of the country. Studies based on general population samples have yet to yield rich findings about devotionalism and politics. Nevertheless, Gallup surveys (see Gallup and Castelli 1987) show increasing activity on those behaviors that compose devotionalism measures, at the same time that the trend on frequency of public religious practices remains steady or goes downward. It is timely to subject the NES 1989 Pilot Study and other general population surveys to rigorous questions concerning devotionalism and politics.

The 1989 and 1990 NES Data on Devotionalism

In the 1989 Pilot Study, a battery of five items tapped the devotional life of NES respondents away from their religious institutional context. The items concern frequency of private prayer, monitoring religious news in print media, watching religious television programs, reading the Bible, and seeking to evangelize others. The item format offered eight response categories ranging from *daily* to *never*. It is important to note that all are reported *behaviors*, thus avoiding the problem of differential measurement error coming from behavior reports and attitude assessments mingled in the same summary scale.

Table 7.1 shows the mean frequency of devotionalism on each behavior, both across the sample as a whole and within each of the current American Christian traditions. The data were also run for non-traditional Protestants, Jews, and Orthodox, but the Ns are too small to report here.

Clearly, private prayer is a universal and frequently practiced devotional activity regardless of religious tradition. Nevertheless, frequent private prayer is more characteristic of evangelicals than of mainline Protestants. Jews (not shown) are much less likely to engage in private prayer frequently. Reading about religion is also common, as is reading the Bible on one's own. There are not great differences among the religious traditions on the former—probably because of its ready accessibility in public and religious presses—but Bible-reading practices differ considerably from evangelicals to mainline Protestants and Catholics. The average evangelical reads the Bible at least weekly, while the average mainline Protestant or Catholic reads it monthly or several times a year. Monitoring religious programs on television and evangelizing others are much less frequently practiced, being *hardly ever* done by the average Catholic and mainline Protestant and infrequently done even by the average evangelical.

The *F* scores and their high levels of significance attest that people from different religious traditions differ in their private devotional practices. It remains unclear whether such differences are the result of self-selection into a denomination or exposure to different norms regarding devotional practices espoused by each denomination.

From a measurement perspective, the items elicit substantial variance that appears consistent with common sense and other studies. The use of eight response categories is probably not warranted in the less-practiced items; what is the difference between *several times a year* and *hardly ever* in religious television viewing? On the other hand, because frequent prayer is so common—64 percent of the respondents report daily prayer—it may be important to distinguish between *daily* and *several times a day* and the type of prayer (table grace, meditation, prescribed prayer such as rosary, conversation with God, etc.); the 1988 NES prayer item shows that more than half of these same respondents identified as praying at least *once per day* in 1989 were actually praying *several times per day*. (Remember that 1989 was a panel sample of the 1988 NES respondents.)

Table 7.1

Frequency of Private Devotional Acts by Religious Tradition
(N = 406)

Devotional Act	Grand Mean*	S.D.	Religious Tradition, Mean			F
			Evan	Main	Cath	
Pray on your own	7.25	1.25	7.56	7.01	7.20	8.65***
Read about religion through magazines, books, or newspapers	4.90	2.32	5.35	4.55	4.73	2.72**
Read the Bible on your own	4.41	2.76	5.60	4.00	3.10	10.94***
Watch religious programs, other than services of local churches, on TV	2.68	2.18	3.62	2.16	1.93	9.78***
Convince others to accept your faith	2.18	2.48	3.12	1.44	1.47	8.61***
Devotionalism Scale	21.32	6.74	25.19	19.19	18.46	14.49**

Source: NES 1989 Pilot Study.

*The closer the score is to 8.0, the more frequently the devotional act is practiced.

**significant beyond the .01 level.

***significant beyond the .001 level.

The private devotionalism items yield a summated scale ranging from 8 (low) to 40 (high) with a mean of 21.32 and a coefficient *alpha* of .73. There are substantial overall differences among evangelical Protestants (mean = 25.19), mainline Protestants (mean = 19.19), and Roman Catholics (mean = 18.46) in private devotionalism. To some extent that is because two of the five items—frequent Bible reading and watching religious television—are characteristics associated with modern-day evangelicals and Protestants generally. The highly significant F score for the summated scale shows that there is some overlap between devotionalism and religious tradition.

As anticipated, the measure also shows overlap with our other summary measures of religiosity, but at the same time it shows a substantial amount of religiosity that is distinct. The Pearson r between the private devotionalism scale and the church involvement scale (see chapter 6) is .65; the salience index, i.e., religion as a guide (see chapter 7), is .57; and the cue-giving index (see chapter 12) is .20. The greatest overlap, as expected, comes on the measures of religious intensity and importance. It is interesting that private devotionalism correlates with a doctrinal item, biblical inerrancy, at .48. Thus, while there is considerable overlap, devotionalism is far from being a surrogate for fundamentalistic religious beliefs.

Of the individual items that compose the private devotionalism scale, prayer is the best predictor of church involvement and salience (.71 and .57), frequent Bible reading is the best predictor of religious tradition (.34) (it is especially an evangelical devotional act), and evangelizing is the best predictor of the cue-giving index (.30), or perhaps vice versa. Yet the private devotionalism scale as a whole is always within .01 or .02 points of these best individual predictors. The scale is clearly measuring common elements of religiosity at the same time that it is offering a unique dimension.

For our purpose, however, we want to assess what gains in knowledge about a person's *political behavior* and *attitudes* derive from knowledge about private devotionalism. On the surface of it, a lot. Using fifteen measures of political dependent variables (data not shown), highly significant relationships are found on eight variables (beyond .01 on three and well beyond .001 on five). The *beta* between private devotionalism and restrictive abortion policy is .34, support for moral traditionalism is .29, opposition to policies reflecting social change is .25, getting tougher with the Soviet Union is .19, opposition to guarantees of rights for homosexuals is .17, support for both the death penalty and school prayer is .11, and support for affirmative action policies in employment is .098. Significant bivariate relationships do not appear between private devotionalism and party identification, presidential candidate preference, turnout, opposition to civil rights leaders, self-classification of liberalism-conservatism, opposition to government assistance for the poor, or support for defense spending. In short, private devotionalism as a summary scale tells a great deal about conservative attitudes on social policy and communism. It does not appear to be important in the understanding of other political behaviors and attitudes. But such findings are based only on the simple regression models often found in the literature. They lack controls for demographic predictors and other dimensions of religiosity.

Yet to be answered, therefore, is this question: While private devotionalism may be one of many measures of religious intensity, does it offer anything *unique* in the understanding of these political behaviors and attitudes? The reader will recall that Lenski (1963) and then Kersten (1970) found devotionalism promising for understanding politics, yet offered few or no controls to assess the unique contribution. Welch and Leege (1988), on the other hand, controlled for many demographic and religious intensification dimensions of Catholics and still found substantial political understanding that derived from knowing a Catholic's *style* of private devotionalism.

The national survey data across all denominations look nearly as promising as Welch and Leege's (1988) Catholic parishioner data. We used multiple regression equations involving (1) five dimensions of religiosity (the private devotionalism scale; the religious tradition classification, with comparisons among Catholics, mainline Protestants, and evangelical Protestants, using no religious affiliation as the suppressed reference category; the church involvement index; the measure of biblical literalism; and the salience index), and (2) controls for six demographic variables (region [South and non-South], race [white and black], age, gender, education, and family income). The results across fifteen political dependent variables are presented in Table 7.2. The table is based on both the 1989 NES Pilot Study sample of 406 usable cases and the NES 1990 Election Study sample of 2,000 cases. The measure of devotionalism in 1989 is based on five items, but in 1990 it is truncated to two: frequency of prayer and Bible reading. The church involvement measure in 1990 was also truncated to frequency of church attendance since the range of variables built into the 1989 measure was not available on the 1990 instrument. Among the dependent variables, three are missing in 1990, and the 1989 general measure of government assistance to the poor is tapped by a specific 1990 measure of support for the poor through food stamps.

Religious and demographic variables are grouped separately in the table, and only significant predictor variables are noted. The F scores for twenty-six of the twenty-seven equations are significant beyond .001, with only government assistance to the poor in 1989 limited in significance to the .01 level. In short, the combination of demographic and religious predictor variables proved very useful.

As a group, the religion variables are quite powerful, with one or more showing significant relationships to political variables in all twenty-seven instances. The demographic variables are also powerful, with one or more showing significant relationships in all twenty-seven instances. The latter is to be expected since sociologists and political scientists have routinely used these demographic variables for predictive purposes. The former is perhaps a surprise in that analysts have often underplayed or ignored potential religious explanations of political outcomes. In the controlled design, unlike the simple relationships, such core political concerns as party identification, candidate choice, turnout, and political ideology are at least as responsive, and often more responsive, to measures of religiosity than they are to other social locational variables. A similar finding can be observed on issues ranging from the "moral agenda" to national defense and civil rights. Quite commonly, when one of the measures of religiosity is not the strongest predictor variable, race, another cultural trait, takes its place.

While devotionalism appears to be a slightly less important predictor of political outcomes than was suggested by simple regression models, it still makes statistically and substantively significant contributions to eight outcomes. It is the most important predictor of abortion positions in 1990. Devotionalism also has an independent impact on abortion attitude in 1989 stronger than any demographic variable, but less important than two other measures of religiosity. Devotionalism does better than any other religious or demographic predictor in accounting for moral traditionalism in the 1990 data set. Devotionalism is also found useful in understanding party identification, candidate choice, liberalism-conservatism, and attitudes toward affirmative action. All of these are matters central either to the understanding of American elections or to the peculiar kinds of issue agendas that have presented themselves to the voters in the past decade. Consistently those who score higher on private devotionalism take political positions that have been identified as conservative.

The relationships between devotional life and race are particularly noteworthy. In an earlier analysis we decided to omit race as a demographic predictor. When the devotional behaviors of both blacks and whites were mingled, party identification and attitudes on several issues, particularly affirmative action and the death penalty, were just the reverse. That is, highly devotional people favored affirmative action, opposed the death penalty, and were more likely to be Democrats. These are characteristics of blacks and reflect the pervasive devotionalism in the black religious community. Once racial distinctions are acknowledged, however, not only does the strength of devotionalism as an explanation diminish, but the direction of its impact changes. In short, models of religious effects that use measures of religious intensity such as devotionalism would be deceptively underspecified if they did not account for racial differences. A future direction for research might involve interaction terms between race and devotionalism; the differential impact of devotionalism by race would be magnified.

By contrasting simple and controlled regression designs, we can see that devotionalism is sometimes subsumed under another dimension of religiosity. For example, when controls are introduced, moral traditionalism can be seen as sometimes more responsive to religious salience and church involvement, while attitudes toward the Soviet Union are more a function of religious fundamentalism (biblical literalism) and education. Nevertheless, performance on many of the political outcomes reflects the unique contribution of private devotionalism. Furthermore, private devotionalism is often more useful in understanding the

Table 7.2

Religious and Demographic Predictions of Political Behaviors and Issue Positions
(multiple regression coefficients based on NES Pilot Study, 1989 N=406, 1990 N=2,000

Year	Party Identification (Positive is more Republican)	Presidential Choice (positive favors Bush)	Turnout (positive means voted)	Liberalism - Conservatism (positive more conservative)	Moral Traditionalism (positive more traditionalistic)	Abortion (positive limits availability)	Death Penalty (positive favors)
1989	Catholic -.168** Salience of Religion .095* Race (white) .272*** income .086*	Catholic -.146*** Biblical Liberalism .133*** Race (white) .266***	Catholic .124* Salience of Religion .092* Education .249*** Age .188*** Region (South) -.177** Income .103**	Biblical Literalism .140** Race (white) .108** Age .087*	Salience of Religion .193*** Church Involvement .158** Catholic -.140* Devotionalism .122 Age .150 Region (South) -.084*	Salience of Religion .242*** Biblical Literalism .216** Devotionalism .125* Mainline -.100* Income -.096** Education -.087*	Salience of Religion -.114** Race (white) .226*** Education -.152** Income .104** Gender (male) .090**
1990	Mainline .079** Devotionalism .063* Race .233*** Income -.116** Age .069** Gender (male) -.054* Education .052* .043	Mainline .119*** Devotionalism .103** Evangelical .076 Age .199*** Education .096*** Income .076*** Region (South) .044	Catholic .166*** Evangelical .114*** Mainline .079*** Church involvement .070** Age .292*** Education .236*** Income .112*** Region (South) .079***	Evangelical .142*** Biblical Literalism .103*** Devotionalism .079*** Mainline .071* Race (white) .119*** Gender (male) .067** Education -.055* Income .048*	Devotionalism .086*** Income .050*	Devotionalism .162*** Church Involvement .145*** Catholic .122*** Biblical Literalism .105** Salience of Religion .098* Evangelical .074* Education -.135*** Gender (male) .088*** Income .067*	Mainline .098*** Salience of Religion -.060* Race (white) .221*** Education -.108*** Gender (male) .077*** Income .068**

Year	Defense Spending (positive favors increase)	Cooperate with Russia (positive opposes)	Homosexual Rights (positive limits protections)	Social Policy (positive is restrictive)	School Prayer (positive Supports)	Government Assistance to Poor (positive opposes)	Civil Rights (positive is push too fast)	Affirmative Action (positive opposes)
1989	Biblical Literalism .183*** Evangelical .145* Race (white) .129*** Income .115** Gender (male) .099*	Biblical Literalism .205*** Education -.194*** Age .084* Income .083*	Biblical Literalism .172* Gender (male) .152*** Race (white) .135*** Education -.128* Region (south) .080*	Biblical Literalism .172*** Evangelical .166** Salience of Religion .127* Race (white) .158*** Gender (male) .127*** Education -.126**	Catholic .148** Salience of Religion .133** Mainline .155** Education -.135*** Region (south) .133**	Church Invovement -.117* Income .272*** Age .094*	Biblical Literalism .098* Race (white) .272*** Education -.119** Region (south) -.099** Gender (male) .099**	Race (white) .339***
1990	Evangelical .109*** Mainline .087*** Catholic .064* Education -.169*** Region (south) .107** Race (white) .085*** Income .057*	N/A	N/A	N/A	Biblical Literalism .150*** Evangelical .142*** Catholic .132** Mainline .096* Education -.051* Age .054*	Evangelical .089* Biblical Literalism .083** Mainline .069** Catholic .062* Race (white) .201*** Income .185*** Region (south) .082** Age .072***	Biblical Literalism .116*** Mainline .100*** Race (white) .211*** Education -.122** Income .065** Age .064** Region (south) .053*	Devotionlism .072* Biblical Literalism .051* Race (white) .325*** Income .122***

Source: NES 1989 Pilot Study, 1990 NES.

* significant beyond .05.

** significant beyond .01.

*** significant beyond .001.

voter than are standard demographic items. In short, its components belong on surveys of the national electorate.

Because the data exist on the 1989 Pilot Study, it is possible for us to test the consequences of making our earlier conceptual distinction between *acts* and *affects* and between *private* (i.e., noninstitutional) and *public* religious behaviors. Recall that many of the early studies confounded all four while we, in our chapter structure, have already separated public (chapter 6) from private (chapter 7). We performed an oblique factor analysis on a battery of items that included not only the five devotional behaviors but also salience and three church involvement variables: church membership, attendance, and involvement in parish organizations. A three-factor solution fit the data nicely. The first factor (percent of variance 39.1, eigenvalue 4.7) included prayer, Bible reading, and salience. The second factor (percent of variance 11.1, eigenvalue 1.3) included religious television and evangelization. The third (percent of variance 9.2, eigenvalue 1.1) included the church involvement acts and reading about religion in newspapers, magazines, etc.

The factors are quite comprehensible. The third involves reading about religion, simply because most denominations send periodicals to church members. The second factor has the common thread of evangelical religious tradition, a tradition served heavily by religious television and promulgating the norm of evangelizing. The first factor is clearly the strongest, incorporating the acts of prayer and Bible reading with the affects associated with salience. Many of the early studies by sociologists of religion simply did not distinguish between the two, and, indeed, King and Hunt's (1972) factorial models found the strongest relationships among devotional acts and salience affects.

Since the first factor involves both elements of private devotionalism and salience, we removed both of those scales from the controlled models that helped explain the fifteen political behaviors and attitudes. The results (not shown) are considerably less promising than before. This mixture of devotional acts and affects is statistically and substantively significant only in the explanation of party identification (.16); curiously, income is the nearest other important variable in party identification at .02. Thus, those who pray a lot, read the Bible a lot, seek guidance from their religion, and feel religion is important in their daily lives are more likely to identify as Republicans. It is important to note that the relationship transcends religious traditions and greatly exceeds any of the demographic variables. Neither of the two policy concerns—death penalty and abortion—is explained by this combined act–affect measure of devotionalism. For the most part, however, the same relationships found in the earlier controlled models continue, and, in many instances, the other measures of religiosity are enhanced as predictors. For example, in the new models, biblical literalism jumps from .16 to .50 in the explanation of opposition to rights for homosexuals, and from .20 to .50 in opposition to policies that reflect social change.

Methodologically, how should the analyst configure the data? Our preference remains for retaining the distinction between *acts* and *affects*, as in the earlier models. Although private devotionalism is a somewhat unique religious dimension, when measured as a set of acts it yielded more understanding of politics than when measured as a combination of both. At the same time, whatever element is common between a belief about the literalism of the Bible and private devotionalism, configured as behaviors, is freed when *acts* and *affects* are combined; biblical literalism becomes an exceedingly powerful explanation in current American politics. Finally, it should be noted that in the factor analysis, *reading about religion*, from factor 3, loaded .46 on factor 1 and *evangelizing*, from factor 2, also loaded .34 on factor 1. Thus, all five of the original NES devotional items continue to have a lot in common, suggesting that the simple summated scale of devotionalism has more desirable properties than the factor scales.

Even when the five items of 1989 are cut back to two private acts in 1990—prayer and Bible reading—private devotionalism remains an independently important predictor of party identification, candidate choice, political ideology, moral traditionalism, and position on issues such as abortion and affirmative action. Thus both the time-honored core of explanations of American political behavior and the positions that voters take on current issues can be uniquely understood through measures of private devotional life.

Discussion

Early studies of devotionalism were never certain where to draw the line between ritualistic associational acts, private devotional acts, and feelings about such acts. In this chapter, we have opted to keep the three distinct as measures of religiosity; in the next chapter, we will recognize the conceptual and empirical overlap among them.

Although earlier studies argued for the utility of devotionalism as a form of religiosity with political consequences, tightly controlled models find it a more important predictor than many standard demographic items but not so strong as other dimensions of religiosity in influencing certain political outcomes. What is it about private devotional acts that may enhance or diminish their political relevance?

To answer this question, we point to at least six functions, any of which may be met through private devotionalism: (1) responding to spiritual norms advocated by church, family, or peers about the appropriate Christian private life; (2) drawing closer to other Christians in base communities centered on the Scriptures and prayers; (3) growing in spirituality and sense of personal righteousness; (4) finding guidance for vexing personal decisions; (5) drawing closer to God, with the attendant confidence and security that comes from perceptions of frequent communication with God; and (6) learning more about the will of God both for one's personal life and the appropriate direction for civic history. It seems to us that the first four functions and perhaps the fifth are either primarily inward-turning or assume such differences between the spiritual life and civic life, valuing the former more highly, that one should not expect political consequences from such devotional acts. These functions are nurtured by all five of the acts measured on the NES 1989 Pilot Study but are especially common in the three most frequently performed—private prayer, Bible reading, and reading about one's religion—and perhaps in the fifth, evangelizing.

Given the content of religious television other than services of local churches, on the other hand, the sixth function is quite likely to be met through this devotional act. It is no surprise, for example, that perceptions of political cue giving by religious leaders were more closely associated with this private devotional item than anything except prayer and evangelization; steadfast prayer, evangelization, and political transformation are the dominant messages of religious television. Yet a kind of personal empowerment deriving from the fifth function could also readily be transferred to politics. Chapter 6 noted that those scoring higher on devotionalism also scored higher on electioneering, a form perhaps of political evangelizing. (The impact of religious television is discussed fully in chapter 13.)

In this respect it is understandable that, in the tightly controlled models, high scores on private devotionalism are now among the best religious and demographic predictors of Republican party identification, especially for whites. The well-to-do and mainline Protestants have traditionally been at the core of the Republican party. But besides becoming a white party through the 1980s, Republicans have attracted evangelical Protestants and more of the religiously devotional whites. In recent years Republican candidates and platforms have held symbols of protest and hope in front of the very people who feel compelled by an agenda of moral traditionalism to pray, evangelize, and transform. At the same time, their policy positions are sometimes better conveyed through other dimensions of religiosity, particularly a beliefs item, Biblical literalism.

As the correlational data and the factor analysis show, prayer and Bible reading are often companions of the religious life. A recent analysis of prayer conducted by Paloma and Gallup (1991) shows that those who have more frequent, intense, and personal prayer experiences are more likely than others to feel that their religion is relevant to their politics and that it is appropriate for their churches to be involved in politics. The finding holds for evangelicals and non-evangelicals and is controlled for some other measures of religiosity. It is not uncommon for them to pray in support of a candidate or an issue, and to vote for the candidate who shares their moral views. Paloma and Gallup argue, "One of the fruits of prayer is a heightened political awareness that lessens the separation between the private religious side and the public political side of life" (78). Seeing the two as a whole cloth, people who pray come to politics with the empowering spiritual energy they derive from devotional activity. Our analysis of the NES data shows that devotionalism cuts differently for devout blacks and devout whites. Ironically, the same "talks with God" often push blacks and whites in opposite directions on parties, candidates, and issues of special relevance to blacks, while maintaining a common core of moral traditionalism. Regardless, the devotional life and politics are partners.

Scholars using general population samples such as the National Election Studies, the General Social Surveys, and Gallup data would be well advised to continue attention to private devotionalism. But they should not pursue this dimension of religiosity at the expense of others. They should not use it in simple correlation–regression models without controls for other dimensions of religiosity or demographic characteristics, particularly race. Finally, they should be aware that how they configure devotionalism will have consequences for understanding American politics.

References

Benson, Peter L., and Williams, Dorothy L. 1982. *Religion on Capitol Hill: Myths and Realities.* New York: Harper and Row.

D'Antonio, William V.; Davidson, James D.; Hoge, Dean R.; and Wallace, Ruth A. 1989. *American Catholic Laity in a Changing Church.* Kansas City, MO: Sheed and Ward.

Fukuyama, Yoshio. 1961. "The Major Dimensions of Church Membership." *Review of Religious Research* 2:154–61.

Gallup, George, Jr., and Castelli, Jim. 1987. *The American Catholic People.* New York: Doubleday.

Gerth, Hans H., and Mills, C. Wright, eds. 1946. *From Max Weber: Essays in Sociology.* New York: Oxford University Press.

Glock, Charles Y., and Stark, Rodney. 1965. *Religion and Society in Tension.* Chicago: Rand McNally.

Greeley, Andrew M. 1984. "Religious Imagery as a Predictor Variable in the General Social Survey." Paper presented at the annual meeting of the Society for the Scientific Study of Religion, Chicago.

Guth, James L.; Jelen, Ted G.; Kellstedt, Lyman A.; Smidt, Corwin E.; and Wald, Kenneth D. 1988. "The Politics of Religion in America: Issues for Investigation." *American Politics Quarterly* 16:357–97.

Hertzke, Allen D. 1988. *Representing God in Washington: The Role of Religious Lobbies in the American Polity.* Knoxville: University of Tennessee Press.

Kersten, Lawrence L. 1970. *The Lutheran Ethic: The Impact of Religion on Laymen and Clergy.* Detroit: Wayne State University Press.

King, Morton B., and Hunt, Richard A. 1972. *Measuring Religious Dimensions: Studies in Congregational Involvement.* Dallas: Southern Methodist University Press.

Leege, David C. 1989. "Toward a Mental Measure of Religiosity in Research on Religion and Politics." In *Religion and American Political Behavior,* ed. Ted G. Jelen, 45–64. New York: Praeger.

Lenski, Gerhard. 1963. *The Religious Factor: A Sociological Study of Religion's Impact on Politics, Economics, and Family Life.* Garden City, NY: Doubleday-Anchor.

Paloma, Margaret M., and Gallup, George H. Jr. 1991. *Varieties of Prayer: A Survey Report.* Philadelphia: Trinity Press International.

Stark, Rodney, and Glock, Charles Y. 1968. *American Piety: The Nature of Religious*

Commitment. Berkeley: University of California Press.

Welch, Michael R., and Leege, David C. 1988. "Religious Predictors of Catholic Parishioners' Sociopolitical Attitudes: Devotional Style, Closeness to God, Imagery, and Agentic-Communal Religious Identity." *Journal for the Scientific Study of Religion* 27:536–52.

――――. 1991. "Dual Reference Groups and Political Orientations: An Examination of Evangelically Oriented Catholics." *American Journal of Political Science* 35:28–56.

Chapter 8

Salience: The Core Concept?

James L. Guth and John C. Green

Social scientists have long suspected that individual religiosity influences political attitudes and behavior. And yet, the connection between religious faith and political consequence has proven elusive (Wuthnow 1973). Part of the problem lies in specifying which aspects of religion should have impact. As the chapters in this volume make clear, the many dimensions of religion influence political attitudes and behaviors in different ways, leaving analysts to sort out the effects. In undertaking this task, scholars have tested measures for concepts such as Christian orthodoxy, religious participation, devotionalism, biblical literalism, denominationalism, and religious tradition.

In view of these theoretical labors, it is ironic that less attention has been given to a core concept, *religious salience*—the importance of religion to the individual. Indeed, within the Judeo-Christian world, salience is not just a condition but a religious duty: "Love the Lord your God with all your heart and soul and with all your strength and with all your mind" (Leviticus 19:18 NIV). Those who follow this prescription, one might assume, should differ politically from those to whom faith is less central or not important at all. And yet, despite a good many theoretical reasons for investigating religious salience, much of the research has been incidental and inconclusive. Some studies find salience to have a considerable impact on attitude and behavior, while others discover only modest effects (cf. Hoge and de Zulueta 1985).

In this chapter, we survey the literature on religious salience and investigate the National Election Studies (NES) salience measure, which we will call the *guidance scale*. We argue that the inconclusiveness of research on salience has a number of sources: the diverging conceptions used by scholars; the different roles played by the concept in competing theories of religion and politics; diverse measurement strategies; and, finally, the ineffectiveness of some items in tapping the basic concept. After reviewing the social, religious, and political correlates of the NES guidance scale, we suggest an alternative measure, an index composed of the guidance scale, a devotionalism scale, and church attendance, which we will label the *religiosity index*. Properly conceptualized and measured, the *importance of religion* is a powerful tool for understanding the role of faith in political life.

Theoretical Perspectives

As Roof and Perkins (1975, 111) observed years ago, salience measures were included in surveys long before their meaning was fully explored. As a result, scholars often mean rather different things by *salience*, utilize the concept in competing theoretical roles, and expect it to exhibit several different kinds of political influences.

First, scholars use the concept in two very distinct ways. *Salience* usually refers to the importance that religion has in a person's life or, sometimes, the strength of religious commitment; this might be called *general salience*. At other times, *salience* means the perceived relevance of faith to an individual's specific attitudes or decisions, or what might be called *religious relevance*. Some analysts argue that only the first should be included within the concept of salience (Hoge and de Zulueta 1985), while others contend that the influence of religion is most likely when individuals perceive, or are reminded of, its relevance to specific attitudes or decisions (Lea and Hunsberger 1990).

This distinction is of more than passing interest. As a recent survey found, many Americans claim that religion is very important but do not see its relevance to political belief or behavior (Patterson and Kim 1991). A more important issue, then, is precisely *how* religion comes to be a factor in making political choices. (After all, religion might be influential without an individual being conscious of that fact.) In any case, the relationship between the two concepts is an empirical one. If measures for both general salience and religious relevance are available, their differing impacts can be assessed. For example, MacIver (1989) uses a general salience measure, asking, "To what extent is God important in your life?" and a religious relevance query, "Do your religious convictions play a role in your political preferences?" She finds that Europeans who score high on the second question are more likely to line up on the ideological right than are equally devout individuals who do not perceive religion's relevance. Wilcox (1992) has reported comparable findings for American evangelicals. Lamentably, the National Election Studies have never included a religious relevance item. Thus, we will focus on general salience and note that religious relevance is an important area for future research.

Even scholars who adopt a *general salience* definition use the concept in two different ways: (1) as an independent variable, directly related to political measures, or (2) as a variable that conditions relationships between another facet of religion and political variables, i.e., as a control. This choice frequently turns on the theorist's assumptions about the most critical dimension of religion.

For many social scientists, the salience of religion is itself at the center of the drama. Secularization theorists, for example, may regard general salience as the best summary assessment of adherence to traditional religious worldviews and institutions, a central variable in their theory. Thus, studies of European politics have found that general salience itself is a powerful determinant of party alignments, with secularists on the left and the devout on the right (Berger 1982). Likewise, analysts who argue that high religiosity diverts citizens from "this-worldly" activity also find such measures a convenient predictor. Marsh and Kaase (1979, 118) have speculated, for example, that "the more important dimension" in suppressing unconventional political activism "is not sectarian affiliation but the extent of a respondent's subjective sense of religiosity." In the same vein, Inglehart's (1990, 177–211) massive longitudinal study of value change in Western democracies contended that the importance of God to an individual was the best indicator of the traditionalist perspectives under assault from "postmaterial" values. What all these theories have in common is an assumption that strength of attachment to religious beliefs and traditions (rather than their specific content) is vital to understanding some aspect of modern political life, whether party affiliation, propensity to unconventional activism, or emerging social attitudes.

On the other hand, many theorists, especially those in the Glock–Stark tradition, regard the specific dimensions of religiosity—beliefs, denominations, or behaviors—as the critical variables. If general salience appears at all, it usually plays a different role: only those who take religion very seriously are influenced by the normative standards of a religious group, whether embodied in denominational tradition, theological beliefs, or religious identity (cf. Wimberly 1989). Thus, general salience itself has no direct influence but interacts with other religious dimensions to produce political beliefs, attitudes, or behaviors.

This approach is quite attractive to American political analysts. Given Americans' extraordinary religiosity, the religious-secular divide typical of Europe has seldom been a factor and other dimensions of religion have been taken more seriously. If, as ethnocultural historians argue, American voters are divided by religious tradition, the distinctive political traits of each tradition should be enhanced by high general salience. There is a good bit of evidence supporting this approach. For example, Kellstedt, Smidt, and Kellstedt (1991) found that in 1988 more religious evangelical and mainline Protestants were more closely tied to the historically Protestant Republican party than were their less devout co-religionists. Even current applications of denominational social teachings may be best acquired by those for whom religion is very important. Kenski and Lockwood (1988) have argued, for example, that the Catholic bishops' peace pastoral changed attitudes among Catholics for whom faith was most salient.

For other scholars, theology is more important than denominational ties. Symbolic interactionists argue that links between *creedal dimensions* of religion and political variables are a function of general salience (Gibbs, Miller, and Wood 1973). Bahr, Bartel, and Chadwick (1971) found that for laity, general salience mediated between Christian orthodoxy and view of the social and political role of the church. Only among the most religious members was orthodoxy correlated with opposition to social and political action by churches. (On the other hand, Bahr, Bartel, and Chadwick [1971] found no direct relationship between general salience and political views.) The impact of other theological beliefs and identifications, such as *fundamentalism*, may be enhanced by greater religiosity as well (cf. Grasmick, Morgan, and Kennedy 1992; Hertel and Hughes 1987). Of course, general salience may behave both as a direct influence under some circumstances and as a conditioning variable under others (see chapter 3).

A final ambiguity involves the type of issues upon which general salience might operate, whether directly or interactively. Here there is somewhat more agreement among scholars. General salience should influence attitudes that are directly tied to religious values and institutions. This means, usually, matters of personal and social morality, sexuality, "family" issues, or the church's role in society. Others have argued that foreign policy and issues of war and peace are also subject to religious interpretation by the more religious, alone or in combination with distinct theological perspectives (Kierulff 1991). The more distant issues are from the central tenets of faith, however, the less impact general salience will have in either direct or interactive ways.

The impact of general salience may also depend on the sample. As Gorsuch (1984) argues, the broader the sample the more that general measures, such as salience, will show predictive power; as the sample is restricted to the religious (as is frequently the case), general salience will be less useful than more nuanced religious measures (but see Rothenberg and Newport 1984). Hoge and de Zulueta (1985) imply that general salience is also subject to attitude constraint: correlations with political variables are strongest in elite rather than mass samples. This insight is supported by Guth and Green (1990), who have shown that among political activists, general salience is not only the best religious predictor of political attitudes but also has the highest loading on a general religiosity dimension, ahead of church attendance, Christian orthodoxy, and commitment to a strict moral code (but for an argument that general salience is *not* a good predictor among one elite, see Benson and Williams 1982, 159–160).

Measures of Salience

Beyond these ambiguities in meaning and use, general salience has been plagued by haphazard development of indicators. The concept has been tapped by a bewildering number of survey items. Indeed, in operational terms, salience might best be considered a family of measures. Nevertheless, two broad approaches predominate. The first involves straightforward queries about the importance of religion (or God) in the respondent's life (e.g., Gorsuch and McFarland 1972; Gallup 1982; Hadaway, Elifson, and Petersen 1984; Inglehart 1990) or, alternatively, a battery of items tapping the subjective importance of religion, which are then combined into a scale (Gibbs, Miller, and Wood 1973; Roof and Perkins 1975; Grasmick, Morgan, and Kennedy 1992). Another strategy uses behavioral indicators, such as church attendance (Kellstedt and Smidt 1991), ritual involvement, or, often, devotional activities (Kauffman 1989). The two approaches are sometimes combined, using both attitudinal and behavioral items, a strategy encouraged by the invariably high correlations among general salience, church attendance, and private devotionalism. For example, King and Hunt (1972) hedge their operational bets, producing two highly correlated subscales, *salience: behavior* and *salience: cognition.*

Thus, the number of items used is extensive. And there has been little analysis of competing strategies, such as that applied to biblical literalism or born-again items (see chapters 9 and 10). Whether multiple indicators might be better than single items (Gorsuch and McFarland 1972) is also a moot point: at best, only one such measure is available on national surveys utilized by political scientists. And, complicating matters further, the National Election Studies use none of the more common questions but have a unique two-item approach from which a general salience measure can be constructed. The respondent is first asked, "Do you consider religion to be an important part of your life or not?" To those who reply, *yes,* a follow-up question is asked: "Would you say your religion provides some guidance in your day-to-day living, quite a bit of guidance, or a great deal of guidance in your day-to-day life?" The resulting four-point scale can then be used as a general salience measure (and we will call it the *guidance scale* for obvious reasons). Interestingly enough, the General Social Surveys have no general salience measure at all, opting instead for an item assessing the strength of denominational preference.

As constructed, the NES guidance scale has a smaller range than many other general salience measures (or many other NES variables that array options along five- or seven-point scales). In operation, the guidance scale concentrates a plurality of respondents in the most religious category, limiting variation somewhat. In 1990, for example, 37 percent said religion provided *a great deal of guidance,* followed by 22 percent saying *quite a bit,* 21 percent reporting *some,* and 21 percent claiming that religion was not important to them. Although it is hazardous to make observations across sample and question types, measures with more categories usually produce stronger effects. On the other hand, having more choices does not mean respondents will take them: 56 percent in a 1982 poll chose point 1 on a ten-point scale on the importance of doing God's will (Gallup 1982).

Inspection of dozens of cross-tabulations between the NES guidance scale and other variables shows that it "works" best at the end points: those to whom religion provides a great deal of guidance and those to whom it is not important are the most distinct and consistent politically. This finding is not surprising. In a sense, one group exhibits high religious salience, the other *high salience of irreligion* (cf. Gibbs, Miller, and Wood 1973, 47–48). The two "inside" categories are less predictable. This result may well be an artifact of the scale's two-step construction or the greater psychological proximity of *some* and *quite a bit*. A social desirability factor could be at work here as well: many Americans find some attachment to religion desirable, even if it plays only a modest role in their lives. Hence, only those who say that religion provides *a great deal of guidance* in day-to-day living can be regarded as highly religious.

Demographic, Religious, and Political Correlates of General Salience

In this chapter, we will primarily utilize the 1990 National Election Study, with its large sample ($N = 2,000$), but we will make some reference to the 1989 Pilot Study (usable $N = 389$), which includes the salience items asked of the respondents in 1988.

Our first task concerns the social location of general salience. Table 8.1 reports the relationships between demographic variables and the guidance scale. There are few surprises in the monotonic relationships shown here. Religion is (uniformly) more important for older people, residents of the South and Midwest, women, African Americans, Hispanics, and those with less formal education and lower income. Although we cannot settle the secularization debate here, evidence certainly suggests some attrition of religiosity among the more "modern" social groups: the well-educated, prosperous residents of the industrial and postindustrial regions of the United States. Family situation is also correlated modestly with the guidance scale: those married or widowed are somewhat more religious than the divorced, who in turn attach more importance to religion than those never married. Surprisingly, size of community and occupation have no consistent impact (data not shown).

The guidance scale follows predictable demographic lines and, if some scholars are correct, provides a good measure of the general importace of religion. But to understand this phenomenon, we must relate it to other measures. Table 8.2 (see page 165) presents data on the religious location of general salience. First, the guidance scale varies by religious tradition (chapter 3). Evangelical Protestants say religion is important more often than do Catholics, who in turn have higher scores than mainline Protestants, followed by Jews and, predictably, those with no denominational preference. Within each religious tradition, ethnic groups vary: Hispanic and African-American evangelicals and Catholics attach more importance to religion than whites, while African-American, but not Hispanic, mainline Protestants show greater attachment than their white counterparts.

The correlations with other religious variables are as expected. The guidance scale correlates most strongly across the sample with frequency of private prayer, church attendance, and Bible reading, and somewhat less strongly with biblical literalism and born-again status. (See chapter 7 for the comparable 1989 data.) The relationships are strongest among evangelical Protestants but are still robust for mainline Protestants and Roman Catholics. Although evangelicals see religion as most important, the guidance scale clearly taps more than just reli-

Table 8.1

NES Guidance Scale by Demographic Groups

	Mean	S.D.	(N)
NATION	2.732	1.158	(1974)
REGION			
West	2.410	1.209	(383)
East	2.429	1.135	(436)
Midwest	2.836	1.097	(513)
South	3.045	1.089	(642)
ETHNICITY			
White	2.608	1.161	(1488)
Hispanic	2.994	1.069	(175)
Black	3.242	1.017	(269)
AGE			
18-29	2.391	1.149	(460)
30-39	2.566	1.173	(461)
40-49	2.761	1.689	(334)
50-59	2.939	1.106	(212)
60-69	3.083	1.047	(242)
70+	3.089	1.046	(265)
GENDER			
Male	2.530	1.201	(894)
Female	2.891	1.093	(1080)
EDUCATION			
Grade 8 or less	3.171	1.007	(187)
Some High School	2.866	1.138	(276)
High School Grad	2.714	1.151	(1006)
Some College +	2.535	1.184	(501)
INCOME			
To $11,000	2.877	1.115	(755)
$11,000 To $20,000	2.728	1.147	(393)
$21,000 To $30,000	2.649	1.166	(305)
Over $30,000	2.445	1.215	(366)

Source: 1990 National Election Study.
a great deal of guidance = 4
religion not important = 1

gious tradition. Among white Protestants, the measure is also modestly associated with theological self-identification: *evangelical, fundamentalist*, or *pentecostal* respondents regard religion as more important than colleagues from the
same religious tradition who do not adopt these labels (data not shown).

The high correlations with devotionalism (an index of Bible reading and
prayer; see chapter 7) and church attendance underscores the conceptual difficulty of separating these three measures. And this universal finding helps explain
why social scientists have often regarded devotionalism and church attendance
as alternative measures of the importance of religion. Indeed, factor analysis of
these variables produces a single factor accounting for 75 percent of the variance, with the guidance scale (.87) and devotionalism (.88) having almost identical loadings, with church attendance (.83) only slightly lower.

Thus, although the guidance scale, church attendance, and devotionalism may
have distinctive political effects, as noted in chapter 7, they are mostly tapping a
common dimension and, indeed, may be interpreted as multiple measures—one
cognitive and two behavioral—of general salience. As Hadaway, Elifson, and
Petersen (1984, 118) note, these three variables, but especially general salience
and prayer, "measure the acceptance or non-acceptance of a religious value
system. Thus, they imply a personal commitment by the believer." Or, as Young
(1992, 80) has commented recently, "Devotionalism is a clear indicator of the
salience of religion in daily life. Regular prayer, Bible reading, and attendance at
worship services indicate more than a situational commitment to religion."

Of the three variables, church attendance is perhaps least useful as part of an
extended measure of general salience. When the guidance scale is arrayed
against church attendance, we find, as expected, that people who say religion is
of little or no importance seldom attend church, read the Bible, or pray. But there
are also many Americans who seldom attend church, but say religion is of great
importance (cf. Bahr, Bartel, and Chadwick 1971; Gallup 1978). Initially, the
analyst might suspect social desirability effects favoring religion, or *indiscrimin-
ant proreligiousness*, but this is not usually the case. Here devotional items
confirm the validity of the guidance scale. Most respondents who say that religion is of great importance—but never attend church—also report high levels of
prayer and Bible reading. Thus, one might argue, devotionalism and the guidance scale both tap the importance of religion—cognitive or behavioral—better
than church attendance, which is subject to constraints of age, mobility, location,
and other nonreligious influences.

How does the guidance scale influence political attitudes? Following Carmines and Stimson (1989), we might argue that the connection between religiosity and a political choice is *easy* on some issues and *hard* on others. The
influence of religious commitments and beliefs is usually strongest on personal
morality and, of course, related social and political issues, such as abortion and
pornography. Civil religion theorists might also argue that general social values
such as patriotism should be held most strongly by those for whom religion is

Table 8.2

NES Guidance Scale and Other Religious Measures

	Means	S.D.	(N)
RELIGIOUS TRADITION			
All Evangelicals	3.293	.931	(656)
Black Evangelicals	3.448	.798	(192)
Hispanic Evangelicals	3.583	.692	(36)
White Evangelicals	3.187	1.001	(411)
All Mainline	2.554	1.103	(484)
Black Mainline	3.296	.912	(27)
Hispanic Mainline	2.429	1.089	(14)
White Mainline	2.507	1.100	(430)
All Catholics	2.709	1.056	(488)
Black Catholics	2.957	1.186	(23)
Hispanic Catholics	2.925	1.034	(107)
White Catholics	2.649	1.057	(350)
Jewish	2.167	1.056	(36)
None	1.685	1.069	(260)

CORRELATIONS OF SALIENCE
WITH OTHER RELIGIOUS MEASURES
(Whites Only)

	Sample	Evangelical	Mainline	Catholic
Prayer	.70**	.67**	.63**	.58**
Church Attendance	.58**	.56**	.48**	.53**
Bible Reading	.56**	.59**	.50**	.41**
Biblical Literalism	.45**	.43**	.31**	.32**
Born Again	.40**	.44**	.32**	.21**

Source: 1990 National Election Study.

salient; similarly, opposition to "godless communism" might influence views concerning the former Soviet Union, defense policy, and nationalism. Expectations concerning other domestic policies are less clear. In elite samples, direct effects of general salience might extend even to *hard* economic and social welfare issues, enhancing conservative responses. But in the mass public, such influences might be interactive, limited to activating or enhancing normative political directions derived from religious traditions or theological beliefs. Thus, perhaps, very religious Catholics should be stronger Democrats or more in favor of tuition aid to parochial schools, while their Protestant counterparts should exhibit the opposite viewpoints.

Table 8.3 reports correlations between the guidance measure and political attitudes, with analysis restricted to white adherents of the four major religious traditions: evangelical Protestants, mainline Protestants, Catholics, and those who identify with no religious tradition or denominations (Nones). The first column reports the *eta* between the guidance scale and a dependent variable. The rest of the table reports *betas* from a multiple classification analysis (MCA) with the guidance scale, religious tradition (as per above), church attendance, and devotionalism entered, along with controls for age, gender, income, and education. This analysis gives us an idea of how salience relates to political variables, alone and in competition with other religious measures with which it is highly correlated.

First, we note that the guidance scale, contrary to some early studies, correlates respectably with quite a few political variables. The pattern is not surprising: it is a good predictor on social issues, such as moral traditionalism, abortion, school prayer, women's roles, civil rights, warmth toward unpopular groups including homosexuals and feminists, and choice of social issues as the "most important problem facing the country." And, with one exception, those for whom religion is most important take more conservative positions. Only on the death penalty were the highly religious slightly more likely to take a liberal stance. All these relationships survive substantively undiminished—or even enhanced—under the demographic controls for age, gender, education, and income (data not shown).

The guidance scale also influences attitudes on nationalism and national defense. Even with the cold war's denouement, very religious whites were more anticommunist and prodefense than the less devout. They claimed a deeper pride in the country and thought that the United States must maintain international preeminence. They were also most offended by flag burning and in favor of amending the Constitution to prevent such protests.

Although the NES has few pure New Deal issues, the guidance scale clearly has less impact on economics. On spending for most social programs, the very religious are often modestly more conservative, especially when priorities touch on social sensitivities. They favor less AIDS and antidrug spending and fewer dollars for school and child care programs than the least religious, but this

Table 8.3

NES Guidance Scale and Political Attitudes
(whites only, major traditions, N = 1,419)

	Bivariate (eta)	MCA ANALYSIS			
		Salience	Devote	Trad	Attend
SOCIAL ISSUES		(with demographic controls)			
Moral Traditionalism	.40**	.10	.30**	.13**	.14*
Abortion Policy	.38**	.14*	.19**	.17**	.17**
Oppose Gays++	.28**	.15	.13	.32**	.12
School Prayer	.24**	.08	.18*	.13*	.13
Women's Role	.24**	.07	.18	.13	.07
Civil Rights Index	.21**	.15**	.09	.07	.08
Social Issue Agenda	.18**	.08	.19**	.08	.08
Cool to Feminists++	.17*	.04	.08	.17	.22*
Death Penalty	-.08*	.10	.10	.11*	.04
NATIONALISM					
Patriotism++	.33**	.20*	.13	.13	.12
Anti-Communist++	.30**	.12	.17	.22**	.11
Defense Attitude++	.25**	.13	.19	.12	.0
Flag Burning	.23**	.10*	.09	.10*	.04
Detente with USSR++	.20*	.20*	.11	.15	.15
DOMESTIC ISSUES					
Spending on AIDS	.14**	.05	.15**	.02	.06
Social Security	-.14**	.15**	.09	.11	.15**
School Spending	.11**	.08	.05	.02	.03
Anti-Drug Spending	.10*	.04	-.09	.13*	.10
Child Care	.09*	.05	.06	.07	.11
Environmental Policy	.07	.08	.10	.10*	.15
Warm to Unions++	.06	.08	.11	.09*	.09
USE PEACE DIVIDEND TO:					
Cut the Deficit	.09*	-.11*	.08	.09*	.14*
Cut Taxes	.08*	.10*	.06	.08*	.06
Expand Social Prog	.08*	.07	.10	.04	.10
PARTISAN/IDEOLOGY					
Ideology	.20**	.09*	.12	.18**	.11
Bush Vote 1988	.19**	.07	.14	.18*	.23**
Warm to GOP Figures	.18**	.08	.11	.11	.25**
Difference GOP/Dems	.14	.14	.12	.19*	.33**
Partisan Strength	.10*	.05	.12	.12*	.10*
Cool to Dems	.06	.11	.12	.09	.08
Party ID	.05	.04	.12*	.13**	.09

Source: 1990 NES and 1989 NES Pilot Study.

* P < .05.

** P < .001.

Positive correlations signify conservative direction.
++Item from 1989 NES Pilot Study, N = 389.

relationship is often inconsistent across the guidance scale, with the *most religious* sometimes moving in a different direction from the *quite religious* category. On other issues, the correlations are sometimes in the expected (conservative) direction but do not reach statistical significance: coolness toward labor unions, less support for environmentalism, and opposition to greater spending on food stamps. The guidance scale is also positively associated with a desire to use the peace dividend from the cold war's end to reduce the deficit rather than to cut taxes or to increase spending for domestic social programs.

The influence of the guidance scale on partisanship and general ideological identifications is mixed. The guidance scale is only modestly related to partisan identification but is a better predictor of other electoral and partisan measures: self-identified ideology, vote for George Bush in 1988, high thermometer ratings toward prominent Republican figures in both 1988 and 1990, low ratings of leading Democrats, and larger differences between Republican and Democratic ratings. The measure also correlates with strength of partisanship. Other partisan measures, such as 1988 ratings of President Ronald Reagan, exhibit very similar patterns (data not shown). The guidance scale is also strongly associated with other variables, including political interest, information acquisition, and concern for the direction of American society (data not shown, but see chapters 3, 6, and 7).

Multivariate analysis provides some additional insight. The MCA reported here and the multiple regressions shown in chapter 7 indicate that the guidance scale is seldom the best predictor of political attitudes, but few other generalizations can be offered. Indeed, the entire pattern is clear only on partisan items, where religious tradition in conjunction with church attendance are the surest guides: very religious evangelical and mainline Protestants deviate to the GOP side, while their counterparts among Catholics and those who identify with no religious denomination tend toward the Democratic. Elsewhere, there is no evident pattern, although devotionalism survives the MCA with larger and more significant *beta*s than the guidance scale or church attendance. Note, however, that all three variables retain some influence on many questions. Indeed, on several issues the individual coefficients are not significant, but the variables in combination are.

This finding returns us to the earlier discussion of the relationship among general salience, devotionalism, and church attendance. Although the three are not so strongly intercorrelated as to create severe multicollinearity problems, further analysis shows, as expected, considerable fluctuations in coefficients when any of the three are omitted from the MCA. To us this finding suggests that the best measure of the importance of religion would be an index utilizing all three items. For illustrative purposes, we constructed a *religiosity index* using standardized scores for the guidance scale, church attendance, and devotional behavior (prayer and Bible reading). The index is highly reliable, with an *alpha* coefficient of .84. (A comparable index was computed for the 1989 Pilot Study.) Although the separate use of general salience, church attendance, and devotionalism measures may be valuable for some purposes, we suspect that the index combining them really taps what most analysts are getting at when they speak of *importance of religion* or *religiosity.*

For MCA analysis, we collapsed the religiosity index into deciles. Inspection of mean scores for political variables shows that the index is stable, exhibiting fewer intransitivities than the component variables. Table 8.4 replicates Table 8.3, using the religiosity index, religious tradition, and biblical literalism (as a rough measure of theological conservatism). The religiosity index has strong bivariate correlations with the dependent variables; high religiosity produces more conservative responses, most strongly on moral and social issues, followed by strong associations with partisan and national defense, and finally, weak connections to other domestic issues. (Again, as with the guidance scale, the controls for demographic variables do not affect these findings.) Interestingly, where identical political items are available from the 1989 Pilot Study, the results are quite comparable (data not shown).

The multivariate analysis also has intuitively pleasing results. The religiosity index retains strength across issue domains, but contributes most to attitudes on moral traditionalism and the contemporary social issue agenda of abortion, prayer in schools, and gender roles—although religious tradition has some power here as well, with evangelicals more conservative and nonidentifiers more liberal. Catholics prove somewhat more tolerant toward homosexuals, more opposed to the death penalty, and more supportive of detente than other groups; the latter two, of course, are consistent with the "seamless garment" social teachings of the American bishops. Biblical literalism influences homosexual rights, civil rights, and women's roles and has a powerful effect on the nationalism and national defense items. All three measures affect partisan and ideological measures, although, as expected, religious tradition is still the best predictor of long-term partisanship and strength of identification. But on the 1988 vote, warmth toward Republican leaders, coolness toward Democrats, and self-identified ideology, the religiosity index matches or exceeds the explanatory power of religious tradition. The index is an especially strong influence on the gap between respondents' evaluations of Republican and Democratic figures.

Clearly, the religiosity index is an economical test of the direct political influence of the importance of religion to an individual. But here we must return to a conceptual issue raised above. Whatever its direct impact, does general salience also activate or enhance effects of other religious identifications or beliefs? We expect, if some theorists are correct, that the influence of religious tradition, orthodoxy, or, perhaps, identity may be enhanced by salience. So, we systematically looked for interactions of both the guidance scale and our religiosity index with these variables. Although the religiosity index produced somewhat stronger interactions than the original guidance scale, they exhibit very similar patterns. We will report on the results from the religiosity index (data not shown).

Table 8.4

The Religiosity Index and Political Attitudes
(whites only, major traditions, N=1,419)

	Bivariate (eta)	MCA ANALYSIS			
		Index	Trad	Bible	R^2
SOCIAL ISSUES		(with demographic controls)			
Moral Traditionalism	.47**	.35**	.13*	.14*	.26
Abortion Policy	.44**	.36**	.15**	.16**	.28
School Prayer	.30**	.20*	.13*	.09	.15
Oppose Gays+ +	.28*	.16	.20*	.31**	.32
Women's Role	.27**	.15	.10	.21**	.18
Cool to Feminists+ +	.25*	.18	.15	.08	.10
Social Issue Agenda	.22**	.21**	.10*	.06	.07
Civil Rights Index	.20**	.12	.04	.16*	.20
Death Penalty	-.13*	-.14*	.11*	.07	.07
NATIONALISM					
Anti-Communist+ +	.26*	.17	.17*	.30**	.28
Flag Burning	.21**	.07	.09*	.21**	.22
Detente with USSR+ +	.22	.19	.09	.28**	.17
Defense Attitude+ +	.23	.16	.08	.29**	.19
Patriotism+ +	.19	.09	.09	.23**	.28
ECONOMIC ISSUES					
AIDS spending	.20**	.19**	.05	.06	.06
Environmental Policy	.16**	.14*	.10*	.09*	.11
Child Care	.14*	.13*	.08*	.02	.05
Anti-Drug Spending	.12	.08	.09*	.16**	.06
Social Security	.12*	.15*	.05	-.18**	.08
Warm to Unions+ +	.11*	.14*	.09*	-.07	.04
School Money	.11*	.08	.02	.03	.05
USE PEACE DIVIDEND TO:					
Cut Deficit	.13*	.17**	.11**	-.18**	.08
Expand Social Prog.	.11	.11	.06	.06	.02
Cut Taxes	-.10	-.14*	.07	.20**	.06
PARTISAN/IDEOLOGY					
Difference GOP/Dems	.32**	.27**	.22**	.14	.16
Warm to GOP Figures	.28**	.20**	.12*	.15*	.12
Ideology	.25**	.15**	.15**	.19**	.13
Bush Vote 1988	.20**	.20*	.13*	.04	.08
Cool to Dems	.16*	.16*	.08**	.07	.05
Partisan Strength	.14*	.09	.13*	.01	.07
Party ID	.11*	.13*	.14**	.02	.05

Source: 1990 NES and 1989 NES Pilot Study.

* p < .05.   Positive correlations signify conservative direction.

** p < .001.   ++Item from 1989 Pilot Study, N = 389.

Reassuringly, there are relatively few interactions, but they occur exactly where expected. Religious tradition and commitment interact on partisanship and a few other issues: very religious Protestants (both evangelical and mainline) are most Republican, most antiabortion, and most opposed to flag burning. Very religious Catholics are also more antiabortion but, unlike Protestants, are not stronger in their traditional Democratic allegiance (in fact, they are warmer toward Republicans) and are more pro-union. Religiosity also interacts with tradition on some spending issues; although the devout in all traditions tend to be more conservative, only among evangelicals is the relationship strong. Very religious evangelicals are *much* more conservative on spending for AIDS, public schools, and child care and more liberal on social security programs. They strongly oppose using the peace dividend to increase domestic spending but rather want to cut the deficit. They are also much warmer toward GOP leaders and much more anti-union than their less devout co-religionists.

Religiosity occasionally interacts with biblical literalism as well. Literalists are much warmer toward Republican leaders and antiabortion activists and more opposed to flag burning if religion (perhaps in the form of fundamentalist leaders) is particularly important. Very religious biblical literalists are also more likely to use the peace dividend to cut the deficit rather than cut taxes. Religiosity seldom interacts with born-again identification but does with fundamentalist, evangelical, and pentecostal identities: these are most strongly associated with conservatism, especially on social and military issues when religion is salient. The most frequent interactions occur with *fundamentalist*, where the very religious, as tapped by the index, are thoroughgoing conservatives on a broad range of issues, including relatively new issues such as environmentalism (data not shown). Thus, there is some evidence supporting the use of general salience as a control variable.

Conclusions

In sum, we find support for both major theoretical approaches regarding general salience outlined in the literature: as an independent variable in its own right and as a conditioning variable for other aspects of religion. On many political and social attitudes, general salience is a good predictor, suggesting that the importance of religion has direct influence. On such issues, the more religious in all traditions and identities tend to resemble each other, fostering broader religious alliances. But we also discover some support for interaction effects. In important instances, general salience intensifies the link between specific religious beliefs, traditions, and identities on the one hand and political attitudes and behaviors on the other. And in these instances, the religious distinctiveness is amplified, sustaining political particularism.

Our analysis of the NES guidance scale reveals both its potential and its limitations. Despite the measure's uniqueness, we have found that it correlates quite strongly with many political variables thought to be influenced by religiosity: traditional moral values, social issues, patriotism, and defense issues. Among whites, it also has a negative relation with support for civil rights policies. Perhaps more important, the measure correlates with orientations toward candidates and parties in recent years, identifying voters amenable to GOP blandishments.

By itself, the guidance scale has some limitations for multivariate analysis, however: most of its influence tends to be absorbed by other highly correlated items such as devotionalism and church attendance. Thus, we have argued that a combined scale using all three items is an effective way to simplify analysis. Our religiosity index is not only a superb means of identifying those who take religion seriously but correlates strongly with a great many political variables and interacts with some other aspects of religion to create distinctive results. At the same time it must be remembered, as pointed out in chapter 2, that church attendance and Bible reading are forms of pietistic religious behavior stressed especially in evangelical churches and that the resulting index must not be viewed as the single best measure of religiosity across all traditions.

A final note. The substantive implications of the results here should not be overlooked. Religious traditions still show distinct characteristics, sometimes activated or reinforced by salience, but these influences are being supplemented (or perhaps supplanted) by a certain style of religiosity itself as a major religious underpinning of the American party system (Green, Guth, and Fraser 1991). However that may be, the fact that general salience, tradition, and theology all have an impact that survives controls for age, gender, income, and education underlines the importance of religion to the future analyst of American politics.

References

Bahr, Howard M.; Bartel, Lois Franz; and Chadwick, Bruce A. 1971. "Orthodoxy, Activism, and the Salience of Religion." *Journal for the Scientific Study of Religion* 10:69–75.

Benson, Peter L., and Williams, Dorothy L. 1982. *Religion on Capitol Hill: Myths and Realities*. New York: Harper and Row.

Berger, Suzanne, ed. 1982. *Religion in Western European Politics*. London: Frank Cass.

Carmines, Edward G., and Stimson, James A. 1989. *Issue Evolution: Race and the Transformation of American Politics*. Princeton, NJ: Princeton University Press.

Gallup, George, Jr. 1978. *The Unchurched American*. Princeton, NJ: Princeton Religious Research Center.

———. 1982. *Religion in America*. Princeton, NJ: Princeton Religious Research Center.

Gibbs, David R.; Miller, Samuel A.; and Wood, James R. 1973. "Doctrinal Orthodoxy, Salience, and the Consequential Dimension." *Journal for the Scientific Study of Religion* 12:33–52.

Gorsuch, Richard L. 1984. "Measurement: The Boon and Bane of Investigating Religion." *American Psychologist* 39:228–36.

Gorsuch, Richard L., and McFarland, Sam G. 1972. "Single vs. Multiple-Item Scales for Measuring Religious Values." *Journal for the Scientific Study of Religion* 11:53–64.

Grasmick, Harold G.; Morgan, Carolyn Stout; and Kennedy, Mary Baldwin. 1992. "Support for Corporal Punishment in the Schools: A Comparison of the Effects of Socioeconomic Status and Religion." *Social Science Quarterly* 73:177–87.

Green, John C.; Guth, James L.; and Fraser, Cleveland R. 1991. "Apostles and Apostates? Religion and Politics among Political Contributors." In Guth and Green 1991, 113–39.

Guth, James L., and Green, John C. 1990. "Politics in a New Key: Religiosity and Participation among Political Activists." *Western Political Quarterly* 43:153–79.

——, eds. 1991. *The Bible and the Ballot Box: Religion and Politics in the 1988 Election*. Boulder, CO: Westview Press.

Hadaway, C. Kirk; Elifson, Kirk W.; and Petersen, David M. 1984. "Religious Involvement and Drug Use among Urban Adolescents." *Journal for the Scientific Study of Religion* 23:109–28.

Hertel, Bradley R., and Hughes, Michael. 1987. "Religious Affiliation, Attendance, and Support for Pro-Family Issues in the United States." *Social Forces* 65:858–82.

Hoge, Dean R., and de Zulueta, Ernesto. 1985. "Salience as a Condition for Various Social Consequences of Religious Commitment." *Journal for the Scientific Study of Religion* 24:21–37.

Inglehart, Ronald. 1990. *Culture Shift in Advanced Industrial Society*. Princeton, NJ: Princeton University Press.

Kauffman, J. Howard. 1989. "Dilemmas of Christian Pacifism within a Historic Peace Church." *Sociological Analysis* 49:368–85.

Kellstedt, Lyman A., and Smidt, Corwin E. 1991. "Measuring Fundamentalism: An Analysis of Different Operational Strategies." *Journal for the Scientific Study of Religion* 30:259–78.

Kellstedt, Lyman A.; Smidt, Corwin E.; and Kellstedt, Paul M. 1991. "Religious Tradition, Denomination and Commitment: White Protestants and the 1988 Election." In Guth and Green 1991, 139–58.

Kenski, Henry, and Lockwood, William. 1988. "The Catholic Vote from 1980 to 1986." In *Religion and Political Behavior in the United States*, ed. Ted G. Jelen, 109–38. New York: Praeger.

Kierulff, Stephen. 1991. "Belief in 'Armageddon Theology' and Willingness to Risk Nuclear War." *Journal for the Scientific Study of Religion* 30:81–91.

King, Morton B., and Hunt, Richard A. 1972. "Measuring the Religious Variable: Replication." *Journal for the Scientific Study of Religion* 11:240–51.

Lea, James A., and Hunsberger, Bruce E. 1990. "Christian Orthodoxy and Victim Derogation: The Impact of the Salience of Religion." *Journal for the Scientific Study of Religion* 29:512–18.

MacIver, Martha Abele. 1989. "Religious Politicization among Western European Mass Publics." In *Religious Politics in Global and Comparative Perspective*, ed. William H. Swatos, Jr., 111–30. Westport, CT: Greenwood.

Marsh, Alan, and Kaase, Max. 1979. "Background of Political Action." In *Political Action*, ed. Samuel H. Barnes and Max Kaase, 97–136. Beverly Hills, CA: Sage Publications.

Patterson, James, and Kim, Peter. 1991. *The Day America Told the Truth*. Englewood Cliffs: Prentice Hall.

Roof, Wade Clark, and Perkins, Richard B. 1975. "On Conceptualizing Salience in Religious Commitment." *Journal for the Scientific Study of Religion* 14:111–28.

Rothenberg, Stuart, and Newport, Frank. 1984. *The Evangelical Voter*. Washington, DC: Free Congress Research and Education Foundation.

Wilcox, Clyde. 1992. *God's Warriors: The Christian Right in Twentieth Century America*. Baltimore: Johns Hopkins University Press.

Wimberly, Dale W. 1989. "Religion and Role Identity: A Structural Symbolic Interactionist Conceptualization of Religiosity." *Sociological Quarterly* 30:125–42.

Wuthnow, Robert. 1973. "Religious Commitment and Conservatism: In Search of an Elusive Relationship." In *Religion in Sociological Perspective*, ed. Charles Y. Glock, 117–32. Belmont, CA: Wadsworth.

Young, Robert L. 1992. "Religious Orientation, Race and Support for the Death Penalty." *Journal for the Scientific Study of Religion* 31:76–87.

Part IV

Doctrinal, Experiential, and Worldview Measures

Chapter 9

Doctrinal Beliefs and Political Behavior: Views of the Bible

Lyman A. Kellstedt and Corwin E. Smidt

After several decades of empirical research, most analysts conclude that religion is best treated as a multidimensional phenomenon. Despite this general agreement, scholars continue to disagree about the number and content of the dimensions of religion. These disagreements result from the use of different definitional and measurement approaches, different analytical frameworks, and different populations for analysis (Cornwall, et al. 1986, 226).

Despite these disagreements, analysts tend to agree that religious beliefs constitute an important component of religion. This centrality of doctrinal beliefs is evident in a variety of ways. First, most definitional approaches to religion tend to be substantive in nature and emphasize that religion relates to some conception of and belief in a supernatural being, world, or force. Even alternative definitions of religion that are broad enough to include nontheistic systems as religious faiths (e.g., secular humanism, nationalism, and Marxism) emphasize the functional nature of religious beliefs for the individual. Second, religious or doctrinal beliefs serve as strong forces in motivating and structuring behavior. Whether one uses illustrations from the past (e.g., the Crusades, the Protestant Reformation, or the Inquisition) or the present (e.g., the conflicts evident within such denominations as the Southern Baptist Convention, the contemporary resurgence of religious fundamentalism both at home and abroad, creation science textbook controversies, or religious conflicts in Northern Ireland or Lebanon), religious beliefs and their attendant institutions serve as powerful forces motivating and directing political behavior.

Scholars have not been blind to the central role of beliefs within religious faiths or to the importance that religious beliefs may play in shaping behavior. Early social scientific studies of religion emphasized religious beliefs. Stark and Glock (1968, 22), for example, stated, "Virtually everyone agrees that the central feature of Christian commitment is belief." These authors developed an empirical measure of religious belief that they labeled the *Orthodoxy Index* (Glock and

Stark 1966; Stark and Glock 1968). The development of this index generated both considerable scholarly activity and criticism. Over time, however, the focus upon religious orthodoxy largely disappeared from social scientific studies of religion, and with its disappearance came a decline in attention given to religious beliefs. None of the major national data collections—e.g., the General Social Surveys (GSS) or the National Election Studies (NES)—adopted the four-item religious orthodoxy measures, and other measures of religious beliefs in these national surveys have been included only periodically. Only questions relating to life after death (GSS) and the Bible (GSS and NES) have been asked with any regularity.

Despite these limitations, this chapter seeks to assess the relative utility of measures of religious or doctrinal beliefs, particularly views concerning the Bible, in accounting for political differences within the American electorate. Obviously, a variety of factors prevent this chapter from providing a definitive answer to such concerns. Both the narrow choice and the particular focus of the available questions found in the major national surveys impose important constraints on the analysis. Nevertheless, this chapter will show that religious beliefs do have important effects politically and that, as a result, political analysts need to be more sensitive to the role that religious or doctrinal beliefs play in shaping political attitudes and behavior.

Doctrinal Beliefs

Previous Studies

Expectations that religious beliefs have important consequences for human behavior were verified in early social scientific studies of religion. Seminal studies of the *consequential dimension of religiosity* (religion and civic life, religion and political attitudes) emphasized the impact of doctrinal beliefs (Glock and Stark 1965, 1966; Hadden 1969; Kersten 1970; Stark and Foster 1970; Stark et al. 1971). However, this emphasis upon doctrinal orthodoxy generated a considerable critique (e.g., Yinger 1969, 1970; King and Hunt 1972; Roof 1979; and Hoge and de Zulueta 1985) that has taken a variety of forms. Some attack the emphasis on doctrinal orthodoxy from a conceptual perspective, while others question its measurement strategy. More specifically, a conceptual approach that requires adherence to specific beliefs attempts to discern whether or not (or to what extent) one is religious rather than *how* one is religious. For example, Yinger (1970, 11) has contended, "It is not the nature of belief, but the nature of believing that requires our study." Moreover, the focus on doctrinal beliefs can generate difficult analytical problems when such beliefs are taken as indicators of religiosity per se. Can we say, for example, that devout Quakers are "less religious" than devout Lutherans and the latter are "less religious" than devout Baptists simply on the basis of lack of adherence to certain doctrinal beliefs?

Obviously, acceptance or rejection of specific religious tenets does not necessarily determine religiosity; it only reveals differences in the level of acceptance of the specific beliefs measured. Similarly, the focus upon acceptance or rejection of traditional forms of belief (i.e., analyzing variation in the level of doctrinal orthodoxy) creates the difficult problem of distinguishing between religious change and religious decline.

Despite such difficulties, the analysis of religious beliefs still has merit for political analysts. For example, the espousal of particular religious beliefs may be associated with important differences in political attitudes and behavior. Given their different substantive interests, political analysts have been less concerned than sociologists of religion with the issue of how best to conceptualize religion. To analyze the political consequences of specific religious beliefs is not to assume that those who espouse such beliefs are more religious than those who do not do so. Rather, such analyses simply seek to ascertain which, if any, religious beliefs have important direct effects upon particular political attitudes and behavior. Nevertheless, despite this more limited concern, it still remains unclear whether the analysis of religious beliefs has any utility in explaining political attitudes and behavior. Even if religious beliefs do aid in explaining political variables, what is the relative level of their utility in such explanations? Are religious beliefs primary or secondary factors in causal explanations? Are the effects of religious beliefs upon political variables largely direct, or indirect, in nature? Are the effects of religious beliefs largely limited to a few unique dependent variables?

The results of studies that link religious beliefs with political attitudes and behavior have been mixed (Wald 1992, 103). Various factors account for these inconsistent findings. First, it may be that the political implications of religious beliefs are not fully comprehended by those who express them. Accordingly, such a lack of comprehension may account for some of the variation in previous findings in that the strongest relationships between the expression of religious beliefs and political attitudes have been found in studies of the clergy (e.g., Hadden 1969; Quinley 1974; Driedger 1974; Olson and Carroll 1989).

Second, it should be remembered that most religious bodies tend to be elastic enough to permit a variety of political perspectives within the framework of their doctrinal system. Thus, the lack of consistent findings among the laity may result from accepted differences in political interpretations of their doctrinal system, while the greater consistency evident among the clergy may result from being socialized to particular political implications of their doctrinal system in their theological or seminary training.

Third, the complexity of doctrinal systems themselves may contribute to the low correlations between religious beliefs and political variables. The particular religious beliefs chosen for analysis may be peripheral facets of the doctrinal system, while crucial aspects are left unanalyzed. Fourth, the growing individualism and privatization within American religion generally (as well as the emphasis on the "priesthood of all believers" within Protestantism specifically), makes linking doctrine and political behavior difficult. American believers tend to be relatively free to develop their own interpretations and understandings of religious doctrines. Individuals even combine facets of different religious creeds in constructing their own, unique religious faith (Bellah et al. 1985, 235). The political linkages of such personalized religious understandings may also be relatively idiosyncratic in nature. As a result, religious beliefs may be important determinants of political behavior, yet, under such idiosyncratic circumstances, they may remain undetected when analyses are based upon mass samples.

Fifth, certain types of religious beliefs may be more closely tied to specific forms of behavior than other types of religious beliefs. For example, Glock and Stark (1965, 24–25) differentiate among three types of religious beliefs: *warranting beliefs*, which "warrant the existence of the divine and define its character"; *purposive beliefs*, which "explain divine purpose and define man's role with regard to that purpose"; and *implementing beliefs*, which "establish what is the proper conduct of man toward God and toward his fellow man." We feel that implementing beliefs are more closely tied to political attitudes and behavior than either warranting or purposive beliefs.

Sixth, the linkages between religious beliefs and political variables vary by religious traditions. Black Protestants are intensely religious, but their political behavior is more likely conditioned by religious themes of oppression and deliverance than that of white Protestants. In contrast, white evangelical Protestants have been mobilized by both religious interest groups and the Republican party during the past decade on the basis of different religious themes. This mobilization would suggest that particular religious or doctrinal beliefs affect the political attitudes and behavior of those who are religiously committed in different ways.

Issues

Before beginning our analysis, it may be advantageous to address certain issues in the study of religious beliefs.

Definitional Approach

Scholars use two major approaches in defining religious beliefs: substantive and functional. Most analysts of religious beliefs adopt a substantive approach and limit the analysis of religious beliefs "to those systems of thought embodied in social organizations that posit the existence of the supernatural" (Stark and Bainbridge 1985, 3). Other analysts contend that it is the specific function which certain beliefs perform, rather than the content of the beliefs, that makes such beliefs religious in nature. In this chapter, a substantive approach is adopted. The same religious belief questions are analyzed across all respondents; it is assumed that the questions analyzed substantively tap religious beliefs.

Measurement Strategy

When one seeks to measure the doctrinal beliefs of respondents, there are two broad approaches to the definition and measurement of components of religious beliefs. One approach, more analytically deductive in nature, attempts to identify potentially important religious beliefs and doctrines and then to develop operational measures to tap those beliefs that have been conceptually derived (e.g., the orthodoxy measure developed by Glock and Stark 1966). A second approach, more inductive in nature, derives important dimensions of religious beliefs by looking for mathematical relationships among sets of items from a large pool of indicators (e.g., the orthodoxy dimension derived by King and Hunt 1972). Given that relatively few religious questions are available in most national surveys, the first approach is typically employed and is used in the analysis of this chapter.

Approaches to Religious Beliefs

When one's analysis of religion is restricted to mental measures, regardless of the measurement approach adopted, there remains the issue of what kind of mental measures to employ. While most analysts using mental measures have focused upon various propositional statements tapping religious beliefs or doctrines, several other approaches using mental measures of religion have attempted to avoid some of the previously noted difficulties. Basically, these alternative approaches have sought to move away from doctrinal questions to *pre-doctrinal* questions and from the question of whether one is religious to the question of how one is religious. As discussed more fully in chapter 2, one such approach has focused upon the holding of religious images (Greeley 1984, 1988; Hoffman 1985; Jelen 1985; Welch and Leege 1988), while another approach has focused on foundational beliefs (Benson and Williams, 1982; Leege 1989; Leege and Welch 1989). In this chapter, however, the focus is upon propositional statements tapping religious beliefs.

Causal Sequence

Regardless of definition, measurement strategy, and/or approach one adopts, a further assumption must be made about whether such beliefs shape or reflect religious affiliations. The relationship between the *believing* and *belonging* components of religion remains unclear. Some have argued that the two are relatively independent of one another. Religious beliefs, for example, may be meaningful and salient for certain individuals; yet these individuals may not belong to or be actively involved in any particular religious group. Others have argued that the two components are related but disagree about how they are related. Some analysts argue that religious beliefs lead to religious belonging (Alston and McIntosh 1979), while others contend that belonging precedes believing (White 1968; Welch 1981). Still others argue that the two cannot be separated in that beliefs and belonging interact to form a single process (Davidson and Knudsen 1977; Roof 1978).

Bases of Constraint

Even if (1) mental measures of religion are strongly associated with political attitudes and behavior, and (2) beliefs lead to religious affiliations, it still remains unclear what accounts for the associations between the religious beliefs and political variables. Is it the beliefs per se, or is it some external factor that forges the link between such religious and political measures? The strength of the relationship between a particular religious belief and a political attitude or behavior is likely to vary across individuals; some people are more *constrained* in their attitudes than others. Two possible sources exist for whatever constraint is present between religious beliefs and political attitudes and behavior: one internal and the other external in nature (Converse 1964). The internal source of constraint is psychological; individuals whose beliefs stand in logical contradiction with each other are posited to experience some psychological pressure to bring such cognitions into consistency. Research has shown that individuals vary in the amount of inconsistency they can tolerate in their cognitive structure. Internal pressure for consistency between religious and political beliefs arises from three sources: the specific nature of the doctrinal beliefs, the level of religious salience for the individual, and the presence of a constraining religious community. For example, those who believe that the Bible is literally true may feel constrained from advocating positions that promote women's equality, freedom of choice on abortion, and homosexual rights. Likewise, those who assign high levels of salience to their religious beliefs should feel more pressure to bring their political cognitions into congruence with their religious cognitions than those whose religious beliefs are less important to them. On the other hand, political beliefs may not necessarily be directly related to religious beliefs in any logical fashion. As a result, religious or political elites feel free to package certain religious beliefs and political positions together. Under such conditions, it is not surprising that level of church attendance is a significant predictor of attitudinal constraint for certain religious groups but not for others (Jelen, Kellstedt, and Wilcox 1990).

Biblical Views and Political Attitudes and Behavior

National public opinion surveys have periodically contained questions that tap doctrinal perspectives. When such questions have been present, items tapping the political attitudes and behaviors of respondents have not always been asked. As a result, the number of potential items tapping religious beliefs that can be analyzed here is rather limited.

In this section we examine attitudes toward the Bible as an indicator of religious or doctrinal beliefs. We do so for several reasons. First, this question has been asked with some regularity in political surveys. The National Election Studies included a Bible measure in 1964 and 1968, picked up the question again in 1980, and have included it in presidential election surveys ever since (as well as in the 1990 Congressional Election Study). Only religious preference and church attendance measures have a longer life in NES studies. Thus, a more extensive time series is available for the Bible item than for any other religious belief question. In addition, the importance of this particular religious belief question is quite high in various religious traditions. Jews and Christians base much of their faith on biblical accounts. In addition, the Bible has, at least historically, served as the basis of religious authority for most doctrinal systems rooted in the Protestant tradition; the cry of *sola scriptura* echoed among Protestant reformers in their opposition to papal authority. Even Roman Catholics, who historically base doctrine on church authority and church tradition, have undergone a renaissance in scriptural interest. In the United States, Bible reading is increasingly common among the laity, and biblical scholarship is increasingly the mark of Catholic theologians (Welch and Leege, 1991). Third, the Bible has served as an important symbol within the American political culture. For example, most American homes contain Bibles, and oaths of public office are still taken upon the Bible. Finally, views of the nature of biblical authority shape, color, and/or determine the nature of many other religious beliefs. For example, responses to questions tapping doctrinal orthodoxy, as discussed above, are likely to be highly correlated with one's view of the nature of biblical authority. Consequently, there is considerable merit in examining the political consequences of differing views concerning the nature of biblical authority.

Question Wording

The nature of biblical authority is a matter of some dispute even among those Christians who subscribe to a "high" view of the Scriptures. Briefly stated, some adhere to an infallible point of view, others to an inerrant point of view, while still others subscribe to a literal point of view (see Smidt 1989, 32–36). While such nuances may escape the awareness of many "Bible believers" (Jelen 1989a; but see Jelen, Smidt, and Wilcox 1990), it is likely that such differences in perspective are related to whether one views the Bible to be (1) the actual word of God, or (2) the inspired word of God.

National surveys have not employed the same question wording for items that tap views of biblical authority. Basically, two different forms have been used. One form has been employed by Gallup polls, and its most authoritative response taps biblical literalism (hereafter called the *literalism measure*). The other form has been used predominately by the National Election Studies, and its most authoritative response taps biblical inerrancy (hereafter called the *inerrancy measure*). The specific response options for the literalism and inerrancy questions are, respectively, "The Bible is the actual word of God and is to be taken literally, word for word," and "The Bible is God's word and all it says is true." The second option for each measure also permits relatively "high" views of the Scriptures to be expressed: for the literalism measure, "The Bible is the inspired word of God but not everything in it should be taken literally, word for word," and, for the inerrancy measure, "The Bible was written by men inspired by God, but it contains some human errors." The other option(s) for these measures generally take a relatively "low" view of the Scriptures. For example, the literalism measure generally uses the following for its final option: "The Bible is an ancient book of fables, legends, history, and moral precepts recorded by men." The inerrancy measure generally has had two final options: (1) "The Bible is a good book because it was written by wise men, but God had nothing to do with it," and, (2) "The Bible was written by men who lived so long ago that it is worth very little today."

Responses concerning belief in biblical authority vary with the particular measure employed. Two particular patterns are evident. First, when the literalism measure is employed, a somewhat smaller percentage of the American people give the most authoritative response to the Bible question than when the inerrancy question is used. For example, the GSS used both forms at different times between 1983 and 1991. While 36.3 percent gave the most authoritative response to the Bible item when the literalism measure was employed over these years, 46.8 percent gave the most authoritative response when the inerrancy measure was employed (data not shown). Likewise, these same patterns are evident in the 1990 NES in which a split-half technique was used with regard to the Bible item. When the literalism measure was employed, 45.5 percent of the respondents reported that the "Bible is the actual word of God and is to be taken literally, word for word," but when the inerrancy measure was used, 50.4 percent reported that "The Bible is God's word and all it says is true." Obviously the two measures do not elicit identical responses but it is unclear whether such differences are associated with meaningful political differences (Jelen 1989a; but see Jelen, Smidt, and Wilcox, 1990).

Second, regardless of which measure is employed, responses are highly skewed. In either format, only 10 to 15 percent of the respondents report a "low" view of biblical authority—that the Bible is simply a human document. Thus, each measure has constricted variation associated with its response options in that the only "meaningful" variation occurs between the first two options. This constricted variation is likely to hamper the ability of these Bible questions to explain variation in any selected dependent variable.

In addition, responses to the Bible questions, regardless of the particular measure employed, vary by certain sociodemographic characteristics of the respondents (data not shown). Nonwhites are significantly more likely than whites to give more authoritative responses to such questions, as are females, southerners, and those with lower levels of education. Finally, older respondents are more likely than younger respondents to give more authoritative responses to the Bible questions, although the differences are not always statistically significant.

Data Analysis

Do responses to the Bible item tap meaningful political differences among the respondents surveyed? Table 9.1 analyzes, through the use of Multiple Classification Analysis (MCA), the relationship between the respondents' expressed views of biblical authority (limited to just the two "authoritative" responses) and three selected dependent variables: partisan identification, presidential vote choice, and attitudes toward abortion.[1] The data are taken from the National Election Studies for those years in which a Bible question was asked. Respondents are divided into three religious traditions: evangelical Protestant, mainline Protestant, and Catholic (see chapter 3). Given that certain demographic variables are associated with expressed views on biblical authority as well as with various political variables, the MCA procedure controlled for the age, gender, education, and region of the respondents. Finally, analysis was limited to white respondents only.[2]

Several important patterns are evident in Table 9.1. First, in terms of partisan identifications, it is apparent that the Bible question serves as an important predictor. Despite controlling for the demographic characteristics of the respondents, and despite restricting analysis to the two most common responses to the Bible item, the Bible question is a significant predictor of partisan identifications in seven out of the fifteen comparisons (i.e., three different religious traditions over five different points of time). For example, in 1964, the mean score for partisan identifications among those evangelicals who reported that the Bible was *inspired* was 2.07. In contrast, the mean score for those evangelicals who reported that the Bible was *true* (i.e., "The Bible is God's word and all it says is true") was 1.90, significantly more Democratic than those evangelicals who reported that the Bible was simply inspired. In fact, the Bible item served as a significant predictor of the partisan identifications of evangelicals in three of the five election studies, while it is a significant predictor for mainline Protestants and for Catholics in two of the five election studies. Equally important to this methodological point, and perhaps contributing to the Bible item's lack of significance in certain elections, is the substantive finding that the *political meaning* of Bible responses has changed for Protestants over time. For example, within all three religious traditions in 1964, those respondents who expressed a *true* view of the Scriptures were more Democratic in their partisan identifications than those who expressed an *inspired* view. By 1980, this pattern had reversed among mainline Protestants, and, by 1984, the same had occurred among evangelical Protestants. Consequently, in 1988, those evangelical and mainline Protestants who expressed *true* views of the Bible were significantly more Republican in

Table 9.1

Political Variables by Views on the Bible among White Respondents within Different Religious Traditions over Time
(a multiple classification analysis controlling for age, gender, education, region)

| | National Election Studies | | | | |
Political Variable	1964	1968	1980	1984	1988
PARTY IDENTIFICATION (scores range 0-6; higher scores = more Rep.)					
Evangelicals					
True	1.90*	2.44	2.50	3.26*	3.22*
(N)	(230)	(262)	(224)	(319)	(308)
Inspired	2.07	2.64	2.64	2.81	2.77
(N)	(79)	(106)	(77)	(92)	(94)
Beta	.08	.06	.05	.10	.09
Mainliners					
True	2.69*	3.11	3.43	3.47	3.88*
(N)	(213)	(231)	(147)	(207)	(184)
Inspired	3.14	3.29	3.22	3.33	3.52
(N)	(265)	(237)	(198)	(250)	(238)
Beta	.10	.08	.05	.04	.07
Catholics					
True	1.70*	2.06	2.38	2.41*	2.63
(N)	(146)	(133)	(96)	(158)	(140)
Inspired	1.99	2.01	2.48	2.61	2.73
(N)	(139)	(141)	(171)	(252)	(207)
Beta	.07	.11	.03	.05	.04
PRESIDENTIAL VOTE (% = GOP vote)					
Evangelicals	1964	1968	1980	1984	1988
True	34%*	65%*	63%	75%*	73%*
(N)	(152)	(113)	(147)	(202)	(194)
Inspired	47%	72%	65%	67%	59%
(N)	(61)	(58)	(47)	(64)	(59)
Beta	.14	.10	.06	.10	.15

Mainliners					
True	37%*	67%*	74%*	73%	66%
(N)	(169)	(153)	(114)	(148)	(142)
Inspired	52%	74%	66%	70%	65%
(N)	(231)	(162)	(135)	(202)	(180)
Beta	.15	.07	.11	.03	.07
Catholics					
True	22%	43%	56%	54%	52%
(N)	(128)	(93)	(58)	(114)	(93)
Inspired	22%	37%	56%	55%	48%
(N)	(118)	(98)	(118)	(206)	(167)
Beta	.01	.11	.01	.05	.04

ABORTION ATTITUDES					
(scores range 1-4;	1964	1968	1980	1984	1988
higher scores = more opposed)					
Evangelicals					
True	not	not	2.76*	2.75*	2.71*
(N)	asked	asked	(216)	(318)	(309)
Inspired	not	not	2.16	2.02	1.96
(N)	asked	asked	(76)	(93)	(94)
Beta			.41	.30	.31
Mainliners					
True	not	not	2.24*	2.35*	2.36*
(N)	asked	asked	(144)	(209)	(184)
Inspired	not	not	1.71	1.79	1.75
(N)	asked	asked	(194)	(247)	(236)
Beta			.33	.30	.32

Catholics

True	not	not	2.83*	2.51*	2.58*
(N)	asked	asked	(97)	(157)	(137)
Inspired	not	not	2.24	2.17	2.28
(N)	asked	asked	(165)	(244)	(205)
Beta			.31	.19	.18

Source: NES 1964–88.

* Mean score differences between the true and inspired response categories are statistically significant at .05 level or higher. Nonorthodox responses are dropped from the analysis because of their small numbers and to reduce the number of coefficients presented in the table. *Betas* are based on inclusion of the nonorthodox responses.

their partisan identifications than their counterparts who expressed *inspired* views, while the opposite pattern was evident among Roman Catholics (though not in a statistically significant fashion).

In terms of the respondents' reported vote for president, views of the Bible have served as significant predictors of presidential voting among Protestant, but not Catholic, respondents. In seven of the ten comparisons reported for Protestant voters, biblical views constituted a significant predictor of vote choice. This was particularly the case for evangelical Protestants, where variation in the views of the Scriptures were significantly related to voting decisions in every election except 1980. Once again it should be noted, however, that the partisan direction of this relationship has changed over time. Whereas during the 1960s "higher" views of scriptural authority were significantly related to lower levels of Republican voting, this relationship has either disappeared (primarily among mainline Protestants) or been reversed (primarily among evangelical Protestants) during the 1980s.

Finally, views of biblical authority were related to a particular political issue, namely, attitudes toward abortion. (Since respondents were not asked their position on this issue during the election studies conducted in the 1960s, comparisons are limited to the three election studies of the 1980s.) It is evident from Table 9.1 that attitudes toward the Bible served as a significant predictor of attitudes toward abortion for respondents within all three religious traditions in all three elections of the 1980s—even after controls for demographic variables have been introduced.

Thus, in conclusion, Table 9.1 reveals several important points about the nature of the relationship between respondents' attitudes toward the Bible and political dependent variables. First, the impact of religious doctrine is most apparent when controls are introduced for the religious traditions of the respondents. Had all respondents been lumped together or had even all Protestants been aggregated, the resultant patterns would be less apparent and less significant. Religious beliefs take place within a social context, and it is important to recognize these differential "starting points" in order to realize the significant impact differences in those doctrinal perspectives make. Second, how doctrinal positions are related to politics can change over time. "Higher" views of scriptural authority were significantly related to Democratic partisanship and voting during the 1960s; they were significantly related in a Republican direction for those same variables in the 1980s. Once again, controlling for religious traditions helps to reveal such changes. Finally, the impact of biblical views upon political variables changes with the nature of the dependent variable. For some variables, it serves as a significant predictor; for other variables (e.g., ideological self-classification, data not shown), it serves as a relatively poor predictor.[3]

Do differences in views of biblical authority continue to have a significant impact on political variables in the 1990 National Election Study? Do differences in views of biblical authority still have politically significant effects even after controlling for differences in frequency of reading the Bible? Controls for Bible *reading* should clarify relationships and alleviate the problem of skewness. Given the skewed distributions that we have noted on the Bible items, are there respondents who give an inerrant view of the Scriptures but who rarely or never read it? After all, frequent Bible readers are likely to attest to its importance in their lives. These questions are addressed in Table 9.2.

Table 9.2 examines the impact that different biblical views had in 1990 upon partisan identification, presidential vote choice in 1988, and attitudes toward abortion within each of the three religious traditions, after the demographic controls have been added.[4] In addition, Table 9.2 examines the impact biblical views have upon the dependent variables controlling for frequency of Bible reading.

Several conclusions emerge from the patterns evident in Table 9.2. First, differences in views regarding biblical authority have a significant impact on all three dependent variables among both evangelical Protestants and Roman Catholics, but not among mainline Protestants. For respondents within the evangelical and Catholic traditions, every comparison made across different biblical views reveals statistically significant differences in their partisan identifications, vote choices, and abortion stances. However, for mainline Protestants, differences in biblical views have a significant impact only with regard to the abortion issue. Thus, once again, it is evident that the impact of differences in biblical views becomes more apparent when one controls for the religious traditions of the respondents.

Second, Table 9.2 reveals the important impact that differences in reported

Table 9.2

Political Variables by Views of the Bible among Whites within Different Religious Traditions
(a multiple classification analysis controlling for age, gender, education, region)

	Party Id.	Vote 1988	Abortion	Party Id. Bible Read		Vote 1988 Bible Read		Abortion Bible Read	
				High	Low	High	Low	High	Low
Evangelicals									
Lit./Inerr.	3.24*	75%*	2.74*	3.28*	3.14*	79%*	68%*	3.01*	2.36*
(N)	(291)	(171)	(297)	(174)	(116)	(118)	(52)	(173)	(123)
Positive	2.56	57%	2.17	2.60	2.57	56%	56%	2.65	2.01
(N)	(98)	(66)	(96)	(28)	(70)	(22)	(44)	(26)	(70)
Non-Orthodox	1.65	59%	1.45	___	2.01	___	___	___	1.52
(N)	(10)	(5)	(10)	(1)	(9)	(1)	(4)	(1)	(9)
Mean Score	3.03	70%	2.57	3.17+	2.88	76%+	62%	2.95+	2.20
Beta	.18	.19	.30	.15	.16	.21	.12	.22	.22
Mainliners									
Lit./Inerr.	3.09	66%	2.02*	2.81*	3.16	75%	61%	2.53*	1.86*
(N)	(126)	(86)	(122)	(35)	(90)	(25)	(61)	(33)	(88)
Positive	3.09	69%	1.74	3.11	3.09	77%	69%	2.14	1.63
(N)	(235)	(174)	(236)	(46)	(188)	(36)	(138)	(45)	(190)
Non-Orthodox	3.37	66%	1.37	___	3.46	___	65%	___	1.37
(N)	(58)	(39)	(58)	(2)	(37)	(2)	(37)	(2)	(56)
Mean Score	3.13	68%	1.77	2.94+	3.17	75%+	66%	2.28+	1.65
Beta	.05	.03	.22	.13	.07	.11	.07	.27	.18
Catholics									
Lit./Inerr.	2.60*	66%*	2.59*	2.64	2.50*	76%	62%*	3.07*	2.53*
(N)	(118)	(69)	(117)	(15)	(102)	(11)	(57)	(16)	(100)
Positive	2.45	50%	2.17	2.86	2.46	76%	47%	2.51	2.13
(N)	(190)	(140)	(187)	(13)	(177)	(11)	(129)	(13)	(174)
Non-Orthodox	1.87	53%	1.79	___	1.88	___	52%	___	1.78
(N)	(31)	(24)	(32)	(2)	(29)	(1)	(23)	(2)	(30)
Mean Score	2.45	55%	2.28	2.67+	2.42	76%+	52%	2.77+	2.23
Beta	.09	.14	.23	.13	.08	.10	.13	.29	.22

Table 9.2 Source: NES 1990.

Higher Party ID and 1988 Vote Scores = a more Republican identification or vote.

Higher abortion scores = more prolife.

* Differences on the Bible measure are significant at the .05 level or higher (comparing vertically).

+ Differences on the Bible Reading item are significant at the .05 level or higher (comparing horizontally).

Beta scores of .1 or higher reflect statistically significant differences between the responses on the Bible item in samples of this size.

levels of Bible reading have upon the dependent variables. As can be seen from the right-hand portion of Table 9.2, the resultant mean scores for all three dependent variables are significantly different for the high and low Bible readers among evangelicals. This same pattern also holds for both mainline Protestants and Roman Catholics. Thus, for all three religious traditions, differences in frequency of Bible reading have a significant impact on all three dependent varables. Consequently, Table 9.2 demonstrates that the control for Bible reading is an important one. It clarifies the relationships between attitudes toward the Bible and the dependent variables. If ongoing national surveys (Gallup, GSS, NES) wish to keep the older Bible items for reasons of continuity despite their skewed distributions, the addition of a Bible reading item will enhance understanding by permitting a control for its effects.

Third, the combined impact of biblical views and levels of Bible reading varies across religious traditions. Among evangelicals, differences in biblical views continue to have a significant impact on the dependent variables even after controlling for differences in level of Bible reading. High Bible reading literal/ inerrantists are the most Republican in partisanship and vote choice and the most prolife among evangelicals. But, among Roman Catholics, differences in biblical views have a significant impact on all three dependent variables only among those Catholics who report low levels of Bible reading, while significant differences are evident only on the abortion issue among those Catholics who report high levels of Bible reading. Finally, still another pattern is evident among mainline Protestants. Differences in biblical views among mainline Protestants have a significant impact on abortion stands among both high and low Bible readers, while differences in biblical views have a significant impact on partisan identification only among those mainline Protestants who report high levels of Bible reading, with literal/inerrant respondents more *Democratic*.

It should be noted that the significant differences reported in Tables 9.1 and 9.2 are evident despite the rather *constricted* variation associated with the current Bible items. Might not a Bible measure that captured a wider variation in biblical views be an even more powerful variable in explaining variance in political dependent variables? This appears to be the case in data gathered in a 1990 study of religious activists.[5] This study included a Bible question that posed several new alternative response options: (1) "The Bible is God's word and is meant to be taken literally, word for word," (2) The Bible is God's word, and all it says is true, but not all of it is meant to be taken literally, word for word," (3) "The Bible is God's Word, and is authoritative for Christian faith and practice, but it is not intended as a book of science or history," (4) "The Bible was written by men inspired by God but does contain some spiritual errors, often reflecting the limitations of its authors and their eras." This particular Bible item permits a finer differentiation between and among differing understandings of the nature of biblical authority.

Table 9.3 presents a Multiple Classification Analysis using party identification, vote choice in 1988, and attitudes toward abortion as the dependent variables and the expanded Bible question as the independent variable, while including controls for age, gender, region, education, church attendance, and religious salience.[6] Once again, the impact of variation in views of biblical authority upon the dependent variables is examined within the three religious traditions of evangelical Protestants, mainline Protestants, and Roman Catholics.

Several patterns are evident in Table 9.3. First, at least among this sample of religious activists, the new Bible question captures greater variation in views in biblical authority than was evident in either of the older measures. Not surprisingly, the distribution in responses to this new Bible item varies according to the religious traditions of the respondents. Second, the resultant scores on the three dependent variables are distributed in a monotonic fashion across answers to the Bible question within all three religious traditions. And, finally, it is apparent that greater variation in the Bible item helps to explain increased variation in the selected dependent variables. In fact, the differences in the amount of variance explained by the Bible item (the R^2) are rather large—ranging from a low of .171 to a high of .285. Thus, it appears that the predictive ability of the NES Bible items, which is already significant for many dependent variables despite the constricted variation of both literal and inerrant options, would likely be enhanced considerably if greater variations were included in the response options.

Conclusions

This chapter has examined doctrinal beliefs and their relevance for an understanding of political behavior. Linkages between doctrine and behavior have been difficult to establish given the paucity and/or inadequacy of doctrinal measures. Questions concerning belief in God; the nature of God; beliefs in the life, death, resurrection, and purpose of Jesus Christ; and beliefs about the Bible are either not asked or are asked infrequently. Time-series analyses of these beliefs are therefore largely impossible. The linkage between doctrine and political behavior through time remains uncharted. This is the case despite the use of some measures of doctrine in Gallup surveys on religion as well as in the NES and GSS surveys.

Table 9.3

Political Variables by Alternative Bible Measure
(a Multiple Classification Analysis controlling for region, education,
church attendance, and religious salience)

	Party ID	Vote Choice in 1988	Abortion (range: 1–7)
Evangelical Protestants			
Literal	4.87	95%	4.92
(*N*)	(980)	(943)	(976)
True	4.43	87%	4.76
(*N*)	(870)	(814)	(848)
Authoritative	3.14	56%	4.11
(*N*)	(346)	(316)	(306)
Errors	2.66	32%	2.55
(*N*)	(53)	(41)	(49)
Mean	4.38	85%	4.69
Beta	.22	.28	.29
Mainliners			
Literal	4.33	80%	4.73
(*N*)	(107)	(100)	(102)
True	3.46	60%	3.76
(*N*)	(318)	(303)	(302)
Authoritative	2.45	31%	2.87
(*N*)	(332)	(311)	(298)
Errors	1.83	20%	1.65
(*N*)	(127)	(121)	(110)
Mean	2.95	46%	3.27
Beta	.19	.19	.34
Catholics			
Literal	3.90	88%	5.25
(*N*)	(11)	(9)	(12)
True	2.44	43%	4.91
(*N*)	(132)	(127)	(124)
Authoritative	1.99	31%	4.58
(*N*)	(216)	(197)	(194)
Errors	1.56	18%	3.80
(*N*)	(130)	(122)	(107)
Mean	2.04	34%	4.50
Beta	.17	.16	.25

Source: 1990 Religious Activist Study.

Note: Higher Party ID scores are more Republican. Vote choice percentages are the Republican percentages. Abortion scores range from 1 to 7; higher scores are prolife.

Empirically, this chapter has focused on responses to questions about the Bible. Given the centrality of the Bible for evangelical Protestants and its importance for other Christians, the development and use of measures tapping attitudes toward the Bible is of great significance. We have found that responses to the literalism and inerrancy measures are highly skewed in the direction of positive or favorable answers to the Bible questions. When two-thirds of the respondents who profess *no religious preference* give *positive* responses to the Bible, as was the case in the 1990 NES (data not shown), something is wrong with the measure if it is to be tapping religious, rather than cultural, responses. Our analysis of the Bible item used in the religious activist study shows that providing more response categories lessens the skewed nature of answers, despite the highly religious audience, and increases the utility of the item for data analysis purposes. If national surveys employ only one Bible item, they should use a measure with more nuanced response categories than the typical options in the literalism and inerrancy measures. If the results from the religious activist study are indicative, such a strategy would reap dividends.

Yet, despite the difficulties with the literalism and inerrancy measures, our analysis still shows that beliefs about the Bible are important predictors of such political variables as partisanship, vote choice, and attitudes toward abortion. The findings are the most robust when examining evangelical Protestants. If, for purposes of continuity, the literalism or inerrancy measures are utilized in future studies, a question concerning frequency of Bible reading should be added to enhance understanding of the relationships between views of biblical authority and political behavior.

Why should these patterns be stronger for evangelical Protestants than for mainline Protestants or Roman Catholics? Perhaps, it is because a monistic, rather than a pluralistic, conception of truth has continued to be most evident within the evangelical tradition. Historically, Protestants separated from the Roman Catholic church over the issue of the Scriptures being the sole basis of religious authority, and, thereby, neither the pope nor religious tradition was viewed to hold any authority for Protestants. However, over time, many segments within mainline Protestantism sought to reconcile their religious teachings with "scientific knowledge," and, thus, at least since the modernist-fundamentalist debate of the 1920s, a counterauthority to biblical authority has been evident within much of mainline Protestantism. Thus, evangelical Protestantism remains the major religious tradition whose very identity is tied to positive affirmations about the Bible. In a church context in which reading the Bible is widespread, Bible studies are everywhere, and biblical exegesis is standard fare in Sunday worship services, it is not surprising that attitudes toward the Scriptures are related to political attitudes and behavior.

Yet, two different trends suggest that differences in biblical views may become more important politically in differentiating among mainline Protestants as well as Roman Catholics. The first trend relates to the increasing cross-fertilization evident across different religious traditions. Various factors (e.g., the growth of religious publishing and broadcasting, para-church organizations, geographical mobility) have permitted different religious ideas and perspectives to cross religious traditions more easily today than in the past. For example, the charismatic movement has had a significant impact on both evangelical and mainline Protestantism as well as on the Roman Catholic church. Therefore, the fact that differences in biblical views among Roman Catholics had, for the first time in 1990, a significant impact on all three dependent variables suggests that answers to the Bible item may be acquiring greater political significance outside of evangelical Protestantism. This finding is consistent with Welch and Leege's (1991) argument and findings about evangelical-style Catholicism, a phenomenon growing in part because of religious renewal movements in Catholic parishes.

Second, some analysts have been arguing that a restructuring of American religion is taking place (Wuthnow 1988). Such a restructuring is dividing American religion along a liberal-conservative divide within and across each religious tradition. If such a restructuring is indeed occurring, then answers to the Bible question may well indicate upon which side of such a religious divide the respondent may fall.

Notes

1. It should be noted, however, that the *betas* reported in Table 9.1 are calculated on the basis of including the *nonauthoritative* responses to the Bible question. Consequently, at times, the *betas* reported in the table may appear surprisingly large given the relatively small difference in mean scores between the two *authoritative* responses presented.

2. Blacks and other nonwhites tend to give more *authoritative* responses to the Bible questions than whites. However, it is not clear just what these responses represent. For example, an analysis of the *Los Angeles Times* survey of July 1986, conducted by the Gallup Organization, reveals that the percentage of black respondents who give *orthodox* answers to four religious belief questions is greater among those blacks who state that the Bible is "an ancient book of fables, legends, history, and moral precepts" (62.8 percent) than those who state that the Bible is "the actual word of God and is to be taken literally, word for word" (52.6 percent). The same is true among other nonwhites; the percentage of those who expressed orthodox religious views is greater in the least authoritative category (73.5 percent) than the most authoritative category (52.4 percent). Among whites, the opposite is the case. While 73.4 percent of those whites who state that the Bible is the actual word of God are *orthodox* in their religious beliefs, only 16.6 percent of those who state that the Bible was "an ancient book of fables, legends, history, and moral precepts" could be classified as *orthodox* in their religious beliefs.

3. For further evidence of the significance of the Bible items as a predictor of political behaviors and issue positions, see Table 7.2.

4. The 1990 NES study employed two Bible questions. One-half the sample was given the literalism measure, while the other half received the inerrancy measure. Given that the pattern of responses to the two items did not vary greatly, and in order to increase the resultant *N* within the analysis, responses to the two questions were combined according to their relative assessment of the authoritative nature of the Bible.

5. During late 1990 and early 1991, a ten-page questionnaire was sent to 7,589 mem-

bers of seven different religious groups: Bread for the World, Concerned Women for America (CWA), Evangelicals for Social Action, JustLife, National Association of Evangelicals, Prison Fellowship, and donors to Americans for the Republic, Pat Robertson's political action committee. Five of the seven organizations provided us with a random sample of the organization's membership. The names of members of CWA were obtained through leadership lists published in the monthly periodical of the organization. The names of donors to Americans for the Republic were obtained through public documents. A total of 4,316 completed questionnaires were returned, for an overall response rate of 56.9 percent. The research team was composed of Lyman A. Kellstedt, John C. Green, James L. Guth, and Corwin E. Smidt.

6. The two religious controls are added to eliminate from the analysis the strongly religious nature of the activist sample, permitting a better test of the adequacy of the Bible measure. On the abortion item for the Religious Activist Study, the metric ranges from 1 (prochoice) to 7 (prolife).

References

Alston, Jon P., and McIntosh, William A. 1979. "An Assessment of the Determinants of Religious Participation." *Sociological Quarterly* 20:49–62.

Bellah, Robert N.; Madsen, Richard; Sullivan, William M.; Swidler, Ann; and Tipton, Steven M. 1985. *Habits of the Heart: Individualism and Commitment in American Life.* Berkeley: University of California Press.

Benson, Peter L., and Williams, Dorothy L. 1982. *Religion on Capitol Hill: Myths and Realities.* New York: Harper and Row.

Converse, Philip. 1964. "The Nature of Belief Systems in the Mass Public." In *Ideology and Discontent,* ed. David E. Apter, 206–61. New York: Free Press.

Cornwall, Marie; Albrecht, Stan L.; Cunningham, Perry; and Pitcher, Brian L. 1986. "The Dimensions of Religiosity: A Conceptual Model with an Empirical Test." *Review of Religious Research* 27:226–44.

Davidson, James, and Knudsen, Dean. 1977. "A New Approach to Religious Commitment." *Sociological Analysis* 10:151–73.

Driedger, Leo. 1974. "Doctrinal Belief: A Major Factor in the Differential Perception of Social Issues." *Sociological Quarterly* 15:66–80.

Glock, Charles Y., and Stark, Rodney. 1965. *Religion and Society in Tension.* Chicago: Rand McNally.

———. 1966. *Christian Beliefs and Anti-Semitism.* New York: Harper and Row.

Greeley, Andrew. 1984. "Religious Imagery as a Predictor Variable in the General Social Survey." Paper presented at the annual meeting of the Society for the Scientific Study of Religion, Chicago.

———. 1988. "Evidence That a Maternal Image of God Correlates with Liberal Politics." *Sociology and Social Research* 72:150–54.

Hadden, Jeffrey K. 1969. *The Gathering Storm in the Churches.* Garden City, NY: Doubleday and Co.

Hoffman, Thomas J. 1985. "Religion and Political Change: The Impacts of Institutional Connectedness and Religious Imagery." Paper presented at the annual meeting of the American Political Science Association, New Orleans.

Hoge, Dean, and de Zulueta, Ernesto. 1985. "Salience as a Condition for Various Social Consequences of Religious Commitment." *Journal for the Scientific Study of Religion* 24:21–37.

Jelen, Ted G. 1985. "Images of God as Predictors of Attitudes on Social Issues among Fundamentalists and Non-Fundamentalists." Paper presented at the annual meeting of

the Society for the Scientific Study of Religion, Savannah.
————. 1989a. "Biblical Literalism and Inerrancy: Does the Difference Make a Difference?" *Sociological Analysis* 49:421–29.
————, ed. 1986b. *Religion and Political Behavior in the United States.* New York: Praeger.
Jelen, Ted G.; Kellstedt, Lyman A.; and Wilcox, Clyde. 1990. "Racism and Religion: Some New Evidence for an Old Question." Paper presented at the annual meeting of the Association for the Sociology of Religion, Washington, DC.
Jelen, Ted G.; Smidt, Corwin E.; and Wilcox, Clyde. 1990. "Biblical Literalism and Inerrancy: A Methodological Investigation." *Sociological Analysis* 51:307–13.
Kersten, Lawrence L. 1970. *The Lutheran Ethic: The Impact of Religion on Laymen and Clergy.* Detroit: Wayne State University Press.
King, Morton B., and Hunt, Richard A. 1972. *Measuring Religious Dimensions: Studies in Congregational Involvement.* Dallas: Southern Methodist University Press.
Leege, David. 1989. "Toward a Mental Measure of Religiosity in Research on Religion and Politics." In *Religion and American Political Behavior,* ed. Ted G. Jelen, 45–64. New York: Praeger.
Leege, David C., and Welch, Michael R. 1989. "Religious Roots of Political Orientiations: Variations among American Catholic Parishioners." *Journal of Politics* 51:137–62.
Olson, Daniel, and Carroll, Jackson. 1989. "Theological and Political Orthodoxy among American Theological Faculty." Paper presented at the annual meeting of the Society for the Scientific Study of Religion, Salt Lake City.
Quinley, Harold E. 1974. *The Prophetic Clergy: Social Activism among Protestant Clergy.* New York: John Wiley.
Roof, Wade Clark. 1978. *Community and Commitment: Religious Plausibility in a Liberal Protestant Church.* New York: Elsevier.
————. 1979. "Concepts and Indicators of Religious Commitment: A Critical Review." In *The Religious Dimension: New Directions in Quantitative Research,* ed. Robert Wuthnow, 17–45. New York: Academic Press.
Smidt, Corwin E. 1989. "Identifying Evangelical Respondents: An Analysis of 'Born-Again' and Bible Questions Used across Different Surveys." In Ted G. Jelen 1989b, 23–43.
Stark, Rodney, and Bainbridge, William Sims. 1985. *The Future of Religion: Secularization, Revival, and Cult Formation.* Berkeley: University of California Press.
Stark, Rodney, and Foster, Bruce D. 1970. "In Defense of Orthodoxy: Notes on the Validity of an Index." *Social Forces* 48:383–93.
Stark, Rodney; Foster, Bruce; Glock, Charles; and Quinley, Harold. 1971. *Wayward Shepherds: Prejudice and the Protestant Clergy.* New York: Harper and Row.
Stark, Rodney, and Glock, Charles Y. 1968. *American Piety: The Nature of Religious Commitment.* Berkeley: University of California Press.
Wald, Kenneth D. 1992. *Religion and Politics in the United States.* 2d ed. Washington, DC: Congressional Quarterly Press.
Welch, Kevin W. 1981. "An Interpersonal Influence Model of Traditional Religious Commitment." *Sociological Quarterly* 22:81–92.
Welch, Michael R., and Leege, David C. 1988. "Religious Predictors of Catholic Parishioners' Sociopolitical Attitudes: Devotional Style, Closeness to God, Imagery, and Agentic-Communal Religious Identity." *Journal for the Scientific Study of Religion* 27:536–52.
————. 1991. "Dual Reference Groups and Political Orientations: An Examination of Evangelically Oriented Catholics." *American Journal of Political Science* 35:28–56.

White, Richard. 1968. "Toward a Theory of Religious Influence." *Pacific Sociological Review* 11:23–28.

Wuthnow, Robert. 1988. *The Restructuring of American Religion.* Princeton, NJ: Princeton University Press.

Yinger, Milton. 1969. "A Structural Examination of Religion." *Journal for the Scientific Study of Religion* 8:88–99.

———. 1970. *The Scientific Study of Religion.* New York: Macmillan.

Chapter 10

The Political Effects of the Born-Again Phenomenon

Ted G. Jelen, Corwin E. Smidt, and Clyde Wilcox

In recent years, the popular culture has devoted a good deal of attention to the political aspects of religious experience. Partly as a result of Jimmy Carter's explicit claim to be a born-again Christian, the political implications of religious experience received a great deal of attention. Indeed, journalistic accounts of Carter's "walk in the woods" with his sister, Ruth Carter Stapleton, which led to Carter's conversion experience, emphasized the dramatic, emotional nature of many such experiences (Witcover 1977). In the 1980 presidential election, all three candidates (Jimmy Carter, Ronald Reagan, and John Anderson) claimed to have been born again. Seemingly, by 1980, the status of *born-again Christian* was considered a highly desirable candidate attribute.

Our main focus in this chapter is on the religious experience or status of being born again. Such an emphasis is appropriate, since being born again is a very common phenomenon in the United States. Many analysts have used the terminology of being born again to refer to large portions of the New Christian Right, or to evangelical Protestantism generally. For example, one of the first studies of popular attitudes toward the Moral Majority carries the title *Born-Again Politics and the Moral Majority: What Social Surveys Really Show* (Stacey and Shupe 1982). A PBS documentary on a fundamentalist church in Massachusetts was titled, simply, "Born-Again" (Boone 1989). In the popular media, and in some scholarly accounts, the concept of being born again is shorthand for an entire range of phenomena relating to doctrinally conservative Protestantism. In this chapter, we attempt to impose some conceptual and empirical order on the phenomenon of being born again and to provide a more precise treatment of the concept.

Born-Again Experiences and Statuses

The task of conceptualizing the notion of being *born again* is complicated by the variety of usages and meanings the term has come to carry. For some, the phenomenon of being born again refers to a direct religious experience. Christianity, as is true for many other religions, calls individuals to repentance and change, i.e., to "experience" conversion. This phenomenon of conversion may be defined as "a profound, self-conscious, existential change from one set of beliefs, habits, and orientation to a new structure of belief and action" (Brauer 1978, 227). While religious conversions transpire within different religious faiths, the phenomenon of conversion within certain segments of the Christian faith is frequently labeled being *born again*. This particular designation is drawn, in part, from the words of Jesus in his conversation with Nicodemus (KJV, John 3:1–21): "I tell you the truth, unless a man is born again, he cannot see the Kingdom of God."

Different Christian traditions understand the born-again phenomenon in diverse ways. Some emphasize "making a decision for Christ," i.e., receiving Jesus as one's personal Lord and Savior. Such a decision not only is understood to occur at a specific moment in time, but it is also understood that such a decision is frequently accompanied with a spiritual struggle or experience, sometimes intense in nature, over whether Christ will "rule" in one's life. In this instance, the status of being *born again* results from a specific *experience*, which one may be able to identify with a particular time, place, or circumstance. Such an experience corresponds to Glock and Stark's (1965, 46) concept of a *responsive experience*, in which an individual has an intuition or feeling about the truth of his or her beliefs, and feels that "the divine has taken specific notice of the individual's existence." The person having a born-again experience has the sense of simultaneously accepting and being accepted by Christ.

Other Christian traditions tend to emphasize that being born again is a condition or status one enjoys in the eyes of God through making a public profession of one's faith in Jesus Christ. Furthermore, the *status* of having been born again may reflect an *identification* with a group of believers or a community of people who have been "saved," with an implicit contrast to those outside the faith. People may adopt the label of *born again* without having had a specific (or more gradual) conversion experience, if such an identification is a community norm. For example, Kellstedt (1990) reports that an identification as a born-again Christian is a much stronger predictor of a variety of political attitudes in the North, where such a status is unusual, than in the South, where the born-again designation is considerably more common. Calling oneself *born again* may simply reflect the expectations of one's congregation (or some larger community) and may or may not correspond to identifiable religious experiences.

What is common to these two senses of being born again is that both making a decision for Christ and making public profession of one's faith can be traced to a distinct moment in time: what is different is that in one tradition, being *born again* is more likely to be accompanied by a deep religious experience than in the other tradition.

Conversely, some Christians have understood being born again to result from more of a process than a discrete act or a particular experience. Two different understandings are evident within this *process* approach. Among those Christians who emphasize a more experiential than confessional understanding of conversion, there are some who remember their born-again experience as a gradual process, occurring over a period of time. Thus, it is not surprising that many psychological studies of conversion experiences divide them into two main types: "a volition type which comes gradually, step by step, and a self-surrender type which comes suddenly" (Brauer 1978, 230).

On the other hand, among those traditions that emphasize a more confessional than experiential approach to conversion, there are those who understand their born-again status simply as a reflection of being baptized and nurtured in the church. For them, the sacrament of baptism is a christening, being reborn in Christ through a divinely sanctioned cleansing of original sin and taking on a new identity. It requires little or no volition, particularly if one is an infant, but simply God's promise of new life. If there is an act of volition, it would come during the teen years in the process of confirmation, i.e., reaffirmation of baptism, and in periodic confession. Both of these are sacramental in nature, that is, they call more attention to God's grace than to the individual striver's action.

Despite the fact that the contemporary evangelical movement is thought to be composed of born-again Christians, not all evangelicals believe that conversion must reflect a sudden "Saul/Paul" experience (e.g., Wells 1991). Rather, in its broadest sense, to be born again is simply to confess and to repent from one's sinful nature and to accept Jesus Christ as one's Savior (Poloma 1982). Thus, a born-again experience may not be the crucial defining characteristic of being an evangelical; rather, it is one's personal commitment to Jesus Christ as the Lord of one's life.

However, because of its narrower connotation as referring to some relatively intense experience that marks a spiritual turning point in one's life, the *born-again* terminology tends to be used more frequently within some segments of doctrinally conservative Protestantism than within others. Evangelicals from more confessional traditions are less likely than evangelicals from more pietistic traditions to understand the conversion experience in terms of a specific, identifiable point in one's life (Hunter 1983, 65). Thus, for example, Lutherans are much less likely to claim a born-again experience than are Baptists (Smidt and Kellstedt 1987).

Gallup (1979) originally differentiated between *conversionalist* and *confessional* evangelicals, and Hunter (1983) later continued to make this distinction. However, while Gallup found some significant differences between the two groups, he viewed the overlap between them to be sufficiently large (in that many conversionalists also met the criteria for being orthodox-confessional evangelicals) that he found it convenient to speak of the two as one conversionalist group. Consequently, Gallup later began to employ a born-again question to identify evangelical respondents operationally.

Subsequently, the born-again question has become a frequently used religious measure in national public opinion polls—particularly for identifying evangelical respondents. However, the specific questions posed to tap this born-again phenomenon have varied from survey to survey, with different percentages of the population admitting to being born again when different question wording is employed (Smidt 1989a; Smidt and Kellstedt 1987). Moreover, Kellstedt (1989) has shown that claims to be born again do not, by themselves, discriminate between orthodox evangelicals and other respondents, which suggests that self-reports of born-again statuses or experiences are inadequate measures of evangelicalism. Consequently, the focus of this chapter is not upon the relationship between the born-again phenomenon and religious communities but upon how, if at all, aspects of being born again may have political effects.

Born-Again Politics: Political Attitudes and Behavior

How might the experience or status of being born again affect a person's political attitudes? It has been shown (Wilcox 1992; and chapters 7 and 9 of this volume) that religious variables such as the respondent's belief in an inerrant Bible become politically relevant when such religious beliefs are given political meaning by religious or political elites. We consider it unlikely that religious experiences carry direct political content. Religious experiences are not intrinsically political but gain their political meaning through the interpretations placed upon them externally (see Glock and Stark 1965).

We can conceive of at least three cognitive mechanisms by which being born again might come to have political meaning. First, the experience of being born again might serve as a political *demobilizer*, by increasing the *otherworldliness* of some conservative Protestants. To use terminology coined by Benson and Williams (1982), conversion experiences may result in religious orientations that are *agentic* (or individualistic) and *vertical* (the individual believer's relationship with God supersedes merely human activities such as politics). Politics may seem extremely unimportant to a person who has directly experienced God.

Second, if the status of being born again refers to a religious *identification*, as opposed to an *experience*, being born again might well serve as a source of political mobilization. It has been shown (Jelen 1991c, 1993) that attitudes about religiously defined groups are often powerful sources of political attitudes. Group-based heuristics are an important means by which individual citizens organize and simplify the political world. To the extent that the status of *born-again Christian* serves to distinguish believers from nonbelievers, such an identification may have important political implications.

Finally, the born-again phenomenon may serve as a *plausibility structure* by which the authority of religious communications might be enhanced. Roof (1976) has argued that religious communications must compete with a variety of secular messages for the allegiance of church members. It has been frequently noted that religious orthodoxy must compete with other, dissonant messages in the modern world and that religion runs the risk of being compartmentalized or compromised through a process of accommodation (see especially Hunter 1983, 1987). Why should religious messages be accorded priority over other cues provided by the larger culture? For Roof, plausibility structures are social in nature, consisting largely of frequent personal interaction with like-minded people. However, the concept of a plausibility structure is potentially much broader than simple social interactions. Indeed, religion itself may enhance the plausibility of its own message, and religious experiences may constitute an important means of such enhancement. Direct experiences with divine phenomena may increase the credibility of the sacred and may increase individual sensitivity to religious messages.

Thus, we can imagine at least three means by which religious experiences, such as being born again, have implications for political attitudes and behavior: (1) born-again experiences may serve as a source of political demobilization, by inducing general orientations that may inhibit the salience of politics; (2) the status of claiming to be born again may serve as a source of political mobilization; or (3) one's self-identification as a born-again Christian may provide a simple cognitive structure through which the political world can be viewed or may serve as a means of enhancing the plausibility of religious communications.

The Born-Again Items

The primary data sources for this chapter are the 1988 National Election Study (NES) and the NES 1989 Pilot Study. Because religion often has different consequences for American blacks (and because the black subsample is extremely small), the analyses presented here are limited to white respondents.

As noted above, our principal focus is on the political effects of a born-again status or experience. The 1988 NES contains the following item, eliciting a sense of the born-again phenomenon as a status or self-identification: "Do you consider yourself a born-again Christian?" A slightly different item appears in the 1989 Pilot Study: "Would you call yourself a born-again Christian—that is, have you personally had a conversion experience related to Jesus Christ?" The latter version of the born-again item is more experiential, connoting a particular experience with Christ at the center. Of course, the conversion experience described in this version of the question could either be sudden or more gradual. The 1989 item is designed to define the *status* of born again with reference to a personal conversion *experience*. Thus, it is an elaborating definition, a context for the respondent to decide whether the term *born-again Christian* fits.

The conceptual difference between the two items is potentially substantial, but the empirical difference is not. Just over one-third of white respondents report being born again, regardless of which item is being considered. Indeed, the 1989 version (the more experiential item) generates a slightly *higher* percentage of born-again respondents than does the item eliciting born-again status

(39.0 percent reporting a born-again *experience*, as opposed to 35.4 percent claiming a born-again *status*). Thus, these items, despite their somewhat different wordings, seem substantially equivalent. These findings stand in contrast with previous patterns reported by Smidt (1989a), who has shown that the proportion of respondents claiming to be born again is reduced in items in which the experiential aspects of being born again are emphasized.[1] It is, of course, possible that positive responses to the 1989 item are inflated by the social desirability of the referent *Jesus Christ*. However, it seems more likely that the phrase *conversion experience* used in the 1989 item is sufficiently elastic to cover a variety of commitments to Christ that might be made by any given respondent.

It should be noted that both born-again items may overestimate the percentage of born-again respondents. Dixon, Levy, and Lowery (1988) argue that many people respond to the term *Christian* in survey questions like these rather than focusing on the *born-again* aspect of the item. For some respondents, a *no* response means that they do not consider themselves Christians, and this interpretation leads to a high number of false positives. When respondents are offered a choice between *Christian* and *born-again Christian*, Dixon, Levi, and Lowery (1988) report that the percentage claiming a born-again status declines dramatically. While we have no clear means for determining the "correct" question wording, it should be noted that the marginal distributions of the born-again items may be quite sensitive to other versions of the item.

Table 10.1 shows the relationships between both born-again items and a number of religious and political variables. In this table we use the respondents from the 1989 Pilot Study in both columns, analyzing both their 1988 and 1989 responses. Although this source results in a smaller number of cases for analysis, we believe that this procedure is preferable to running the analyses separately for the 1988 NES and 1989 Pilot Study. Since the respondents for both columns of Table 10.1 are the same, the only differences between the two sets of correlations are the question wordings themselves (provided one assumes that there is relatively little religious status or experience change between the two waves of the panel). We can, for practical purposes, eliminate sampling error as a source of difference between the two items.

The data in Table 10.1 suggest that the two born-again items are substantially equivalent. With respect to the relationships between the born-again items and religious variables, the coefficients are generally in the expected direction. Both versions of the born-again item are strongly related to membership in an evangelical or pentecostal denomination, to the frequency with which the respondent monitors religious communications, and to religious salience and church attendance. Catholics are much less likely to report being born again than Protestants, and respondents who identify with particular sect movements within conservative Protestantism (evangelical, charismatic, or fundamentalist) are relatively likely to claim a born-again status or experience.

Turning to the relationships between the born-again items and political

Table 10.1

Alternative Versions of the Born-Again Item, by Criterion Variables
(product-moment correlations)

	1988 NES	1989 Pilot
Religious Variables:		
Religious Salience	.42	.44
Evangelical Denomination	.36	.43
Catholic	-.31	-.30
Pentecostal Denomination	.21	.23
Left/right self-placement	.14	.15
Church attendance	.35	.38
Region	.26	.25
Frequency reading religious material	.21	.22
Frequency watch religious TV	.12	.17
Pastor Preaches politics	.13	.22
Fundamentalist ID	.36	.23
Evangelical ID	.35	.36
Charismatic ID	.38	.34
Combined religious ID[1]	.46	.38
Political Variables:		
Party Identification	.06*	.11
Moral traditionalism	.24	.27
Defense spending	.12	.19
Spending for the poor	-.14	-.13
Rating Moral Majority	.28	.37
Presidential vote	-.08*	-.11*
Social issues	.30	.34
Rating Ronald Reagan	.10	.14
Rating Pat Robertson	.33	.33
Vote turnout	.04*	.01*

Source: Data are taken from 1989 Pilot Study for both items.

*not significant at .05.

[1]Counts number of self-identifications with conservative Protestant traditions (fundamentalist, evangelical, charismatic-pentecostal.)

Born-again variables are coded 0 (not born-again) and 1 (born-again). Political variables are coded so that higher scores indicate greater conservatism, greater Republicanism, or higher levels of support for Christian Right figures.

attitudes, we again find that the items are substantially equivalent. The experiential item has a slightly stronger relationship with attitudes toward defense spending and affect toward the Moral Majority than does the item eliciting the respondent's born-again status, but these differences are not large. As might be expected, attitudes toward issues of personal morality exhibit stronger relationships with both born-again items than do attitudes toward spending to help the poor or for national defense.

What is also interesting is the pattern of weak bivariate relationships between the born-again items and partisan attitudes. The relationships between the born-again items and presidential vote in 1988, party identification, and affect toward Ronald Reagan are quite weak and occasionally insignificant. This non-finding is somewhat surprising, given that the born-again items are both related to a number of attitudes and behaviors with partisan implications. Many religious communications (including exposure to religious television) present clear partisan cues. Moreover, the respondent's born-again credentials are also related to a number of issues on which the parties at the national level have taken unambiguous and opposing stands. The lack of connection between issue positions and partisan attitudes suggests that being born again may indeed serve as a political demobilizer as we hypothesized (see Jelen 1987, 1991a). The status of being born again may increase the perception that politics is unimportant relative to the individual's relationship with God. Further analysis suggests that neither born-again item is significantly related to voting turnout, either by itself or in combination with other variables. However, as we shall see below, there may be an important regional component of the relationship between partisanship and born-again experiences.

Further evidence (not shown) suggests that being born again may also serve as a plausibility structure, by which the credibility of religious messages is enhanced. Using the full data set from the 1988 NES (to ensure a large sample size), bivariate correlations between the respondent's born-again status and a variety of political attitudes were computed separately for African-Americans, white evangelical Protestants, white mainline Protestants, and Roman Catholics. Each of these groups was divided further into frequent and infrequent church attenders.

Among African Americans, being born again has a slight conservatizing effect on issues of personal morality, and a slight liberalizing effect on economic issues. Conversely, white evangelical Protestants who claim a born-again status are more conservative on social issues and moral traditionalism, and this effect is more pronounced among frequent church attenders. Born-again mainline Protestants tend to be somewhat more liberal than other mainliners on social issues, with the effect again being stronger among frequent attenders. For all three groups, the effect of being born again is to exaggerate the political tendencies of the theological traditions in question. Thus, our data suggest that, among blacks and white Protestants, the status of being born again enhances the credibility of religious communications.

Being born again has a conservatizing impact on Roman Catholics who do not attend religious services regularly. This suggests that evangelically oriented Catholics (who may be poorly integrated into parish life) may be politically distinctive. While there are too few born-again Catholics in the 1988 NES to sustain a thorough multivariate analysis, this set of results may indicate that such Catholics merit further investigation (see Welch and Leege 1991; Jelen 1992b).

Multivariate Analysis

Another set of concerns relates to the independent impact of the respondent's sense of being born again on political attitudes. Table 10.2 is intended to provide two sorts of information. First, Table 10.2 presents those political attitudes on which being born again has an independent effect once other religious variables have been controlled. Second, the data in this table show the effects of being born again in a multivariate model in which the respondent's born-again experience is used in interaction with other religious and demographic variables. These other variables include the respondent's view of the Bible, region (South, non-South), the subjective importance of religion in everyday life, membership in an evangelical denomination, Roman Catholicism, frequency of church attendance, frequency of viewing religious television, and identification as fundamentalist, evangelical, or charismatic.[2] The intention here is to determine the extent to which the respondent's self-reported born-again experience enhances the political effects of other variables.[3] The dependent variables used on the equations on which Table 10.2 is based are those listed in Table 10.1, as well as the components of the social issues index (women's rights, homosexual rights, abortion, and school prayer). Only those issues on which the effects of the born-again item attain statistical significance in the multivariate model (either by itself or as part of an interaction term) are included. To permit comparison of the effects of being born again across different regression equations, the entries in Table 10.2 are unstandardized regression coefficients (b).

As the data in Table 10.2 suggest, the respondent's sense of being born again is not significantly related to most political attitudes once the effects of other religious variables have been controlled. By itself, however, the respondent's report of a born-again experience is significantly related to attitudes on abortion, capital punishment, and party identification. Interestingly, the effects of a born-again experience on party identification are *increased* when the effects of other religious and demographic variables have been controlled (*beta* = .15 in the multivariate model, as compared to a zero-order correlation of .11). Inspection of the correlation matrix on which this equation is based suggests that it is the control for region which generates this result. That is, a born-again experience is related to partisanship in the North but not in the South. As previously noted, being born again is apparently a politically distinctive attitude in the North but is part of the common political culture in the South (see Kellstedt 1990; Smidt

Table 10.2

Comparison of Born-Again, Biblical Inerrancy, and Interaction Terms on Selected Dependent Variables
(unstandardized regression coefficients)

	Born-again	Bible	Interaction
Rating Robertson	*	8.26	12.62
Abortion	.30	.32	.47
Death Penalty	.34	.31	*
Defense spending	*	.26	.31
Party ID	.67	*	*

Source: NES 1989 Pilot Study.

*not significant at .05.

Controls include born-again status; respondent's view of the Bible; education; sex; age; region (South, non-South); marital status; importance of religion in everyday life; membership in an evangelical denomination; Roman Catholicism; frequency of viewing religious television; fundamentalist, charismatic, and evangelical self-identifications; church attendance; and whether the respondent was exposed to political topics in sermons at his or her own church. Religious variables were omitted from equations when used as components in interaction term. When used in interactions, religious variables were dichotomized and coded 0 or 1 to preserve metric of the born-again item.

1989b). Alternatively, it may be that Republican elites have exploited the symbolic aspects of the born-again experience and have perhaps divorced the status of being born again from its theological context. For example, Ronald Reagan claimed to have been born again even though he could point to no *specific* conversion experience. Even Episcopalian George Bush, while not employing the *born-again* vocabulary directly, used the conversional language of having "accepted Jesus Christ as [his] personal Savior." Having had a born-again experience is also independently related to a conservative attitude on the death penalty.

With respect to attitudes toward Pat Robertson, abortion, and defense spending, a born-again status achieves its greatest effect in interaction with biblical inerrancy. For these issues, the respondent's sense of having been born again appears to enhance the credibility of particular interpretations of the Bible, in contrast to more secular communications. In this context, then, the born-again phenomenon appears to provide a plausibility structure within which a biblically based heuristic can compete with messages in the secular world.

When interaction terms between other religious variables and the 1989 Pilot

Study born-again item are included in multivariate equations, in no case does the interaction with the born-again item improve the performance of the control variable. In other words, being born again does not enhance the effects of any other religious variable on any other political attitude.

Thus, being born again does have an independent effect on certain political attitudes. This effect is generally strongest when the effects of being born again are considered in combination with a strict view of the Scriptures. This result confirms findings reported by Kellstedt (1989), in which he compares doctrinally conservative Protestants with "suspect" evangelicals (i.e., people who have only one characteristic associated with evangelicalism). By itself, the status or experience of being born again does not have great political importance. In some instances, religious experience increases the effects of a belief in an inerrant Bible. However, what stands out about Table 10.2 is the large number of political attitudes that are *not* included because the effects of the born-again measure do not attain statistical significance. The effects of a born-again status or experience, as a discrete variable, are thus rather limited. One possible explanation for this set of largely null findings is that the born-again phenomenon is a component of a rich tapestry of religious meanings and that the *unique* effects of being born again cannot be isolated from this larger set of religious meanings.

However, it is also possible that a simple dichotomous variable tapping whether or not an individual perceives himself or herself as a born-again Christian or reports a born-again experience fails to capture important variation in how an individual understands that label. Given that Christians hold different understandings concerning how religious conversions occur, it may be advantageous to distinguish between and among such understandings.

A recent national survey of activists from seven groups that draw their memberships primarily from evangelical Protestants contained a question that permits a preliminary test of the potential utility of a more-refined measure.[4] In the survey, respondents were asked, "Do you consider yourself a born-again Christian?" Respondents answering affirmatively were then asked: "Which of the following applies BEST to you? (1) It was a specific moment in my life I can remember, (2) It is a condition I enjoy by profession of faith in Jesus, (3) It was a gradual experience that occurred over a period of time, (4) It is the result of being nurtured in Christ's church throughout my life."

Even restricting analysis to Protestant respondents, responses to this more-refined measure are revealing. First, given that this was a largely evangelical sample, it is not too surprising that relatively few respondents (4.9 percent) refused to classify themselves as born-again Christians. Secon, a majority (52.9 percent) of those classifying themselves as born-again Christians reported that they could remember a specific moment in their lives whereby they became born again. Nevertheless, nearly one-half of born-again Protestants understood being born again as reflecting something other than a specific-moment conversion experience—with 14.2 percent reporting that it reflected a condition they enjoyed by profession of faith, 18.1 percent that it reflected a gradual experience which occurred over a period of time, and 14.8 percent that it resulted from having been nurtured in the church throughout their lives.

Is variation in one's interpretation of being a born-again Christian related to differences in political attitudes and behavior among these activists? Table 10.3 contains the percentage of respondents falling within each category of the born-again variable that exhibited the specified characteristics. The top portion of Table 10.3 presents the percentage of respondents within each category with respect to certain religious, social, and political variables, while the bottom portion examines the relationships between the born-again variable and four political variables (attitudes toward abortion, partisanship, political ideology, and reported vote for president in 1988), while controlling for selected variables.

Several different patterns are revealed in Table 10.3. First, the relationships between the born-again item and other religious variables are rather modest (except for the Bible item). In particular, the relatively weak relationships between the born-again item and other religious experiences (a feeling of well-being, experiencing God's presence) lend credence to the hypothesis that the born-again phenomenon relates to a psychological identification and not necessarily a discrete experience. Further, the largest percentage differences for the various religious measures tend to be between those who did not regard themselves as born-again Christians and all others. In other words, those respondents expressing differing interpretations of being born again tend to be closer together than those who refuse to label themselves *born again*.

On the other hand, the same is not true with respect to political variables. Not only are consistent monotonic patterns evident for all four political variables, but those who report different understandings of being born again tend to differ more with each other than some do with those who do not consider themselves born again. Moreover, these relatively strong relationships persist even after controlling for several religious variables and educational attainment, and obtain across a number of other political attitudes as well. One is struck by the relative strength of such relationships as well as the consistent monotonic patterns across a variety of dependent variables.[5]

Discussion

The contrast between the results presented in Table 10.1 and Table 10.2 suggest that the political effects of being born again are rather complex. The strong correlations between born-again status and experience reported in Table 10.1 suggest that being born again is a component of a rich set of religious attitudes relating conservative theology to politics. However, the attribute of being born again by itself, when measured simply as a dichotomous variable, has little independent effect.

Nevertheless, the apparent unimportance of the born-again variable in the

Table 10.3

Selected Characteristics of Different Types of Born-Again Christians
(Protestants only)

	Not Born Again (N=173)	Nurtured in Faith (N=479)	Gradual Experience (N=613)	Profession of Faith (N=501)	Specific Experience (N=1786)	r
Religious and Social Characteristics						
% religion is center of one's life	32.7%	68.2%	69.2%	66.7%	75.6%	.12
% Feel Regularly:						
Well Being	27.2%	42.9%	41.1%	44.6%	57.5%	.18
God's Presence	21.4%	29.9%	28.8%	30.7%	39.4%	.14
Divinely Inspired	9.4%	11.8%	12.3%	14.2%	20.6%	.18
% Attend Weekly	71.2%	92.9%	90.3%	88.4%	93.1%	.09
% Evangelicals	24.3%	71.8%	77.7%	78.4%	82.8%	.22
% Charismatic/Pent.	4.0%	15.2%	24.5%	25.3%	38.0%	.22
% Bible Inerrantist	19.6%	54.4%	69.7%	72.5%	84.7%	.39
% Graduate Degree	54.7%	49.5%	39.5%	36.7%	29.8%	.17
Political Characteristics						
% Abortion Never	3.2%	7.5%	12.9%	15.8%	20.3%	.40
% Republican	21.8%	46.1%	52.5%	60.5%	74.4%	.33
% Conservative	11.8%	33.3%	39.9%	47.5%	67.7%	.37
% Bush in 1988	26.1%	54.6%	64.7%	73.2%	87.5%	.37

Source: 1990 Religious Activist Study.

1989 Pilot Study may be attributable to the fact that such a simple dichotomy masks important variation in the understanding and interpretation of the born-again designation. The meaning of being born again varies among groups of born-again Christians, and variations in these meanings appear to be systematically related to some important political variables.[6]

In addition to work on refining the born-again measure to reflect such differences in meaning, future research on the political effects of being born again might profitably focus on the consequences of the born-again phenomenon at the level of the local congregation. Whether being born again is a political demobilizer, a group identification, or a politically relevant plausibility structure seems likely to depend on the content of elite communications in communities in which born-again Christians are numerous. Jelen (1991b) has shown that the main political effects of born-again status occur at the congregational level. That is, the relationship between congregational-level frequency of being born again and various political attitudes is stronger than the same relationship at the individual level. Isolated individuals who claim a born-again status or experience may not change their political attitudes in response to their religious conversions. At the mass level, religious experiences appear to gain their political relevance from elite-level communications that take place within religious communities.

Conversely, more research is needed on the meaning of the born-again phenomenon within sacramental traditions. While the panel resulting from the 1988 NES Presidential Election Study and the 1989 NES Pilot Study contains too few born-again Catholics to sustain multivariate analyses, Leege, Kellstedt, and Wald (1990) have shown that Roman Catholics adopt a born-again *status* more easily than they report having had born-again *experiences*. Since some previous research (Welch and Leege 1991; Jelen 1992b) has suggested that evangelical Catholics constitute a politically interesting group, further investigation of the meaning of the *born-again* label in nonevangelical settings seems warranted. In particular, open-ended questions, asking respondents to describe their own senses of being born again, seem a promising avenue of future research.

Leege, Kellstedt, and Wald (1990) show that the more *experiential* item does a better job of discriminating evangelical Christians and others who may report being born again. While we believe that both a status item and an experiential item may be useful in future research, the results reported by Leege, Kellstedt, and Wald suggest that, if forced to choose, the experiential item may be more promising. However, this recommendation carries two caveats. First, the *experience* depicted in any future item should be described in sufficiently general terms to capture the diverse meanings that respondents may apply to the term. As Table 10.3 indicates, there are a variety of senses in which respondents may come to regard themselves as born again. While it may not be feasible to pose all of these alternatives in a national survey, any single item should be worded broadly enough to tap these several meanings. Second, the work of Dixon, Levy, and Lowery (1988) serves as a useful reminder that many born-again items contain socially desirable terms, such as *Christian, Jesus Christ*, etc. Future items designed to measure the born-again phenomenon should include an explicitly *religious* or *Christian* alternative by which the respondent can report having a religious identification *without* claiming a born-again status or experience. For example, Dixon, Levy, and Lowery (1988) use an item in which respondents are asked to choose among being a *Christian, born-again Christian*, or *neither of these*. While this identification item does not pose the issue of born-again experience, it may ameliorate the social desirability problems of other versions of the measure. While we do not regard the results reported by Dixon, Levy, and Lowery (1988) as definitive, future research into the born-again phenomenon must address the issue of socially desirable responses.

More generally, this chapter has raised more questions than it has answered. The phenomenon of being born again has important implications both within and outside the evangelical community, and the concept appears to have political relevance for a large percentage of American citizens. Thus, the born-again phenomenon deserves the attention of political scientists in future analyses of American political attitudes and behavior. Nevertheless, the conceptual and measurement issues that this chapter has raised admit of no simple solutions. Quantifying an essentially spiritual phenomenon remains an elusive (and imperative) task.

Notes

1. Several factors may account for these differences. First, the lead-in portion of both questions frame the item in terms of self-classification as a born-again Christian. Only after the relatively similar lead-in question has been asked does the 1989 Pilot Study qualifying the lead-in ask whether the respondent has had a conversion experience. Second, given that the 1989 Pilot Study was based on reinterviews of the 1988 NES respondents, the same respondents are responding to similar lead-in portions of the two questions.

2. These analyses employ the 1989 Pilot Study (experiential) version of the born-again item.

3. When used as components of interaction terms, other variables are coded 0 or 1 to preserve the comparability of the unstandardized regression coefficients.

4. The seven groups were Bread for the World, Concerned Women for America, Evangelicals for Social Action, JustLife, National Association of Evangelicals, Prison Fellowship, and donors to Americans for the Republic, Pat Robertson's political action committee. These interest groups are some of the largest and most significant organizations in the religious sector. They also run the gamut of the evangelical community, from activists at the core of the New Christian Right to members of the Evangelical Left, with many centrists in between. The questionnaire was mailed to a stratified random sample of 7,589 activists, with 4,316 completed questionnaires being returned—a 56.9 percent response rate. The study was conducted by Lyman A. Kellstedt, John C. Green, James L. Guth, and Corwin E. Smidt.

5. The major exceptions to these monotonic patterns tend to be evident among the charismatic and pentecostal respondents—with those self-classified charismatic-pentecostal respondents falling into the *not born again* column breaking the pattern. However, only

214 DOCTRINAL, EXPERIENTIAL, AND WORLDVIEW MEASURES

five respondents fell into that category, making the resulting percentages rather unstable and suspect.

6. The differences between the 1989 Pilot Study and the 1990 Religious Activist Study may also reflect differences in levels of sophistication. Religious activists have more internally consistent belief systems than do members of the mass public.

References

Benson, Peter L., and Williams, Dorothy L. 1982. *Religion on Capitol Hill: Myths and Realities.* New York: Harper and Row.

Boone, Kathleen C. 1989. *The Bible Tells Them So: The Discourse of Protestant Fundamentalism.* Albany: State University of New York Press.

Brauer, Jerald C. 1978. "Conversion: From Puritanism to Revival." *Journal of Religion* 58:227–43.

Dixon, Richard; Levy, Dianne E.; and Lowery, Roger C. 1988. "Asking the 'Born-Again' Question." *Review of Religious Research* 30:33–39.

Gallup, George. 1979. "The Christianity Today–Gallup Poll: An Overview." *Christianity Today* 23:1663–73.

Glock, Charles Y., and Stark, Rodney. 1965. *Religion and Society in Tension.* Chicago: Rand McNally.

Hunter, James Davison. 1983. *American Evangelicalism: Conservative Religion and the Quandary of Modernity.* Brunswick, NJ: Rutgers University Press.

————. 1987. *Evangelicalism: The Coming Generation.* Chicago: University of Chicago Press.

Jelen, Ted G. 1987. "The Effects of Religious Separatism on White Protestants in the 1984 Presidential Election." *Sociological Analysis* 48:30–45.

————, ed. 1989. *Religion and Political Behavior in the United States.* New York: Praeger.

————. 1991a. "Church–State Relations: The View from the Pulpit." Paper presented at the annual meeting of the American Political Science Association, Washington.

————. 1991b. "The Political Effects of Religious Experience: A Contextual Analysis." Unpublished paper, Illinois Benedictine College.

————. 1991c. *The Political Mobilization of Religious Beliefs.* New York: Praeger.

————. 1992. "Religion and Attitudes toward Foreign Policy." Paper presented at the conference on the Political Consequences of War, American National Election Studies and the Brookings Institution, Washington, DC.

————. 1993. "The Political Consequences of Religious Group Attitudes." *Journal of Politics* 55:178–90.

Kellstedt, Lyman A. 1989. "The Meaning and Measurement of Evangelicalism: Problems and Prospects." In Ted G. Jelen 1989, 3–22.

————. 1990. "Evangelical Religion and Support for Social Issue Policies," In *The Disappearing South: Studies in Regional Change and Continuity,* ed. Robert P. Steed, Laurence W. Moreland, and Tod A. Baker. Tuscaloosa: University of Alabama Press.

Leege, David C.; Kellstedt, Lyman A.; and Wald, Kenneth D. 1990. "Religion and Politics: A Report on Measures of Religiosity in the 1989 NES Pilot Study." Paper presented at annual meeting of the Midwest Political Science Association, Chicago.

Poloma, Margaret M. 1982. *The Charismatic Movement: Is There a New Pentecost?* Boston: Twayne Publishers.

Roof, Wade Clark. 1976. "Traditional Religion in Contemporary Society: A Theory of Local-Cosmopolitan Plausibility." *American Sociological Review* 41:195–208.

Smidt, Corwin E. 1989a. "Identifying Evangelical Respondents: An Analysis of 'Born-

Again' and Bible Questions Used across Different Surveys." In Ted G. Jelen 1989, 23–43.

———. 1989b. "Change and Stability among Southern Evangelicals." In *Religion in American Politics,* ed. Charles W. Dunn, 147–60. Washington, DC: Congressional Quarterly Press.

Smidt, Corwin E., and Kellstedt, Lyman A. 1987. "Evangelicalism and Survey Research: Interpretive Problems and Substantive Findings." In *The Bible, Politics, and Democracy,* ed. Richard J. Neuhaus, 81–102, 131–67. Grand Rapids, MI: William Eerdmans.

Stacey, William A., and Shupe, Anson. 1982. *Born-Again Politics and the Moral Majority: What Social Surveys Really Show.* New York: Edwin Mellen Press.

Welch, Michael R., and Leege, David C. 1991. "Dual Reference Groups and Political Orientations: An Examination of Evangelically Oriented Catholics." *American Journal of Political Science* 35:28–56.

Wells, David F. 1991. "Conversion: How and Why We Turn to God." *Christianity Today* 35:28–31.

Wilcox, Clyde. 1992. *God's Warriors: The Christian Right in the Twentieth Century* Baltimore: Johns Hopkins University Press.

Witcover, Jules. 1977. *Marathon.* New York: Random House.

Chapter 11

Religious Worldviews and Political Philosophies: Capturing Theory in the Grand Manner through Empirical Data

David C. Leege and Lyman A. Kellstedt

The Enduring Questions: God, Humankind, and Country

Embedded within every religion are the basic elements of political philosophy. This is the case because religion is built through stories of origin and destiny and offers both proclamations and explanations of freedom and order, judgment, meaning, and hope. Religion is often the source for founding myths that collect a people into a political community and give them purpose. Religion holds up transcendent standards of justice by which a people can measure its collective actions. In prescribing a path to salvation, religion, as Max Weber noted (Gerth and Mills 1946), tells a people not only what it is saved *from* but what it is saved *for*. In short, religion offers models *of* and *for* personal and collective reality.

The adhesive that binds together religious worldviews and political philosophy is culture. Geertz (1973, 44) argues that culture is not simply a complex of "*concrete behavior patterns*—customs, usages, traditions, habit clusters—but . . . a *set of control mechanisms*—plans, recipes, rules, instructions—for the governing of behavior." At the heart of culture, according to Geertz (1966, 129–31) is a system of sacred symbols that seem "to mediate genuine knowledge, knowledge of the essential condition in which life must, of necessity, be lived. . . . What a people prize[s] and what it fears and hates are depicted in its world view, symbolized in its religion, and in turn expressed in the whole quality of life." Culture, particularly through its religious beliefs, rituals, and worldviews, has a regulating function.

Religion becomes collective memory, but politics becomes collective action. Religion gives cultural expression to the main problems of existence perceived by a people. It not only addresses the fundamental problems of human existence but prescribes the process of their solution and envisions the outcome. Because politics involves the legitimate use of the means of coercion to achieve societal goals, it can have a peculiarly binding way of "enforcing salvation." Most religious worldviews allow for the possibility of nonconformity through freedom of the will; religion will offer identity and norms for behavior, but any individual is free to cope with the consequences of a personal decision not to conform. The political order, by its very definition as collective action and its capacity to use coercion, has the potential to impose swift and often devastating sanctions on nonconformity. The religious nonconformist, in the self-confidence of the mind, can typically tolerate and perhaps welcome separation from a religious community. The political nonconformist, particularly where the state is driven by a monistic salvational purpose, is likely to be forcibly separated from the political community and perhaps from life itself.

The culture that developed in the United States, as so aptly described by Alexis de Tocqueville, had, as its centerpiece, individualism. Its democracy was a social condition characterized by the sovereignty of *all* the people. Anglo-Americans, according to Tocqueville ([1835, 1840] 1958, 45), had incorporated into their culture two apparently contradictory elements—the spirit of religion and the spirit of liberty. Americans could pursue "with equal eagerness material wealth and moral satisfaction; heaven in the world beyond and well-being and liberty in this one." Because only their religion could be salvational if it were not to contradict the spirit of liberty, the state was always circumscribed in its use of coercive powers. But because of the moral imperative of religion in this life, the state always had a purpose in creating a climate that fostered moral behavior, personal welfare, and the commonweal. In fact, if the American polity failed to further these ends, it was to be held accountable to the transcendent standards of religion.

The partnership between religion and politics was uneasy from the start—especially when one considers the theocracies and religious particularism of some early colonies and the later doctrines of manifest destiny for the American nation. But it foretold an extraordinary emphasis on the personal piety of the citizen: if God has fixed salvation in the hereafter, then the individual must tend industriously to well-being in the here and now. Personal conduct becomes the measure of worth. And since the society values equality, not hierarchy, the expectation is that each, regardless of station, is accountable. Weber (Gerth and Mills 1946, 321), viewing religion in the United States, argues that "it is not the ethical *doctrine* of a religion, but that form of ethical *conduct* upon which premiums are placed that matters." The American cultural form of religion is concerned with an individual's standing in the community. An individual's religious conduct, such as honesty, integrity, piety, and concern for others, predicts whether that person is to be trusted both in the economic market and with the reins of government. Because American sect-type religion is voluntary, admission and continuation of membership in a church is already a community judgment that the individual measures up to the standards of worth. Evidence of belief in God and moral conduct become part of the curriculum vitae for political and economic leadership.

This uneasy partnership between religion and politics, however, did not blue-print the entire role of the state or the range of public policies it must pursue. Nevertheless, religion did place its imprint on American politics. It was a reli-gious impulse, Reformed or Calvinist in origin, that led Americans to believe that political structures could be improved. Familiarity with religious discourse also encouraged political leaders to legitimate whatever policy options they se-lected through the revivalistic language of a moral crusade (cf. Noll 1988). American politicians could use different components of religious worldviews to justify both limited government and active intervention, waging war and refrain-ing from armed conflict. The same Judeo-Christian source documents could be used to argue for submission to authority and to call the same authority to justice.

Consider the Pauline perspective on the function of government:

> Every person must submit to the supreme authorities. There is no authority but by act of God, and the existing authorities are instituted by him; consequently anyone who rebels against authority is resisting a divine institution, and those who resist have themselves to thank for the punishment they will receive. For government, a terror to crime, has no terrors for good behavior. But if you are doing wrong, then you will have cause to fear them; it is not for nothing that they hold the power of the sword, for they are God's agents of punishment, for retribution on the offender. That is why you are obliged to submit. It is an obligation imposed not merely by fear of retribution, but by conscience. (Ro-mans 13:1–6, NEB)

In a world where one must have a low estimate of the capacity of humans to do good works of their own accord, according to Paul, the state is instituted by God to punish those who do not live in harmony with others. The capacity to maintain order is by divine institution. To disobey the state apparently is to disobey God. Respect for order must be inculcated into the human conscience, that is, it must stimulate *self*-control rather than being based simply on the threat of punishment. Other than the implied obligation of the state to create a climate for good works, this passage offers little basis for collective action to change the status quo.

However, the prophetic books of the post-Davidic monarchy provide much clearer arguments that the state itself is subject to divine sanctions and that citizens who fail to hold it accountable will suffer at the hand of God. Amos offers particularly strong indictments for those of means and power who oppress the poor: "You trample on the poor and force him to give you grain. . . . You oppress the righteous and take bribes and you deprive the poor of justice in the courts. . . . Hate evil and love good; enthrone justice in the courts" (Amos 5:11–15, NIV).

Nations that turn from injustice to live righteously, in the Judeo-Christian prophetic tradition, will subdue their enemies. Isaiah says: "The sons of your oppressors shall come forward to do homage, all who reviled you shall bow low at your feet; they shall call you the City of the Lord, the Zion of the Holy One of Israel" (Isaiah 60:14, NEB).

And when the one whom Christians call the Messiah comes, his mother prophesies in the famous Magnificat: "The arrogant of heart and mind he has put to rout, he has brought down monarchs from their thrones, but the humble have been lifted high. The hungry he has satisfied with good things, the rich sent empty away" (Luke 1:51–53, NEB). And in the words of Jesus himself: "[God] has anointed me to preach good news to the poor. He sent me to proclaim freedom for the prisoners and recovery of sight for the blind, to release the oppressed" (Luke 4:18, NIV).

Thus, in this worldview, God watches the nations and peoples; when they fail to do justice, their social orders are turned topsy-turvy: the humble are exalted, the lambs rule the lions. That is a demanding set of standards for the rulers and the rich; even though their power and station are derived from the divine order of things, the way they use it determines whether they dare keep it. The notions of stewardship and service permeate this penetration of political philosophy by religious worldview. It becomes the basis for biblical republicanism and, in its more secular permutation, the classical republicanism embedded in the Declaration of Independence and the Preamble to the Constitution (Bellah et al. 1985, 27–31, 35–39).

While this religious worldview makes assumptions about the nature of humans, the nature of God, and the purpose of the political order, it still does not spell out the process by which justice comes to a nation. Is it the steadfast, selfless love shown by communities of believers operating through civil society that transforms a nation? Or is it their enlistment of the power of government to bring low the mighty and exalt the humble? That is a peculiar dilemma of a nation in which the spirit of religion and the spirit of liberty are both embraced.

Biblical interpretation, then, provides two models for appropriate religious worldviews. One model is based on obedience to authority and assumes that such obedience will provide a context for individuals to pursue right relationships with God. Since government is God-ordained, such a religious worldview comes to legitimate existing social hierarchies. Order itself implies hierarchy. Hierarchies are based on acquisitiveness: power, health, wealth, strength, or whatever. In free societies that manifest themselves in capitalist economies, hierarchies of power and wealth become intertwined. Thus, what religion legitimates, what it affirms as "goodness" in citizens, is respect for free market dealings through which the industrious can acquire means. This worldview, *religious individualism*, maintains a passive view of government except in terms of punishing individual wrongdoing and providing encouragement for pietistic lifestyles. In this sense, although its origins are in the anticlerical sentiments of the Scottish enlightenment (see chapter 1), liberal individualism can be grounded in a religious worldview.

On the other hand, a second religious worldview fosters altruism. It is unjust that those who have should hoard. Acquisitiveness may serve both just and unjust ends. But it is unclear whether justice calls for private or collective action. Is the hierarchical system itself so unjust that power must be wrested from it? Should the collective order be used to redistribute wealth and equalize protection and opportunity for those on the lower rungs? Or are these efforts toward justice to be confined to charitable individuals or groups in the civil society? Generally, proponents of this worldview, *religious communitarianism*, hold an activist orientation that favors governmental assistance to the poor or oppressed. This worldview legitimates as "goodness" the quest for the public good.

The problems of making religious worldviews compatible with political action, in the Western liberal philosophical heritage, are as old as the social contract theorists. If humans are not to be trusted, why should some people be authorized to govern? If the state is to create a climate in which justice flourishes, should it do this by (1) limiting itself and providing incentives for individual action, or (2) maximizing itself so that it has the resources for collective action? Can the state transform the hearts of people so that they can live together more cooperatively and altruistically? Obviously, assumptions about the will of God, the nature of humankind, and the purpose of the state, as found in Western religious constructions of "reality," bear on such eternal questions. It would be difficult to separate any apparently secular political philosophy from the religious culture, the religious worldviews, that initially spawned the questions it addresses.

Measuring Religious Worldviews

Empirically oriented social scientists have not made a frontal assault on the measurement of linkages among beliefs about God, assessments of human nature, and the roles of the political system and civil society in fostering order and justice. The National Election Studies (NES) have not provided data suitable for this purpose. While the General Social Surveys (GSS) added a battery of questions concerned with images of God during the 1980s, factor analyses of these items yield a standard *attributes-of-God* composite and a *maternal, nurturant* factor. Neither factor, however, is of much moment in understanding the limited range of political variables on the GSS. In the middle of the decade, the GSS also tried a battery of worldview measures; these also fail to yield interpretable factors and the battery has been reduced to only two items in succeeding surveys. Thus, we are not yet capable of modeling and estimating the problem from the large national data collections. Yet fragments of special-purpose empirical work exist. The remainder of the chapter is devoted to their illumination and critique.

Glock and Stark (1965) explored the multiple dimensionality of American religion through data collected in the San Francisco Bay area. Their ideological (or religious beliefs) dimension is most germane for understanding religious worldviews. It has three components—(1) *warranting beliefs*, i.e., definitions regarding the existence and nature of the divine, usually containing the basic conceptions of God, (2) *purposive beliefs*, i.e., beliefs about the meaning of life, including ideas about God's relationship to the world, human purpose and potential, and (3) *implementing beliefs*, i.e., norms that tell humans how to behave toward God and toward fellow humans if they are to realize the divine plan. The second and third components are most likely to offer a religious worldview and to provide a source for political philosophies. In their study, directed primarily to Christians, measures for the first (Stark and Glock 1968) include belief in the existence of God, belief in the divinity of Jesus, and related beliefs about his life. Measures for the second included belief in original sin, belief in the nature of redemption and salvation, and belief in the afterlife. Measures for the third included various forms of ethical behavior.

Stark and Glock (1968) named their measure of the third component, *ethicalism*. They viewed the measure as an alternative to Christian orthodoxy. An index of ethicalism was constructed that asked respondents to assess the importance for gaining salvation of *doing good for others* and *loving thy neighbor*. Although the orthodoxy measure of Stark and Glock attracted scholarly attention, attack, and rebuttal, it is the ethicalism index that has had relevance for our efforts in the area of religious worldviews. Although it was unfortunate that Stark and Glock complicated their ethicalism measure by linking *doing good for others* or *loving thy neighbor* with the *requisites* of salvation instead of asking about their importance for the Christian life, they did raise the possibility that religion could motivate its adherents in a communitarian fashion. In other words, religion is not simply about relationships between human beings and God but also about relationships among humans. As Stark and Glock (1968, 75) put it: "Ethicalism and orthodoxy can be mutually exclusive roots of religious identity." Or in language that we would prefer, communitarianism and individualism are potentially opposing religious worldviews, the former emphasizing *horizontal* relationships with others, the latter emphasizing *vertical* relationships with God. As we argued previously, both worldviews are grounded in the biblical text and in Christian tradition.

The studies of Glock and Stark have had a profound effect on the sociology of religion in the United States. In fact, a whole generation of scholars has dissected the concepts and empirical findings of these pioneers. For our purposes in this chapter, the work of Roof (1972, 1975) is of particular relevance. Although Roof uses conceptual terminology that varies from Glock and Stark and from that which we have developed in this chapter, he makes significant contributions to our understanding of religious worldviews. Roof developed a series of questions in two surveys, one of Episcopalians (1972) and one of Southern Baptists (1975), that measure a communitarian perspective held by individuals. Examples include: "The church should stick with religious matters and not get involved in social and economic issues of the day"; "An ideal religion includes involvement in social and political issues of the day" (1975, 128); "Do you think a minister should encourage church members to study political issues and candidates?" (1972, 7). Disagreement with the first item and agreement with the last two (called *church activism*) are negatively correlated with orthodoxy (1975, 117).

Davidson (1975) also builds on Glock and Stark's (1965) distinction of five separate dimensions of religious commitment. From an analysis of prior conceptual schemes of religious commitment, Davidson argues that two underlying religious orientations can be distinguished in these dimensions. One perspective "reflects the other-worldly, personal, and unquestioning type of commitment which is most often associated with religious conservatism" (Davidson 1975, 85). Institutionally, this perspective is more likely to be present in sects than in churches. The other orientation "reflects the social, rational-critical, and community-oriented type of commitment which is most often associated with religious liberalism" (85). Davidson applies this distinction to Glock and Stark's ideological or belief dimension and argues that this dimension has two components—one conservative and the other liberal in orientation. The former Davidson labels *vertical*, which "concern[s] man's relationships to the supernatural order" (85). Davidson includes beliefs in God, in life after death, and in the divinity of Jesus in his vertical beliefs component. In contrast, Davidson posits *horizontal* beliefs "concerning man's social relationships and activities in social institutions" (85). Here he includes items concerned with the importance of helping others and the need to love one's neighbor in contrast to engaging in traditional religious practices (87). Davidson finds that vertical and horizontal belief measures are negatively correlated (−.45) in survey results from a sample of two Baptist and two Methodist congregations in Indiana completed in 1968 (88). Davidson treats these belief measures as properties of churches.

The notion that horizontal and vertical dimensions of belief are properties of the local congregation is developed more comprehensively in an analysis of Hartford churches in which Roozen, McKinney, and Carroll (1984) analyze the different responses of churches to urban life. They borrow from the work of church historian, Marty (1970), who istinguished between *private* and *public* Protestantism. The former is individualistic in its interpretation of the Gospel, and it emphasizes individual salvation and a pietistic life-style. The latter is social in orientation and has found historical expression in the Social Gospel movement (Roozen, McKinney, and Carroll 1984, 9). The authors label the former as *other-worldly* and the latter as *this-worldly* (34). As the distinction suggests, the latter involves a concern for others, "the establishment of the Kingdom of God in society," cooperation with other churches, and emphasis on participation in public life and concern for social issues. The otherworldly dimension, as its names implies, stresses salvation after death, a clear distinction between the secular and the spiritual, acceptance of the legitimacy of contemporary political institutions and opposition to worldly life-styles (87). The authors develop measures of these dimensions with a focus on the importance of each for congregational life. The items could be adapted to apply to individuals as well. We think the this-worldly dimension is measuring *religious communitarianism* and the otherworldly dimension, *religious individualism.*

The research done by Roof, Davidson, and Roozen and his colleagues serves as a natural bridge between Glock and Stark and the more explicit attention given to religious worldviews in Benson and Williams (1982). In a seminal study linking the religious beliefs of members of Congress to their political ideologies and legislative roll-call votes, Benson and Williams employ both God imagery and a new measure of foundational outlooks on the world. The latter, a summary measure of *individualism-preserving religion* and *community-building religion,* does a remarkably good job of distinguishing between political conservatives and liberals. Based on analysis of both fixed-alternative and open-ended questions about God, humanity, and how the society and polity should be structured to respond to these beliefs, Benson and Williams find four pairs of opposing religious themes: (1) *agentic*—individualistic and me-centered religion—versus (2) *communal*—we-centered, interdependent religion unifying one with other humans; (3) *vertical*—religion primarily as a relationship between the individual and God—versus (4) *horizontal*—religion pushing the individual toward compassionate, caring stances toward others; (5) *restricting*—religion primarily as a set of restrictive controls or discipline—versus (6) *releasing*—religion as freeing and enabling experiences; (7) *comforting*—religion as solace, support, and relief—versus (8) *challenging*—religion as a stimulus to action. Despite the opposing nature of these themes, Benson and Williams (1982, 108) argue that "as they appear in human lives they are mixed in varying amounts and intensities" and form patterns. Generally, those who score high on some combination of 1, 3, 5, and 7 call themselves *political conservatives* and vote that way, while those who score high on some combination of 2, 4, 6, and 8 are *liberals.*

What is impressive about these results is that these worldviews serve as far better predictors of liberal or conservative voting patterns in the Congress than other measures of religiosity. Part of the success of these measures as predictors is that they tap what Davidson (1975) had earlier called liberal and conservative orientations toward religion. Yet Benson and Williams's (1982) design still leaves us short of an operational set of measures for a general population sample. It is based in large part on open-ended questions, coder-classification judgments, and an elite sample of people who have exceptional verbal facility. We also suspect that the agentic and vertical themes are highly interrelated and difficult to distinguish from each other conceptually. A similar argument can be made about the communal and horizontal themes. It is also likely that these combined individualist and communitarian themes are accounting for the greatest share of the variance in the predictions of congressional voting patterns in comparison to the restricting-releasing and comforting-challenging dimensions. This theoretical suspicion cannot be empirically checked, given that Benson and Williams's data are not available for secondary analysis. However, studies by Leege, discussed below, suggest the plausibility of this surmise.

Leege and Welch have tried to apply the Benson–Williams logic to mass populations through Catholic samples—parishioners, lay leaders, staff, and pastors. The initial attempt was to devise a measure of foundational religious beliefs (religious worldviews) (Leege 1989; Leege and Welch 1989; Welch and Leege 1988). They devised an instrument shown in the appendix to this chapter. Based on a back-translation of Benson and Williams's coding classifications, it asks people to draw lines connecting their responses to each of three questions: (1) What do you think is the basic human problem that religion deals with? (2) What do you think is the path to salvation? and (3) What do you think is the outcome of salvation? The options provide structure and at the same time allow for the unique ordering of idea-elements. To save the benefits of the latter design, then, analysis was done in terms of the paths respondents selected rather than correlations of individual components. (See Brown 1980 for arguments regarding the superiority of Q-methodology to standard survey correlational analysis.) The paths yield clearly identifiable religious worldviews classified as *individualistic* (38 percent), *communitarian* (18 percent), and *integrated* (29 percent). The measure is validated by predictions to variables known to be related to individualism and communitarianism, and its utility is shown by contrasting the variance explained through this approach as opposed to multiple-item indices drawn from related variables on the instrument.

The religious individualism-communitarian measure was useful in predicting a number of political attitudes and behaviors. In Table 11.1 we present the results of multiple regression analyses that use six demographic factors (family income, sex, region, race, age, education) and individualism-communitarianism as independent variables, and party identification, ideological self-classification, and abortion attitudes as dependent variables. In all three instances, the religious worldview measure is a significant predictor of the dependent variables. Individualists are more likely to be Republican, conservative, and prolife than communitarians; next to race no other factor in these equations is a better predictor of political ideology than religious individualism-communitarianism. In other analyses not presented in the table, the religious worldview measure was helpful in predicting attitudes on such social issues as women's rights, male-female family roles, and the threat of secular humanism. In addition, religious individualists were more likely than communitarians to claim that their religious values influence their voting behavior, and in a Republican direction.

In short, there is every reason to believe that religious worldviews do bear a strong relationship to both political-philosophical orientations and to feelings about specific political issues. While the Leege–Welch measure is suggestive, it was validated only for a special-purpose Catholic sample and requires administration through a paper-and-pencil format.

In a recent survey of religious activists conducted by Kellstedt (1991) and his associates, the measurement of religious worldviews is simplified so that it can compete for scarce space on general data collections. Four items were included

Table 11.1

Individualism-Communitarianism: Demographics and Political Attitudes among Catholic Parishioners
(multiple regression analysis)

	Party ID	Political Ideology	Abortion Attitudes
Individualist/Communitarian	−.05*	−.11	−.11
Income	.18	.08	NS
Sex	−.06	−.05	.05
Region	−.04	.06	NS
Race	.16	.16	.05
Age	NS	.04	.11
Education	.11	−.06	NS
Adjusted R^2	.11	.05	.03

Source: Notre Dame Study of Catholic Parish Life, N=2,667.
NS = Not significant
* Coefficients are *beta* weights, all significant at least at the .05 level.
Codes for the independent variables are as follows:
Individualist/communitarian: low scores = individualist, high scores = communitarian.
Family income: high scores = highest income.
Sex: low scores = male, high scores = female.
Region: low scores = non-South, high scores = South.
Race: low scores = black, high scores = white.
Age scores: low = youngest, high = oldest.
Education: highest scores = graduate degrees.
Codes for the dependent variables are as follows:
Party ID: low scores = Democrat, high scores = Republican.
Political ideology: low scores = liberal, high scores = conservative.
Abortion attitudes: low scores = prochoice, high scores = prolife.

in the survey. Individuals were asked to choose, if possible, between two attractive alternatives: "The church should attempt to encourage individual morality" (individualist), or "The church should attempt to encourage social justice" (communitarian). The second two alternatives were: "The best way to address social problems is to change the hearts of individuals" (individualist), or "The best way to address social problems is to change societal institutions" (communitarian). (This second set of items was actually used as one of the validators for the Leege–Welch measure.) For the third set of items, the two alternatives were: "Individuals are poor because of individual inadequacies" (individualist), or "Individuals are poor because of social, economic, and political factors" (communitarian). Respondents were asked to circle the number from 1 to 7 that came closest to their point of view on these pairs of statements. Finally, a standard *strongly agree* to *strongly disagree* item was included that read: "If enough people were brought to Christ, social ills would take care of themselves." Agree answers were coded *individualist* and disagree responses were coded *communi-*

tarian. The first and last of the four items are directed to churched people; it would make little sense to ask these questions of the "unchurched." The second and third questions also measure worldviews but could be directed to anyone. The four worldview items were highly intercorrelated, ranging from a low of .32 to a high of .57. They load on an *individualist-communitarian* factor, with loadings ranging from .65 to .81. They form an acceptable scale with a coefficient *alpha* of .734. Scores on the individual variables were multiplied by the factor loadings for each item and then added together to form a scale. Scale scores were then divided into an *individualist* third, a *mixed* third, and a *communitarian* third.

In data not shown here but interpreted by Kellstedt (1991), multiple regressions with the individualist-communitarian scale were run using partisan identification, 1988 presidential vote choice, and attitudes toward abortion as dependent variables and other religious variables, and numerous demographic items as independent variables. The individualist-communitarian scale and a group affiliation measure (in which the seven organizations in the study were arranged from left to right) were invariably the major predictors of partisanship, vote choice, and abortion attitudes. As a result of this prior analysis, in this chapter we are using the Multiple Classification Analysis (MCA) procedure to measure the impact of individualism and communitarianism on partisanship, vote choices and abortion attitudes, controlling for organizational affiliation, education, age, and gender. MCAs are run separately for evangelical Protestants and mainline Protestants as well as for Roman Catholics. This separation stems from the findings in chapter 3, which showed the importance of religious traditions. The results are presented in Table 11.2 and are limited to white respondents only.

Turning first to partisanship and to the uncontrolled data, evangelical Protestant activists are more likely than either mainline Protestant or Roman Catholic activists to identify as Republicans. Controls for demographic factors, and particularly for group affiliation, reduce but do not eliminate these differences. As expected, individualists are significantly more likely to identify as Republicans than communitarians within all three religious traditions, and the differences remain when controls are instituted. The results show in dramatic fashion that individualist-communitarian attitudes matter in the partisan identification of religious activists, although they do not eliminate the impact of religious tradition.

Next, in Table 11.2, we turn to the relationship between religious worldviews and vote choice in the 1988 presidential election. Note that evangelical Protestant activists are the most supportive of George Bush, followed by mainline Protestant and Catholic activists. The controls reduce the differences substantially but, again, do not eliminate them. Differences between individualists and communitarians in all three traditions are massive and remain large, if somewhat diminished, when controls are introduced. Bush was the favorite candidate of individualists in 1988 regardless of religious tradition.

Finally, in Table 11.2, we examine the relationship between religious worldview and abortion attitudes. Both evangelicals and Catholics are more

Table 11.2

Religious Worldviews, Religious Tradition, and Political Behavior
(a multiple classification analysis, whites only)

PARTISAN IDENTIFICATION

WORLDVIEW	Evangelical Protestant		Mainline Protestant		Roman Catholic	
	Mean	N	Mean	N	Mean	N
All	4.39	2476	2.99	986	2.03	524
All + controls*	3.93	2476	3.57	986	3.18	524
Individualists	4.95	1389	4.72	261	3.86	60
+ controls	4.61	1389	4.00	261	3.33	60
Communitarians	2.92	513	1.92	504	1.50	369
+ controls	3.51	513	2.30	504	1.61	369

BUSH VOTE IN 1988

WORLDVIEW	Evangelical Protestant		Mainline Protestant		Roman Catholic	
	%	N	%	N	%	N
All	86	2355	48	928	31	491
All + controls	74	2355	61	928	58	491
Individualists	97	1332	90	246	84	56
+ controls	92	1332	70	246	70	56
Communitarians	50	463	22	471	17	347
+ controls	63	463	32	471	20	347

ABORTION ATTITUDES

WORLDVIEW	Evangelical Protestant		Mainline Protestant		Roman Catholic	
	Mean	N	Mean	N	Mean	N
All	2.36	2463	3.80	947	2.61	502
All + controls	2.66	2463	2.41	947	2.86	502
Individualists	2.10	1372	2.61	259	1.95	59
+ controls	2.19	1372	3.24	259	2.30	59
Communitarians	3.16	491	4.59	471	2.77	347
+ controls	2.92	491	4.24	471	2.71	347

Source: 1990 Religious Interest Group Study, principal investigators: Lyman C. Kellstedt, John C. Green, James L. Guth, and Corwin E. Smidt.

Means for partisan identification range from 0 to 6, with 0 = Strong Democrat, 3 = Pure Independent, and 6 = Strong Republican.

Means for abortion attitudes range from 1 to 7, with 1 = never permit; 2 = permit only when mother's life is at stake; 3 = previous exception plus in cases of rape or incest; 4 = previous exceptions plus in cases of birth defects; 5 = previous exceptions plus in cases of poverty; 6 = previous exceptions plus in cases where a career may be threatened; and 7 = always permit.

*Controlling for age, gender, education, and interest group affiliation (in which groups are arranged from most liberal to most conservative).

prolife than mainline Protestants, and this pattern continues when controls are introduced. As expected, individualists are much more likely to hold prolife attitudes than communitarians. As with partisanship and vote choice, the controls reduce the differences between worldviews but in no way eliminate them.

The findings in Table 11.2 are promising. The questions developed to measure religious worldviews work as expected. Individualists are more Republican in both identification and vote choice and more prolife in abortion attitudes than are communalists. Still, the fact remains that this sample is of religious activists, and questions involving religion nvariably work well with such a sample.

Discussion

This chapter has argued the case that neither sociologists of religion nor mainstream political scientists have yet realized the full potential for understanding how religious worldviews shape political ideologies andattitudes among general populations. Our examination of several special-purpose surveys suggests that the potential to do so exists. As an agenda for future research, preferably through the National Election Studies, we propose experimentation with a series of individualist and communitarian questions that explore the appropriate role for both individuals and the church: Should individuals concentrate on their vertical relationships with God, or should they reach out to assist others in need? Should the church concentrate on building individual morality or turn to social justice concerns?

Where should the experimentation take place? Access to national samples for purposes of instrument experimentation is not readily available. The National Election Studies have provided some opportunity for experimentation through the Pilot Study series, one of which has served as the basis for this book. One possibility, then, is that individualist-communitarian questions be devised for testing in the Pilot Study series. Certainly, the results from the special-purpose surveys we have examined in this chapter suggest that such an endeavor appears promising.

There are also substantive reasons to encourage continued research on religious worldviews. In the presidential election of 1996, a fight within the ranks of the Republican party between mainline and evangelical Protestants can be foreseen. Recent research suggests that there are clear policy differences between the mainline and evangelical Protestant members of the Republican party coalition (Kellstedt 1990, 14). A candidate who takes a strong prolife stance on abortion and favors the positions of the New Christian Right on other "family" issues could face opposition in 1996 from another candidate who responds to the traditional probusiness concerns of the Republican party. Earlier research by the Times-Mirror organization (Ornstein, Kohut, and McCarthy 1988) has shown that Enterprisers and Moralists compose the core of the Republican party in about equal proportions. Leege (1992) has demonstrated how strategic politics places these groups in an uneasy alliance that, sooner or later, could explode as the requirements of a governing coalition frustrate promises made to an electoral coalition. Abortion, in the post-*Webster* era, could well be the fragmenting issue.

This chapter suggests that the core of the difference between these two Republican factions is rooted in their contrasting religious worldviews. These differences will not be bridged easily. Furthermore, the chapter has shown that individualist and communitarian religious worldviews can account for part of the difference between Republicans and Democrats. Hence, continued research into contrasting religious worldviews would be a timely investment.

References

Bellah, Robert N.; Madsen, Richard; Sullivan, William M.; Swidler, Ann; and Tipton, Steven M. 1985. *Habits of the Heart: Individualism and Commitment in American Life.* Berkeley: University of California Press.

Benson, Peter L., and Williams, Dorothy L. 1982. *Religion on Capitol Hill: Myths and Realities.* New York: Harper and Row.

Brown, Steven R. 1980. *Political Subjectivity: Applications of Q Methodology in Political Science.* New Haven, CT: Yale University Press.

Davidson, James. 1975. "Glock's Model of Religious Commitment: Assessing Some Different Approaches and Results." *Review of Religious Research* 16:83–93.

Geertz, Clifford. 1966. "Religion as a Cultural System." In *Anthropological Approaches to Religion,* ed. Michael Bainton, 1–46. London: Tavistock.

———. 1973. *The Interpretation of Cultures.* New York: Basic Books.

Gerth, Hans H., and Mills, C. Wright, eds. 1946. *From Max Weber: Essays in Sociology.* New York: Oxford University Press.

Glock, Charles Y., and Stark, Rodney. 1965. *Religion and Society in Tension.* Chicago: Rand McNally.

Kellstedt, Lyman A. 1990. "Religion and the U.S. Party System." *Public Perspective* 2(1):12–14.

———. 1991. "Religious Worldviews and Political Behavior." Paper presented at the annual meeting of the American Political Science Association, Washington, DC.

Leege, David C. 1989. "Toward a Mental Measure of Religiosity in Research on Religion and Politics." In *Religion and Political Behavior in the United States,* ed. Ted G. Jelen, 45–64. New York: Praeger.

———. 1992. "Coalitions, Cues, Strategic Politics, and the Staying Power of the Religious Right." *PS: Political Science and Politics* 22:198–204.

Leege, David C., and Welch, Michael R. 1989. "Religious Roots of Political Orientations: Variations among American Catholic Parishioners." *Journal of Politics* 51:137–62.

Marty, Martin E. 1970. *Righteous Empire.* New York: Dial Press.

Noll, Mark A. 1988. *One Nation under God?* San Francisco: Harper and Row.

Ornstein, Norman; Kohut, Andrew; and McCarthy, Larry. 1988. *The People, the Press and Politics.* Reading, MA: Addison-Wesley.

Roof, Wade Clark. 1972. "The Local-Cosmopolitan Orientation and Traditional Religious Commitment." *Sociological Analysis* 33:1–15.

———. 1975. "On Conceptualizing Salience in Religious Commitment." *Journal for the Scientific Study of Religion* 14:111–28.

Roozen, David A.; McKinney, William; and Carroll, Jackson W. 1984. *Varieties of Religious Presence: Mission in Public Life.* New York: Pilgrim Press.

Stark, Rodney, and Glock, Charles Y. 1968. *American Piety: The Nature of Religious Commitment.* Berkeley: University of California Press.

Tocqueville, Alexis de . [1835, 1840] 1958. *Democracy in America.* Trans. Phillips Bradley. New York: Vintage Books.

Welch, Michael R., and Leege, David C. 1988. "Religious Predictors of Catholic Parishioners' Sociopolitical Attitudes: Devotional Style, Closeness to God, Imagery, and Agentic-Communal Religious Identity." *Journal for the Scientific Study of Religion* 27:536–52.

Appendix

Now we are going to ask you to be an artist. Religion always identifies a basic human problem, something that is wrong with humans and their world. Then religion talks about a path to salvation, that is, a way that basic human problems can be overcome. Finally, religion talks about outcomes of salvation—a change in persons' lives or the way the world is as a result of salvation. The figure on the next page is part of a picture that shows several kinds of basic human problems, paths to salvation, and outcomes of salvation. Think about your religious beliefs. Now you be the artist. What do you think is the basic human problem that religion deals with? What do you think is the path to salvation? When you decide these, draw an arrow from the box that describes the basic human problem (under A) to the box that describes the path to salvation (under B). Finally, what do you think is the outcome of salvation? Now draw an arrow from the box you have chosen under B to the box you have chosen under C—the outcome of salvation. If any of our descriptions in the boxes under A or B or C do not really describe what you think is the basic problem, or the path, or the outcome, then you can try to describe it in your own words. We have left some open boxes for you to write in something if you want. But be sure to connect whichever boxes you choose for A, B, and C with arrows.

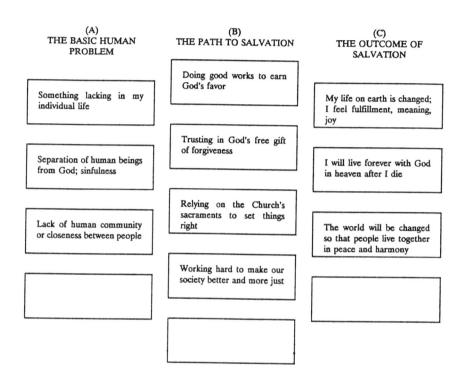

(A)
THE BASIC HUMAN
PROBLEM

(B)
THE PATH TO SALVATION

(C)
THE OUTCOME OF
SALVATION

Doing good works to earn God's favor

Something lacking in my individual life

My life on earth is changed; I feel fulfillment, meaning, joy

Trusting in God's free gift of forgiveness

Separation of human beings from God; sinfulness

I will live forever with God in heaven after I die

Relying on the Church's sacraments to set things right

Lack of human community or closeness between people

The world will be changed so that people live together in peace and harmony

Working hard to make our society better and more just

SOURCE: Notre Dame Study of Catholic Parish Life.

Part V

Leadership Stimuli and Reference Groups

Chapter 12

Are the Sheep Hearing the Shepherds? Cue Perceptions, Congregational Responses, and Political Communication Processes

Michael R. Welch, David C. Leege, Kenneth D. Wald, and Lyman A. Kellstedt

American politics has changed dramatically in the past generation. The days when the friendly precinct captain knocked on doors to ask for votes have long since passed, and television is now a major source of information for citizens. Political parties no longer play the intermediary role that they did formerly. Churches now have the potential to fill the void, for Americans are more involved in churches than in any other voluntary organization. Berger and Neuhaus (1977) emphasize this importance of churches as intermediaries between individuals and public life. Roozen, McKinney, and Carroll (1984, 27–28) make a similar point: "Relatively few institutions can 'mediate' effectively between society's megastructures and individuals, but congregations are clearly among them. They mediate in the sense that they intersect with both worlds: the 'outer' world of structures, institutions, and social movements and the 'inner' world of individual meaning and purpose." And, as Wald, Owen, and Hill (1988, 532–33) have demonstrated, church congregations function quite effectively as political communities in shaping the viewpoints of members. Overt political messages and subtext are often interwoven in the conversations among parishioners, the context of church bulletins, and other symbols (e.g., artwork and posters) of a congregation's collective stance on sociopolitical issues. All reinforce the orientation being transmitted.

Perhaps the most important role in this process of political communication is played by the clergy, for they are often in the best position to transmit overt or symbolic political messages and to mobilize their flocks for political action (Beatty and Walter 1989, 131; see also Morris 1981, 1984; and Walton 1985, for a description of the role of black ministers in the civil rights movement). Among the mainline Protestant denominations during the 1960s and 1970s, most of these efforts included highly directive sermonizing (Nelsen 1975; Nelsen, Yokley, and

Madron 1973) geared toward the promotion of liberal causes (see Wald 1992, 243–44, for an overall summary). A few ministers, nevertheless, sought to avoid controversial issues and preached on more narrowly religious themes, e.g., concern for personal salvation (Koller and Retzer 1980; Nelsen 1975). In a recent study of ministers from ten denominations, Beatty and Walter (1989) discovered substantial variations across denominational families in how frequently ministers preached overtly politicized sermons and addressed liberal and conservative political issues in church. They conclude that clergy from conservative, evangelical denominations engage in political cue giving just as intensely as their counterparts in liberal, mainline denominations, but not so *widely*: i.e., their political activism and directiveness are more narrowly focused on a select set of moral issues, such as abortion, prayer in schools, pornography, and the transformation of women's roles. This finding challenged prevailing characterizations about the relative political quiescence of evangelical clergy during the 1960s and 1970s (Beatty and Walter 1989, 131). Reporting on similar findings but based on a sample of 5,100 ministers from three denominations, the Southern Baptist Convention, the Presbyterian Church in the USA, and the Christian Church (Disciples of Christ), Guth (1989, 15) characterizes the current political cue-giving situation as "close to true 'two party' mobilization in American Protestantism between 'modernist this-worldly clergy' and 'their traditionalist, other-worldly colleagues.'" Working with still other data sets, other scholars report findings congruent with these (Harder 1988; Langenbach 1988).

Strong political cue giving has also emanated from the Roman Catholic clerical leadership in the United States. Since the creation of the U.S. Catholic Conference and the National Conference of Catholic Bishops after Vatican II, a vigorous social action orientation has been growing within the administrative hierarchy of the American church (Wald 1992, 225). Beginning in the late 1960s and continuing since then, the bishops have issued a series of high-profile pastoral letters that criticized the military role of the United States in Vietnam (1968), the doctrine of nuclear deterrence (1983), and social inequalities generated by free market capitalist economies (1984). Research has not yet clarified whether this leftward direction in pronouncements from the church hierarchy has been consistently reflected in the stances taken by local pastors.

Up to this point, research on political cue giving has yielded insights about the activities and orientations of clergy but revealed little as to whether ordinary laypersons understood such cues and nothing about the implications of cue perception for political attitudes and behavior. Previous studies have either dealt with experiments on political perceptions (e.g., McKeown and Carlson 1987) or been based on analyses of televangelism (Abelman and Pettey 1988; Mobley 1984), inferences drawn from congregational analyses (Wald, Owen, and Hill 1988, 1990; Jelen 1989), and the kind of clergy self-reports discussed earlier (Beatty and Walter 1989; Guth 1989). Thus it identified what clergy said or claimed to have said about politics but not what congregants heard. In view of the many mechanisms that intervene between communicator and target audience—inattention, selective perception, distortion (e.g., Kinder and Sears 1985, 710; McGuire 1985, 143)—it is unwise to assume that church members perceive clearly the messages intended by clergy. This is an important issue for the study of political mobilization and one to which we now turn our attention.

Measuring Perceptions of Political Cues:
New Data from the NES 1989 Pilot Study

The NES 1989 Pilot Study collected data on perceived cue-giving efforts by pastors from all respondents who expressed a church affiliation.[1] The panel design of the Pilot Study allowed analysts to use both the new data on cue giving and data collected in 1988 and 1989 on other aspects of religiosity and political attitudes and behavior. While the relevant subsample is quite small (a maximum of 375 cases), it is large enough to permit comparison of congregants grouped by religious tradition.

The 1989 Pilot Study items asked respondents to indicate whether local religious leaders "spoke out" on the following selected sociopolitical issues:

> Political issues often times reflect moral concerns. Some religious leaders like pastors, rabbis, or bishops speak out on public issues through sermons, newsletters or other public statements. Others feel it is better not to speak out on public issues. How about religious leaders in your place of worship? Do they speak out on prayer in schools? The economy? Abortion? Housing and homelessness? Proper sexual behavior? Nuclear disarmament? Candidates for political office?

To paraphrase W.I. Thomas (Thomas and Thomas 1928, 572), perceptions *are* the reality on which individuals base their actions, *regardless* of the accuracy of those perceptions. In utilizing the NES Pilot Study data, we recognize that we have no control over whether the pastor actually gave the cue. Although the data limit our focus to respondents' *perceptions* about whether clergy present positions on various public issues, it can be argued that cue *perceptions themselves* are the central component in political communications.

Cue Perception and Religious Traditions

It is clear from the data presented in Table 12.1 that local religious leaders are perceived by their religious constituencies as offering cues on sociopolitical issues in a highly selective fashion (see final column for total sample) and that differences in cue perceptions become more pronounced when comparisons between divergent religious traditions are made. Respondents have been categorized into one of three traditions based on their reported affiliation, in accord with procedures described in chapter 3. (Because of their small Ns, other religious groups such as Jews, Orthodox, and nontraditional Protestants are excluded from the table.) Data are presented for white respondents only because of the small number of blacks in the sample.

Based on previously cited studies of cue giving by the clergy, we expect that evangelicals would be most likely to report hearing messages about issues of personal behavior such as sexual mores, abortion, and school prayer. Perceived messages in the mainline churches should tilt more toward broad economic issues. Finally, the recent pastoral letters on peace and the economy and the constant attention given to abortion suggest that messages focusing on these issues are more likely to be perceived by Catholics. As expected, substantial differences appear among the three main categories of respondents on four of the seven issues. If respondents' perceptions are to be trusted, leaders from denominations within each of these religious traditions appear to attach considerably greater moral priority to some issues, as communicated in their public teaching and other prophetic aspects of their ministry.

Lingering effects of conflicts from the 1960s and 1970s may be discernible in the response patterns of mainline Protestants. If the perceptions of these mainliners are accurate, clergy in mainline Protestant denominations across the country are most likely to speak out on housing policy and problems of the homeless—issues that may evoke sympathy from most members and about which there is likely to be little disagreement within the congregation. The percentage of mainline respondents indicating that their leaders speak out drops noticeably for other issues that have proven to be more controversial and contentious, (e.g., abortion, sexual conduct, school prayer, and the economy).

The seeming reluctance of mainline pastors, as perceived by their flock, to speak or offer religious guidance on several controversial issues contrasts with patterns reflected in the responses of evangelical Protestants and Roman Catholics. In the perceptions of evangelicals, clergy are quite willing to comment publicly on issues that have most recently provoked the greatest controversy: sexual conduct, abortion, and school prayer. This finding is not especially surprising given the centrality and prominence of these issues within the well-publicized agenda of the New Christian Right.

Concentration on provocative issues is seen even more clearly among Catholic respondents. Fully 83 percent of the Catholics perceive cues on abortion, a finding that further emphasizes the pervasiveness of concern about this issue among Catholic leaders throughout the country. Again, not surprisingly, many Catholics also perceive general cues on sexual behavior, as represented by the high percentage (67.3 percent) of Catholics who report that their local clergy comment on this issue. These findings further confirm the importance of sexual issues to both Catholics and evangelicals. Moreover, they reinforce conclusions about religious cue giving drawn from other recent studies demonstrating that the effects of religious orientations on political opinions are strongest when church

Table 12.1

Respondents Indicating Local Pastors "Speak Out" on Selected Sociopolitical Issues
(in percents, whites only)

Perceived Topics of Cues	Mainline Protestant[a]	Evangelical Protestant[b]	Roman Catholic[c]	Chi-Square	Total Sample[d]
Housing, Homelessness	70.6	48.5	69.8	.003	60.2
Proper Sexual Behavior	51.2	70.6	67.3	.018	62.0
Abortion	41.2	65.3	83.3	.001	60.4
Prayer in Public Schools	35.6	51.5	31.5	.021	40.2
The Economy	31.4	38.2	38.9	N.S.	35.8
Nuclear Disarmament	20.2	19.0	28.3	N.S.	21.0
Speak About Candidates for Political Office	12.6	12.7	9.3	N.S.	11.6

Source: NES 1989 Pilot Study.
[a]Size of subsample varies from 84 to 108.
[b]Size of subsample varies from 100 to 112.
[c]Size of subsample varies from 52 to 73.
[d]Size of subsample varies from 252 to 375.

teaching or guidance is most clear, as is characteristic of many church positions on sexual conduct (e.g., Welch and Leege 1991).

On other issues, however, this convergence of cue perceptions between Catholics and evangelicals disappears or is reduced. Evangelicals clearly display their most distinctive emphases, relative to the others, on school prayer and abortion, while Catholic respondents more closely resemble their mainline Protestant contemporaries on school prayer.

No statistically significant differences in cue perceptions distinguish the respondents on the remaining issues (i.e., the economy, nuclear disarmament, and political candidates). Relatively few (less than 40 percent) indicate that their clergy speak out on any of these issues. Failure to perceive cues about candidates probably reflects the intensely controversial nature of this topic. But altogether these results seem remarkable, especially for Catholics, when one considers the degree of emphasis attached by the Catholic bishops to their pastoral letter on peace and nuclear disarmament.[2]

We constructed a summated index of cue giving, composed of the number of *yes* responses to these seven issue items. This index measures the overall perception of cue giving, or directiveness. The index shows an *alpha* of greater than .74.[3] For purposes of analysis, the index was recoded into an eight-category polytomy, with low levels of perceived cue giving receiving a score of 1 and high levels receiving a score of 8. Although some cross-tradition differences in mean scores on the overall cue-giving index are detectable (in general, mainliners report the lowest level of cue giving, Catholics the highest), these differences are *not* highly significant ($F = 2.58, p = .078$).

In summary, when comparing our data to results drawn from earlier research, there seems to be a relatively close correspondence between what clergy in the respective religious traditions say they preach about and what congregants hear. Thus, these perceptions data validate clergy self-reports. The data also undermine a stereotype about the subculture of American evangelicalism: namely, its inherent otherworldliness and lack of interest in secular affairs. Clearly, present-day evangelicals view their clergy as no less likely than other clergy to "talk politics." Although the emphases given certain topics vary across religious traditions, clergy in each of the traditions tend to focus this emphasis on only two or three issues as opposed to a wider array.

One important question that we have not addressed to this point concerns whether congregants "approve" of clergy offering political cues. Considering the resistance to such cue giving shown in the past by members of various denominations (e.g., Hadden 1969; Luidens and Nemeth 1989; Wald 1992), and the overt backlash that often resulted, the answer to the question may signify whether clergy and congregants have reached a consensus on formerly controversial issues or whether a new round of confrontations is beginning over clergy activism and political directiveness.

The NES 1989 Pilot Study presents an opportunity to examine this question in the form of the item: "In general, do you feel it is alright or not alright for religious leaders like pastors, preachers, rabbis, or bishops to speak out on political issues in their places of worship?" For analysis, responses were classified into the following categories: *alright, depends on the issue, not alright*. Although it would have been desirable to have included additional issues and the direction of the teaching on each, time constraints imposed on the interview schedule precluded this.

When we break down the percentage of congregants who view clergy cue giving as legitimate and approve of the activity, a rather uniform pattern emerges across religious traditions. A little more than 46 percent of mainline Protestants, 49 percent of Catholics, and nearly 52 percent of evangelical Protestants approve of such cue giving (percentage differences not statistically significant at $p < .05$). The relative uniformity of this nearly 50:50 split in approval across the three groups clearly indicates substantial potential for backlash against clergy if they are perceived to overstep the imaginary boundary line between legitimate pastoral guidance and crass political "jawboning." Although the critical mass needed to produce such a backlash is unknown, the force of the reaction (powerful) and the triggering stimulus (excessive clergy activism in support of unpopular, radical causes) have unfortunately been observed before. These uniformities in the data also further underscore a point that was made earlier: evangelicals are just as receptive *and approving* toward political cue giving by their clergy as are members of other religious traditions. This finding is simply one more piece of evidence on which to indict the lingering stereotype of the apolitical or otherworldly evangelical.

Interest in Political Processes and Receptivity to Social Influence

Although the preceding findings establish that cue perception varies substantially [content, not level,] by religious tradition and issue domain, quite likely other traits of parishioners would make some more attentive for cues and others less attentive (Zaller 1989). In general, cognitive theory suggests that individuals who are more interested, involved, and attuned to political processes within the nation at large, as well as their local communities, would also tend to be more sensitized and more receptive to political messages, whatever their source. We would expect these individuals, in particular, to have their political antennae primed; thus, they would be more likely to perceive cues emanating from local clergy than individuals who are less interested in things political. This hypothesis further specifies the relationship between religious tradition and cue perception, suggesting that political interest enhances an individual's search for information and, ultimately, the reception of religious-based political cues.

To test this hypothesis, relationships among the degree of political interest shown by respondents, their religious tradition, and cue perception were investigated through tabular analyses, with the political interest variable representing a specification factor.[4] The results (data not shown) provide at least partial support for our political specification hypothesis. Substantial differences in cue perception among Catholics, evangelicals, and mainline Protestants are limited to those respondents who display moderate to high levels of interest in political campaigns and activities; no statistically significant differences emerged across religious traditions for those individuals who showed little or no interest in politics.[5]

These significant differences ($p < .05$ or greater for all) in cue perception are confined to four issues, namely, abortion, school prayer, sexual behavior, and homelessness. The most notable increases in the percentages of Catholics and evangelicals who report that their local clergy have offered cues on proper sexual behavior occur among those respondents who are most interested in politics (for Catholics, 85.0 percent; for evangelicals, 76.3 percent), compared to their counterparts who report only moderate interest (Catholics, 53.6 percent; evangelicals, 68.0 percent). The same pattern is reproduced among evangelical Protestants for perceptions of cues about prayer in public schools (those with high interest who perceive cues, 55 percent; those with moderate interest who perceive cues, 48 percent).

A somewhat different pattern emerges when we turn our attention to perception of cues on homelessness and abortion, however. On these issues Catholics and evangelicals exhibit thresholds of awareness that diverge substantially from what they reported about sexual cues and cues related to school prayer. Catholics who are at least *somewhat interested* in political campaigns show a much greater proclivity toward perceiving clergy cues on abortion (89.7 percent) and homelessness (79.3 percent) than their less-interested contemporaries (75 percent perceive cues on abortion; 25 percent perceive cues on homelessness). Evangelicals duplicate this pattern, but only for cue perceptions about homelessness (those with moderate interest who perceive cues, 51 percent; those with low interest who perceive cues, 35.7 percent).

Taken together, these patterns clearly suggest the existence of threshold effects that may attest to processes of selective attention operating especially among Catholics and evangelicals. These intervening cognitive processes may indeed enhance the reception of political cues among attuned congregants, particularly for issue domains in which clergy are sending signals both loudly and clearly.

Who Is Most Likely to Be Affected? Cue Perceptions and the Significance of Religious Elites in the Social Influence Process

Although the preceding findings establish that cue perception varies by religious tradition, issue domain, and interest in politics, it remains unclear whether cues transmitted by local religious leaders have any import. Do they, for example, bear any relation to the political orientations church members display or the positions they take on specific issues? Indeed, this is a crucial question for any theory that posits religious influence as a salient force for political communication (and ultimately political mobilization), and it is the linchpin that connects clergy influence to more comprehensive processes of social influence.

Prior research (Welch and Leege 1991) suggests a general hypothesis that relates the effects of perceived political cues to the salience of denominational teaching: the more clear and salient the position displayed by a denomination's leadership on a specific political issue, the more members' cue perceptions are likely to show a positive relationship to political orientations that are consistent with that position. This *position clarity* hypothesis leads to several different predictions for Roman Catholics, mainline Protestants, and evangelical Protestants. First, given the apparent high salience of positions taken by evangelical Protestant clergy relating to abortion, sexual behavior, and prayer in schools, members' cue perceptions on these issues should display relatively strong and significant relationships to political orientations that are consistent with evangelical leaders' emphases (H_1). For mainline Protestants, relationships between cue perceptions and political orientations should be strongest and most consistent with denominational positions primarily on issues relating to homelessness and sexuality (H_2). Finally, we predict that Catholics should exhibit the strongest and most consistent relationships between cue perceptions on abortion, housing-homelessness, and sexual behavior (H_3); that is, Catholics who perceive that cues are given should tend to display more conservative positions on abortion and sexual conduct and more liberal positions on housing and aid to the homeless.

Simple correlations (measured by tau_c) between the cue perception measures and six items that represent respondents' positions on corresponding issues (abortion, homosexual rights, school prayer, federal spending for the homeless, relations with the former Soviet Union, and support for Reaganomics) provide some support for the position clarity hypothesis (data not shown). However, most of the statistically significant bivariate relationships are only modest in size (e.g., tau_c values vary from .11 to .38). Evangelical Protestants who perceive cues on key issues most important to their clergy, such as abortion, proper sexual behavior, prayer in schools, and homelessness, *do* tend to take positions that correspond to the direction of clergy cues: specifically, they tend to hold more conservative positions opposing abortion and laws protecting homosexuals against job discrimination and favoring federal aid to the homeless and allowing or requiring prayer in public schools. It may seem somewhat surprising that evangelicals who perceive clergy cues are *less* approving of Reaganomics than their counterparts who fail to perceive such cues, but it must be remembered that evangelicals are moralists, not enterprisers (Ornstein, Kohut, and McCarthy 1988).

Relationships between the perception measures and issue positions taken by Catholic and mainline Protestant respondents are somewhat surprising. Consistent with the hypothesis, Catholics who perceive clergy cues on housing and homelessness do tend to be more supportive of federal aid to solve such problems. But, strangely enough, perception of clergy cues about abortion does *not* seem to guarantee congruence with the Roman Catholic church's views; rather, it is the reception of cues directing sexual behavior that seems to have a more important connection for Catholics (i.e., those perceiving sexual cues tend to display stronger antiabortion sentiments). Among mainline Protestant respondents, perception of clergy cues about homelessness bears no relationship to views about federal aid for the homeless. Moreover, despite the generally liberal themes about sexuality that are transmitted by many mainline clergy, mainline congregants who perceive cues on sexual behavior actually tend to hold more conservative positions on sexual issues such as homosexual rights. This finding may be an instance of the distance between mainline clergy and their congregations noted by Hadden (1969).

To examine whether cue perception is related to a more general sense of conservatism that underlies various sociopolitical issues, we include a four-item scale (*alpha* = .62) representing moral traditionalism (see Conover and Feldman 1986 for its development). Correlations between this scale and the individual cue perception measures show some patterns that offer support for the position clarity hypothesis, but these are largely confined to evangelical respondents. Among evangelicals, cue perception on the central issues of abortion, sexual behavior, homelessness, and school prayer is uniformly linked to more traditionalistic responses (*taus* ranging from .22 to .40, all $p < .05$). Again, somewhat surprisingly, this pattern is reproduced among mainline Protestants for relationships between cue perceptions about abortion and sexual behavior (tau_c of .14 and .20, respectively, both p .05); however, perception of clergy cues on the homelessness issue is linked to less traditionalistic responses ($tau_c = -.34$).

Finally, correlations between the overall cue-giving index and the measures of issue positions also reveal that relationships exist, although they again seem to be primarily among evangelicals. In general, evangelical respondents who report high levels of cue giving emanating from their clergy tend to take more conservative positions on such issues as abortion, homosexual rights, school prayer, and moral traditionalism and more liberal positions on government spending for the homeless. No statistically significant correlations are observed among mainline Protestants; however, among Catholics, high levels of perceived cue giving are related to more conservative positions on abortion and more liberal positions on aid for the homeless.

Although these findings provide some support for the position clarity hypothesis, we decided to investigate the relationship between cue perception and issue positions a little more closely. There are good theoretical reasons for doing this.

As we indicated earlier, a growing number of researchers have confirmed that church congregations function as contexts for the transmission and reinforcement of political attitudes (Wald, Owen, and Hill 1988, 1990; Gilbert 1989a, 1989b, 1990; Jelen 1990). Most of these studies posit various sources of this religious influence, such as direct cue giving from clergy (e.g., in sermons and informal conversations) and from other congregants, as well as by more indirect means such as *behavioral contagion* (Wald, Owen, and Hill 1988, 533). But others, such as Jelen (1990, 2), question the impact of political messages delivered via the pulpit and point to alternative interactional processes as being more influential. This emphasis on direct interaction as the principal mechanism for the transmission and perception of political cues within religious contexts can be traced back to earlier studies of group influence (e.g., Festinger, Schachter, and Back 1950) and White's (1968) work on interaction as the basis for social influence within religious congregations. Although, as Gilbert (1990, 2) notes, scholars (e.g., McPhee, Smith, and Ferguson 1963; Sprague 1982) have recognized the importance of both direct (i.e., interactional) and indirect (e.g., behavioral contagion) mechanisms in political communication processes, recent studies of social influence within religious contexts have tended to focus on the former. For example, in describing forces that shape political cohesiveness within churches, Wald, Owen, and Hill (1990, 200) are led to conclude that

> High levels of social interaction magnify the exposure of members to the collective consensus and increase the likelihood that commitment to group norms will be reinforced in conversation with other members. *Moreover, to the extent that church authority figures support the group political norm in either overt or covert fashion, involvement in church activities exposes the membership to persuasive communication. Accessibility should thus magnify the susceptibility of the individual to group influence.* [italics added]

Thus, higher levels of contact with one's congregation and religious subculture should enhance the effects of perceived political messages.

But is it possible for religious elites to transmit political cues to individuals who are not highly involved in the life of their congregation? If, for example, one controls for levels of involvement, will cue perception necessarily be diminished? It is clear that the moral leadership clergy exert may extend far beyond the congregation. For issues that attract widespread community attention outside one's church or coverage by local or national media, for example, the influence of religious leaders is not confined to sermonizing and may indeed reach many individuals who are relatively inactive within their congregation but nevertheless attach a high degree of legitimacy to the moral pronouncements of clergy.

To test links between cue perceptions and political orientations of individuals, we must therefore control for levels of involvement in religious activities and the salience of religion in an individual's life. If the relationship between perceived cue giving by clergy and individuals' political orientations is primarily a function of religious involvement or interaction within a congregation, then appropriate controls for level of religious involvement should render the net relations involving cue perceptions unimportant.

In addition to controlling for the effects of religiosity, we have also controlled for interest in politics, which we found earlier to specify the relationships between cue perceptions and religious tradition. Given what we discovered about reception of cues, we would hypothesize that net relationships between cue reception and issue positions should be strongest among those individuals who are most interested in politics and thus perhaps more likely to be seeking direction on political issues or to be influenced by pronouncements from knowledgeable community leaders such as clergy. We also hypothesize that the strongest net relations are most likely to involve those issues that are most emphasized within the various religious traditions: i.e., abortion, sexual behavior, homelessness, and school prayer among evangelicals; abortion, sexual behavior, and homelessness among Catholics; and sexual behavior and homelessness among mainline Protestants.

To test these relationships, multiple classification analyses (MCAs) were performed separately on white evangelical Protestant, mainline Protestant, and Roman Catholic respondents who showed different levels of interest in politics. Age, gender, education, region of residence, and socioeconomic status were included as demographic controls in all analyses. We also introduce three measures of religiosity as alternative controls for exposure and commitment to one's religious subculture and the salience of religion in one's life.

Results of the MCA analyses examining the net relationships between cue perceptions and the political attitude variables, with demographic characteristics and levels of religiosity controlled, are reported in Table 12.2 for respondents having different religious traditions and levels of political interest. Only the results of statistically significant equations are reported in Table 12.2 to conserve space.

Although it is apparent that some of the zero-order relationships discussed earlier become nonsignificant when controls are introduced, several significant relationships still appear. Most of these relationships exist among evangelical respondents, although two occur among Catholics. It is also evident that only two types of clergy cues seem to have any bearing on the kinds of political stances individuals take or the attitudes they exhibit: cues about abortion and those concerning appropriate sexual behavior. Similarly, these cues display statistically significant relationships only with attitudes toward abortion and moral traditionalism. In general, the patterns of relationships offer some support for the position clarity hypothesis and our hypothesis about the effects of political interest, although the support is rather limited.

Among evangelicals, for example, individuals who display *high* levels of political interest and report that their local clergy provide cues on the abortion issue are also substantially more likely to express strong views against abortion than their counterparts who failed to perceive such cues. With each of the sets of demographic and religious variables controlled, statistically significant coefficients representing relationships appear only among highly interested individuals; moreover, all of the coefficients are quite sizable, ranging from .48 ($p < .05$) to .78 ($p < .05$). A somewhat similar pattern of relationships also appears among evangelicals who are *moderately* interested in politics, except in this instance

Table 12.2

Results of MCA Analyses Examining Net Relationships between Cue Perceptions and Selected MEasures of Political Attitudes and Issue Positions among Evangelical Protestants, Mainline Protestants, and Roman Catholics
(controlling for selected demographic and religious variables*)

Topics of Cues and Religious Control		Level of Political Interest								
		High Interest			Moderate Interest					
		ABORTION			ABORTION			MORAL TRADITIONALISM		
			Adj. Dev.			Adj. Dev.			Adj. Dev.	
		Beta	1	2	Beta	1	2	Beta	1	2
ABORTION[a] (Controlling for DEVOTIONALISM)	EVAN	.48[b]	-.45	.20				.41[b]	-.68	.45
	MAIN									
	CATH									
ABORTION[a] (Controlling for SALIENCE)	EVAN	.66[b]	-.69	.30				.43[b]	-.82	.47
	MAIN									
	CATH									
ABORTION[a] (Controlling for INVOLVEMENT)	EVAN	.78[b]	-.78	.34				.43[b]	-.81	.49
	MAIN									
	CATH									
SEXUAL BEHAVIOR[a] (Controlling for SALIENCE)	EVAN									
	MAIN									
	CATH				.56[b]	-.56	.49			
SEXUAL BEHAVIOR[a] (Controlling for INVOLVEMENT)	EVAN									
	MAIN									
	CATH				.65[b]	-.69	.55			

Source: NES 1989 Pilot Study.

1 = Pastor doesn't speak on issue

2 = Pastor speaks out

*Demographic controls include: age (coded in years), gender (0 = male, 1 = female), education (1 = 8th grade or less, through 7 = advanced or graduate degrees), South, non-South (0 = southerner, 1 = nonsoutherner), and socioeconomic status. Because no statistically significant net relationships appeared among respondents who showed only a low degree of interest in politics, the low interest category is not included. *N*s for analyses vary from 33 to 46.

[a] All overall equations with coefficients represented in the table are significant at least at $p < .05$ level or beyond.

[b] Relationship significant at least at $p < .05$ level or beyond.

perception of clergy cues about abortion is linked to the expression of highly traditionalistic views on moral issues. All of the coefficients are again significant and sizable (.41 to .43, all $p < .05$). Thus, cue perceptions about abortion are connected to the political viewpoints expressed by evangelical Protestants, but *only* among those individuals who are at least moderately (or somewhat) interested in politics.[6] (Those with low interest in politics are not shown because there were no significant relationships on any issues.)

Among Catholic respondents, an entirely different set of net relationships is revealed. With relevant demographic and religious effects controlled, Catholics who perceive that their local clergy speak out on issues related to sexual conduct are more likely to express strong opposition to abortion than Catholics who have not perceived such cues. As can be seen, however, these relationships are substantial in magnitude (.56 and .65, both $p < .05$) but apply only to Catholics who report a *moderate* degree of interest in political processes.

Our findings clearly suggest that cue perception varies by religious tradition and level of political interest and that perceived cues from local clergy do relate to positions individuals take on certain issues. The extent of relationships between these cue perceptions and positions on selected political issues also varies substantially by religious tradition and level of interest; fewer connections exist among mainline Protestants and Roman Catholics, many more exist among evangelical Protestants. But these fundamental insights are really only preliminary, for our findings prompt the exploration of other questions.

Discussion

Pastors as Cuegivers: The Authoritative Force of Pastors within Evangelical Churches

One of the most notable findings that surfaced in our analyses is the importance of perceived pastoral cues among evangelical Protestants. This importance is reflected in the fact that perceived cues from clergy relate to a respondent's stance on political issues independent of his or her level of religiosity. But why should such cues necessarily assume greater importance for evangelicals than for mainline Protestants and Catholics? Perhaps the answer lies in the essentially sectarian character of most evangelical churches and the role of the pastor within the sectarian milieu.

First, it is apparent that a democratic form of religious organization (see Sommerfield 1968; Leege 1992) is a concomitant of sect-type religion. Second, it is clear that in the absence of a rigid clerical hierarchy, a meaningful system of sacramental symbols, and a millennia or two of authoritative conciliar decisions on doctrinal issues, sectarian churches look directly to the Scriptures for moral and spiritual guidance. When problems confront these sect-type bodies and conflict naturally arises from the operation of democratic processes, scriptural authority is often consulted for a solution (Leege 1992, 8). But whose interpretation of the Scriptures sets the course of action? Typically, that derivative authority resides with the individual who shows the greatest evidence of gifts of the Spirit when applied to interpreting and preaching the Scriptures—most often the pastor. Over time, despite the leveling effects of theological principles (e.g., priesthood of all believers) and nonhierarchical church polities, evangelical pastors exert a high degree of moral authority over their congregants. The local pastor takes on characteristics of a pope on matters of faith and life. It is this exceptional power for moral suasion that we believe is reflected in our data.

This investment of moral authority in the pastoral role also occurs among mainline Protestants and Catholics, but its effects may be diminished by several factors. More of these local churches and parishes belong to hierarchically ordered denominations rather than having an independent local church status or being part of a loose confederation. More of their pastors have been ordained through centuries-old training regimens and rituals and are subject to the disciplinary and assignment authority of a higher power (bishop, synodical president, etc.). And many of them judge sin and mediate grace sacramentally rather than through the judgment of the pastor or the local elders. Further, those mainline and Catholic bodies that evolved from minority ethnic groups were often careful to avoid public preaching on politics as a way of displaying their loyal and quietistic citizenship in this world while focusing on the world beyond. Mainline groups who constituted the traditional educational, social, and economic leadership of local communities, on the other hand, stressed political involvement through individual rather than corporate action; thus their pastors had to be careful to present a problem with many policy alternatives and leave the political course of action to individual congregants (see Roozen, McKinney, and Carroll 1984 for a classification of alternate *religious presences* in the community). In many respects, then, the democratic model of church polity and the social characteristics of evangelicals combined to produce more potential for authoritative pastoral leadership.

Catholic "Pelvic" Politics:
The Connection between Clerical Cues on Sexuality
and Attitudes toward Abortion

The connection between perceived clerical cues on sexual behavior and the positions held by Roman Catholics on the abortion issue is another finding that deserves further comment. Although it seems most likely that the relationship between abortion cues and abortion attitudes proves insubstantial largely because of the extremely limited variance exhibited by the abortion cues variable, it is still noteworthy that Catholics associate sexual cues so strongly with restrictive positions on abortion. It is also notable that they fail to make a similarly consistent connection between perceived clerical pronouncements on sexual behavior and issues relating to gender roles. What does this reflect about the prevailing mind-set of American Catholics?

It is probable that Catholics continue to discern a punitive subtext in clerical messages about how they should express their sexual nature. The church has continually emphasized responsibility in the use of one's sexuality, delimiting the appropriate social context (i.e., within marriage), form (i.e., heterosexual vs. homosexual union), and goal (i.e., reproduction rather than recreation) of sexual expression. As a result, many Catholics impute the stigmatizing connotation of sexual irresponsibility to unwanted pregnancies. And to exculpate sexual irresponsibility in the act of abortion only compounds the moral wrong.

This connection with sexual restrictiveness seems to suggest that the politics of abortion as practiced by American Catholic parishioners may be motivated as much by a substrate of Jansenism as by a genuine concern for the sanctity of life. Although the data offer only limited clues about this phenomenon, they are suggestive and offer a starting point for future research. They are consistent with the findings of others (e.g., Jelen 1990; Cleghorn 1986) regarding the seams in the "seamless garment" of human life issues.

Pastoral Influence or Voluntary Affiliation?
The Direction-of-Effect Question

One question that looms throughout this research concerns the direction of effects. Do political cues transmitted by local clergy influence the political attitudes of individual denomination members on selected issues? Or do individuals voluntarily choose to affiliate or reaffiliate based on their perceptions that the moral message preached by the pastor agrees with their own attitudes? Because of the cross-sectional nature of the data and the small subsamples, we cannot be confident about the causal directionality of the relationships we are studying. And especially when we consider that, among evangelicals, self-selection is a prominent mechanism that may account for membership (see Roof and McKinney 1987; Wuthnow 1988), we recognize how the problem may be compounded. The subsample N for each group and the missing data problem on key control or dependent variables could not sustain appropriate path analyses.

It does seem to us, however, that the evidence of greater voluntary affiliation among evangelicals is compelling. Both Roof and McKinney (1987) and Wuthnow (1988) have shown how the cleavages in contemporary Protestantism relate especially to life-style and moral responsibility. In the analyses presented in chapter 5, it was shown that not only was switching toward evangelical bodies greater than switching toward Catholic or mainline bodies, but that those who switched to evangelical bodies generally had as conservative or more conservative sociopolitical views than those who had lived all their lives as evangelicals. Many evangelicals seem to expect a sociopolitical message and, if our data are correct, they find it. But which came first—the attitude or the hearing of the message? It may take larger subsamples than we have to untangle that question, but it seems unlikely to us, in this day of voluntary church affiliation, that the *switchers* would join the new church with no expectations about moral directives and the *stand-patters* would stay in a church where reprehensible positions are preached.

Methodological Implications: Which Measures of Religiosity Matter Most?

In the competition for scarce interview schedule space in the NES 1990 Congressional Election Study, the cue-giving items did not appear. Has an important advance been lost? The experience with the independent variables and the controls suggests that sensitive questions to elicit and code denomination, to screen for social desirability in church affiliation and attendance, to capture the salience of religion in one's life and his or her private devotional practices will take us a long way in understanding both contextual religious effects and cue giving. We now know that findings from studies of pastoral cue giving are paralleled by our findings on parishioners' perceptions of cues. We would not be far amiss, then, in inferring the presence or absence of cues and cue effects from the measures of religiosity that have survived on the 1990 study.

At the same time, there is enough difference from cue to cue, issue to issue, and tradition to tradition, to make us still want to pursue issues examined in this chapter with a full NES national sample. Particularly for evangelicals, the most rapidly growing and youngest sector of the American religious universe, there are many questions we still want to untangle. Religio-moral concerns will remain on the public agenda because there is electoral advantage in their presence (Leege 1992). There is a limitless potential for religious dogfights in politics because they constitute one of the clearest forms of cultural politics that readily subsume economic interests (Leege, Lieske, and Wald 1991). To understand these processes more completely, we need to study further the nature of political communication processes and gain better measures of relevant variables.

Notes

1. Through a series of filter questions controlling for social desirability, the 1989 NES Pilot Study has a far more accurate estimate of religious apostasy, 18 percent rather than the 8 percent reported by the panel in 1988 (Leege, Kellstedt, and Wald 1990). Thus, there is less noise in the perception data than would be yielded for religiously affiliated subsamples of general population surveys.

2. Although the most recent pastoral letters from the Catholic bishops have addressed the economy and peace, Catholic parishioners do not sense much attention to such issues—certainly not as much as is paid to abortion. Despite Archbishop Cardinal Bernardin's effort to formulate a consistent life ethic through his "seamless garment" metaphor, studies have shown that few Catholics relate the teaching on economic and

peace issues to the life ethic in the manner that they relate the abortion teaching (cf. research cited in Jelen 1990; Welch and Leege 1991). In fact, the level of recognition of the teaching on both peace and economic justice is quite low; D'Antonio et al. (1989, 166), analyzing a 1987 Gallup survey, show that only 25 percent of all Catholics have heard or read about the peace pastoral and 29 percent have heard or read about the economy pastoral. In the Gary diocese, 85 percent of the respondents in a 1988 survey "did not know what is in the economic pastoral." Wald (1992) also notes the generally limited nature of efforts made to publicize the peace pastoral at the parish level. We can only speculate that Catholic pastors and priests say little about these pastorals in their homilies and newsletters. Certainly our findings are consistent with the D'Antonio et al. (1989) findings.

3. Despite the desirability of such internal consistency, it is unclear whether a response set may have shaped answers to the separate cue-giving items.

4. Political interest was measured by an item from the NES 1989 Pilot Study that asked respondents to indicate their level of interest in political campaigns on a five-point response scale. For purposes of the analysis, original scores on this item were reverse-coded and collapsed into the following scale: 1 = not very interested, 2 = somewhat interested, and 3 = very much interested.

5. Because of the small subsample Ns on which some of these analyses are based, we have used the .10 level of significance as the basic threshold for interpreting relationships.

6. MCA analyses were also used to examine the net relationships between our index of cue giving and the measures of political orientations. Three significant ($p < .05$) net relationships appeared among evangelicals who are moderately interested in politics and the level of perceived cue giving and moral traditionalism. Thus, the more likely one is to perceive high degrees of clergy directiveness, the more traditionalistic one's views—provided, of course, that one has at least some moderate interest in politics. No such connections were observed among Catholics and mainliners or other evangelicals who showed little interest in political affairs.

References

Abelman, Robert, and Pettey, Gary. 1988. "How Political Is Religious Television?" *Journalism Quarterly* 65:313–21.

Beatty, Kathleen, and Walter, Oliver. 1989. "A Group Theory of Religion and Politics: The Clergy as Group Leaders." *Western Political Quarterly* 42:129–46.

Berger, Peter, and Neuhaus, Richard John. 1977. *To Empower People*. Washington, DC: American Enterprise Institute.

Cleghorn, J.S. 1986. "Respect for Life: Research Notes on Cardinal Bernardin's 'Seamless Garment.'" *Review of Religious Research* 28:129–41.

Conover, Pamela Johnston, and Feldman, Stanley. 1986. "Morality Items in the May 1985 Pilot Study." Ann Arbor, MI: NES Pilot Study Committee.

D'Antonio, William V.; Davidson, James A.; Hoge, Dean R.; and Wallace, Ruth A. 1989. *American Catholic Laity in a Changing Church*. Kansas City, MO: Sheed and Ward.

Festinger, Leon; Schachter, Stanley; and Back, Kurt. 1950. *Social Pressures in Informal Groups: A Study of Human Factors in Housing*. New York: Harper.

Gilbert, Christopher P. 1989a. "The Political Influence of Church Discussion Partners." Paper presented at the annual meeting of the American Political Science Association, Atlanta.

———. 1989b. "Voting, Party Identification, and Church Political Environments: A Contextual Analysis." Paper presented at the annual meeting of the Midwest Political

Science Association, Chicago.

———. 1990. "Religious Environments and Political Attitudes." Paper presented at the annual meeting of the American Political Science Association, San Francisco.

Guth, James L. 1989. "Pastoral Politics in the 1988 Election: Protestant Clergy and Political Mobilization." Paper presented at the annual meeting of the American Political Science Association, Atlanta.

Hadden, Jeffrey K. 1969. *The Gathering Storm in the Churches.* Garden City, NY: Doubleday and Co.

Harder, Kathleen. 1988. "Pastors and Political Mobilization: Preaching Politics." Paper presented at the annual meeting of the American Political Science Association, Washington, DC.

Jelen, Ted G. 1992. "Political Christianity: A Contextual Analysis." *American Journal of Political Science* 36:692–714.

———, ed. 1989. *Religion and Political Behavior in the United States.* New York: Praeger.

———. 1990. "Religious Belief and Attitude Constraint." *Journal for the Scientific Study of Religion* 29:118–25.

Kinder, Donald R., and Sears, David O. 1985. "Public Opinion and Political Action." In Lindzey and Aronson 1985, 659–742. New York: Random House.

Koller, Norman B., and Retzer, Joseph D. 1980. "The Sounds of Silence Revisited." *Sociological Analysis* 41:155–61.

Langenbach, Lisa. 1988. "Evangelical Elites and Political Action." Paper presented at the annual meeting of the American Political Science Association, Washington, DC.

Leege, David C. 1992. "Coalitions, Cues, Strategic Politics, and the Staying Power of the Religious Right." *PS: Political Science and Politics* 22:198–204.

Leege, David C.; Kellstedt, Lyman A.; and Wald, Kenneth D. 1990. "Religion and Politics: A Report on Measures of Religiosity in the 1989 NES Pilot Study." Paper presented at the annual meeting of the Midwest Political Science Association, Chicago.

Leege, David C.; Lieske, Joel A.; and Wald, Kenneth D. 1991. "Toward Cultural Theories of American Political Behavior: Religion, Ethnicity, Race, and Class Outlook." In *Political Science: Looking to the Future*, vol. 3, ed. William J. Crotty, pp. 193–238. Evanston, IL: Northwestern University Press.

Lindzey, Gardner, and Aronson, Elliot, eds. 1985. *Handbook of Social Psychology*, vol. 2. 3d ed. New York: Random House.

Luidens, Donald A., and Nemeth, Roger J. 1989. "After the Storm: Closing the Clergy–Laity Gap." *Review of Religious Research* 31:183–95.

McGuire William J. 1985. "Attitudes and Attitude Change." In Lindzey and Aronson 1985, 233–346.

McKeown, Bruce, and Carlson, James M. 1987. "An Experimental Study of the Influence of Religious Elites on Public Opinion." *Journal of Political Communication and Persuasion* 4:93–102.

McPhee, William; Smith, Robert B.; and Ferguson, Jack. 1963. "A Theory of Informal Social Influence." In *Formal Theories of Mass Behavior*, ed. William McPhee, 74–103. London: Collier-Macmillan.

Miller, Arthur H., and Wattenberg, Martin P. 1990. "Politics from the Pulpit: Religiosity and the 1980 Elections." *Public Opinion Quarterly* 48:301–17.

Mobley, G. Melton. 1984. "The Political Influence of Television Ministers." *Review of Religious Research* 25:314–20.

Morris, Alden. 1981. "Black Southern Student Sit-In Movement: An Analysis of Internal Organization." *American Sociological Review* 46:747–67.

———. 1984. *The Origins of the Civil Rights Movement.* New York: Free Press.

Nelsen, Hart M. 1975. "Why Do Pastors Preach on Social Issues?" *Theology Today* 32:56–73.

Nelsen, Hart M.; Yokley, Raytha; and Madron, Thomas. 1973. "Ministerial Roles and Social Actionist Stance: Protestant Clergy and Protest in the Sixties." *American Sociological Review* 38:375–86.

Ornstein, Norman; Kohut, Andrew; and McCarthy, Larry. 1988. *The People, the Press, and Politics.* Reading, MA: Addison-Wesley.

Roof, Wade Clark, and McKinney, William. 1987. *American Mainline Religion.* New Brunswick, NJ: Rutgers University Press.

Roozen, David A.; McKinney, William; and Carroll, Jackson W. 1984. *Varieties of Religious Presence: Mission in Public Life.* New York: Pilgrim Press.

Sommerfield, Richard A. 1968. "Conceptions of the Ultimate and the Social Organization of Religious Bodies." *Journal for the Scientific Study of Religion* 7:178–96.

Sprague, John. 1982. "Is There a Micro Theory Consistent with Contextual Analysis?" In *Strategies of Political Inquiry,* ed. Elinor Ostrom, 99–128. Beverly Hills, CA: Sage Publications.

Thomas, W.I., and Thomas, D.S. 1928. *The Child in America.* New York: Knopf.

Wald, Kenneth D. 1992. *Religion and Politics in the United States.* 2d ed. Washington, DC: Congressional Quarterly Press.

Wald, Kenneth D.; Owen, Dennis E.; and Hill, Samuel S., Jr. 1988. "Churches as Political Communities." *American Political Science Review* 82:531–48.

———. 1990. "Political Cohesion in Churches." *Journal of Politics* 52:197–215.

Walton, Hanes. 1985. *Invisible Politics: Black Political Behavior.* Albany: State University of New York Press.

Welch, Michael R., and Leege, David C. 1991. "Dual Reference Groups and Political Orientations: An Examination of Evangelically Oriented Catholics." *American Journal of Political Science* 35:28–56.

White, Richard. 1968. "Toward a Theory of Religious Influence." *Pacific Sociological Review* 11:23–28.

Wuthnow, Robert. 1988. *The Restructuring of American Religion.* Princeton, NJ: Princeton University Press.

Zaller, John R. 1989. "Bringing Converse Back In: Information Flow in Political Campaigns." *Political Analysis* 1:181–234.

Chapter 13

Preaching to the Converted: The Causes and Consequences of Viewing Religious Television

Ted G. Jelen and Clyde Wilcox

During the 1980s, the power of religious television became an important issue in American national politics. While the Federal Communications Commission has always encouraged religious broadcasting, changes in communications regulation, broadcast technology, and the political climate have brought the televangelists into a position of high visibility in recent years (Hadden and Swann 1981; Hoover 1988). Although easier access to electronic media has allowed religious programming of several types to be seen on television, the most visible and largest (in terms of audience) programs have been associated with evangelical Protestantism. Such programs as "The Old Time Gospel Hour," "The 700 Club," "Hour of Power," and "PTL Club" have combined an explicitly evangelical, "old-fashioned" religious message with the techniques of modern mass communication. (For a comparison of modern televangelism with the recurring historical phenomenon of *urban revivalism*, see Frankl 1987.)

Many, although not all, of these programs offer explicitly political messages. Of particular interest to political scientists is the fare provided by Jerry Falwell, host of "The Old Time Gospel Hour" and founder of Moral Majority, and Marion (Pat) Robertson, host of "The 700 Club" and unsuccessful candidate for the Republican presidential nomination in 1988. Each of these televangelists has attempted to address a political agenda, ranging across a wide array of political issues, with an explicit biblical basis (see especially Falwell 1980; Kellstedt 1988). In addition to traditional evangelical concerns with issues of personal morality, both Robertson and Falwell have taken conservative positions on issues of economics, women's rights, and foreign affairs. Each of these televangelists has offered rather transparent partisan cues, and Falwell has claimed to have recruited several million Christians into political activity (for a contrary view, see Lipset and Raab 1981; Wilcox 1992).

This chapter is intended to address two questions. First, what types of people constitute the audience for religious television? Is this audience made up of traditionally religious people, who seek to supplement their more standard religious activity with telecommunications? Or, has religious television eroded support for local congregations, by providing a substitute worship or observance experience? Does the money contributed to televangelists come at the expense of the local congregation's collection plate? Thus far, the empirical evidence has been rather mixed. Support for the hypothesis that religious television serves as a substitute for attendance at religious services (under certain circumstances) has been provided by Pettersson (1986) for a Swedish sample and by Gaddy and Pritchard (1985) in the context of the United States. However, religious television usage has been shown to be most frequent among people who are active in their local congregations (Tamney and Johnson 1984; Korpi and Kim 1986; Hoover 1988).

Second, what are the effects of religious television on political attitudes and behavior? Does the political content of religious television actually influence the attitudes of viewers, or does the audience consist of people who already believe the conservative message the televangelists seek to convey? In other words, does religious television preach to a self-selected audience of the converted? The work of Hadden (1983, 1987; Hadden and Swann 1981) has suggested that religious television serves the needs of a large population of religious conservatives who are concerned about the secular, relativist direction of modern life. Religious television programming can thus be expected to mobilize people who might otherwise feel isolated and alienated from contemporary society. Empirical evidence suggesting that televangelism increases acceptance of religious involvement in political affairs has been reported by Gaddy (1984). By contrast, Mobley (1984) has presented evidence showing that religious television is a rather ineffective shaper of political attitudes, and he has challenged the notion that televangelists are able to influence voting behavior. Bruce (1990) has suggested that the popularity of particular religious programs is likely to vary inversely with their political content, since the target audience for these programs have apolitical, world-withdrawal orientations. Thus, issues involving the uses to which religious television is put and effects of such uses have generated considerable (and, occasionally, acrimonious) debate (see especially Gerbner et al. 1984, 1989; Frankl and Hadden 1987; Hadden and Frankl 1987, 1989; Shriver 1989; Fore 1989). In sum, this chapter seeks to assess the causes and effects of viewing religious television.

Measurement Issues

The focal variable in our analysis is whether the respondent views religious television and, if so, how much. The analyses presented in this chapter are limited to white respondents only. The 1988 NES contains the following series of questions: "In the past week, did you watch or listen to religious programs on radio or TV?" Respondents who answered *yes* were asked: "About how many times did you watch or listen?" Unlike the NES 1989 Pilot Study version, this question also elicits the extent to which the respondent listens to religious radio, which may contain more local (and perhaps more parochial) programming. The 1989 Pilot Study contained a slightly different version of this item: "How often do you do each of the following?" The following items were listed: Bible reading, prayer, witnessing, reading religious periodicals, watching religious programs, other than services of local churches, on TV. Response categories were *"daily, two or three times a week, once a week, two or three times a month, once a month, several times a year, hardly ever,* and *never.*

Inspection of the marginal distributions of the 1988 item suggests that the follow-up (measuring frequency of viewing) contains some nonrandom measurement error. A few respondents report very frequent viewing (or listening) (20–50 occasions per week). Since many of these same respondents participate in the paid labor force, such reports of viewership are very likely exaggerated. Therefore, we have conducted analyses with this item in an unrecoded form and have computed another version of the 1988 measure in which respondents are dichotomized into *nonviewers* (who report never watching religious television) and *viewers* (who report any religious television usage).

Table 13.1 contains the product-moment correlations between the unrecoded 1988 item, the dichotomous 1988 item, and the religious television item from the 1989 Pilot Study and external variables. In general, this table shows that the dichotomous version of the 1988 item performs better than the unrecoded version. We attribute this finding to the highly skewed marginal distribution of the unrecoded item and the high probability of substantial measurement error. Table 13.1 also shows that the 1989 Pilot Study item, with its multiple, closed-ended responses, performs slightly better than either version of the 1988 item, although the differences between the dichotomous 1988 version and the 1989 Pilot Study version are typically not large. It should be noted that only the 1989 Pilot Study version exhibits strong relationships with the Bible-reading or reading religious material items. We attribute this set of results to a probable response-set bias, in that these religious activity items were grouped together in the 1989 questionnaire. This finding, in turn, suggests that the 1989 Pilot Study item may be affected by its proximity to other religious activity items.

The Causes of Religious Television Usage

Table 13.1 shows that less-educated people are more likely to view religious programming than are people with higher levels of education, and that southerners are more likely to watch religious television than are those outside the South (Hoover 1988). Religious television usage is also related to a variety of measures of religiosity (church attendance and subjective importance of religion in every-

Table 13.1

**Comparison of Relationships between Religious Television Items and
Selected Criterion Variables**
(product-moment correlations, whites only)

	1988 NES	1988 recode[a]	1989 Pilot
Demographic Variables:			
Age	.02	.15*	.24*
Education	.01	-.15*	-.23*
Region	.09	.14*	.17*
Religious Variables:			
Born-again	.17*	.33*	.26*
Biblical inerrancy	.40*	.34*	.37*
Evangelical denomination	.01	.09	.14*
Pentecostal denomination	.08	.16*	.19*
Fundamentalist ID	.05	.12*	.07
Charismatic ID	.18*	.22*	.10
Religious salience	.13*	.27*	.24*
Church attendance	.14*	.17*	.16*
Religiosity index	.15*	.27*	.16*
Read Bible frequency	.003	.02	.30*
Read religious periodicals	.03	.08	.23*
Issue Attitudes:			
Social issues index	.18*	.30*	.33*
Death penalty	.04	.01	.09
Moral traditionalism	.14*	.22*	.21*
Defense spending	.08	.14*	.14*
Abortion	.14*	.19*	.29*
Women equal	.08	.12	.11
Women work	.13*	.15*	.27*
Women family role	.03	.03	.08
Group related Attitudes:			
Racial minority rating	-.03	-.19*	-.20*
Liberal rating	-.17*	-.13*	-.19*

Robertson rating	.20*	.24*	.25*
Moral Majority rating	.18*	.26*	.28*
Political Orientations:			
Party identification	.07	.06	.003
Internal efficacy	.01	.06	.02
External efficacy	-.03	-.04	.06
Vote turnout	.005	.03	.03
Presidential vote	.06	.04	.13
Reagan rating	.08	.04	.09

Source: 1989 NES Pilot Study, 1988 NES.
[a]Dichotomized version of the 1988 religious television item, which distinguishes all viewers from nonviewers.
*significant at .05.

day life as well as an index combining these variables), born-again status, and the respondent's view of the Bible (Hadden 1987; Hoover 1988; Korpi and Kim 1986). Membership in an evangelical denomination and fundamentalist self-identification (see chapters 3 and 4) exhibit relatively weak relationships with religious television viewership, while the effects of charismatic self-identification and membership in a pentecostal denomination (consisting primarily of Assemblies of God) are slightly stronger.

Most of these relationships are rendered statistically insignificant after multi-variate controls. Table 13.2 contains the results of a multiple regression model, describing the effects of religious and demographic variables on viewing religious television (using the 1989 version of the religious television item as the dependent variable). As this table shows, the only variables with significant effects on frequency of religious television viewing are an index of religiosity (combining church attendance and religious salience) and status as a homemaker or homemaker's spouse. Fundamentalist self-identification and belief in an inerrant Bible approach significance at .10. Affiliation with an evangelical or pentecostal denomination, charismatic self-identification, and born-again status have no effect on religious television usage.[1]

These data thus suggest that religious television supplements, rather than supplants, more traditional forms of religious observance. When the equation in Table 13.2 is recomputed substituting the separate components of the religiosity index, both church attendance and subjective religiosity emerge as significant (and positive) predictors of religious television viewership, despite the fact that these two variables are highly multicollinear. This is an important finding, since, if religious television were a substitute for more standard forms of religious

Table 13.2

Mulivariate Predictors of Religious Television Usage
  (OLS regression, whites only)

	b	beta	t
Religiosity index	.55	.20	3.17**
Education	-.002	-.002	-.04
Region	.24	.04	.51
Housewife	.97	.11	1.86+
Fundamentalist ID	.20	.08	1.15
Charismatic ID	.09	.04	.53
Evangelical denom.	.41	.05	.81
Sex	-.13	-.02	-.39
Biblical inerrancy	.48	.08	1.16
Born-again	.13	.02	.31

Source: NES 1989 Pilot Study.
$R^2 = .11$
**significant at .01.
+significant at .10.

activity, the relationship between attendance and viewership should be negative once subjective religiosity is controlled. It is also of interest to note that, despite the strong emphasis on evangelical Christianity among the more popular religious programs, the effects of evangelicalism, fundamentalism, or other aspects of doctrinally conservative Christianity are insignificant. This finding suggests that the appeal of such programs may be more ecumenical than previous research may have suggested (see Jelen 1991; Wilcox 1988; Bruce 1990), although these results might be quite different if respondents had been asked about viewership of specific religious programs.

The Political Effects of Religious Television

When considered as an independent variable, we can see from Table 13.1 that religious television viewing by whites is associated with negative feelings toward racial minorities and liberals and with conservative positions on a variety of social issues.[2] Viewing religious television is also strongly related to affect toward New Christian Right symbols such as Pat Robertson and the Moral Majority. Religious television is moderately related to negative attitudes toward female participation in the paid labor force and to attitudes toward equal social roles for women and men. Interestingly, the zero-order correlations between viewing religious television and manifestly political attitudes, such as party identification, 1988 presidential vote, and affect toward Ronald Reagan, are generally very weak and nonsignificant. The sole exception is that the 1989 Pilot Study item is weakly, but significantly, related to 1988 presidential vote. Frequency of religious television usage is also unrelated to general political orientations such as internal political efficacy (sense of personal competence), external efficacy (political trust), or political cynicism. Thus, the data in Table 13.1 suggest that there are substantial limits to the role of religious television as a political mobilizer or as a source of partisan cues.

With respect to certain political attitudes, the effects of religious television appear to be contingent on the religious environment of the viewer. In particular, religious television may be a means by which cognitive dissonance, induced by inconsistent religious cues, may be resolved. Table 13.3 contains correlations between religious television usage and selected political attitudes for two sets of respondents. *Mismatched* respondents are those who belong to nonevangelical denominations (including Roman Catholic) and who believe in an inerrant Bible, while *nonmismatched* respondents are those whose beliefs about the Bible are more congruent with their denominational affiliations.[3] As Table 13.3 shows, the relationship between religious television usage and several different political attitudes is strongest for mismatched respondents. The effects of such viewership on mismatched respondents is stronger with respect to affect toward New Christian Right symbols Robertson and the Moral Majority, moral traditionalism, defense spending, 1988 presidential vote, and a seven-point scale concerning equal social and economic roles for women. By contrast, the effects of religious television are stronger among nonmismatched respondents for internal political efficacy or subjective political competence.

The data presented in Table 13.3 suggest that, among respondents whose personal theological orientation is more conservative than their religious environment, religious television is a moderately influential source of political attitudes. Such mismatched believers, who do not take the apparently drastic step of changing denominational families, appear to supplement and balance their more traditional religious activity with religious television. Although such mismatched persons are only slightly more likely to view religious television than members of evangelical denominations who hold an inerrant view of the Bible, they appear considerably more likely to be affected by such media usage. Religious television appears to be a partial source of political cues for those whose religious environments do not provide information about the political consequences of their doctrinal beliefs. (For a similar analysis, see Welch, Johnson, and Pilgrim 1990). Unfortunately, there are too few mismatched respondents to subject these findings to multivariate controls.

This finding is potentially quite important but should be viewed with a good deal of caution. It is not clear from these data that the results presented in Table 13.3 would survive even relatively simple multivariate controls. Moreover, even

Table 13.3

Comparison of Effects of Religious Television in Mismatched and Nonmismatched Respondents
(product-moment correlations, whites only)

	Mismatched	Non-mismatched
Robertson rating	.22*	.09
Moral Majority rating	.20*	.04
Moral traditionalism	.23*	.14*
Defense spending	.13*	-.03
Presidential vote	.15*	-.009
Women equal	-.16*	.01
Internal efficacy	-.01	.12*

Source: NES 1989 Pilot Study.
*significant at .05.

the zero-order results reported here apply to only a few variables. When these correlations are rerun using the 1988 NES (providing a large N and a slightly different version of the religious television item), the results are generally similar, except that there are no differences between mismatched and nonmismatched respondents with respect to internal efficacy or defense spending, and the difference between the two groups is reduced with respect to the effects of viewing religious television on attitudes toward Pat Robertson.

This last set of results raises the more general issue of self-selection. Does religious television have an independent effect on political attitudes and behavior, or is the audience for religious programming comprised of those already receptive to the messages put forth by televangelists? While it is impossible to answer this question definitively without data gathered over time,[4] we can determine whether the effects of viewing religious television persist after the imposition of multivariate controls. Can other variables account for the robust zero-order relationships reported in Table 13.1?

Table 13.4 summarizes the effects of religious television on a variety of political attitudes and behaviors after controls are introduced for religiosity, education, residence in the South, sex, membership in an evangelical denomination, self-identification as a fundamentalist or charismatic, beliefs about the Bible, age, born-again status, and status as a homemaker (or having a homemaker as a spouse). As these data show, religious television has a significant independent effect on attitudes toward abortion and has effects on the social issues index and internal efficacy, both of which are significant at .10. On all other issues, including party identification and presidential vote, the effects of viewing religious television can be accounted for by other variables.

Table 13.4

Effects of Religious Television on Selected Political Attitudes, after Multivariate Controls
(OLS regression, whites only)

	b	beta	t
Group related attitudes:			
Liberal rating	-.34	-.05	-.98
Robertson rating	.50	.06	1.03
Moral Majority rating	.32	.04	.72
Issues and Attitudes:			
Social issues index	.02	.08	1.74+
Death Penalty	-.007	-.01	-.35
Moral traditionalism	.03	.07	1.40
Defense spending	.003	.009	.17
Spending for poor	-.01	-.04	-.77
Abortion	.04	.11	2.21*
Women work	.002	.01	.16
Women family role	.01	.04	.53
Women equal	.01	.04	.59
Political Orientations:			
Party identification	.05	.07	1.21
Presidential vote	-.002	-.01	-.21
Reagan rating	.76	.07	1.33
Vote turnout	-.005	-.03	-.63
Internal efficacy	.03	.08	1.65+
External efficacy	-.03	-.08	-1.27

Source: NES 1989 Pilot Study.
*significant at .05.
+significant at .10.

A number of tests were run to determine whether religious television has an effect on political attitudes in interaction with other variables. We computed multiplicative interactive terms between the religious television item and respondent views of the Bible, a dummy variable measuring theological *mismatching*, fundamentalist and charismatic self-identification, and membership in an evangelical denomination, religious salience, and church attendance. The interactive term was then included in the equation in place of both the religious television and interaction variable. The only interaction effect that made a noticeable difference is the combination of religious television and church attendance. In this instance, the interactive term was significantly related to the social issues index, abortion, and internal efficacy as well as to affect toward liberals, moral conservatism, and all three indices of feminism (a seven-point scale about women's equality, beliefs about female participation in the paid labor force, and attitudes toward women as homemakers; see Wilcox and Jelen 1991, for a discussion of the dimensionality of feminist attitudes). The attendance–television interaction is also significantly (at .10) related to a conservative position of opposition to government spending to assist the disadvantaged. The interaction between church attendance and religious television was also significantly related to voting turnout in 1988.[5] This finding suggests that the claims of televangelist Jerry Falwell to have mobilized conservative Christians into political activity may contain an element of truth. Although the magnitude of these relationships is not large (the absolute values of the standardized regression coefficients range from .11 to .17), the effects of the attendance–television interaction persist in the face of elaborate multivariate controls.

This set of findings suggests that religious television may well have a reinforcing effect on norms learned in other settings. That is, the effects of viewing religious television are fairly limited on those respondents whose religious beliefs are individualized and private. In isolation, religious television is a relatively weak agent of political socialization. By contrast, religious television usage appears to have a somewhat greater effect on those who interact frequently with others in religious settings. It has been shown (Wald, Owen, and Hill 1988; Peterson 1992; Jelen 1992) that the local congregation is an important source of political learning and that these effects are stronger in evangelical churches (Wald, Owen, and Hill 1990). Although this hypothesis cannot be tested directly with available data, it may be that politicization occurs as the result of the combination of social and political skills learned in public settings and the messages provided by televangelists. While religious television remains a weak source of partisan cues, the combination of frequent church attendance and religious television usage may serve to reinforce messages of social conservatism and to generate beliefs in the efficacy of political activity.

Finally, it is of some interest to note that religious television is not a particularly strong source of political knowledge or political sophistication. In contrast to the effects of viewing local or national television news or regular newspaper reading, viewing religious television has no measurable effect on political knowledge.[6] Religious television has a slight effect on attitude constraint,[7] although most of the increase in attitude consistency arises from greater constraints across the components of the index of moral traditionalism. This effect is not large ($r = .20$), but does retain its statistical significance under controls for education and church attendance. Religious television does not increase constraint across the components of the social issues index or the defense index.[8]

Discussion

This chapter has shown that religious television has limited, but significant, effects on political attitudes and behavior. While the political consequences of viewing religious television have perhaps been exaggerated by some observers, televangelism does seem to have contributed in a modest way to the politicization of religious conservatives. Based on the results of this study, we regard the religious television variable as a potentially important one and urge that such an item be included in future surveys of the American public.

When viewed as a dependent variable, religious television appears to supplement, rather than supplant, more traditional forms of religious activity. Religiosity (measured as the combination of church attendance and religious salience) is the strongest predictor of religious television viewing. Thus, the fears of some that televangelism may replace the local church as the focal point for religious communications seem unwarranted. Our data also show that the appeal of religious television is generally ecumenical, with variables measuring adherence with specific traditions (e.g., fundamentalism, pentecostalism, etc.) having very limited effects. Of course, this finding may be an artifact of the religious television question. Were we to inquire about viewership of specific religious programs (e.g., "The Old Time Gospel Hour," "The 700 Club,") the effects of particular religious traditions might be much stronger.

The effects of religious television usage are limited and subtle. In general, religious television has its strongest effects in conjunction with church attendance and affects attitudes only on issues of personal or social morality. The effects of televangelism do not extend to the full range of economic and international issues to which spokespersons such as Falwell and Robertson address themselves. Thus, televangelists have not provided a "Christian agenda" for the full range of issues affecting the American political system. Moreover, the effects of viewing religious television on explicitly partisan attitudes such as party identification or presidential voting are extremely limited.

We cautiously advance the hypothesis that the effects of viewing religious television are strongest for doctrinal conservatives who attend theologically liberal churches. Some very preliminary evidence suggests that religious television has an effect on such *mismatched* respondents with respect to several political attitudes. Our caution is derived from the fact that the relatively small number of mismatched respondents makes our estimates extremely unstable and precludes multivariate analysis with these data. This potentially important finding thus cries out for replication and reanalysis with larger samples.

The combination of religious television and church attendance has its greatest effects on attitudes concerning personal political efficacy and voting turnout. Although the effects of the interaction term are moderate (*beta* = .16 for turnout, .11 for internal efficacy), they are significant and persist in the face of very elaborate multivariate controls. Thus, the claims of a Jerry Falwell to have mobilized large numbers of Christians may have been exaggerated but do appear to contain an element of truth. Religious television is apparently ineffective in converting Democrats into Republicans, but may well have the effect of turning some nonparticipants into participants. If conservative Christians receive partisan cues elsewhere, religious television may serve to counteract the world-withdrawal tendencies of some conservative Christians (see Jelen 1987; Hoover 1988). While it would be a mistake to exaggerate the mobilizing effect of religious television, it would also be inappropriate to ignore its role in connecting religion and politics.

Future research in this area could benefit from smaller-scale studies measuring the causes and effects of viewing particular religious programs. Are viewers of the explicitly political messages of Falwell and Robertson more or less particularistic than those who are exposed to less political televangelists such as Oral Roberts? Do explicitly partisan messages enhance or detract from political learning from religious television?

The question of the religious television–church attendance interaction also merits closer investigation. Our data suggest that the effects of viewing religious television are enhanced by church attendance and that this interaction effect is relatively insensitive to the type of church the viewer attends. This set of results leads us to hypothesize (very tentatively) that religious activity is a source of social, interactive *skills* (as opposed to specific *attitudes*) that religious television extends to the larger world of politics. Obviously, this hypothesis deserves investigation by much more direct methods than are permitted by a national survey.

The *indirect* effects of viewing religious television also deserve further attention. Even if the effects of religious television usage on a mass sample are somewhat limited, these effects might be stronger on opinion leaders: clergy or lay leaders within specific congregations. Perhaps televangelists alter political attitudes through the familiar *two-step* flow of political information.

Finally, monitoring these effects over time would contribute to our understanding of the effects of religious television. As noted above, the results of previous research on the effects of viewing religious television have been mixed. Here, we find moderate, subtle, effects during a period when many televangelists were in a period of decline. During the 1988–89 period, televangelists Jimmy Swaggart and Jim Bakker suffered personal scandals, Jerry Falwell discontinued Moral Majority (after first subsuming the organization into the Liberty Federation), and Pat Robertson's presidential campaign ended unsuccessfully. It seems plausible to suppose that the effects of religious television are sensitive to *period effects* and that such effects rise and fall in response to political events.

Despite the recent troubles of several televangelists, the structural changes in television technology and regulation suggest that religious television has become a permanent fixture in the American political landscape. The effects of such religious programming will undoubtedly occupy the attention of researchers for some time to come.

Notes

1. Experimentation with an interactive term between evangelical denomination and religiosity yields a null result. The effects of the interactive term are insignificant, and the substitution of this multiplicative interaction for the religiosity and evangelical denomination variables reduces the adjusted R^2 from .11 to .006.

2. In subsequent analyses, religious television is measured using the 1989 Pilot Study item. The social issues index is the mean of the normalized scores on the equal roles for women, homosexual rights, abortion, and school prayer items. The moral traditionalism index consists of the respondent's mean rating of normalized scores across the following Likert items, after these questions had been recoded to a common direction: "The world is always changing, and we should adapt our view of moral behavior to those changes"; "We should be more tolerant of people who choose to live according to their own moral standards, even if they are very different from our own"; "This country would have many fewer problems if there were more emphasis on traditional family ties"; "The newer lifestyles are contributing to the breakdown of society."

3. The *nonmismatched* column includes members of evangelical denominations who do not hold a "high" view of the Scriptures. Because very few of these respondents watch religious television, the exclusion of these respondents from Table 13.3 does not affect the results reported.

4. The number of people who reported not watching religious television in 1988, but watching in 1989, is extremely small and barely exceeds those who report watching in the 1988 survey but not in 1989. Thus, over the brief period of the 1988–89 panel, there is too little change in the independent variable to isolate direct effects.

5. For the attendance–television interaction, controlling for theological mismatching makes no difference in the results reported here. Further, the effects of the interactive term are very similar for members of evangelical and nonevangelical denominations.

6. The index of political knowledge was computed by summing the correct responses for items asking respondents to name the offices held by Edward Kennedy, George Shultz, William Rehnquist, Mikhail Gorbachev, Margaret Thatcher, Yasser Arafat, and James Wright and the parties controlling each house of Congress.

7. *Constraint* is computed by recoding normalized scores on political attitudes to a common range and computing individual respondents' standard deviations across the domain of attitudes in question. (See Jelen 1990; Kiecolt and Nelsen 1988; Luskin 1987; Campbell 1983; Mueller and Judd 1981; Barton and Parsons 1977; and Wilcox 1987, for applications of this procedure.)

8. *Defense index* is the individual mean of normalized scores across three questions: a seven-point scale concerning whether defense spending should be increased or decreased; a forced-choice item asking whether we should *have a very strong military* or whether it is better to work out differences at the negotiating table; and an item asking respondents to rate the importance of a strong military.

References

Baron, Allen H., and Parsons, R. Wayne. 1977. "Measuring Belief System Structure." *Public Opinion Quarterly* 41:159–80.

Bruce, Steve. 1990. *Pray TV: Televangelism in America.* New York: Routledge.

Campbell, James. 1983. "Ambiguity in the Issue Positions of Presidential Candidates: A Causal Analysis." *American Journal of Political Science* 27:284–93.

Falwell, Jerry. 1980. *Listen, America!* Garden City, NY: Doubleday and Co.

Fore, William F. 1989. "Response." *Review of Religious Research* 31:100–102.

Frankl, Razelle. 1987. *Televangelism: The Marketing of Popular Religion.* Carbondale, IL: Southern Illinois University Press.

Frankl, Razelle, and Hadden, Jeffrey K. 1987. "A Critical Review of the Religion and Television Research Report." *Review of Religious Research* 29:111–24.

Gaddy, Gary D. 1984. "The Power of the Religious Media: Religious Broadcast Use and the Role of Religious Organizations in Public Affairs." *Review of Religious Research* 25:289–302.

Gaddy, Gary D., and Pritchard, David. 1985. "When Watching Religious TV Is Like Attending Church." *Journal of Communication* 35:123–31.

Gerbner, George; Gross, Larry; Hoover, Stewart; Morgan, Michael; and Signorielli, Nancy. 1984. *Religion and Television: A Research Report by the Annenberg School of Communications.* 2 vols. Philadelphia: University of Pennsylvania and the Gallup Organization.

————. 1989. "Responses to 'Star Wars of a Different Kind: Reflections on the Politics of the Religion and Television Research Project' by Jeffrey K. Hadden and Razelle Frankl." *Review of Religious Research* 31:94–98.

Hadden, Jeffrey K. 1983. "Televangelism and the New Christian Right." In *Religion and Religiosity in America: Studies in Honor of Joseph H. Fichter,* ed. Jeffrey K. Hadden and Theodore E. Long, 114–27. New York: Crossroad.

————. 1987. "Religious Broadcasting and the Mobilization of the New Christian Right." *Journal for the Scientific Study of Religion* 26:1–24.

Hadden, Jeffrey K., and Frankl, Razelle. 1987. "Star Wars of a Different Kind: Reflections on the Politics of the Religion and Television Research Project." *Review of Religious Research* 29:101–10.

————. 1989. "Rejoinder: Star Wars of a Different Kind." *Review of Religious Research* 31:102–4.

Hadden, Jeffrey K., and Swann, Charles E. 1981. *Prime Time Preachers: The Rising Power of Televangelism.* Reading, MA: Addison-Wesley.

Hoover, Stewart M. 1988. *Mass Media Religion: The Social Sources of the Electronic Church.* Newbury Park, CA: Sage Publications.

Jelen, Ted G. 1987. "The Effects of Religious Separatism on White Protestants in the 1984 Presidential Election." *Sociological Analysis* 48:30–45.

————. 1990. "Religious Belief and Attitude Constraint." *Journal for the Scientific Study of Religion* 29:118–25.

————. 1991. *The Political Mobilization of Religious Beliefs.* New York: Praeger.

————. 1992. "Political Christianity: A Contextual Analysis." *American Journal of Political Science* 36:692–714.

Kellstedt, Lyman A. 1988. "The Falwell Issue Agenda: Sources of White Evangelical Support." In *Research in the Social Scientific Study of Religion,* ed. Monty L. Lynn and David O. Moberg, 109–32. Greenwich, CT: JAI Press.

Kiecolt, Jill K., and Nelsen, Hart M. 1988. "The Structuring of Political Attitudes among Liberal and Conservative Protestants." *Journal for the Scientific Study of Religion* 27:48–59.

Korpi, Michael F., and Kim, Kyong Liong. 1986. "The Uses and Effects of Televangelism: A Factorial Model of Support and Contribution." *Journal for the Scientific Study of Religion* 25:410–23.

Lipset, Seymour Martin, and Raab, Earl. 1981. "The Election and the Evangelicals." *Commentary* 71(3):25–31.

Luskin, Robert C. 1987. "Measuring Political Sophistication." *American Journal of Political Science* 31:856–99.

Mobley, G. Melton. 1984. "The Political Influence of Television Ministers." *Review of Religious Research* 25:314–20.

Mueller, Carol M., and Judd, Charles M. 1981. "Belief System Constraint and Belief Consensus: Toward an Analysis of Social Movement Ideologies." *Social Forces* 60:182–87.

Peterson, Steven A. 1992. "Church Participation and Political Participation: The Spillover Effect." *American Politics Quarterly* 20:123–39.

Pettersson, Thorleif. 1986. "The Audience's Uses and Gratifications of TV Worship Services." *Journal for the Scientific Study of Religion* 25:391–409.

Shriver, Peggy L. 1989. "Response." *Review of Religious Research* 31:98–100.

Tamney, Joseph B., and Johnson, Stephen D. 1984. "Religious Television in Middletown." *Review of Religious Research* 25:303–13.

Wald, Kenneth D.; Owen, Dennis E.; and Hill, Samuel S., Jr. 1988. "Churches as Political Communities." *American Political Science Review* 82:531–48.

——. 1990. "Political Cohesion in Churches." *Journal of Politics* 52:171–215.

Welch, Michael R.; Johnson, C. Lincoln; and Pilgrim, David. 1990. "Tuning in the Spirit: Exposure to Types of Religious TV Programming among American Catholic Parishioners." *Journal for the Scientific Study of Religion* 29:185–97.

Wilcox, Clyde. 1987. "America's Radical Right Revisited: A Comparison of Activists in Christian Right Organizations from the 1960s to the 1980s." *Sociological Analysis* 48:46–57.

——. 1988. "The Christian Right in Twentieth Century America: Continuity and Change." *Review of Politics* 50:659–81.

——. 1992. *God's Warriors: The Christian Right in Twentieth Century America.* Baltimore: Johns Hopkins University Press.

Wilcox, Clyde, and Jelen, Ted G. 1991. "The Effects of Employment and Religion on Women's Feminist Attitudes." *International Journal for the Psychology of Religion* 1:161–71.

Part VI

Does Religion Matter in Studies of Voting Behavior and Attitudes?

Chapter 14

Religion, the Neglected Variable: An Agenda for Future Research on Religion and Political Behavior

Lyman A. Kellstedt

Religion matters. It matters politically. That is the thesis of this volume. Religion matters, it seems, regardless of how it is conceptualized: whether in terms of social group affiliation, religious group identification, ritualistic or private devotional practices, doctrinal beliefs, salience, or religious worldviews. Despite multivariate controls, each of these variables has an independent impact on political attitudes and behaviors. And this is the case even though the measures are often methodologically flawed.

The argument that religion matters should come as no surprise, for as Wald (1992) has shown, Americans invariably identify with a religious group of some sort and, in addition, engage in religious practices with great frequency. They have far greater religious involvement than their sporadic involvement in politics. And something this pervasive should be expected to have considerable impact. However, it is not simply its pervasive quality that leads us to expect a political impact. Religious institutions, and especially churches, serve as "intermediary organizations for politics, that array of organizations which stand between the individual citizen and the institutions of government" (Shafer 1991, 43). The presidential campaigns of Jesse Jackson in 1984 and 1988 and of Pat Robertson in 1988 certainly demonstrated that churches play this role. Given the decline of local organizations of the major political parties as intermediaries, churches may have an even greater impact than in the past, for they are places where people congregate (no pun intended). But in addition, religion is important in terms of linking social base characteristics and politics. Shafer (1991, 43) identifies four "inherent divisions of group identification" within the society that impact electoral politics: race and ethnicity, social class, region, and religion or culture. He argues that attitudes toward politics are formed in these *group* contexts. Political scientists have focused on all four of these divisions but have given the least attention to religion. This book has sought to initiate a research dialogue that will remedy the imbalance.

This final chapter summarizes the arguments made in the preceding chapters. It highlights key findings and promising measurement innovations to begin with and then develops a model of religious commitment from previous theoretical efforts and from the analyses presented in this volume, including a brief empirical test of the model. Finally, the chapter points to the future, sketching a tentative agenda for research on religion and politics.

In reexamining the theoretical developments, measurement innovations, and substantive findings of the preceding chapters, one finds the subfield of religion and political behavior in ferment. The NES 1989 Pilot Study opened up new opportunities and possibilities for greater dialogue with other students of voting behavior. Yet the new developments have not produced consensus in conceptual usage, measurement strategies, approaches to error, or statistical techniques. This lack of consensus makes it difficult for a reader to get a "quick fix" on the relationships between religion and political behavior. In the social sciences, however, such consensus develops slowly. Hence the diversity and ferment in this book should be seen as a sign that serious work is under way.

Religion as Group Affiliation and Identification

Political scientists have given only sporadic attention to group affiliation and identification. Over a generation ago, the classic studies of voting behavior (cf. Berelson, Lazarsfeld, and McPhee 1954; Campbell et al. 1960) gave emphasis to the group basis of partisanship and voting behavior. Attention then languished until the 1980s, when political scientists rediscovered the importance of groups (cf. Conover 1984; Conover and Feldman 1984). Part II of this volume examined carefully the role of religion in terms of its group meaning. Chapter 3 looked at religious group affiliations. Chapter 4 examined religious group identifications. Finally, chapter 5 explored whether change in religious group affiliation across the life cycle had an impact on political behavior. In this section of the final chapter we examine some implications of the findings from these three chapters.

Denomination and Religious Tradition

Denominational attachments and religious traditions make a difference politically. Historical evidence (see Swierenga 1990) attests to the connections, paralleling our contemporary data analysis. This finding should not come as a surprise since, for many people, local church and denominational affiliations as well as their aggregates, religious traditions, provide answers to ultimate questions, the ones unanswerable by scientific methods or philosophical reasoning. As a result, these religious structures acquire legitimacy in the eyes of their adherents and become potent socializers about such things as attitudes toward abortion, pornography, the role of women, homosexuality, racial prejudice, communism, patriotism, war and peace, the free enterprise system, and social justice, and such overtly political phenomena as partisan identification and vote choice.

Local churches provide answers not only to the unanswerable but also fulfill a need for affiliation. As Emile Durkheim noted long ago, affiliation and interaction with group members nurtures legitimacy well beyond the allure of a belief. What is thought to be held in common overpowers the fear of social isolation. Its yield is a propensity toward conformity.

Denominations and religious traditions, then, provide a context within which many Americans make political choices. Grouping of Protestant denominations into religious traditions serves as an aggregating mechanism, allowing the great number of denominational groups to come together to provide support for issue positions, political parties, and candidates for public office. These religious traditions, and particularly institutions that have developed to serve them, become the focal point of campaign efforts on the part of candidates and parties. Hence, in an overt appeal for political support, not only did Vice-President Dan Quayle deliver a keynote address to the Southern Baptist Convention, but President George Bush addressed prolife groups, religious broadcasters, national prayer breakfasts, and even the annual convention of the National Association of Evangelicals. The expectation, or hope, on the part of the candidate is that positive messages about such events will reach the mass of evangelical voters—across many churches—in the pews. By implication, politicians seem to grasp that differences among religious traditions (evangelical Protestant, mainline Protestant, Roman Catholic) matter. Social scientists have been slower to recognize the salient divisions in Aerican religion and the workways of politicians.

Nonetheless, a generation ago, Stark and Glock (1968, 55) argued that the "theological fragmentation of Protestantism" had serious research implications. They noted that the theological and cultural differences within American Protestantism were profound and that these differences both reflected and affected demographic cleavages within Protestant denominations as well as social and political attitude differences. The Stark and Glock findings "seriously challenge the common social science practice of comparing Protestants and Roman Catholics" (55). They continue: "When we speak of 'Protestants,' as we so often do in the social sciences, we spin statistical fiction. . . . Protestantism [in contrast to Catholicism] includes many separately constituted groups and the only possible ground for treating them collectively would be if they shared in a common religious vision. Since this is clearly not the case, we shall have to change our ways" (56). The findings in this book reaffirm the conclusions of Stark and Glock from a generation ago. We find consistent differences between evangelical and mainline Protestants in political attitudes and behaviors. Political scientists need to recognize that these differences are often more important politically than the gulfs between rich and poor, between young and old, or on some policy questions, even between black and white.

The measurement implications of these findings are profound as well. Accurate assessment of denominational affiliation is essential to valid classification into religious traditions. Even if denominational attachments are accurately measured, aggregation into religious traditions is difficult because there is little consensus concerning the existence or makeup of religious traditions. We have opted in this volume for a distinction between evangelical and mainline Protestants. Empirically, the distinction between the two appears to have great validity, for in chapter after chapter, evangelical and mainline Protestants were found to differ politically. These differences are rooted in socioeconomic status, religion, and culture.[1]

Our distinction between evangelical and mainline Protestants is not without problems, however. First, classification is not always easy: some denominations could be assigned to either category (for example, Lutheran Church–Missouri Synod, American Baptist Churches USA, Reformed Church in America). Second, the growing numbers of nondenominational Protestants cause problems in determining assignment to the appropriate religious tradition. Third, new denominations come into being, but there is little or no information available about them. Fourth, denominations change over time. For example, the Congregationalists (one component of the United Church of Christ today), pillars of orthodoxy in the colonial period, are currently among the most religiously liberal of the mainline denominations; and their partner in a 1958 merger, the Evangelical and Reformed Church, once had even stronger emphases on doctrinal orthodoxy. Analysts need to stay alert to these changes. Fifth, classification of black denominations into evangelical and mainline Protestant religious traditions needs to be reassessed, as it is not clear where some of these denominations belong in such a classification.

Despite these problems, some classification scheme is needed or the Protestant category will be used without differentiation, as has been the case in most political behavior research. Although the specifics of our categorization are new, the distinction between the two groups of Protestants is often made (cf. Wuthnow 1988) and, as noted above, is rooted in differences that are cultural, socioeconomic, and, above all, religious. Furthermore, as this volume attests, the empirical results from such a distinction are promising.

Real progress has been made by NES surveys beginning with the 1989 Pilot Study and continuing with the 1990 and 1992 studies. First, ascertaining a respondent's correct denominational affiliation has been facilitated by in-depth probes about his or her local church. Without significantly increasing scarce interview time, accuracy in recording responses has been enhanced. Second, a set of coding categories has been created to classify the detailed set of denominations obtained in the interview. Within a few years, scholars will be able to aggregate across election cycles to portray more accurately than heretofore the political attitude and behavior differences among denominations within a family (such as the Lutherans). If the General Social Surveys (GSS), the Gallup Poll, and other leading commercial pollsters would adopt the changes pioneered by the NES, denominations and religious traditions would come out from under a bushel and demonstrate their importance as predictors of all types of social and political phenomena. Of course, there is nothing stopping individual scholars from using these changes in special-purpose surveys of their own. Third, initial efforts, as exemplified by the findings in this book, demonstrate the efficacy of aggregating Protestant denominations into evangelical and mainline traditions. Of course, other possibilities for aggregation exist, and scholars should explore these possibilities with the reliable measures of denomination now available in the NES surveys.

Denominational Change and Political Behavior

The chapter on denominational change reveals that the vast majority of Americans remain within the religious tradition in which they were raised. The changes that do occur tend to "enhance the political distinctiveness of religious traditions" (p. 114). Yet a strong case is not made for the importance of denominational change when compared to political change within traditions emanating from other sources. Differential birthrates and immigration patterns are posited as other sources of change within religious traditions that may have greater impact on political behavior than denominational change. Nonetheless, the growth of the secular category is a potential change to watch.

Denominational change data were available in the 1989 Pilot Study but not in the 1990 or 1992 NES. Such data are available in the General Social Surveys. Despite some difficulties with the coding of denominations in the GSS, political scientists intrigued with the possibilities for research raised by chapter 5 should turn to that source. It will provide both larger Ns and an extended time period to test hypotheses of interest.

An Ethnoracial Interlude: Race, Religious Tradition, and Political Behavior

This volume has focused on whites in examining the linkages between religion and politics. The main reason for this emphasis is straightforward—black Americans since 1964 have been overwhelmingly Democratic. Hence, there is little or no within-group variance. Moreover, most examinations of NES data ignore Hispanics. We know of no table in the extant literature that looks at the political behavior of Hispanics controlling for religious affiliation. In this book, chapter 8 did report differences among whites, blacks, and Hispanics in terms of religious salience and religious traditions (see Table 8.2). There were differences in salience scores among the three categories and within the categories among the different religious traditions.

Table 14.1 (pages 280–81) explores these ethnoracial and religious differences in much more detail, comparing the political attitudes and behaviors of whites, blacks, and Hispanics within categories of religious affiliation. We begin our analysis with three items concerning abortion, the so-called hot button issue for many American religious groups. Whites as a group are more positive toward "supporters of abortion" and less positive toward "opponents of abortion" than either blacks or Hispanics, and on the general abortion item take a much stronger prochoice position. Evangelicals within all three racial-ethnic groups are the most strongly negative toward abortion supporters, most favorable toward abortion opponents, and most prolife. Differences in religious tradition are a much more important factor on abortion-related positions for whites and Hispanics than for blacks. A similar pattern emerges when we examine thermometer ratings toward the women's movement. All ethnoracial and religious groups rate the women's movement positively, but the evaluations by white and Hispanic evangelicals are less favorable. Ideologically, Table 14.1 shows that whites and Hispanics consider themselves more conservative than blacks (among whom there is little ideological variation), with evangelicals as the most conservative religious tradition and the group with no religious affiliation the most liberal.[2]

How interested and active politically are the racial and religious groups? All three ethnoracial groups exhibit only modest levels of interest in politics and vote turnout. Whites tend to outrank blacks and Hispanics in interest but not to a significant extent. The racial and ethnic differences in vote turnout are more significant, with whites far outpacing blacks and Hispanics. This finding has implications for the Democratic party and its candidates, who tend to be strongly supported by blacks and, to a lesser but still significant degree, by Hispanics. Within ethnoracial groups, interest and turnout are lowest among those with no religious affiliation. The lower turnout rate among white evangelicals when compared with white mainline Protestants and Catholics is worth noting. Although white evangelicals were wooed by the Republican party in the late 1970s and early 1980s and won by the GOP in the late 1980s and early 1990s (Kellstedt 1990), their contribution is lessened by their lower rates of turnout.

There are enormous differences among racial-ethnic groups and their religious subgroups in terms of partisan preference and vote choice. Whites as a whole lean toward the Democratic party in their partisan identifications, but the two Protestant subgroups do not. Hispanics are strongly identified with the Democratic party, and blacks are even more so.[3] George Bush won the support of whites in 1988, fared less well among Hispanics, and did poorly among blacks. Yet the Bush vote varied by religious tradition, especially among whites (both Protestant groups high, Catholics near the national average, those with no religious affiliation low). Hispanic evangelicals gave Bush well over half of their votes (although we should be cautious because of the relatively small size of this subgroup). The vote for Republican House of Representatives candidates in 1990 fell far below the Bush percentages in 1988, although the ethnoracial and religious group differences noted for the Bush vote variable are present here as well.

What are the implications of the findings from Table 14.1? First, the differences between evangelicals and other religious traditions among whites, which this book has highlighted, appear to hold for Hispanics as well. Hispanic evangelicals are quite conservative in political attitudes if not in partisanship and vote choice. Almost half of them identify as charismatic.[4] Second, Hispanic Catholics differ from white non-Hispanic Catholics, with lower interest and turnout, greater Democratic identification, and stronger support for Democratic candidates. This finding suggests that examining Catholics as an undifferentiated mass in survey research may make no more sense than failing to distinguish between evangelical and mainline Protestants. In a book that has driven home the latter point again and again, it is important to suggest that exploration of the prior argument may prove just as fruitful.

Religious Group Identifications

As chapter 4 concludes, religious group identification is a promising area for research about religion and politics. These identities serve as cues for appropriate attitudes and behaviors, including political attitudes and behaviors. The identifications act as organizing devices to categorize and evaluate political phenomena. Hence, when fundamentalist pastor Jerry Falwell calls for the election of Ronald Reagan, fundamentalist identifiers pay attention. Or when charismatic pastor Pat Robertson speaks, charismatic identifiers listen.

The concept of religious group identification suggests agreement about appropriate attitudes and behaviors associated with particular identities. Such agreement implies communication networks between leaders and followers and among followers. This relationship suggests that religious group identifications should have the greatest impact among those whose religious commitments are strongest, who are in the position to pick up political cues. Although anyone can label herself or identify himself as a *fundamentalist*, a *charismatic*, or whatever, these identities will be most meaningful for those with strong religious commitments. The identities may also be most salient within the religious traditions from which the identities sprung. Hence a fundamentalist identity may most likely have impact among respondents who affiliate with churches and denominations associated with the evangelical religious tradition.

These hypotheses are contextual in their origin and have not received a full test in this book. Nonetheless, a preliminary examination of data from the 1990 NES is promising. All Protestants were asked to pick the religious identification that best fits them from among four choices (fundamentalist, evangelical, charismatic-pentecostal, and moderate to liberal). Let us focus our analysis on *fundamentalist* identifiers. Prior research (Kellstedt and Smidt 1991) has linked fundamentalism to literal beliefs in the Bible and born-again identifications. We would expect that individuals who identified as fundamentalists but who were neither Biblical literalists nor born again would not have the political behavior hypothesized. (Fundamentalists should have greater Republican identification,

Table 14.1

Religious Tradition, Race, and Political Behavior

	Total Sample	Whites				
		Total	Evan	Main	Cath	None
Supporters of Abortion Thermometer	46.0	46.9	31.9	56.3	41.8	57.8
Opponents of Abortion Thermometer	53.8	52.3	67.4	44.4	57.8	37.2
Attitudes on Abortion	2.18	2.09	2.57	1.77	2.27	1.68
Women's Movement Thermometer	65.5	62.5	56.7	62.5	65.1	66.8
Ideology	4.13	4.17	4.49	4.16	4.09	3.80
Interest in Politics	1.87	1.90	1.93	1.92	1.94	1.68
1990 Turnout	46	50	46	54	57	32
Party ID	2.58	2.82	3.02	3.12	2.45	2.64
1988 Bush Vote	55	60	70	67	54	43
Republican House Vote 1990	36	42	50	42	40	30
N =	2000	1493	414	431	356	220

Table 14.1 *Continued*

	Blacks					Hispanics				
	Total	Evan	Main	Cath	None	Total	Evan	Main	Cath	None
Supporters of Abortion Thermometer	43.1	40.8	48.5	51.2	54.7	43.2	29.6	58.3	44.9	60.0
Opponents of Abortion Thermometer	58.3	59.4	53.7	51.2	52.3	58.7	70.3	48.1	57.5	46.3
Attitudes on Abortion	2.43	2.47	2.0	2.47	2.14	2.48	2.69	1.8	2.52	1.58
Women's Movement Thermometer	76.9	76.7	84.0	87.5	66.9	72.9	62.4	71.1	77.6	70.0
Ideology	3.91	3.94	3.73	4.0	3.82	4.16	4.6	4.0	4.05	3.92
Interest in Politics	1.83	1.88	1.96	1.65	1.53	1.76	2.02	1.8	1.69	1.5
1990 Turnout	40	42	46	35	18	33	40	30	32	08
Party ID	1.34	1.14	1.12	2.88	2.0	2.08	2.0	2.4	2.07	1.91
1988 Bush Vote	21	21	25	43	0	44	57	40	39	50
Republican House Vote 1990	6	7	0	0	0	19	33	0	15	0
N =	259	192	26	17	17	177	40	10	109	12

Source: 1990 NES

Attitudes on abortion range from 1 (pro-choice) to 4 (pro-life). Ideology scores range from 1 (liberal) to 7 (conservative) with a 4 as the midpoint. Interest in politics scores range from 1 (not much) to 3 (very much). Party identification scores range from 0 (strong Democrat) to 6 (strong Republican) with 3 as the midpoint. The 1988 Bush vote, 1990 turnout, and 1990 Republican House vote are simple percentages.

vote at higher rates, and vote more Republican than nonfundamentalist evangelicals.) The results, by religious tradition, are reported in Table 14.2.

Fundamentalist identifiers from the evangelical religious tradition are more Republican than the nonfundamentalists and the nonliteral/non–born-again fundamentalists (the *yes, with error* column). Note that for mainline Protestants, fundamentalist identification is rare (not surprising, given that the origin and base of fundamentalism is within the evangelical tradition) and has little impact on partisanship. Vote turnout in 1990 is lower for evangelicals (46 percent) than for mainline Protestants (55 percent), but fundamentalists within evangelical ranks voted in 1990 at higher levels than the religious tradition as a whole. In contrast, the few fundamentalists within the mainline had the lowest turnout rate. A similar pattern can be observed for both religious traditions in the 1988 presidential vote. Table 14.2 also includes a column within the evangelical tradition for fundamentalists with very high religious commitments (the logic and specifics of this measure are developed later in this chapter). Although the numbers for this group are small, the resuts are dramatic; the high religious commitment fundamentalist group is very Republican in partisanship and presidential vote and active in the political process as attested by the 1990 turnout rate. Hence fundamentalist identifiers who accept the group norms of a literal Bible and born-again identification differ from fundamentalists who do not accept these norms.

Some questions remain about religious identifications. What is their theoretical relationship to other political variables? How are they best measured? Are there some identities that are valid across religious traditions and others that are applicable only within certain religious traditions? Are the identities used in the 1990 NES survey—fundamentalist, evangelical, charismatic-pentecostal, moderate to liberal—exhaustive and mutually exclusive? Are these identities valid for Catholics as well? Can a set of identifications be developed for each religious tradition? Answers to these questions must come from special-purpose surveys, as the survey measures are unlikely to be available from the large national surveys, at least in the short term.

Religious Practice and Salience

To some extent, part III of this book, chapters 6–8, is the centerpiece of the volume. Why is this the case? Sociologists of religion as well as political scientists have found that public religious practices (like church attendance), private devotional practices (like prayer), and the perceived importance of religion make a difference in the lives of most Americans. What part III demonstrates, in rather conclusive fashion, is that public religious practices, private devotional acts, and religious salience matter politically. In all three cases, there is some measurement continuity that helps make the case for religious influence even stronger. Nevertheless, as the three chapters show, there are both conceptual and measurement questions that remain to be resolved.

Table 14.2

Religious Tradition, Fundamentalist Identification, and Political Behavior (whites only)

	White Evangelical Protestants Fundamentalist Identification			Highest Religious Commitment/Yes	White Mainline Protestants Fundamentalist Identification		
	No	Yes, With Error	Yes		No	Yes, With Error	Yes
Party ID	2.91	2.51	3.84	3.89	3.13	3.19	3.08
1990 Turnout	46	41	48	54	55	44	38
1988 Bush vote	68	60	74	85	66	78	62
N =	299	42	69	47	386	27	13

Source: 1990 NES.

The highest category on the commitment measure includes respondents with a religious affiliation who pray on a greater than daily basis, attend church at least weekly, accept an *orthodox* position on the Bible, and attach a great deal of importance to their religion.

See Table 14.1 for explanations of the dependent variables. All scores and percentages presented in the table control for age, gender, education, region, and marital status.

Church Involvement

Chapter 6 makes a strong case for the local church and clergy as sources of political influence. There are many mechanisms of political communication available in a local church (Wald, Owen, and Hill 1988, 532–33), including sermons, other pastoral messages, Sunday school and adult education classes, church publications, visual messages such as banners, and word-of-mouth among parishioners and between parishioners and church leaders. It follows that individuals need to be in the pews to pick up the cues. Hence, questions involving church attendance have an almost hallowed place in the American tradition of survey research, although it has been only recently that political scientists have paid them much attention. Sociologists such as Lenski (1963), however, have used the measure in a more systematic fashion.

Chapter 6 makes the point that church attendance means different things in different religious traditions. Prior to Vatican II, for example, attendance at mass was much more normative for Catholics than it is today. Among evangelical Protestants, outward signs of piety, like church attendance, are taken much more seriously than among mainline Protestants or Jews. As a result, church attendance rates are higher among evangelicals. Hence, the chapter argues that church attendance is an insufficient measure of public religiosity. Fortunately, by design, the 1989 Pilot Study included three other measures of public religiosity: identification or affiliation with a religious tradition, formal church membership, and participation in a religious organization outside of one's place of worship. A church involvement index was created from these four measures to serve as the basis for the data analysis in the chapter. In most respects, the composite measure works as expected.

With respect to measurement, the thrust of chapter 6 is to encourage scholars to broaden their conception of church involvement beyond attendance. This is sound advice in that an attendance measure skews results in the direction of religious traditions that place great emphasis on appearance at worship services. Where only this item is available, researchers can utilize "an attendance scale with fewer categories at the high end" (p. 135) in order to deal with potential bias and, in multivariate analysis, include separate variables for religious tradition and attendance. Unfortunately, formal church membership as an aspect of church involvement is not without problems either. If attendance skews results in an evangelical direction, formal membership does the same thing for other religious traditions. In many evangelical churches and denominations, regular attenders are often not members for one or more reasons: membership is not emphasized, or the criteria for membership are difficult to meet.[5] In addition, the question concerning participation in groups *outside* the church seems to have confused 1989 NES respondents in that over half who stated that they participated in such groups mentioned *within*-church activity in the follow-up questions that requested specifics. Still, it is important conceptually to recognize that church involvement is more than church attendance. It may be more useful to develop a measure of within-church involvement (e.g., singing in the choir, serving on the church board, teaching Sunday school, serving as an usher) followed by an *extra*-church religious involvement measure (e.g., membership in the Knights of Columbus, the Christian Legal Society, or Bread for the World, or working at a church-sponsored homeless center or food pantry). It is particularly important to document the church involvement of the American public, both *within* the church (beyond mere attendance) and *outside* the local church. Religious activities are a big part of the lives of many Americans, and it is reasonable to assume that those who are most active are likely to be heavily involved in civic activities as well. In other words, activity in one sphere begets activity in another.

Private Devotionalism

Chapter 7 argues that private acts of devotion (prayer, Bible reading, and the like) are related to political behavior. This argument may strike the political scientist as less obvious than the findings from the preceding chapter. *Private* devotionalism would not seem to have *public* consequences. Nonetheless, as the chapter suggests, private devotionalism can have public implications. First, for example, as people draw closer to their co-religionists in small group prayers, Bible studies, reading groups, and the like, their interactions will invariably touch on other topics. Second, even private activity of this sort is still activity, and like other types of involvement (labor union, business group, church) it can have public consequences. Some of the devotional activity may be directed at public figures (prayer for the president) or concern for public events (the war in the Persian Gulf, the opening of an abortion clinic) and, hence, directly link the private activity of prayer to the political process.

One of the difficulties in dealing with private devotionalism is to determine which elements or aspects of the concept to measure, particularly where interview time is scarce. Prayer seems to be the best choice in that its practice, if not its meaning, cuts across religious traditions. As with church involvement, however, what may be needed is a set of devotional acts that are specifically tailored to religious traditions. Bible reading seems to fit for evangelicals, but it does not appear to be normative for mainline Protestants or Catholics. Maybe the best course of action in general social surveys is to limit the measurement of private devotionalism to prayer and to give attention to other aspects of religious commitment instead of developing further measures of this dimension.

Salience

Chapter 8 shows the utility of the *guidance* measure used in NES surveys since 1980. The measure behaves as expected when related to demographic variables, religious traditions (evangelicals highest, seculars lowest), other religious variables, and all kinds of social and political attitudes and behaviors. Politically, the higher the salience, the greater the conservatism. The chapter illustrates that a composite measure of religiosity combining church attendance, private devotionalism, and salience has an even stronger impact on political attitudes and behaviors than the individual measures. In addition, this composite measure generally outperforms religious tradition and biblical literalism in explaining political attitudes and behaviors (see Table 8.4).

Has the survey research millennium been reached with the analysis and results of chapter 8? Not according to the authors. As impressive as the findings presented may be, they call for two innovations: a straightforward five- or seven-point scale on the importance of religion and a similar type of measure on the relevance of religion to political choices. Why would they reach such a conclusion? First of all, a general salience measure might more closely approach the properties of a normal curve than the bifurcated NES measure. Second, after asking whether religion is "an important part of your life," the guidance follow-up ("Would you say your religion provides *some* guidance in your day-to-day living, *quite a bit* of guidance, or *a great deal of guidance* in your day-to-day life?") seems to focus on a personal, privatized religion in contrast to a more abstract, public-focused faith. In this sense, the guidance follow-up may have a subtle bias toward the evangelical religious tradition. A five- or seven-point scale would seem to alleviate that possible problem.

Part III of this volume makes a strong argument for measures of church involvement, private devotionalism, and religious salience. Debates can and should continue about the best ways to measure these phenomena. But the chapters provide convincing, close to unassailable, evidence for the conceptual importance of these religious dimensions. No survey of American public opinion that attempts to understand the nature of that public can afford to be without measures of church involvement, private devotionalism, and salience. That is a strong statement, but the evidence bears it out. Combined with a reliable measure and valid code of religious traditions, a "minimalist" measurement strategy emerges that includes church attendance, prayer, and the importance of religion. Such a strategy would go a long way toward helping scholars grasp the impact of religion on American politics.

Doctrinal, Born-Again, and Religious Worldviews Measures

Doctrinal Beliefs

Early studies of religion and American public life (Stark and Glock 1968, 22) emphasized the centrality of religious belief: "Virtually everyone agrees that the central feature of Christian commitment is belief. But contemporary theologians disagree considerably over what it is that Christians ought to believe. As a result, it is nearly impossible to select any universally acceptable standards either to distinguish the believer from the non-believer or to reflect degrees and kinds of convictions among those who profess faith." Note that the authors talk about "Christian commitment." Does this suggest that belief is not central to understanding religious commitment in other, non-Christian communities? Sociologists have answered in the negative: "The most important dimension [of religious commitment] is obviously that of belief" (Wilson 1978, 446). Christians and Jews, the prominent faith traditions in the United States, make beliefs central. If belief is central to understanding religious commitment, and religious commitment is central to understanding political behavior, political scientists are going to have to contend with the conceptualization and measurement of beliefs. An obvious question is: Where do we begin?

Sociologists have grappled with this problem for a generation. Lenski (1963, 56) developed a measure of doctrinal orthodoxy designed for classifying Christians only. Fukuyama (1961) utilized a *creedal* dimension in his work. Glock and Stark (1965, 1966, 1968) built on the insights from this prior research and on earlier work by Glock (1959) to develop a doctrinal orthodoxy measure (belief in the existence of God, the divinity of Christ, biblical miracles, and the existence of the devil) that served as the basis of much of their research (cf. 1968, 58–61) and the focus of much criticism (cf. Fichter 1969). Scholars have argued that the belief component gave too great an emphasis to items that were salient to conservative Christian groups and not to other religious traditions or to other religions. Major efforts were made by survey researchers to develop belief measures (Faulkner and DeJong 1966; King 1967; King and Hunt 1969, 1972, 1975), but these scholars worked in the psychometric tradition of lengthy scales. Not only was no consensus reached by these efforts, but the omnibus surveys like the NES and GSS have never identified one or two items that best capture the belief dimension. The result has been that the major academic surveys like the NES and GSS have not provided a consistent set of religious belief measures over the years.

As a consequence of the above, the NES and GSS, and hence chapter 9, have focused attention on views of the Bible, asked in a literalism format or an inerrancy format. Chapter 9 shows that beliefs about the Bible are important predictors of attitudes toward abortion, partisanship, and how respondents voted in presidential elections. The chapter also demonstrates that a Bible item with more response categories lessens the skewed nature of responses to the standard NES measure and would be preferable to the latter. Nonetheless, that standard Bible item does produce significant findings, especially for evangelical Protestants (where the Bible is central to their identity) and especially when a control for Bible reading is instituted.

Political scientists have tended to ignore doctrinal measures of religious commitment, despite the arguments of sociologists concerning their centrality. It is easy enough for political scientists to argue that there is no necessary theoretical link between religious beliefs and political behavior and to leave discussions about how best to conceptualize and measure doctrinal beliefs to the sociologists of religion. Chapter 9, however, while avoiding some of the important questions about doctrinal beliefs, demonstrates the importance of beliefs about the Bible for understanding political behavior (chapter 7 provided some evidence for this as well). We are left with the need for special-purpose surveys to provide us with guidance in this area in the future.

The Born-Again Phenomenon

Jimmy Carter raised the born-again phenomenon to the conscious attention of many Americans for the first time in the 1976 presidential campaign. Even the survey research community responded, albeit tardily, to this thing called *born again*. Since 1980, but unfortunately not in 1976, a born-again question has been included in the NES Presidential Election Studies (such an item also appeared in the 1990 Congressional Election Study). Chapter 10 attempts to sort out the conceptual meaning of the born-again questions that have been asked in recent years and the political implications of the phenomenon. In terms of the latter, the chapter findings show rather modest results based on the 1989 Pilot Study data. Only with respect to attitudes toward Pat Robertson, abortion, and defense spending does the born-again item make much of an impact, and then only in interaction with biblical inerrancy. Results from a special-purpose survey are more promising. Instead of dichotomous responses to the question, in this case, respondents could check one of four types of born-again responses (nurtured in faith, gradual experience, profession of faith, and specific experience). Relationships between this measure and abortion attitudes, partisanship, ideology, and presidential vote are strong (see Table 10.3).

Scholars have not given much attention to the conceptual status of the born-again phenomenon. Is it a religious experience or a religious identification (or status)? It may be both. It might include a mountaintop or "Saint Paul" *experience*, a gradual turning around of a life over a period of time, or a sacramental marking such as infant baptism when the individual is claimed by God. But it also is a badge of *identification* or status for a person who is far removed from the *experience*. It does seem conceptually different from religious experiences like "feeling the presence of God," "receiving an answer to prayer," "feeling inspired by God to act," or "speaking in tongues." These are experiences that can recur, while being born again is a one-time occurrence in most traditions. It seems best to approach the born-again phenomenon in a manner similar to the religious identifications (fundamentalist, for example) discussed in chapter 4. These identifications seem to make a substantial impact on political behavior within the religious traditions in which thy were spawned and among the most religiously committed. Following this logic, a born-again identification should have the largest impact politically within the evangelical community. In fact, this is the case in analysis done using the 1990 NES data. Born-again evangelicals were more likely to identify as Republicans than evangelicals who were not born-again. Such was not the case for mainline Protestants or Roman Catholics. And the relationship for evangelicals held up even with controls for demographic variables and other religious variables (church attendance, prayer, salience, and biblical inerrancy).

Whether the born-again variable would hold up to extensive, multivariate analysis as a significant predictor of political behavior remains to be determined. Further efforts should be made to clarify the conceptual status of the born-again phenomenon. Is the concept best viewed as an identification or an experiential measure? Finally, efforts should be made to get at the meaning of the born-again language when used by respondents in survey situations.

Religious Worldviews

Chapter 11 explores the relatively uncharted area of religious worldviews. Religious individualism and religious communitarianism are posited to be on opposite ends of a continuum, with the former favoring a less activist view of government in contrast with a preference for proactive government and collective action by the latter. Both perspectives are found to be rooted in the Judeo-Christian tradition, and both have biblical sources of support as well. The chapter demonstrates that the survey research tradition had virtually ignored this topic until the pathbreaking study of Benson and Williams, *Religion on Capitol Hill* (1982). Authors of this volume as well (Leege 1989; Leege and Welch 1989; Welch and Leege 1988; Kellstedt 1991) have explored the concept of religious worldviews in the context of a national sample of Catholics and a survey of activists in religious interest groups. Although the measures used were different in these special-purpose surveys, the results are remarkably similar. Individualists in both studies tend to be more Republican in identification and vote choices, more conservative generally, and more prolife on abortion than communitarians. As the chapter suggests, the next step would appear to be experimentation with agree-disagree or other closed-ended formats that could be used later on national surveys.

The Sources of Religious Influence

In an era when the local organizations of national political parties are far less active in intermediary roles between the citizenry and their government, religious institutions are one possible means to fill the gap. Given the substantial involvement in churches by large portions of the American electorate, political cues emanating from religious leaders in person or through the medium of television can be effective. During the campaign season, candidates for public office can communicate with voters directly in local churches. In fact, Jesse Jackson has shown the potential utility of this direct contact strategy in his runs for the presidency in 1984 and 1988 (Wilcox 1991). Whether through direct contacts by candidates or through attempts by pastors or religious broadcasters to influence the faithful, the potential is there for religious influence in politics. Only the strong tradition of separation of church and state and the antipathy of many Americans toward things "political" has minimized this potential for religious influence.

Part V examines two potential mechanisms for religious influence. Chapter 12 looks at pastoral cues, while chapter 13 explores the impact of religious television. Of course, there are other possible sources of religious influence, most notably word-of-mouth by family and friends. Nonetheless, the local pastor is likely to have a great deal of legitimacy in the eyes of his or her congregants, particularly the most committed members. The legitimacy of religious television has been called into serious question in recent years due to scandals associated with televangelists. Nevertheless, it is a source of information about the world, including the political world, and still has many adherents.

Pastoral Cue Giving

Chapter 12 on pastoral cuegiving shows that pastoral cues are perceived quite differently depending on religious tradition and issue content. Evangelicals are more likely to perceive pastoral cues on proper sexual behavior and prayer in schools than are mainline Protestants and Catholics. They also recall hearing their pastors speaking out on abortion, but at lower rates than Catholics. Mainline Protestants report hearing from their pastors on issues like housing and homelessness. Multivariate analysis shows that cue perception varies by religious tradition and level of political interest, with the effects being greatest among those whose interest in politics is moderate.

It takes a major investment of survey resources to come to grips with the potential political roles of pastors. The evidence in chapter 12 suggests that most pastors do not attempt to influence their parishioners on candidate choice. But this finding is based on mass perceptions and, in fact, could underestimate the subtle cues that exist in any local church. Before we fully grasp the political role of pastors in American church settings, special-purpose surveys need to document their influence on parishioners in such convincing fashion that attention is given to the topic in omnibus national surveys. And these special purpose surveys must consider that the church political context includes more than pastoral cues (cf. Jelen 1991 for a comparative congregational study in one locale, and Leege 1987 for a national study comparing parishes within one denomination).

Religious Television Viewing

Chapter 13 examines another potential religious source of political attitudes, religious television viewing. It concludes that the medium has made a modest contribution to the politicization of religious conservatives. Religious television viewing, in combination with church attendance, has an impact on "issues of personal and social morality" (p. 265). In a most intriguing finding, the chapter argued that religious television had its largest impact on "doctrinal conservatives who attend theologically liberal churches" (p. 265). In terms of conventional political behavior, the combination of religious television viewing and church attendance has important effects on vote turnout and internal political efficacy.

The authors conclude that questions concerning religious television viewing habits should continue to be included in national surveys. They make the case that the item in the 1989 Pilot Study with response categories ranging from *daily* to *never* works better than the 1988 NES version (see Table 13.1). To provide more definitive answers to the importance of religious television as a political socializer, future research will need to develop a more detailed picture of how much viewing goes on and of what programs. Then comparisons can be made of the political impact of other sources of religious influence (e.g., pastors).

Toward a Theory of Religious Commitment and an Empirical Test

The preceding section of this chapter has reviewed and evaluated the conclusions from the empirical chapters of this book. Here we build on the earlier chapters by developing a summary model of religious commitment. We agree with Roof's (1979, 18) conceptualization of religious commitment as embodying "an individual's beliefs and behaviors in relation to the supernatural." The remainder of this chapter advances an argument for the model's importance for students of religion as well as for political scientists. The section examines some of the practical measurement difficulties associated with such a model, proposes specific measures of religious commitment, and provides a brief empirical test of its utility.

Theoretical Concerns

The study of religious commitment owes its greatest debt to the work of Glock and Stark (1965, 1966, 1968), although the earlier publications of Lenski (1963) and Fukuyama (1961) are important as well. Initially, Glock and Stark (1965) argue that religious commitment has five core dimensions: belief, practice, knowledge, experience, and consequences. However, by the writing of *American Piety* (1968, 16), the authors appear to have abandoned the *consequences* dimension: "it is not entirely clear the extent to which religious consequences are a *part* of religious commitment or simply *follow from it.*" Not all sociologists who have since written about religious commitment have used Glock and Stark's terminology (some prefer *religiosity* to *commitment*) or have identified the same dimensions, but all have been influenced by their work.

Glock and Stark distinguish between two types of religious practice: ritual and devotional. Many scholars have identified these aspects of practice in their research, and the components correspond closely to the *church involvement* concept developed in chapter 6 of this book and the *private devotionalism* concept in chapter 7. Given that church involvement and private devotionalism are conceptually and empirically distinct (albeit highly correlated), we prefer to identify them as separate dimensions of religious commitment.

The belief component measured by Glock and Stark through an orthodoxy index has been criticized as a measure biased toward doctrinally conservative Christians. Yet, as we argue in chapter 9, the belief dimension itself was not attacked, only the particular operationalization of it by Glock and Stark. Although the development of measures of a belief component that can be applied across different religions and Christian traditions is crucial for the future, in the past both the GSS and the NES have used a Bible item as the sole consistent measure of religious beliefs. This is certainly not the place to argue against the inclusion of a Bible item in omnibus surveys. Without question, various books of the Bible are central to Christianity and Judaism, although their centrality varies within these faith communities. However, the belief dimension of religious commitment would be much better served with a measure that applies more universally across religions. Stark and Bainbridge (1985, 5) strike the right chord when they argue that "religions involve some conception of a supernatural being, world, or force, and the notion that the supernatural is active, that events and conditions here on earth are influenced by the supernatural." Another belief is usually associated with the first, a belief that some form of life is experienced by individuals beyond the one they know here on earth. Often this takes the form of belief in an afterlife. Acceptance or rejection of life after death is the place to start in terms of conceptualizing religious beliefs. The argument raised by Stark and Bainbridge explicitly asserts that ideational systems that do not acknowledge the supernatural do not qualify as *religions*. It follows that a belief component is paramount to understanding religion, making it all the more ironic that in the omnibus survey research tradition, this component has rarely been explored.

Glock and Stark acknowledged the importance of salience of beliefs, but did not include it as a dimension of religious commitment or provide a measurement strategy for it. Chapter 8 documents the independent effect of salience on political attitudes and behaviors while at the same time noting its high correlations with church involvement and private devotionalism. A choice has to be made whether to consider *salience* as an independent predictor or an antecedent predictor of religious commitment (the latter defined in terms of beliefs and practices) or, in other words, to consider it a *peripheral* dimension (Cornwall et al. 1986). We feel that the salience component, or the importance of religion to the individual, is not peripheral to religious commitment but central to it and should be measured apart from beliefs and practices.

Stark and Glock described the experiential dimension of religious commitment in detail (1968, 43–66), noting four types of experience: confirming, responsive, ecstatic, and revelational. The omnibus survey research tradition has ignored this dimension, unless one considers the born-again phenomenon as belonging here.[6] As noted previously, our preference is to regard *born again* as a religious identification and to argue that religious experience is best defined as intimate or mystical contacts with the supernatural that can occur rarely or frequently. The concept would include such experiences as "feeling the strong presence of God," "receiving an answer to a prayer request," and the like. The relationship of these experiences to political attitudes and behaviors has not been explored until recently (Poloma and Gallup 1992). Whether experience should be considered a component of religious commitment is a question that can be left to others to explore (and avoided completely by political scientists until evidence of its relevance is forthcoming). For purposes of this research, a religious experience dimension will be considered *peripheral*.

Briefly, the intellectual or knowledge dimension advanced by Stark and Glock can be dismissed for purposes of political research. Certainly a religiously committed person will be informed and knowledgeable about the tenets of his or her faith. But a person can be informed *about* something while having little commitment to it. Hence, knowledge is a correlate of commitment but not necessarily a component of commitment.

This volume has argued for religious tradition as a key variable in understanding religion and politics. Now we include this variable as a dimension of religious commitment. The argument is that social group affiliation per se is part of what it means to be religious, just as are public and private practices, beliefs, and salience. Figure 14.1 spells out the core dimensions of religious commitment and a *minimalist* set of measures to tap each of these dimensions.

No doubt, these dimensions are affected by religious socialization in the home, by friends, by the local church context (including pastoral cues), and by the religious media. These dimensions are likely to have their greatest impact on the political process when associated with religious identifications or with religious worldviews.[7]

A Test of Religious Commitment

Can we test the model of religious commitment developed in the preceding pages? There are relatively unambiguous measures of denominational affiliation, church involvement, private devotionalism, and religious salience in the 1988 and 1990 NES surveys. There is, however, no relatively unambiguous measure of beliefs. Nonorthodox responses to the Bible questions ("The Bible is a good book because it was written by wise men, but God had nothing to do with it"; "The Bible was written by men who lived so long ago that it is worth very little today"; "The Bible is an ancient book of fables, legends, history, and moral precepts recorded by men") can be used as surrogate measures of unbelief. In

Figure 14.1

Dimensions of Religious Commitment and Measures Associated with These Dimensions

DIMENSIONS		MEASURES	
1.	Church Involvement	1a.	Church Attendance
		1b.	Other Activity within the
2.	Private Devotionalism		Church
		1c.	Religious Activity
3.	Salience		outside the Church
4.	Belief	2.	Frequency of Prayer
5.	Affiliation	3.	The Importance of
			Religion in one's Life
		4a.	Belief in the
			Supernatural
		4b.	Belief in the Afterlife
		5.	Denominational
			Affiliation

other words, at least in the Christian faith, the small percentage of respondents who give these *nonorthodox* answers can be considered *nonbelievers* in terms of this dimension of religious commitment, while those who give *orthodox* responses can be considered *believers*.

We constructed religious commitment measures from the 1988 and NES 1990 surveys.[8] The religious commitment scale ranges from high to low, as follows: *highest commitment*—respondents must profess a religious affiliation, attend church at least weekly, pray daily, attach great importance to religion in daily life, and give *orthodox* Bible responses; *second level of commitment*—respondents do not meet the above criteria but attend church more than once or twice per year, pray more than weekly, attach at least *quite a bit* of importance to their religion in daily life, and give *orthodox* Bible responses; *third level*—respondents meet only three of the criteria in level two; *fourth level*—respondents meet only two of the criteria in level two; *fifth level*—respondents meet only one of the criteria in level two; *sixth level*—respondents meet none of the above criteria; and finally, *lowest commitment*—respondents claim no religious affiliation.

Table 14.3 presents the frequency distributions of the religious commitment measure for the 1988 and 1990 NES surveys. The results are very similar in both years. The fact that the 1988 findings show somewhat higher levels of religious commitment is based on the measurement error built into the 1988 NES religious preference question.[9] These findings have significance beyond the specific numbers and the similarities between the two years. They provide insight into the levels of religious commitment in the United States. In analysis not shown, we find that the three least religious categories behave similarly when related to external variables, suggesting that the respondents who affiliate with a church or denomination but meet one or none of the criteria for religious commitment are most like those who are nonaffiliated. This similarity leads to the conclusion that a higher percentage of Americans—25–30 percent—fit a *secular* label than has traditionally been assumed.

The second portion of Table 14.3 examines the internal consistency of the commitment measure. It is not surprising to find that the two practice dimensions and the salience dimension are so highly correlated. The affiliation dimension is a dichotomy, with nonaffiliates badly outnumbered by those with some religious affiliation, and yet this skewed measure achieved respectable correlations with the other dimensions. The belief dimension is also a badly skewed dichotomy and yet showed good correlations. The reliability coefficient for the four measures is a respectable .74.

How do the components of the commitment measure relate to the ten attitudinal and political variables examined in Table 14.1? The affiliation dimension relates to the three abortion variables at lower rates than the other dimensions of commitment, while the belief dimension has lower correlations with a number of political behavior items. On the other hand, the church attendance item is more strongly correlated with vote turnout and congressional vote choice than the commitment index as a whole. Although this volume has argued at times for a multidimensional approach to religion (an argument echoing most sociologists of religion), the fact that the measures of the five dimensions of religious commitment tend to behave similarly when related to the ten political variables suggests that religious commitment, at least, is more *unidimensional* than is generally appreciated.[10]

Table 14.4 examines the relationships between the religious commitment measure and political behavior, controlling for demographic variables. The three least religious categories are combined and compared with the highest category of religious commitment. The findings are robust: the most religious whites differ from the least religious on all ten variables. When white evangelical Protestants are examined, the relationships are stronger than for whites as a whole, in most cases. The *betas* for whites *and* white evangelicals are statistically significant in each instance. Demographic variables are controlled for and, hence, are not having the impact here, but religious commitment is.

In multiple regressions not shown, religious commitment and religious tradition are the most significant predictors of attitudes toward abortion supporters, abortion opponents, and the women's movement (all "feeling thermometers")

Table 14.3

Religious Commitment: Stability, Internal Consistency, and Construct Validity

Stability of Religious Commitment

	Highest Commitment	Second Level	Third Level	Fourth Level	Fifth Level	Sixth Level	Lowest Commitment
1988	11%	29%	24%	13%	12%	3%	9%
1990	11%	27%	21%	13%	12%	4%	15%

Internal Consistency of Religious Commitment Measures
(Whites Only)

	Attendance	Prayer	Salience	Beliefs
Affiliation	.41	.34	.28	.25
Attendance		.47	.48	.25
Prayer			.56	.32
Salience				.25

Coefficients are Pearson Product Moment Correlations. Coefficient Alpha = .74

Construct Validity of Religious Commitment Measures
(Whites Only)

	Affiliation	Attendance	Prayer	Salience	Beliefs	Index
Supporters of Abortion Thermometer	.15	.28	.25	.27	.25	.37
Opponents of Abortion Thermometer	-.22	-.30	-.26	-.27	-.24	-.39
Attitudes on Abortion	-.17	-.31	-.28	-.32	-.24	-.43
Women's Movement Thermometer	.08	.15	.08	.09	.07	.17
Ideology	-.15	-.15	-.14	-.10	-.14	-.20
Interest in Politics	.12	.20	.14	.14	.02	.22
1990 Turnout	-.15	-.22	-.13	-.12	-.001	-.21
Party ID	-.04	-.06	-.04	-.01	-.03	-.06
1988 Bush Vote	-.14	-.14	-.13	-.11	-.08	-.19
1990 Republican House Vote	-.08	-.12	-.03	-.02	-.04	-.10

Coefficients are Pearson product-moment correlations.

Sources: 1988 and 1990 NES.

Table 14.4

Religious Commitment and Political Behavior

	Whites only Religious Commitment			White Evangelicals only Religious Commitment		
	Lowest	Highest	Beta	Lowest	Highest	Beta
Supporters of Abortion Thermometer	59.9	19.6	.37	61.9	12.7	.44
Opponents of Abortion Thermometer	39.1	75.1	.38	49.3	79.8	.32
Attitudes on Abortion	1.64	2.97	.41	1.80	3.11	.41
Women's Movement Thermometer	65.3	49.4	.19	67.9	43.0	.32
Ideology	3.92	4.81	.23	3.99	4.98	.28
Interest in Politics	1.72	2.03	.19	1.71	1.99	.20
1990 Turnout	37	56	.17	28	52	.16
Party ID	2.65	3.42	.11	2.31	3.62	.23
1988 Bush Vote	47	80	.20	44	85	.26
Republican House Vote 1990	35	52	.11	27	65	.21
N =	458	153		50	98	

Source: 1990 NES.

The highest category on the commitment measure includes respondents with a religious affiliation, who pray on a greater than daily basis, attend church at least weekly, accept an *orthodox* position on the Bible, and attach a great deal of importance to their religion. The lowest category combines the three lowest levels on the religious commitment measure.

See Table 14.1 for explanations of the dependent variables. All scores and percentages presented in the table involve controls for age, gender, education, region, and marital status. The findings in this table are the result of a series of Multiple Classification Analyses.

and toward single issues like abortion and school prayer, and toward a series of questions concerning traditional morality. In multivariate models, religious commitment is also significantly related to politicization variables like vote turnout and interest in politics.

Given the primacy of economic explanations in voting behavior research, how do religious commitment and religious tradition stand up to economic variables in relationships with party identification and vote choice? Table 14.5 provides an initial answer for whites and white evangelicals. Income is used as a current economic variable, along with predictions about prospective assessments of the economy twelve months into the future. The two religious measures outperform the economic measures slightly on party identification among whites. For white evangelicals, religious commitment has a very strong impact on partisanship. Religious variables perform just as well as economic indicators in our vote choice model, and, for evangelicals, religious commitment is a powerful predictor of vote choice.

The preliminary analysis of the religious commitment measure developed in this chapter is promising. Even when controlling for demographic factors, the measure produces significant findings in terms of the social issue agenda as well as in relationship to interest in politics and vote turnout. Religious commitment held its own as an important predictor of partisanship and vote choice when compared to economic indicators. With more adequate measures of beliefs, church involvement, and salience (see Figure 14.1), religious commitment would take its proper place as a measure essential to the understanding of political behavior.

Conclusions

This chapter has analyzed the results from chapters that preceded it and made additional suggestions for future research in religion and political behavior in light of the findings from this book. Readers, no doubt, will have many ideas of their own. Substantial progress has been made by scholars in utilizing data from omnibus national surveys like NES. In addition, studies of local congregations (e.g., Wald, Owen, and Hill 1988; Jelen 1991) have provided insight into the political context of churches. This latter type of research should continue for it can be done rather inexpensively and can provide new questions and question formats as well as alternative conceptualizations for the variables under study.

As new research in religion and politics is undertaken, careful attention should be given to the theoretical context provided by chapter 1 and the measurement considerations advanced in chapter 2. The former firmly places religion into cultural theories, demonstrates how religion can be a force for change as well as stability, and makes a theoretical argument for religion as a mediator between citizen and government. Chapter 2 advocates careful, self-conscious measurement strategies linked to theoretical concerns.

We conclude on a note of optimism. Although the literature on religion and

Table 14.5

Religion, Economics, and Political Behavior
(a Multiple Classification Analysis, whites only)

	Partisan Identification		1988 Bush Vote	
	All Whites	Evangelicals	All Whites	Evangelicals
Religious Tradition:				
Evangelicals	3.10		66	
Mainline	3.10		69	
Catholics	2.34	N.A.	55	N.A.
None	2.73		49	
Beta	.16		.15	
Religious Commitment:				
Highest	3.39	3.62	79	85
Second Level	2.90	3.08	65	69
Third Level	2.81	2.50	60	58
Lowest	2.71	2.73	55	56
Beta	.10	.19	.16	.25
Income:				
Below $20,000	2.61	2.74	50	62
$20-$30,000	2.90	3.07	61	72
Above $30,000	3.00	3.28	69	74
Beta	.08	.11	.16	.12
Economy 12 months from now:				
Better	2.97	2.93	71	77
Same	3.07	3.37	67	80
Worse	2.71	2.84	58	64
Beta	.08	.12	.11	.16
R Squared:	.08	.16	.09	.18

Source: 1990 NES.

Partisan scores range from 0 (Strong Democrat) to 6 (Strong Republican). The George Bush vote is a simple percentage. The lowest category of religious commitment combines the four lowest levels on the measure. All scores and percentages control for social/demographics. NA = not applicable.

politics has not permeated the study of political behavior in the manner that the authors of this book would like, the decade of the 1980s was productive and profitable. If scholars working in the field continue their labors and new additions from graduate schools around the country join the ranks, the decade of the 1990s should be even better. Religion may have been hidden under a bushel two decades ago, but it has now emerged as salt to season the study of politics and light to illuminate for our colleagues and interested citizens the role religious faith plays in American democracy.

Notes

1. To oversimplify somewhat, there are doctrinal differences between evangelical and mainline Protestants. The former are, for the most part, biblical inerrantists; believe in a particularistic salvation and a personal God; accept Jesus as God; emphasize missions and evangelism; are *conversion*-oriented; and are individualistic in their religious worldviews. The latter interpret the Bible more symbolically; believe in a universalistic salvation and a more transcendent, less companionate God; accept Jesus as a great religious example, if not the Son of God; emphasize the Social Gospel; are *confession*-oriented; and are more communitarian in their religious worldviews. The evangelical base is predominantly from congregational denominations, pietistic denominational families, and sect movements. In contrast, members of the mainline are more often from hierarchical denominations, ritualistic and sacramental denominational families, and church movements. Socially, the evangelical tradition is more southern, female, and lower class, while the mainline tends in the opposite directions. Culturally, evangelicals tend to be separatist and the mainline accommodationist. Organizationally, evangelicals are associated with the National Association of Evangelicals, while mainline Protestants tend to be involved in the National Council of Churches. For evangelicals, politics is centered around issues of moral traditionalism; for mainline Protestants, the focus is a complex mixture of economic conservatism and social justice. Other classifications, beside evangelical and mainline categories, have been proposed. Smith (1990) categorizes denominations along a fundamentalist-liberal continuum, making assignments to *fundamentalist, moderate,* and *liberal* categories based on prior scholarly designations, membership in interdenominational organizations, clergy's beliefs, and the theological orientations of the denominations. Nonetheless, such a categorization is far from foolproof, based as it is on inadequate probes to clear up ambiguous responses, dubious assignments (e.g., Christian Scientists to the fundamentalist category), and lack of clear theoretical criteria.

2. It should be pointed out that Table 14.1 offers no demographic controls of the sort offered in the remaining tables in this chapter.

3. There are significant differences in partisan orientations within the Hispanic community: Mexican Americans and Puerto Ricans are Democrats, while Cuban Americans are strongly Republican. The pro-Democratic tilt for the community as a whole results from the higher proportion of Hispanics who descend from Mexican roots.

4. These Hispanic evangelicals are strongly religious. There is every reason to suspect that their numbers will grow rapidly in the next decade in the United States, following a similar pattern that has been documented in Latin America (cf. Martin 1990; Stoll 1990). Most of this growth is likely in the charismatic-pentecostal sectors of evangelicalism. There are too few cases to test the overlay between religious tradition and whether the respondent is Mexican American, Puerto Rican, or Cuban American.

5. In unpublished data from a study of religious activists, 77 percent of donors to Evangelicals for Social Action are church members (ESA is an organization whose membership is almost exclusively evangelical), while 91 percent of members of Bread for the World, an organization whose roots are in mainline Protestantism and Roman Catholicism, are formal members. In all other respects, ESA donors outrank Bread for the World in frequency of religious practices.

6. As a one-time, specific experience, a born-again experience can be said to contain all four types of experience noted by Glock and Stark (1965). It is confirming, responsive, ecstatic, and revelational—all wrapped into one. But the born-again *experience,* that is, the event of conversion, is not what is relevant politically. It is that the person who has had the experience takes on an identity (of a born-again Christian) that is linked to certain social and political attitudes, such as opposition to abortion.

7. Further research may extend the promising findings on religious worldviews presented in chapter 11 in such a manner that a measure or set of measures could be included with the core measures in Figure 14.1.

8. These measures were close to, but not exactly, identical. Readers should consult the respective codebooks for details.

9. In 1988 the focus of the question was on religious preference, which tends to produce a higher proportion of affiliated people than the 1990 questions, which ask whether a person considers himself or herself a part of a church or denomination *before* asking for a specific affiliation. More important, the 1990 denominational question is preceded by several questions that make it more socially desirable to admit to no religious practices or affiliation.

10. A pattern similar to the one on the bottom of Table 14.3 was found when a construct validation was run on the 1988 data. These unidimensional findings are somewhat surprising given the common assertion (cf. Lenski 1963; Stark and Glock 1968; King and Hunt 1975) of the multidimensionality of religious commitment. This apparent contradiction may be resolved in several ways. First, only one underlying dimension of religious commitment may account for political behavior. Second, times may have changed from the 1960s to the 1990s. Third, measurement models and the instruments themselves are improved and may be responsible for the differences. Fourth, evangelical respondents, a growing proportion of samples over recent decades, account for a disproportionate number of the highly committed cases. Further research should examine this issue.

References

Benson, Peter L., and Williams, Dorothy L. 1982. *Religion on Capitol Hill: Myths and Realities.* New York: Harper and Row.

Berelson, Bernard; Lazarsfeld, Paul; and McPhee, William. 1954. *Voting.* Chicago: University of Chicago Press.

Campbell, Angus; Converse, Phillip; Miller, Warren; and Stokes, Donald. 1960. *The American Voter.* New York: Wiley.

Conover, Pamela Johnston. 1984. "The Influence of Group Identification on Political Perceptions and Evaluations." *Journal of Politics* 46:760–85.

Conover, Pamela Johnston, and Feldman, Stanley. 1984. "Group Identification, Values, and the Nature of Political Beliefs." *American Politics Quarterly* 12: 151–75.

Cornwall, Marie; Albrecht, Stan L.; Cunningham, Perry H.; and Pitcher, Brian L. 1986. "The Dimensions of Religiosity: A Conceptual Model with an Empirical Test." *Review of Religious Research* 27:226–44.

Faulkner, J.E., and DeJong, Gordon F. 1966. "Religiosity in 5-D: An Empirical Analysis." *Social Forces* 45:246–54.

Fichter, Joseph H. 1969. "Sociological Measurement of Religiosity." *Review of Religious Research* 10:169–77.

Fukuyama, Yoshio. 1961. "The Major Dimensions of Church Membership." *Review of Religious Research* 2:154–61.

Glock, Charles Y. 1959. "The Sociology of Religion." In *Sociology Today,* ed. Robert Merton, Leonard Broom, and Leonard Cottrell, 153–77. New York: Basic Books.

Glock, Charles Y., and Stark, Rodney. 1965. *Religion and Society in Tension.* Chicago: Rand McNally.

———. 1966. *Christian Beliefs and Anti-Semitism.* New York: Harper and Row.

Jelen, Ted G. 1991. *The Political Mobilization of Religious Beliefs.* New York: Praeger.

Kellstedt, Lyman A. 1990. "Religion and the U.S. Party System." *Public Perspective* 2 (1):12–14.

————. 1991. "Religious Worldviews and Political Behavior." Paper presented at the annual meeting of the American Political Science Association, Washington, DC.

Kellstedt, Lyman A., and Smidt, Corwin E. 1991. "Measuring Fundamentalism: An Analysis of Different Operational Strategies." *Journal for the Scientific Study of Religion* 30:259–79.

King, Morton B. 1967. "Measuring the Religious Variable: Nine Proposed Dimensions." *Journal for the Scientific Study of Religion* 6:173–90.

King, Morton B., and Hunt, Richard A. 1969. "Measuring the Religious Variable: Amended Findings." *Journal for the Scientific Study of Religion* 8:321–23.

————. 1972. *Measuring Religious Dimensions: Studies in Congregational Involvement.* Dallas: Southern Methodist University Press.

————. 1975. "Measuring the Religious Variable: National Replication." *Journal for the Scientific Study of Religion* 14:13–22.

Leege, David C. 1987. "The Parish as Community." *Notre Dame Study of Catholic Parish Life*, Report 10. Notre Dame, IN: University of Notre Dame.

————. 1989. "Toward a Mental Measure of Religiosity in Research on Religion and Politics." In *Religion and Political Behavior in the United States*, ed. Ted G. Jelen, 45–64. New York: Praeger.

Leege, David C., and Welch, Michael R. 1989. "Religious Roots of Political Orientations: Variations among American Catholic Parishioners." *Journal of Politics* 50:137–62.

Lenski, Gerhard. 1963. *The Religious Factor: A Sociological Study of Religion's Impact on Politics, Economics, and Family Life.* Garden City, NY: Doubleday-Anchor.

Martin, David. 1990. *Tongues of Fire: The Explosion of Protestantism in Latin America.* Cambridge, MA: Basil Blackwell.

Poloma, Margaret M., and Gallup, George H., Jr. 1991. *Varieties of Prayer: A Survey Report.* Philadelphia: Trinity Press International.

Roof, Wade Clark. 1979. "Concepts and Indicators of Religious Commitment: A Critical Review." In *The Religious Dimension: New Directions in Quantitative Research*, ed. Robert Wuthnow, 17–45. New York: Academic Press.

Shafer, Byron E., ed. 1991. *The End of Realignment? Interpreting American Electoral Eras.* Madison: University of Wisconsin Press.

Smith, Tom W. 1990. "Classifying Protestant Denominations." *Review of Religious Research* 31:225–45.

Stark, Rodney, and Bainbridge, William Sims. 1985. *The Future of Religion: Secularization, Revival, and Cult Formation.* Berkeley: University of California Press.

Stark, Rodney, and Glock, Charles Y. 1968. *American Piety: The Nature of Religious Commitment.* Berkeley: University of California Press.

Stoll, David. 1990. *Is Latin America Turning Protestant? The Politics of Evangelical Growth.* Berkeley: University of California Press.

Swierenga, Robert P. 1990. "Ethnoreligious Political Behavior in the Mid-Nineteenth Century: Voting, Values, and Cultures." In *Religion and American Politics*, ed. Mark Noll, 146–71. New York: Oxford University Press.

Wald, Kenneth D. 1992. *Religion and Politics in the United States.* 2d ed. Washington, DC: Congressional Quarterly Press.

Wald, Kenneth D.; Owen, Dennis E.; and Hill, Samuel S., Jr. 1988. "Churches as Political Communities." *American Political Science Review* 82:531–48.

Welch, Michael R., and Leege, David C. 1988. "Religious Predictors of Catholic Parishioners' Sociopolitical Attitudes: Devotional Style, Closeness to God, Imagery, and Agentic-Communal Religious Identity." *Journal for the Scientific Study of Religion* 27:536–52.

Wilcox, Clyde. 1992. *God's Warriors: The Christian Right in Twentieth-Century America*. Baltimore: Johns Hopkins University Press.

Wilson, John. 1978. *Religion in American Society*. Englewood Cliffs, NJ: Prentice Hall.

Wuthnow, Robert. 1988. *The Restructuring of American Religion*. Princeton, NJ: Princeton University Press.

Index

Kinder, Donald, x, 44
King, Morton B., 143, 152, 161, 181
Knights of Columbus, 285
"knowing God's many people," 53, 65
Kornhauser, William, 20
Kulturprotestantism, 5

labor unions, religiosity (salience) and
    attitude to, 167, 168, 170, 171
Laing, R. D., 88
Leege, David C., x, xiii, 3–25, 72–99,
    121–56, 143–44, 148, 212, 216–31,
    223–24, 229, 235–54
Lenski, Gerhard, 123–24, 128, 134, 142,
    143, 148, 284, 287, 291
Levy, Dianne E., 204, 212–13
Liberty Federation, 266
life cycle factors in denominational
    change, 101–2
study of major religious traditions
    (table), 108–11
Lincoln, Abraham, 13, 16
Lincoln, C. Eric, 15
LISREL, 96n20
religious identity studied by (table),
    91–94
lobbyists, religious, 36
Lockwood, William, 159
Lowery, Roger C., 204, 212–13
Lutheran Church—Missouri Synod, 58,
    60–63, 276
Lutherans, 201

McCready, William C., 9
MacIver, Martha Abele, 158
McKinney, William, 14, 222, 235, 250
Madison, James, 5–6, 22
Mamiya, Lawrence H., 15
Marsh, Alan, 159
Marty, Martin E., 222
Marx, Karl, 5, 6, 14, 15
mass society hypothesis, 19
Mayflower Compact, 13
measurement
multidimensional approach to, 124,
    126–27

measurement (continued)
strategies of, 26–49
See also sample surveys
mediating institutions, 19–23, 235, 273
Merriam, Charles E., 5
Midwest Political Science Association, x
Miller, Warren, x
mismatched respondents, 37, 261–62,
    265
Mobley, G. Melton, 256
Moral Majority, 40, 75, 83–85, 199,
    205, 255, 259, 260, 266
mismatched TV viewers and
    attitude toward (table), 261, 262
Protestant religious identities
    compared for (table), 89, 90
religious identity and (table), 80–82
moral traditionalism
political participation—church
    involvement and (table), 131, 132
Protestant religious identities
    compared for (table), 90, 91
religiosity (salience) and (tables), 166,
    167, 170, 171
religious and demographic predictors
    of (table), 148–51
religious identity and (table), 80–82
religious television viewing and
    (tables), 258, 261, 262
Mormons, 66n2
Muslims, 67n2

National Association of Evangelicals,
    36, 39, 196n5, 275
National Council of Churches, 39
National Election Studies (NES), ix–x,
    56, 59, 76–77, 155, 220, 228
1960, 56, 59
1964, 183
1968, 183
1980, 183, 288
1984, 186–88
1988, 186–88
born-again items in (tables), 203–7
religious commitment measures
    constructed from, 293–96, 301n9

National Election Studies (NES)
  (conrtinued)
  religious television in, 257–59, 262
  1989 Pilot Study, x, 27, 42–43, 60,
    75–77, 87, 88, 92, 136*n3*, 274,
    276, 277
  born-again items in *(tables)*, 203–9
  church involvement studies *(tables)*,
    123, 125–34, 284
  cue-perception data, 237, 240–41
  on denominational change *(tables)*,
    103–13
  devotionalism data of *(tables)*, 141,
    145–53
  recoding of, 82–83, 96*n9*
  on religious identity *(tables)*, 77–82,
    84, 85, 88–91
  religious television in, 257–59, 263,
    291
  salience items in, 162
  small sample size, 103
  1990, x, 27, 56, 76–77, 87, 91, 251,
    276, 277, 279, 283, 288, 298
  Bible questions in, 184, 195*n4*
  on denominational preference and
    political behavior *(tables)*, 60–65
  devotionalism data of *(table)*, 141,
    150–51
  religious commitment measures
    constructed from, 293–96, 301*n9*
  on religious identity *(table)*, 77–82,
    85
  salience items in, 162, 163, 165
  1992, 276, 277
  Bible measure in, 183, 186–88,
    190–92, 292, 293
  Catholics in, 86
  guidance scale (salience measure),
    157, 158, 161–72, 285–86
nationalism, Protestant religious
    identities compared for *(table)*, 90,
    91
National Socialism, 15–16, 20
National Survey of Religious
    Identification, 59
NES. *See* National Election Studies
Neuhaud, Richard John, 235

Neumann, Franz L., 20
New Age groups, 67*n2*
New Christian Right, 22, 85, 199, 228,
    238, 260, 261
Noll, Mark A., 8
nondenominationals
  Protestant, 276
  See also
    evangelicals—nondenominational;
    secularists
nonwhites
  political participation and church
    involvement of *(table)*, 130
  See also African-Americans
Northern California churches, study of,
    124–25
Notre Dame Study of Catholic Parish
    Life, 42, 225
nuclear weapons
  Catholic bishops' pastorals on, 236
  perceived cues on, by major tradition
    (table), 238–40
numinous, the, 9

orientation dimension, 124
orthodoxy index, 37–39, 177–78, 292
Otto, Rudolf, 9
Owen, Dennis E., 75, 235, 245

Paloma, Margaret M., 154
para-church organizations, 107, 115*n4*
particularism, religious, 83–85
partisanship. *See* party identification
party identification
  Bible questions and *(tables)*, 185, 186,
    190–95
  born-again status and attitude to
    (table), 208
  denominational change and *(table)*,
    111–13
  denominational preference and, 55
  high social status and, 114
  Protestant religious identities
    compared for *(table)*, 90
  race, religious tradition and *(table)*,
    277–81